The Edge of
Organization

The Edge of Organization

Chaos and Complexity Theories of Formal Social Systems

Russ Marion

SAGE Publications
International Educational and Professional Publisher
Thousand Oaks   London   New Delhi

For information:

SAGE Publications, Inc.
2455 Teller Road
Thousand Oaks, California 91320
E-mail: order@sagepub.com

SAGE Publications Ltd.
6 Bonhill Street
London EC2A 4PU
United Kingdom

SAGE Publications India Pvt. Ltd.
M-32 Market
Greater Kailash I
New Delhi 110 048 India

Printed in the United States of America

Library of Congress Cataloging-in-Publication Data

Marion, Russ.
    The edge of organization: Chaos and complexity theories of
formal social systems / by Russ Marion.
        p.   cm.
    Includes bibliographical references and index.
    ISBN 0-7619-1265-7 (cloth: alk. paper)
    ISBN 0-7619-1266-5 (pbk.: alk. paper)
    1. Social systems.   2. Complex organizations.   3. Chaotic behavior
in systems.   4. Complexity (Philosophy)   I. Title.
    HM131 .M3355   1999
    910'.2'02—dc21   98-40063

This book is printed on acid-free paper.

99   00   01   02   03   04   05   7   6   5   4   3   2   1

Acquisition Editor:	Harry Briggs
Editorial Assistant:	Anna Howland
Production Editor:	Astrid Virding
Editorial Assistant:	Nevair Kabakian
Designer/Typesetter:	Marion Warren/Lynn Miyata
Indexer:	Teri Greenberg

*This book is dedicated to the people in my past—
my father and grandparents—
whose presence in this work is indelible;
and to my wife Gail, daughter Cathy, and mother Lois,
whose presence in this labor was indispensable.*

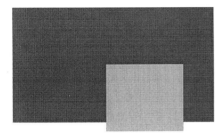

Contents

Preface

▓ The Edge Premise

Modern apologists (modern being the past 250 years or so) make much of the differences between faith and science, but, ironically, both science and faith are premised upon common assumptions. Granted, assumptions about the origins of life differ, as do assumptions about biological causality (need vs. accident), the nature of life itself, and the role of humans in the grand scheme of things. Nonetheless, the ancient Hebrews and Charles Darwin agreed that life resulted from the sifting of order from chaos, that chaos is an ambiance of disorder and useless randomness from which useful order is separated. To put it another way, the religious and the scientific have a common lack of appreciation for chaos and a common appreciation for order.

But I (and Chaologists in general) maintain that chaos is not receiving due respect in all this. I do not intend to engage the Hebrews over theology, but I do argue that our perception of chaos as random, useless dynamic is sophistry. Far from being meaningless void, chaos is the source of creativity and construction in nature and in social dynamics (the focus of this book). Many unpredictable systems are quite ordered, although that order is quite complex. Weather patterns, brain waves, insect populations, and the economy are all unpredictable systems with hidden structures. Conversely, much of what we assume to be ordered behavior is actually quite complex and, in many ways, unpredictable. Many formal social organizations, for example, may appear stable in general—market share, organizational form, and products may change little from year to year—but details, such as personnel, technology, and clientele, are quite dynamic.

I also argue, along with Stu Kauffman (who coined the coming aphorism) and other Complexity theorists, that "order is free." It requires no external force, no "sifting." Not only are chaos and order not what we think them to be, not only are their roles misunderstood, but the emergence of order does not necessarily follow the paths historical science has laid out for it.

There are two issues here: (a) our mis-definition of chaos, and (b) our misunderstanding about the emergence of order. We will address the last, first. Again, faith and science have similar premises: Order is considered the product of sifting, and sifting represents external force, or work. The one attributes sifting to the efforts of God, the other to the efforts of natural selection; but both see order as the fruit of work. Biologist Brian Goodwin explains that our culture is characterized by an almost primal or subconscious acceptance of the work ethic, the conviction that good results from effort. Sifting, whether by God or by selection, he continues, represents work done to produce order. Just as hard work draws men and women from the jaws of poverty and meaningless life, the work of a sifter rescues us from the void of chaos. This is powerful metaphor in our culture, and to argue against it is, well, work. How else could order arise if not through effort of some sort?

Chaos Theory, or rather that branch of Chaos Theory that we will identify as Complexity Theory, responds that order emerges naturally because of unpredictable interaction—interaction is the vehicle by which this occurs and unpredictability is the stimulus that promotes novelty (but I'm getting ahead of myself). The argument proposed in this book is that interacting entities—atoms, molecules, people, organizations—tend (a) to correlate with one another because of their interaction, and (b) to catalyze aggregation. Correlation is what happens when two or more people exert interactive influence over one another; a husband and wife, for example, will gravitate together in their attitudinal structures because they discuss and live their beliefs together. Autocatalysis—the second point—begins when the behavior of one system stimulates certain behaviors in another system that in turn stimulates another and another; eventually the chain of stimulation returns to motivate, or catalyze, the original system and the cycle is reinforced. Order, then, emerges not because someone or some thing expends energy to create it; rather, order emerges from the natural, and free, consequences of interaction.

Unpredictability is an important element of this process. This argument is captured by the U.S. historian Henry Adams, who said, "Chaos often breeds life, when order breeds habit." Novelty does not arise from formula. The mistake of traditional science is its presumption that events are the formulaic and linear results of stimulus, that time is reversible (more on this later), that everything that is or will be was predestined at the moment of the big bang. The Greek philosopher Epicurus said that "it would have been better to remain attached to the beliefs in gods rather than being slaves to the fates of physicists . . . [for] the latter . . . brings with it inviolable necessity" (Prigogine, 1996, p. 10). A flipped coin can produce only heads and tails; an action can produce only an equal and opposite reaction; the output of a linear equation is determined by, and functionally related to, its input variables; an uninspired man or woman produces only the mundane and predictable. The unpredictable, the free will, the chaotic creates novelty, and novelty is the author of new order. It was unpredictability that made possible the Theory of Relativity, Newton's Laws of Motion, and Heisenburg's Uncertainty Principle; it is unpredictability that underlies inventions and mobs and rumors and informal groups and organization. Correlation and autocatalysis build, but unpredictability is that twist of events that inspires creation and renewal. Without it, there are no happenstance meetings, no flashes of creativity, no Schumpeter-ian gales of creative destruction; there is only predictable routine with everything in its place following its predetermined course. Chaos is the spice of order.

The second issue raised in the early paragraphs of this preface had to do with the nature of chaos and order. We usually assume that chaos means random disorder and that order means predictable stability. Both notions are true, but they are less often true than we think. Order is not always ordered and symmetrical (particularly in nature and in society), and chaos need not be random.

Unpredictability comes in two forms: the random and the Chaotic (Chaos is capitalized here because of its specialized meaning). Random behavior exists when an entity, given choices, is likely to perform any one with equal probability. A molecule in fluid, given the choice of moving right or left, is just as likely to move one way as the other and there is no knowing ahead of time which it will do. Chaotic behavior, by contrast, is more structured, stable, and deterministic; nonetheless it, like random motion, is still unpredictable.

Chaos is descriptive of systems rather than entities. Systems, of course, are composed of entities, but the corporate behavior of these entities is organized by correlation and autocatalysis. Consequently the dynamics of Chaotic structures, like weather systems, fluid turbulence, families, mobs, and organizations, are, to varying extents, patterned and stable; even so, their trajectories over time are unpredictable, again to varying extents.

It is the unpredictable nature of Chaotic systems that inspires the order of which we spoke earlier. The isolated, random behavior of an individual, we will argue, is not up to this task. Individuals (such as Newton, Einstein, Martin Luther King, and Henry Ford) may be credited with the emergence of new order, but their achievements are possible only within the context of the correlated, autocatalytic dynamics of a system of actors. An individual may be the symbol of change; he or she may even be the catalysis about which change dynamics collapse. The individual within a Chaotic system, however, is influenced and delimited by correlation with the whole. One could suppose that the completely idiosyncratic behavior of an individual could catch on and influence the whole, but new order more usually involves the evolution of a system rather than the peccadilloes of an eccentric.

We need to narrow our perspective of Chaos a bit in order to describe social systems properly. Chaotic order per se is actually too violent, too changing to describe much that goes on among living beings. Complexity theorists, who are conceptually related to Chaos theorists, argue that life tunes Chaos's intensity down a bit to a transition band between Chaos and predictable stability called the Edge of Chaos. Dynamics in this band are still Chaotic but they also possess characteristics of order. Full-blown Chaotic systems have little memory; living systems must be able to map their past. Chaotic systems flit a bit too readily from novelty to novelty; living systems need to consolidate gains. Predictable, stable systems, by contrast, possess none of the panache needed to create new order or even to respond adaptively to creative environments. Complex systems lie between these poles, at the Edge of Chaos, and they have both panache and stability sufficient to serve life.

Chaos and Complexity theories are themselves, ipso facto, Chaotic and Complex systems, and as such are case studies in the emergence of new order (in this case, the new order is a way to describe reality). This emerging order "catalyzed" my interest in applying its ideas to formal social systems. I was helped along the way by a network of similarly interested academicians. The American Educational Research Association has a special interest group dedicated to such study; The Society for Chaos Theory in Psychology and Life Sciences has an international conference and a journal devoted to the subject; and numerous writers, such as Stu Kauffman, William Doll, Brian Arthur, Jeff Goldstein, Brian Goodwin, and Claire Gilmore, are exploring the explanatory power of these theories in the social sciences. This book, then, is part of a growing network of academics, resources, and ideas devoted to understanding the Chaotic and Complex nature of human social and psychological structures, and the study of formal social systems is its special niche in that network.

I would like to give special thanks to two members of this emerging network of Chaologist and Complexity theorists. Raymond A. Eve, Professor of Sociology at the University of Texas at Arlington, and Sara Horsfall, a recent Ph.D. graduate in sociology from Texas A&M, provided valuable insights about this manuscript, insights that had a significant impact on the overall structure and direction of the book. I would also like to thank Kristin Bergstad for her editorial work. She has found errors that I never would have found, and I am indebted to her for that. Finally, I appreciate the efforts of Harry Briggs and Anna Howland, Sage editors who decided to give this book a go.

CHAPTER

1

The Edge of Organization

Why is there something rather than nothing?

—Martin Heidegger

Thought experiments are experiments that are solved by rational thinking rather than by empirical observation. They are appealing because of their compelling logic and because they help the uninitiated to visualize the dynamics of phenomena that might otherwise be obscured by mathematical complexity. Einstein and Galileo were masters of the art. Galileo Galilei destroyed Aristotelian belief that heavier bodies fall faster than light bodies by visualizing a light body chained to a heavier one. Einstein visualized himself racing a light beam within an electromagnetic field, and mulled over the sensations one experiences in a falling elevator. Many others have employed thought experiments as well. James Maxwell imagined a demon controlling the movement of molecules between a chamber of hot gases and one of cool gases. Newton conjectured about relative motion by imagining a spinning bucket of water. Erwin Schrödinger helped us understand certain arguments of Quantum Theory by asking us to visualize a closed box containing a cat that may, or may not, be killed by poison gas while enclosed.

This book begins in such tradition by posing a thought experiment that I call Einstein's Island. The experiment introduces the unifying theme of the book, that of complex, interactive systems. It poses a dilemma regarding the nature of paradigm shifts, or changes in the way humans perceive reality. Einstein's Island is also about the sudden death of the USSR and the ensuing turmoil that that event triggered. It relates to the recent domination of the electronics market by Japan, the emergence of technological standards, the onset of riots, sudden changes in the stock market, labor strikes, public opinion, and the evolution of markets and industry. It is about planning, rationality, organizational culture, administrative intervention, organizational development and change, environmental change, the diffusion of innovation, the evolution of organizational climate, the evolution of leadership, indeed the evolution of organizational theory itself. Einstein's Island is about how things emerge and how they change.

■ Einstein's Island

Imagine that Albert Einstein's mother was the sole survivor of a shipwreck and that Einstein himself was born on a deserted island. There was plenty of food and water on the island and no dangers threatened survival. Among the items that washed ashore from the wreck were numerous crates of scientific and mathematical books, enough to provide young Einstein a timely (at least as of the ship's sailing date) and complete background of pertinent scientific knowledge. Einstein's mother was able to provide him with the basics of an education, and from the books he was able to develop an understanding of more complex mathematics and physics.

Under these conditions, would he develop his famous theories of relativity? Would he, at age 16, imagine himself riding a light beam? Could he have visualized the behavior of photons in a moving train as that train approached the speed of light?

A logical response to this puzzle might be that, after all, it was Einstein's uniquely creative intelligence that solved the problems of relativity. Because of the books, his command of calculus and physics certainly would be equal to the task.

But perhaps this quick faith is too glib. There are 26 years or so of knowledge lost to Einstein, those scientific developments that occurred between the time the doomed ship set sail and his early adulthood (Einstein was born in 1879, and the texts from the ship would have predated his birth; he first published his Special Theory of Relativity in 1905). If the development of knowledge is a slow evolutionary process in which fact builds on fact, then our Einstein would have had to overcome an arrested source of knowledge— 26 years of scientific discovery by a number of scholars would need to be reconstructed before Relativity could be derived. From his books he would have learned about the prevailing (19th-century) theory that light flows through an invisible "ether" and would have known a bit about the growing concern with this theory (such critique did not become significant until the 1890s, however). Einstein would not have known about Michelson and Morley's light experiment that failed to find expected confirmation of the effect of ether; nor would he have known about Maxwell's theories of electromagnetism or Lorenz's work with contraction in rigid bodies. Between 1880 and 1900, these and other scientific findings created a crisis in the existing theory of motion that Relativity eventually resolved. It would seem unlikely that even Einstein's prodigious intellect could have filled these voids in his knowledge. If scientific development is a process of climbing to progressively higher levels of understanding on a gradually inclined learning slope, a stranded Einstein would be two decades behind the pack.

Even so, Einstein's creative intellect is compelling. One might, therefore, argue that Relativity is a major leap away from the physics of Newton and is consequently less dependent upon building blocks than on the sudden insight of which an Einstein is capable. Maybe he didn't need Michelson and Morley's experimental results to imagine what would happen if photon guns were simultaneously fired from the exact middle of a moving boxcar toward its two ends. It might even be argued that isolation would have fed Einstein's creativity because he would not have been confused or seduced by the pressure of academic peers whose perceptions of reality were Newtonian. Einstein's discoveries required that he think in a completely different dimension of physical reality, thus existing trends regarding the traditional perceptions of physics would seem of little use to him. From this perspective, new leaps of understanding would appear to be the result of rethinking rather than gradual building, in which case Einstein may very well have been able to derive at least elements of his famous theories.

These perspectives pose an important question: Does knowledge expand in a gradual, evolutionary way, or is insight more spontaneous? Was Relativity the end product of 19th-century scientific development (a gradual, sequential process we will call gradualism) or did it arise from genius that brilliantly and precipitously shook off the past and blazed entirely new synaptic paths unfamiliar to Newtonian physics (let's call this punctuation)? Both gradualism and punctuation are problematic. *Punctuation* has difficulty explaining the many linkages between old paradigms and new ones. An equation for electromotive force, known as the Lorentz contraction, that was derived in the late 19th century, is an important component of Einstein's famous formula, $E = mc^2$, as are Maxwell's equations regarding electromagnetism. The notion that new paradigms may be, in essence, without history seems insupportable. *Gradualism,* on the other hand, cannot explain the obviously divergent nature of new paradigms. The Copernican universe "flew in the face" of terracentrism; Pasteur's experiments completely contradicted notions of spontaneous generation; Galileo usurped Aristotelian logic about falling bodies; and Einstein turned Newtonian order on its ear. The problem is that punctuation trips over gradualism and gradualism trips over punctuation. Paradigm shifts seem on the one hand to be little more than the culmination of existing knowledge, yet shifts are so dramatic as to seem to break almost completely with the preceding paradigm.

This mind experiment contains some element of the Great Man/Cultural determinism debate, but the reader should focus on more than that. The question I pose here involves more than great people; it is about sudden, dramatic change of any sort. It asks about the dynamics of change, why change seem to appear out of a void, why certain ideas catch on and others don't. Ultimately it is about the dynamics of complex interactive systems.

An answer to this puzzle lies in a recent, eclectic evolution in knowledge (one that some feel is itself a dramatic paradigm shift; see, for example, James Gleick, 1987). It is eclectic in that it has proven applicable in biology, chemistry, physics, astrophysics, and medicine; and, as is argued in this book, it may very well prove to be of similar value to the social sciences—indeed it is already making significant contributions in economics and is beginning to show up in other social science literature. This theory is called Complexity, and it has roots in yet another dramatic advance known as Chaos Theory. The solutions that Chaos and Complexity provide for Einstein's Island are neither gradualistic nor punctuated, yet in another sense they are both gradualistic and punctuated. These theories will turn our cherished notions of evolution and causality on their ears, and by *evolution* I refer to the emergence of both biological species and social movements. With them, we will explore an alien logic in which punctuation and gradualism are brothers rather than adversaries, order is merely a submanifestation of disorder, cooperation and competition are synonyms rather than antonyms, and Einstein implodes rather than explodes Newtonian physics.

▦ A Brief Overview of Chaos and Complexity

Many people's first foray into Chaos Theory (myself included) was through James Gleick's popular best seller, *Chaos: Making a New Science,* published in 1987. This book introduced us to new perspectives of reality, new ways of conceptualizing cause/effect and seemingly random behavior and system dynamics. To some social scientists, it seemed to drip with metaphors of organizational theory and social behavior (see, for example, Cronbach, 1988). Complexity Theory, which is related to Chaos Theory, was popularized a few years later by books such as Roger Lewin's 1992 work, *Complexity: Life at the Edge of Chaos,* and M. Mitchell Waldrop's book from that same year, *Complexity: The Emerging Science at the Edge of Order and Chaos.*

There is some debate about the technical meanings of the terms *Chaos* and *Complexity,* and about their respective fields of influence (see Goldstein, 1995). Many argue that Chaos Theory is a general theory of nonlinear dynamics and Complexity Theory is a subset of Chaos. Some would argue just the opposite, and yet others see little to distinguish the two. Another school of thought maintains that Chaos and Complexity are two sides of the same issue (Briggs & Peat, for example, compared them in terms of Alice's mirror in Lewis Carroll's *Through the Looking Glass*). To make matters even more confused, complexity has meaning within Chaos Theory that differs from our definition of it. Edward Lorenz argues that the term *complexity* is often used interchangeably with Chaos, but that it is sometimes used in a specialized sense to refer to irregularity in space while Chaos refers to irregularity in time. Alternatively, complexity may refer to the length of a set of instructions required to depict a system.

I argue, however, that Complexity, while exhibiting characteristics of Chaos, is nonetheless distinct from it. The two share general nonlinear premises, yet they represent different phenomena. This is the perspective of early advocates of Complexity Theory, such as Chris Langston and Stephen Wolfram (see the introduction to Chapter 3) and is the perspective adopted by this treatise.

Both Chaos and Complexity theorists propose that a system's dynamics involve more than "if A, then B" relationships in which outcome is the simple function of inputs. They argue instead that system behavior more often results from complex, nonlinear interactions among constituent parts and that, because of this nonlinearity, behavior is difficult or impossible to predict. Nonlinearity—a central concept in Chaos and Complexity theories—means that response is disjointed with cause. That is, a change in a causal agent does not necessarily elicit a proportional change in some variable it affects, rather it may elicit no response, dramatic response, or response only at certain levels of cause. Consider, for example, the behavior of dogs, and assume for the moment that the only emotions these animals experience are fear and anger. As two dogs approach each other, they may express anger at the intrusion of the other and bark furiously. A simple model of causality would predict that the anger of each dog would increase in proportion to the proximity of the other until a fight results. Nonlinear theories argue that a fight is not a foregone conclusion; rather when the situation reaches a certain level of intensity, the emotional state of one dog may precipitously flip to fear, leading it to tuck tail and run. Fight or run: The outcome is sensitively dependent upon the precise state of each dog's emotions, upon subtle nuances of interaction between the dogs, and between each dog and—goodness knows what.

Chaos Theory itself tends to focus on systems in which nonlinearity is intense and mechanical—weather systems, for example, or fluid turbulence or soil percolation. Such systems respond sensitively to, and magnify, minute differences in initial conditions, thus they are unpredictable. Chaotic systems are mathematically deterministic but their descriptive equations cannot be solved. These systems are stable but their behaviors are not repetitive, and they carry only limited memory of their past.

Shortly after James Gleick's book on Chaos was published, articles on social applications of Chaos Theory began to appear in the social science literature. In 1990, Henry Geller and A. P. Johnston, for example, analyzed three cases of public policy implementation and explained the flow of events (what they called the "flowing geometries") with Chaos Theory. In 1988, John Sterman used computer simulations (a stock management game and a beer distribution game) to collect data representing the decisions of players; plots of the data revealed patterns recognizable as what Chaologists call "strange attractors." T. J. Cartwright, writing in 1991 about Chaos's sensitivity to minute changes, argued that organizational theorists should abandon the perception that one can predict the future if one only has enough data and should instead focus on what he calls an ensemble of forecasts.

Despite the potential applications, however, something is amiss when Chaos Theory is used to describe social systems. Chaos Theory is a bit too mechanical, although there certainly is an element of the mechanical in social behavior. It seems more appropriate for describing physical systems such as weather and fluid turbulence than for describing human behavior. There is an element of life missing in Chaos Theory. Where it has been applied to living systems, it has tended to deal either with the "physics" of those systems—the rise and fall of insect populations or epidemics, the rhythm of the heartbeat, or the growth patterns of urban areas—or with generalized population dynamics such as systemic stability and change (Guastello, Dooley, & Goldstein, 1995, for example, described change relative to Chaotic bifurcation). It is not very helpful in explaining or dealing with such issues as adaptation, deliberative behavior, intelligent behavior, reproduction, and evolution.

Adaptation, deliberative behavior, and the such are conscious and unconscious activities that are based on past experiences and, often, anticipated outcomes. Social systems, for example, carry information about themselves and their environments, and are able to act on such information. That information allows them to spawn reproductions of themselves or to replicate their ideas at remote sites; it allows them to make reasonably accurate predictions of the effects of their behaviors; it lets them interact with their environment without being at the mercy of the vagaries of that environment. Chaotic systems fluctuate too unpredictability and mechanically to carry information of this sort, but Complex systems do not.

Complexity Theory layers Chaos Theory on top of more traditional theories of stability, but the result is a unique theory in its own right. A Complex system is more stable and predictable than are Chaotic systems; even so, it borders on the state of Chaos—it possesses sufficient stability to carry memories and sufficient dynamism to process that information. This balance between order and Chaos enables the ability to reproduce, to change in an orderly fashion, and, as we shall see, to self-organize, or emerge without outside intervention. Complexity Theory is useful for describing biological phenomena such as evolution, ecological niches, and even social processes, and many of its more notable advocates (such as Stuart Kauffman, John Holland, Murray Gell-Mann, Craig Reynolds, and Brian Goodwin) have written of such applications. Researchers such as Brian Arthur and Per Bak have used it to describe human behavior and the economic system, and its ramifications are being explored in psychology and other social science fields.

In fairness, one must note that adaptive and mechanical systems aren't entirely delineable by Complexity and Chaos. Per Bak, as an example, has used Complexity Theory to analyze phenomena that would seem the province of Chaos Theory, such as earthquakes and traffic patterns. In the experiment that established his place in the field, he observed that common sandpiles can exhibit Complex characteristics. Further, one can identify Chaotic and Complex patterns within the same system; economic systems have been analyzed by some for their Chaotic structure (see Claire Gilmore, T. Willey, and even one of my own papers) and by others, such as Per Bak, for their Complex characteristics. This does not confuse the definitional matter, for life and non-life are not the sole delineating characteristics of the two theories. Rather it underscores the point that, while all living things are Complex, they can behave Chaotically; similarly, physical systems can exhibit characteristics we attribute to Complexity.

These definitions are only a beginning; we will extend them considerably in the pages that follow. The theme about which these definitions are to be woven is social behavior, and in particular the behavior of systems that are called "formal organizations." The book is about how they emerge, change, and self-organize, for these are central issues of the eclectic fields of Chaos and Complexity.

▓ Implications

New hypotheses based on existing theory answer previously unanswered questions. New theories ask previously unasked questions. New theories often focus on questions that were always there but that were ignored to some degree or another. We tend, as humans, to find solutions, then to ask questions for those solutions rather than to ask questions and then find solutions (see the discussion of the Garbage Can Model of Decision Making in Chapter 10, for example). Thus we often brand as inconsequential those questions for which existing theory provides no context. A goal of this book is to ask unasked questions, such as: Why do humans organize themselves, anyhow? Or: If free market philosophy is all that powerful, why do ineffective leaders and second-rate industries so often do well? The answers to these questions (and to others we will ask) may appear obvious or even flippant. They are neither.

Chapters 2 and 3 of this book will further define Chaos and Complexity theories—the context within which such questions can be explained. Chapters 4 and 5 develop a general theory of complex social systems that will be used to organize more specific, subsequent observations, and the different elements of this theory are fleshed out and applied to organizational behavior in Chapters 6 through 14. Chapter 15 develops mathematical procedures for analyzing Chaotic and Complex systems—this is for the novice and expert alike—and the final chapter returns to the questions posed by Einstein's Island.

We conclude this first chapter by posing some of the questions that will be addressed in the pages that follow. The questions will likely give the reader a glimpse of the solution to Einstein's Island.

- Where do informal groups, cliques, fads, rumors, organizational myths, market demand, riots, social movements, and new paradigms come from, and why do they tend to appear suddenly?

- Why do similar social structures emerge in very different cultures separated by vast distances? Is it, as the Darwinian would suggest, because of common descent, or are there other forces at work?

- Why are governmental agencies so sensitive to the whims of social mood swings, yet nothing really ever seems to change?

- Why does change so often appear out of the blue, with little advance notice? How, for example, did conservative Republicans sweep to power in the U.S. legislature (and in many state governments) in 1994 with no apparent warning and after years of minority status?

- Why is it that social systems often seem coordinated as if by an invisible hand? Why do husbands tend to experience the various phases of sleep—deep sleep, restlessness—at the same time as their wives? How do flocks of birds manage to move as a unit, as if controlled by a super-efficient traffic controller? Why do women in the same household tend to experience coordinated menstrual cycles? Why does a crowd assume a "personality," as if it were a single entity rather than a multitude of entities? On a shop floor, why does it seem that when things start to go wrong, everything goes wrong? We usually attribute coordination to "top-down" control by a central coordinating agent, but these examples, and many others, are spontaneous and emergent. How can we account for such spontaneity?

- Why do organizations sometime get by making bad decisions? Why do they sometimes persist in using inefficient technology when better, more economically beneficial technologies are available (why, for example, did the American auto industry take so long to adopt Japanese-like manufacturing procedures during the 1980s, despite the economic consequences of having an inferior product)? Why do organizations persist with seemingly archaic and ill-adaptive structures or competitive strategies (e.g., 5 & 10 cent stores)?

- Why, as publishers will testify, is it difficult to predict which new book will be successful and which will not? What happens to 5-year plans? Why, despite all our theories and our statistics, have organizational theorists been so unsuccessful at predicting the futures of their organizations? Why is it difficult to predict the ramifications of our decisions? Where do those unintended consequences come from? Why is it difficult to implement plans as they were designed to be implemented?

• Churchill quipped that history is "just one damn thing after another"; that is, it is the victim of simple accidents with no direction or form. Is it indeed? If the Minutemen had failed to make their appointment at Concord Bridge, would the history of the United State have been dramatically altered? Can a leader's decision inalterably change the future of an organization?

• Mitchell Waldrop began his book, *Complexity: The Emerging Science at the Edge of Order and Chaos,* with a series of questions similar to these. Several are appropriate in the context of this book; they include the following:

> Why did the Soviet Union's forty year hegemony over eastern Europe collapse within a few months in 1989? . . . Why did the stock market crash more than 500 points on a single Monday in October 1987? . . . If evolution (or free-market capitalism) is really just a matter of the survival of the fittest, then why should it ever produce anything other than ruthless competition among individuals? In a world where nice guys all too often finish last, why should there be any such thing as trust and cooperation? (pp. 9-10)

We turn now to an exploration of these, and many other, questions—and to a solution for Einstein's Island.

Chaos and Organization

In many ways, humans don't have a grasp on reality. I don't mean that in a flippant or critical way, I mean, we really don't know what reality is. Our perceptions of reality are just that: perceptions. We call them models or theories. They are our best shot at explaining reality. Models can explain a broad variety of behaviors and can help us predict what will happen in similar future circumstances. Even so, they are still models, metaphors based upon what we sense around us, our explanation of the mysterious manifestations of reality.

Model building is a lot like the folk tale of three blind men describing an elephant. One blind man feels the tail and says the elephant is like a rope. The second feels the elephant's leg and concludes it must be a tree. The third feels the trunk and says it is like a snake. Each man focuses on different perspectives and creates a different explanation of elephant.

A test of model goodness is in its generalizability, thus the snake model, if reasonably accurate, should work for the opposite end of the mammoth, but of course it doesn't. Our blind scientists could argue that the elephant is so complex that theorists must focus on one part of the animal at a time. When models are restricted to their intended uses, they are reasonably appropriate. Still, these models are problematic because they do not impart a full sense of elephant, and the blind scientists will inevitably be bothered by the lack of connection among the theories.

As a folk tale, the story ends here; as a metaphor, we need to follow events in the blind culture a bit further. Eventually some other blind man or woman reconciles the shortcoming of the original models by creating a new one that focuses on skin texture, a feature that is constant over much of the elephant. There is the matter of the elephant's feet and soft tissue (eyes, inside the ears, etc.), but these are conveniently labeled inconsequential. The new model is more generalizable, although its detractors argue that, in addition to the problem of feet and soft tissue, it ignores structure—the focus of the original theories. The critics, however, are old fashioned, and eventually their arguments are all but forgotten. Over time scientists learn more and more about skin texture, but increasingly the problem of the feet and soft tissue stands in the way of further understanding. When the difficulties become intolerable, someone revives the structural arguments and, with brilliant insight, produces a model that connects texture and structure. Understanding in the blind culture is advancing.

The moral of the story is simple: Reality is an elusive commodity, and the best one can hope for are closer and closer approximations of it. We may never arrive at absolute and total reality, and even if we did our blindness would likely prevent us from being able to confirm our arrival. Nonetheless, our models serve us well, for we learn eventually to ride our elephants and use them for work. Model building is a process of building and rebuilding, with each cycle pushing back the darkness a bit farther than did the previous one.

Back to reality (so to speak). Current theories of organization are reasonably effective descriptions of organizational behavior. We've focused extensively on the nature of organizational life over the past century, and our models have grown in sophistication. Each new organizational theory in this period of organizational theory building has dealt with problems in its predecessor. Machine Theory, from the early part of the 20th century, rescued human volition from the jowls of Spencer's epic social evolution models; human relations models rescued human psychology from Machine Theory's mechanical perspectives; and Systems Theory added the environment to previously closed theories.

Current metaphors for organization struggle with complexity, complexity within the environment and within organizations themselves. For the most part, complexity is considered an unknowable, largely undifferentiated condition that organizational theorists call ambiguity or uncertainty. It is treated by many models as a random force, the product of multiple interactions, lack of knowledge about cause and effect, unforeseen events, human whimsy, and the such. For example, one current metaphor, called the Garbage Can Model, argues that humans make decisions randomly; indeed we often select solutions before we select problems on which to implement the solutions.

In this, and the next, chapter we propose new metaphors that deal directly with the nature of complexity. They are called Chaos Theory and Complexity Theory (we will consistently spell these words with an uppercase C to distinguish them from more common usage of the words). This chapter deals with Chaotic dynamics; the next introduces Complexity Theory. Since these theories are largely mathematical and scientific, this chapter, and the one that follows, will be something of a science primer. Though our theme requires this scientific digression from organizational theory, the goal is to provide a crucial foundation for pushing back the darkness surrounding complexity in social structures, to provide yet another way for blind scientists to understand nature, including human nature.

▓ The Blind Scientists

In the 17th century, Sir Isaac Newton pushed back the darkness of mysticism by introducing us to calculus and to a new logic of understanding. Calculus is about motion and prediction; if one knows the starting position and velocity of an object, one can determine where it will be at any given point in time. Calculus divides time into tiny chunks; the position and velocity of an object at a point in time is related to its position and velocity at the immediately preceding chunk of time, which in turn is related to where it was and how fast it was moving before that. With calculus, we can send rockets to the moon, predict where a cannonball will fall, describe chemical reactions, and project where traffic jams are most likely to occur during the morning rush hour.

Calculus assumes that some variable B is proportionately related to some variable A, thus a small change in A translates into a small change in B and a large change in A translates into a large change in B. For example, if a cannonball hits its target when the cannon is set at an angle of $45°$, then it will just barely miss that target if set at $45°0'1''$.

Calculus, however, won't explain everything. It hasn't been particularly useful, for example, at predicting the stock market, the outcome of a poker game, or next year's achievement test scores at the local elementary school. So researchers have turned to probability and statistics to explain such complex, random phenomena. As gamblers know, there is pattern to many seemingly unpredictable events, and this is the premise for theories of probability and statistics. In the social sciences, however, statistical analysis has been largely restricted to the study of static phenomena—the state of events as they exist at a given moment. There is much to be gained from studying the dynamics or trajectories of behavior, but statistical designs have not lent themselves to such examination.

An evaluation of the evolution of a conflictive situation, for example, could reveal far more than one that looked simply at statistical pre- and post attitudes. A classic analysis published in 1969 by George Brager of employee behavior in a social agency besieged by negative public attitudes illustrates. Brager's statistical analysis revealed a general relationship between commitment to organizational goals and level of dissension. However, in his discussion he tantalizes the reader with stories of bifurcating reactions (as when splinter groups emerge from an originally unified group) and of spontaneous internal conflicts. The stories he told about the agency's emerging problems were more interesting than were his findings. Such clues indicate that a dynamic model of the conflict would have offered an interesting perspective of what transpired in this social agency.

Although statistics was conceived to deal with randomness, even it must concede the existence of unexplained residual behavior. This is noise, or variation in the dependent variable that is left over after independent variables have explained all they can explain. Variation in any given variable, then, can be divided into that which is explainable and that which is not, and the latter is not particularly interesting.

Chaologists—scientists who study Chaos—approach the notion of noise with a different level of appreciation. Blind scientists have "invented" a new explanation because the previous ones didn't cover everything they were observing.

■ An Alternative Explanation of
   Complex Behavior: Chaos Theory

In many ways, the evolution of organizational theory over the past 50 years, like the evolution of physical explanation over the past 300 years, is about trying to come to terms with internal and external ambiguity, or noise. Chaos Theory promises to provide new theories of noise that are useful to both physicist and social scientist. Chaos Theory proposes that a certain type of noise exists in nature that is not removable by refinement of experimental procedures or by the addition of extra explanatory variables. David Ruelle calls this type of noise "deterministic noise," and argues that:

> In a real experiment . . . noise . . . in a signal is usually considered to be the result of the interplay of a large number of degrees of freedom over which one has no control. This type of noise can be reduced by improving the experimental apparatus. But we have seen that another type of noise, which is not removable by any refinement of technique, can be present. This is what we have called the deterministic noise. Despite its intractability it provides us with a way to describe noisy signals by simple mathematical models, making possible a dynamical system approach to the problem of turbulence. (p. 16)

Ruelle's argument gets at the heart of Chaos. His notion of noise suggests that simple events can generate behaviors so complex that one is tempted to call them random, yet they are entirely deterministic and can be modeled with simple mathematical equations. A simple equation for predicting the birthrate of insects can produce results that are devilishly complex and unpredictable. The most powerful computers cannot predict the trajectories of three inter-acting bodies in space (this refers to a problem known as Hill's reduced model). Mathematically, Chaos happens when equations used to describe seemingly simple systems just won't behave as expected. They will not yield a stable response, or the answers they give jump wildly when the quantity of an input variable is even slightly perturbed. These equations are called "nonlinear" because their inputs are not predictably related to their output.

Attractors

Conventional science has focused on predictable, repetitive phenomena, like the motion of a pendulum. Differential calculus allows scientists to visualize systems' dynamics as trajectories, and it provides the ability to make line graphs of those trajectories much as one might represent the flight of a bumblebee by drawing its trajectory as a line on a piece of graph paper. The graphs of primary interest to scientists, the ones that allow prediction, are periodic or repetitive. The trajectory of a pendulum, for example, can be drawn as a regularly fluctuating, predictable time line, much like the oscilloscope representation of a heartbeat or a sine wave. Alternatively, it can be plotted as a circle, with the graphical axes representing velocity and position (i.e., time is ignored; see Figure 2.1b). The latter type of graph is called a phase space portrait, and has important uses in mathematics.

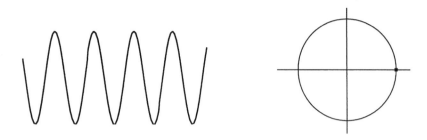

Figure 2.1. Periodic motion of a pendulum. 2.1a, on the left, is a plot of periodic motion over time; 2.1b, on the right, is a phase space plot of periodic motion.

A trajectory to which motion gravitates, such as that represented in Figure 2.1b, is called an attractor. An attractor is stable; if it is perturbed, it will return to its original motion. A pencil lying on its side is stable; lift the pencil a bit, let it go, and it will return to its stable, prone position. A pencil on end is not stable; small perturbations will cause it to topple. The range of points that move to an attractor represents its "basin of attraction." A pendulum exhibits two stable attractors: back and forth motion, called a periodic attractor, and no motion, which is represented by a point on a phase space plot—thus it is called a point attractor.

An attractor is also finite; that is, its behavior is bounded—its phase space portrait will not spill out of a confined area. In the classical definition, an attractor is periodic or quasi-periodic; that is, the behavior is repetitive or, at least, nearly so. Importantly, attractors of the sort described thus far represent the predictable motion that scientists seek.

The point and the periodic attractors were mainstays of classical Newtonian physics; all stable motion was believed to assume some variation of these states. In the early 1960s, Edward Lorenz, a meteorologist at MIT, discovered another attractor that has been labeled the "strange attractor" by David Ruelle and Floris Takens. Like its more conventional siblings, this attractor is patterned (possesses a geometric structure that exists within finite phase space) and stable (the system, if disturbed, readily returns to the state represented by the attractor). Unlike other attractors, however, it is neither periodic nor quasi-periodic: The behavior of the system it represents never repeats itself.

This strange attractor is the product of nonlinearity and interactivity. Scientists usually focus on relationships in which the motion of one variable is directly related to that of another. Nonlinear dynamics are asynchronous; motion in one variable generates nonproportional motion in another. A single grain of sand added to a pile of sand may, for example, have no effect or it may precipitate a landslide.

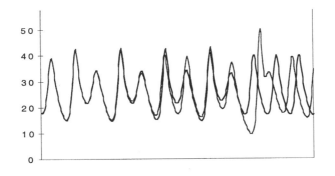

Figure 2.2. Plot of the *X* variable in Lorenz's attractor across time rather than in phase space. The *X* variable is plotted twice; the first begins at *X* = 1.0, the second at *X* = 1.001. Despite the minuscule difference, the ultimate results are uncorrelated. This is the butterfly effect.

Nonlinear behavior is unpredictable. The uncertainty about what might happen with each new grain of sand in the above example illustrates this. Will the pile simply grow by one grain? If there is a "sand slide," what size will it be?

The lack of predictability in strange attractor behavior is a function of two phenomena. It is related first to what Lorenz has called "sensitive dependence on initial conditions." Lorenz found that nonlinear systems, such as weather, are sensitive to minor changes in conditions. This means that something as minor as the flapping of a butterfly's wings can reverberate through an interactive system and lead to outcomes that are significantly different than those that would have occurred without the change (see Figure 2.2).

This alone is enough to mess up prediction, but there's more. The conditions of a given system cannot be accurately measured at any given point in time. Even if a system could be defined with a few localized variables, those variables may very well defy accurate measurement (measure to five decimal places, and there is always a sixth). Traditional science would say that such minor measurement errors translate into trivial error when the system is plotted to its conclusion. The butterfly effect (as it is called), however, tends to magnify those minor inaccuracies and the results are anything but trivial. So not only are minor differences blown out of proportion by Chaos, the initial differences can't be accurately gauged as well. Prediction is impossible under such conditions.

The second reason for unpredictability is, according to Ilya Prigogine, even more compelling; it has to do with interaction and what the famous

19th-century mathematician Jules-Henri Poincaré referred to as resonance.
Every particle, Poincaré argued, possesses kinetic energy, the source of its
current behavior, and potential energy, the source of possible future behavior.
The motion of isolated particles can be easily described by deterministic
formulas because evaluation must account only for the known quantity,
kinetic energy. Numerous particles in close proximity, on the other hand, will
interact, releasing potential energy in unpredictable sorts of ways. This has
unpredictable effects on the trajectories of particles. Thus, even if one could
measure the initial conditions of a system of particles to the infinite-th degree,
Chaos would still exist because of interaction and potential energy.

Interacting particles exhibit yet another important phenomenon called
correlation. When two particles collide, their behaviors assume some measure
of sync-ness, their frequencies begin to reverberate with a degree of harmony.
This helps explain the emergence of Chaotic stability, or attractors. I shall
argue in this book that the same thing occurs at the macro level of human
social behavior: Individual particles (people) interact with one another, and
their behaviors correlate as a result. Imagine such interactions on a large scale
with bi-directional causality and complex, convoluted chains of inter-
relationship, and one can begin to see where Chaos and Complexity will take
us in this examination of social behavior.

One can sense correlation and unpredictability in the phase space portraits of strange attractors (see the Julia attractor, and the sidebar on the Lorenz
attractor). Correlation results in bounded behavior, and the portraits clearly
remain within certain behavioral limits. Notice also the convoluted pastry-like
appearance of the attractors. Two points can be very close together, yet be on
different "layers" of the "pastry"; consequently their trajectories can move in
very different directions.

Parameter Space

Phase space describes the fluctuation of a system whose concentration of
constituent variables is not altered by outside forces. A phase space portrait
for a pendulum exhibits fluctuation over different values of its constituent
variables (position and velocity), but does not show what happens if the bob
were progressively raised. The phase space portrait for a chemical reaction
shows the fluctuating amounts of reacting chemicals, but does not reflect what
happens if the chemist slowly increases one of those chemicals. When the
variables of a dynamical system are altered by external activity, obviously the
system's phase space portrait will be altered—the circular attractor describing

The Lorenz Butterfly Attractor

Edward Lorenz, a meteorologist at MIT, discovered the Chaotic attractor illustrated below in the early 1960s while modeling simple air convection equations on his computer. His model had only three variables—modern simulations for predicting weather just a few days ahead have more than a million variables—yet his simple system proved beyond doubt that accurate weather prediction is outside our grasp.

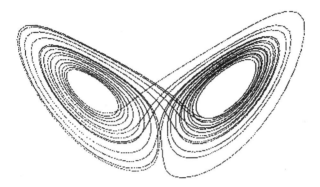

The lines on this attractor represent the trajectory of air currents, and the "wings" represent two different patterns of convection. Let's assume that the left wing represents convection patterns that bring generally warm weather while the right represents patterns that create generally rainy weather. Three variables create those convections, and they interact so Chaotically that two points separated by a mere fraction of a unit will quickly drift apart. Predicting what will happen with any one point, then, is impossible, because its trajectory can be seriously compromised by the slightest error in measuring initial conditions. A forecaster might measure current conditions and predict warm weather in 7 days. If it rains in 7 days, the mistake will not necessarily be because the meteorologist was inept, it will more likely be because accurate forecasting requires impossibly accurate measurements of initial conditions. Small errors of measurement can translate into major prediction errors.

One can sometimes get around this problem by plotting the trajectories of an ensemble of initial conditions. The forecaster plots measured initial conditions along with several possible initial conditions that lie near the measured one. If the trajectories all wind up on the left side of the attractor, one could reasonably predict warm weather. If some trajectories wind up on the right and others on the left, prediction would be little more than the flip of a coin.

The Lorenz attractor represents a stable system because, although the weather patterns it describes never repeat themselves exactly (an infinite number of lines can be crammed into the finite space represented by the attractor), it generally restricts itself to two conditions: warm weather or rain. Perturbation of the system will not change this fact, for the perturbed trajectories will merely return to the attractor.

a pendulum's motion gets smaller as the bob is raised, for example. External activity can even cause a system to jump from one attractor to another. We can represent the effects of such external activity on phase space portraits with a parameter space plot.

Attractors come in different forms. This one is called the Julia Attractor.

One can depict a phenomenon's parameter space by visualizing the constituent variables as axes of a coordinate plot. A coordinate point within such a plot represents the current level of all the parameters that influence a given phenomenon. That single point also locates the phase space portrait that would exist given that particular combination of parameters. Thus each possible combination of parameters defines a particular phase space portrait (see Figure 2.3).

As we said above, gradual changes in a system's parameters cause gradual change in a system's phase space portrait. As a system floats across parameter space, the shape of its attractor slowly transforms. Donut-shaped attractors may expand or contract; they may evolve into simple periodic attractors, or they may die out into point attractors. These transformations are usually rather undramatic, and the various phase space portraits in a given region of parameter space look pretty much alike.

There are certain locations in parameter space, however, where changes are explosive. The system crosses over an invisible boundary and the landscape of attractors alters dramatically. Such changes are called *bifurcations.* The phase space portraits in the new region of parameter space again change gradually just as they did in the first region, but they may differ dramatically in form from those in the former region. As parameters continue to change in the new region of parameter space, the attractors in this region slowly alter until, once more, a bifurcation boundary is reached and the phase space portraits again change. This pattern of relative constancy, then bifurcation, occurs repeatedly as parameters change. Some bifurcation regions are quite large and stable over many values of the corresponding parameters; in others, however, the distance between bifurcation boundaries has shrunk until parameter space is a catacomb of regions so small that minor parameter changes in any direction trigger bifurcation. Chaos, with its sensitive dependence and unpredictability, exists in these catacombs.

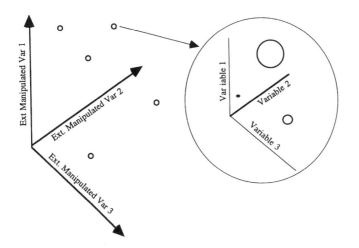

Figure 2.3. A three-dimensional state space embedded within a three-dimensional parameter space ("Ext." = externally).

Figure 15.17, in Chapter 15, illustrates these phenomena. The graphs map the population size of an exploited system, such as commercial fish. The different maps are generated by slowly increasing the birthrate of the system under investigation. When the birthrate is low (as in the map labeled $r = 1.9$), an initial population size of about 43% of niche (from the vertical axis) increases to around 47% of niche, then drops rapidly and spirals into an equilibrium point (point attractor) of about 31% of niche. This single map represents the phase space portrait of this system for the given configuration of parameters (birthrate, profit from harvesting, and cost of harvesting). The different plots in Figure 15.17 are phase space portraits for different birthrates; thus, taken together, they represent a walk through parameter space. Note that the original portrait gradually grows and becomes a circular attractor—the population cycles through a repeating range of behaviors. At about $r = 2.45$ the circle re-forms as a still larger circle, and the population fluctuates over a broader range of sizes. Then at about $r = 3.19$ the attractor breaks up and begins transforming into something entirely different. It has crossed a bifurcation wall, and the new attractor is Chaotic. The trajectories are no longer predictable; before they spiraled inward or revolved around a circle, now they jump from one position to the next in random sequence. The period-to-period size of the population is largely unknowable—we can expect that a small population will likely follow a large population, but that's about the best we can predict.

Social Attractors

So where are we going here? What does all this have to do with social systems? I propose that nearly all social activity can be metaphorically described with a strange attractor (or variation thereof), and that if proper indices can be identified, many social behaviors can be physically described with an attractor. This is a bold statement given the paucity of study to support it, but social Chaos Theory is, after all, a developing hypothesis.

The strange attractor is an obvious metaphor for social phenomena. It is stable but its trajectory never repeats itself; likewise, social behavior is stable but never quite repeats itself. The strange attractor has the capacity to change. It can grow or it can shrink to encompass a broader or a narrower range of behaviors; it can alter its appearance; it can convert to a dramatically different attractor; and it can even fade away. Social behavior is similarly more inclusive at times, less inclusive at others. In the mid-1990s, for example, the social attractor we call "moral sensibility" expanded to the point that it became accepting of what was once considered crude language. Like mathematical attractors, social behavior drifts across time: Fads come and go, mores change, our relationship to institutions alters, our definition of family evolves. Social attractors occasionally experience radical change—witness what happened to the USSR in the late 1980s, for example. Systems, like attractors, even fade away: An Incan empire once flourished in South America, the Romans once dominated the Western world, and the Turkish empire was the supreme authority in the Middle East, and all have dissolved back into the social ambiance that created them.

As we shall argue in Chapter 3, certain types of attractors can learn, they can carry information about their past, they can anticipate the future, and they can reproduce. With computers, we can create attractors that are difficult to differentiate from life itself. These attractors can spontaneously migrate across a computer's memory chips and throughout its storage space; they can reproduce themselves and move from computer to computer (we call these types of attractors "computer viruses"). *In-silico* attractors can mutate their structure to adapt to environmental demands; some can even learn chess so well that they are all but unbeatable.

Such metaphorical comparisons don't prove, of course, that social behaviors are Chaotic attractors, but, as the old saying sort of goes, if it looks like a dog and barks like a dog, why don't we see if it will tell us something about dogs.

Organization at the Edge

■ Complexity and Chaos

Social systems, actually any biological system, differ from the physical systems discussed thus far in that they are adaptive and they carry information about their environment and their past. Social and biological systems learn from their experiences and adjust their behaviors accordingly. They have the ability to anticipate their future and to attempt to manipulate that future. Chaos Theory has spawned a theory of such adaptive systems called Complexity.

Complexity is a hybrid state that lies between stability and Chaos. G. M. Zaslavsky, R. Z. Sagdeev, D. A. Usikov, and A. A. Chernikov, all with the Space Research Institute of Russia's Academy of Science, have analyzed the thin transition zone where stability ends and Chaos begins; the system they examined was the damped pendulum, which, under certain circumstances, can behave Chaotically. The phase space portraits of this zone reveal "hole-riddled structures in which regions of Chaos alternate with regions of stability" (p. 58; see Figure 3.1). Imagine a machine that could move a system from Chaos to stability and back again, all with the turn of a knob. A Chaotic phase space portrait placed in this machine would look like a tangle of very fine lines, and actually is one very long line balled into some sort of shape. Imagine now that we "turn down the heat," so to speak, on this Chaotic system. As we

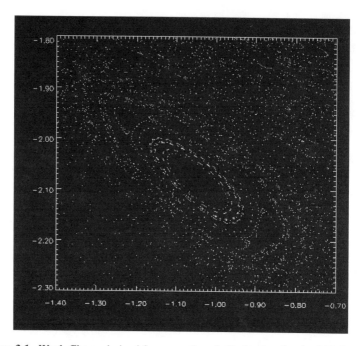

Figure 3.1. Weak Chaos, derived from equations in Zaslavsky, Sagdeev, Usikov, and Chernikov, *Weak Chaos and Quasi-Regular Patterns,* 1991.

near the transition zone, we would see islands of stability appear; as we slowly turned our knob down even farther, these islands would increase in size and number like ice crystals appearing in water as it approaches 0°C. At the divide between Chaos and stability, the islands occupy about as much space as do the areas of change. If you were to magnify a frozen region of this portrait you would find it shot through with regions of Chaos; similarly, Chaotic regions are shot full of stable regions.

Chris Langston, who has been at the center of Complexity study since its inception, has conducted Complexity experiments with something called "cellular automata" (see Sidebar titled Complexity and Cellular Automata: Life in a Computer). Cellular automata is a checkerboard game in which players live or die, and communities ebb and flow, depending upon the availability of resources. While the game is somewhat mechanical, it differs from Zaslavsky's work with damped pendulums in that the players maintain a history of their past and are able to reproduce themselves. Langston played the game with a "tuning knob," just as we imagined above. When he turned the knob up, the pattern of play was Chaotic; if he turned it down, the play

Complexity and Cellular Automata:
Life in a Computer

One of the interests of the famous mathematician John von Neumann was the notion of self-reproducing automatons. To make this particular story short, he did solve the problem, and in the early 1970s, a grad student at the University of Arizona named Chris Langston actually created a self-reproducing automaton on his Apple computer. But this isn't the part of the story that we want to focus on; our focus deals with the tool von Neumann needed to solve his problem. Von Neumann was stymied by self-reproduction until one of his colleagues, Stanislaw Ulam, suggested he try an approach called "cellular automata."

Cellular automata (or CA) is a dynamical process for transmitting information from one entity to another. John Conway, a mathematician from Cambridge University, introduced what is undoubtedly the most famous version of this process in a 1970 edition of *Scientific American*. Conway's game is played on an extended chess board, and is simple enough that the reader may want to pull out a checkerboard and experiment. Each cell of the board is either "alive" or "dead"—if you are trying this for yourself, use checkers to indicate that given cells are alive. Starting with a random clump of "live" cells, evaluate each cell of the board. A given cell will remain alive if it has two or three live neighbors in contiguous cells; it will die from over-crowding if there are more than three live neighbors (mark the dead chip for removal); and it will die from exposure if it has fewer than two live neighbors. A empty cell becomes alive if three of its neighboring cells are alive. Cells should be repeatedly evaluated by these rules. Experimenters will observe, after a while, interesting, emergent behavior: New clumps will develop and break off the "mother" clump, some clumps will fall into repeating on/off patterns, some will freeze with no activity whatsoever, some will disappear, and some will grow and contract with no discernible pattern. If you are lucky, you may even have a clump break away and move across the board (see the sequence below).

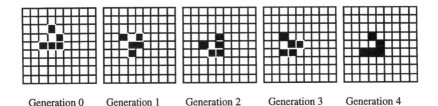

| Generation 0 | Generation 1 | Generation 2 | Generation 3 | Generation 4 |

There is a quicker although less interactive way to play this game. Professor Conway programmed the above rules on a computer, creating what we now call the Game of Life. The game does remind one of life's dynamics, such as the ebb and flow of civilizations, of biological niches, cities, or of species. The computer version is widely available and, for those with computer skills, easy to program.

Another version, called one-dimensional cellular automata, is useful for more precise, mathematical discussions. Start with a single row of cells (a one-dimensional grid), a set of rules similar to those used by the Game of Life, and a few live cells. Evaluate the cells according to the rules, but instead of changing the original row to its new state (thus losing its information), place the revisions in a new row immediately below the parent row. Evaluate the second row to create a third, and so forth. The obvious strength of this approach is that, unlike Conway's Life, one-dimensional CA maintains a visual history of its evolution, hence its usefulness.

(continued)

Complexity and Cellular Automata:
Life in a Computer (Continued)

There are more complex forms of CA. The units in von Neumann's original version, for example, didn't just turn on and off, alive and dead; each assumed 1 of 29 possible states. This sort of complexity was required to achieve self-reproduction. Years later a doctoral student at the University of Michigan, E. F. Codd, demonstrated that the same thing could be achieved with just eight states, or bits of information.

Chris Langston used Codd's idea with his self-reproducing automatons. Langston was interested in exploring what happens when the eight-state CA is tuned in certain ways. He simplified his CA grids a bit and allowed each unit to interact only with four other units, those directly above and below and to the left and right of it. Even so, with eight possible states for each unit, there are 8^5, or 32,768, possible states for the resulting system of five interacting units. If each of the eight possible states were represented by a color, then each generation could assume one of 32,768 color combinations.

One of the eight states (colors) of a unit represents the "off," or dead, state; the other seven are "on," or active states. Langston programmed his system so that he could chose the probability that a given unit would be alive in the next generation. He labeled this probability lambda, and called it his tuning knob. If lambda were tuned to 0.20, then each unit had a 20% chance of being alive in its next generation and an 80% chance of dying. He found that when lambda was low (say around 0.17), his systems froze much as water freezes. The units were in a state in which there was no change and no movement. This state was ideal for maintaining information—each unit knew what color it was, is, and would be—but there was nothing dynamic going on. A unit could not pass its color (information) on to the next generation because there were no new generations. The system was in what Stephen Wolfram has called Type I order, the same order you get with a pendulum at rest. When Langston tuned his system up a bit (lambda about 0.19) he saw Type II, or periodic order. Here, systems would rotate through several states repeatedly, in much the same way that a swinging pendulum repeats its back-and-forth motion over and over. Like Type I order, such systems are frozen with no information being shared. When Langston tuned his tuning knob high (say, lambda = 0.45 or better) he got Type III, or Chaotic, order. There was lots of movement and state change in this system; his computer screen looked like one big mass of dots all changing colors madly and with no observable pattern. Information was lost as soon as it was created, and there was no predicting where the system would go.

Somewhere between these extremes, with lambdas between 0.2 and 0.4 and best illustrated at lambda = 0.273, a different sort of order emerged. This state came on suddenly as Langston slowly edged his knob upward; the change was much like the phase transition that occurs when ice is warmed to slightly above $0°C$. This new state was somewhat like the ordered states created by lower levels of lambda because there was some sense of predictability to what was happening on the screen, yet it was also akin to the Chaotic states of higher lambdas because units were sharing information with one another (affecting each other's color). Unlike the Chaotic state, however, units clumped together into small colonies and each colony tended to assume specific, largely predictable characteristics—much like a biological niche with different types of animals. Some of these clumps would move around on the screen, and others would create new colonies. Occasionally clumps would bump into each other; such collisions typically resulted in the destruction of one of the clumps. However, the destroyed clumps were being replicated at about the same rate they were being destroyed, thus the relative proportion of clump types remained fairly constant. The system was stable—there were recognizable patterns and stable relationships, yet at the same time it was dynamic and changing. The whole thing was amazingly life-like. Langston called this nonfrozen, nonchaotic state, Type IV order, or order at the Edge of Chaos.

became stable and repetitive. At a carefully tuned point in between, a different kind of behavior emerged. Communities appeared that were dynamic, neither repetitive nor spread so large as to be Chaotically uncontrollable. Other communities appeared that were repetitive, but dynamic enough to actually move about the board. Still others created offspring, and some were just stodgy-stable. It was a dynamic diversity that was eerily reminiscent of life.

This region of dynamical system behavior has been labeled the Edge of Chaos by Chris Langston and Class IV stability by Stephen Wolfram. It represents a fourth type of stability (period, point, and Chaotic stability were introduced in the last chapter). This area of attraction provides "enough stability to store information and enough fluidity to send signals over arbitrary distances—the two things that are essential for computation [processing information]" (Mitchell Waldrop, p. 232). In contrast, information added to point and periodic systems is frozen and unusable, while information added to Chaotic systems is lost in the static of irregular activity.

Langston argued that here at the Edge of Chaos one finds "biological evolution, . . . cultural evolution, concepts combining and recombining and leaping from mind to mind over miles and generations" (in Roger Lewin, p. 214). He argued that life processes (social activity, food chains, etc.) are simultaneously stable and Chaotic, unchanging and changing, able to store information reliably yet process it dynamically. Organization, like Langston's automatons, emerges out of a Chaotic/stability soup, persists for a time, then dissolves back into the soup. Some of the organizations may be largely unchanging while others are quite dynamic. While in a protracted tendril of Complex stability, the organized state carries information that helps assure its survival and reproduction. Complex system outcomes typically cannot be predetermined, yet there is a sense of the predictable about them; their dynamics don't necessarily favor efficiency; and once a stability is established, the system tends to lock in to that steady state and to exclude other possible steady states. The emergence of educational movements, culture, organization, organizational climate, roles, and technologies can all be described by Complexity.

Complexity and Organization

Steven Levy defines complex systems thus:

A complex system is one whose component parts interact with sufficient intricacy that they cannot be predicted by standard linear equations; so many

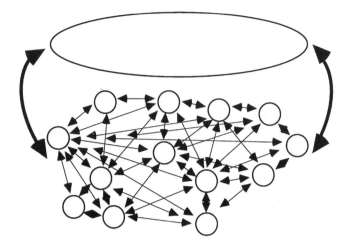

Figure 3.2. Chris Langston's depiction of complexity as related to Roger Lewin, *Complexity: Life at the Edge of Chaos* (1992).

variables are at work in the system that its overall behavior can only be understood as an emergent consequence of the holistic sum of all the myriad behaviors embedded within. Reductionism does not work with complex systems, and it is now clear that a purely reductionist approach cannot be applied when studying life: in living systems the whole is more than the sum of its parts. . . . [T]his is the result not of a mysterious dram of vital life-giving fluid but rather the benefits of complexity which allows certain behaviors and characteristics to emerge unbidden. The mechanisms of this may be hammered out by evolution, but the engine of evolution cannot begin to fire until a certain degree of complexity is present. Living systems epitomize complexity, so much that some scientists now see complexity as defining characteristics of life. (pp. 7-8)

Chris Langston envisioned Complexity as depicted in Figure 3.2. A system, shown as the large structure in the top half of the figure, emerges from the interactions of individual units, shown as small circles. The units in this depiction are driven by local rules, rather, and are not globally coordinated. Adaptive actors are in large degree guided by local interests and have limited understanding of the "big picture." Behaviors are based upon projections (however imperfect or primitive) of future outcome, thus they are adaptive in a teleological sense. They interact in some fashion, be it through language, hormones, or simple reaction to the presence of another. Because of the dynamics of interaction among these individuals, a system emerges. The system is not, of necessity, deliberately created; it may, and very often does, just happen. The individuals may know that they are supposed to organize, as would be the case with human systems, and in this sense it is deliberative. However, they may not remember why or how organization first occurred or why the given organizational structure is chosen over other possible forms.

The emergent system is truly greater than its parts. The whole has a grasp of a "larger picture" that is unavailable to the parts; it is far more functional than are its constituents or even the sum of constituent capabilities; it can carry and use a great deal of information; it can reproduce itself, often even producing replicas more complex than itself; it violates the second law of thermodynamics by growing and becoming stronger rather than dissipating (entropy); and it can maintain its integrity in the face of perturbation. The arrows from the emergent system back to the individuals (in Figure 3.2) indicate that the system exerts a commanding influence on the behavior of the individuals, thus further assuring its vitality and survival.

Emergence

So how do these ordered systems come about? Do they, as Darwin argued, evolve because natural selection separates order from disorder, fit from unfit, or are other forces at work? Complexity theorists are reaching a rather surprising, and certainly heretical, conclusion. Order emerges because of the "physics" of interaction. No work is required, no force is pushing an evolutionary snowball up an ever fitter hill. Order is free, as Complexity theorist Stuart Kauffman has argued; it just happens. Natural selection is a secondary player in this process; its role is to refine what interaction creates.

Stu Kauffman, one of the earliest researchers to observe emergence, contends that the odds in favor of organization through Darwinian accident are remote. Darwinism suggests, for example, that the 100,000 human genes have evolved into about 250 cell types through blind mutation. However, 100,000 genes exhibit $10^{30,000}$ possible activity states; this exceeds the number of hydrogen molecules in the universe. Kauffman argued, "to suggest that 'blind' natural selection will successfully lead you through the swamps of all $10^{30,000}$ states in the system, eventually hitting the 250 that you want," is naive (in Roger Lewin, p. 27). Using computer simulations, he demonstrated that an interactive network of 100,000 units switching each other on or off as is observed among genes (F. Jacob & J. Monad) will quickly gravitate to a small number of stable systems. The number of groups that evolve is approximately the square root of the number of units in the original pool, or, in this case, about 316 patterns—close to the 250 cell types found in humans.

Stability, Kauffman concludes, emerges from the adaptive interactions of a network of units. These stable patterns do not evolve because of hit-or-miss natural selection, rather the stabilities are a product of interaction dynamics. Further, such stable patterns are not randomly generated; were Kauffman's system reset to its original state of 100,000 independent units, roughly similar patterns would evolve, as if drawn by attractors.

How Structure Emerges

Stu Kauffman described a dynamic that explains how systems emerge. His goal was to explain how life emerged from the pre-biotic soup of nonliving chemicals that once existed on this planet, but the dynamic can be invoked to explain the emergence of many phenomena—including social phenomena. He called this dynamic *autocatalytic* interaction; it involves, not surprisingly, catalysts. A catalyst is something that speeds up a process that could conceivably occur without the catalyst, but that would take forever to do so. In cruder terms, a catalyst makes things happen that wouldn't likely happen otherwise. Typically we see a catalyst as an otherwise inert substance that smooths the way for substance X and substance Y to get together—like a matchmaker who quietly manipulates lives to make it possible for boy to meet girl and fall in love.

Kauffman had something a little different in mind, however. Autocatalism is a process in which event A catalyzes event B, event B catalyzes event C, C catalyzes D, and D (perhaps in combination with B and/or C), catalyzes A. Here matchmakers are not silent third parties; they are active participants in, and beneficiaries of, the process, for they themselves are catalyzed by it. A network of catalytic and noncatalytic substances or events emerges and grows out of the process. Event A has indirectly catalyzed the rapid development of D, which in turn catalyzes the rapid development of more A. Events B and C, meanwhile, might catalyze yet another event, F, which finds G, and F and G together create more C. You can see how this system could spread like wildfire, involving a growing number of spin-offs and new catalysts.

The emergence of riots can be described with this process. Perhaps a feeling of alienation and oppression within a certain group of people spawns (catalyzes) hatred of perceived antagonists. Angry groups emerge and begin to spread their message. The message increases the feeling of alienation. Also emerging out of this soup is a sense of anomie, or, broadly, a sense that one owes nothing to the larger society. Such anomie catalyzes, among other things, criminal behavior that widens the gap between the focal group and the larger society (increases alienation). Anomie is also a disincentive for advancing oneself within the dominant society, thus a certain level of poverty is assured. The web grows, and the ambiance for riot emerges. Once a critical level of alienation/anomie/anger/poverty/and so on is reached, a relatively innocuous event can trigger riot. In Los Angeles in 1992, the Rodney King verdict brought just such a network to the edge of riot—it pushed an autocatalyzed powder keg to the critical level. Shortly thereafter, a routine arrest in a critical community triggered the riot. A "living" entity that we call a mob emerged out of the social soup of Los Angeles in the early 1990s in much the same way that (according to Kauffman) life emerged from the pre-biotic soup of the Earth.

Autocatalysis is a bottoms-up, or local, phenomenon: It is not coordinated by an external manager, a queen bee if you like. This local principle is central to a type of computer simulation known as artificial life. Computer programs are typically coordinated from the top down. Most arcade games, for example, have algorithms that specify how the game is to respond to any given input by the human operator. The word processor I am currently using has rules to cover any action I may take. If I click on the button labeled "B" at the top of my screen, the program has instructions to bold any text that is highlighted. If I pressed the command and "S" keys, it knows to save my work. Word processors and games are unified systems that are centrally coordinated; this is top-down programming.

Artificial life algorithms are programmed to respond from the bottom up. There are no global rules of behavior, no unified algorithm. Instead there are a lot of small simple algorithms specifying local behavior patterns. Craig Reynolds of Symbolics computer company, for example, created a bird-like figure on his computer screen and gave it instructions to behave in certain ways. Among other things, it was instructed to move about on the screen, to avoid getting too close to any object on the screen, but not to get too far away from other bird-like figures. He generated a handful of these figures (which he called "boids") and turned them loose in his computer. They immediately exhibited flocking behavior. He created an environment of obstacles for his boids, and they flew around them—even splitting the flock and reassembling it on the other side. Organized behavior emerges from localized rules; structure need not be coordinated to exist. The same principle applies to Kauffman's autocatalytic sets: Order emerges from the spontaneous, local interactions of such networks.

Networks and Phase Transition

Everyone has seen phase transition. When water turns to ice, or steam turns to water, there is phase transition. If you were to experience a sudden mood swing, that's a phase transition. That point at which a crowd becomes a mob, when scattered tribes become a city-state, and when a new technology catches on—these are all phase transitions. Transitions represent the point at which one organized state converts to another, as when tribes become a city-state. They can also represent a point between orderly behavior and disorderly behavior, as when a crowd becomes a mob—or when stability becomes Chaos. They occur rather rapidly and are often unexpected. With autocatalytic sets, phase transitions to ordered systems occur when a critical number of units are linked.

Kauffman illustrates this rather neatly in his 1995 book. He asks that we imagine a pile of buttons before us. Take a piece of string and tie two randomly selected buttons at either end. Select two more buttons at random and string them together, then two more, and so forth. Eventually you will select a button that is already attached to another, and you'll have a network of three. Later a network of four will appear. The networks will, in all probability, remain rather small, however, until the number of draws equals approximately half the number of buttons. Then, precipitously, with the tying of just a few more buttons, a large network will emerge. You'll pick up a single button and find that perhaps 80% of your buttons are lifted with it. A phase transition from small, isolated networks to a massive network has occurred, and order has emerged.

We need to consider this dynamic on two metaphorical levels. At one level, the analogy helps us understand what happens when crowds change into mobs or when tribes make the transition to city-state. Up until the transition, linkages are forged but nothing significant or noticeable appears. Then, with just a few more pieces in place, something explosive happens, order emerges. For example, small groups of people may begin to pull together over some event (such as perceptions of prejudice), and linkages begin to form piece by piece. Then one or more events occur that complete an interactive critical mass, and the group becomes a coordinated, rampaging mob. Tribes in a given region increase in number and interact with one another. Events begin as small networks, two or three tribes at a time bonded by intermarriage or common good. Ties across these small alliances begin to appear here and there, then, almost overnight, a few alliances are forged (whether peacefully or by conquest) that pull together a large number of the small networks, and a civilization emerges. Transistors were invented in the 1950s and began to appear in small radios and similar appliances. Logic boards emerged about the same time and became useful for compressing the circuitry of televisions and computers. Iron oxide storage devices (such as tape recorders) were refined during this period. LEDs linked with circuit boards and transistors in the late 1960s, and hand calculators resulted. Different technologies were emerging and tentatively linking together in different innovations. Then in the mid 1970s, inventors pulled together a number of these innovations, linked them, and the microcomputer exploded onto the market. Order can appear quite suddenly, as if by magic, but it results only after numerous small pieces of the whole have set the stage.

At yet another metaphorical level the analogy with the buttons helps us understand something of the nature of life. A network of buttons can assume one of three general states. The first is a stable state in which buttons exist separately or in small, isolated networks. This is an unworkable metaphor for life. Each button carries information about itself—which is indeed one of the characteristics of life. It knows exactly where it is now, it knows where it was yesterday and where it will be tomorrow. One can read the geological history and future of the world in rocks. Yet stones, like the isolated buttons, aren't doing anything with the information. They aren't modifying it, they're not passing it on to offspring, they aren't adapting to environmental conditions—they are inert. Although memory is important to life, life simply cannot live with that level of stability. The second state our buttons can assume is a Chaotic state in which the buttons are so interlinked that a small tug on any one button causes nearly every button to shift position. Weather patterns, for example, are interlinked such that the flapping of a butterfly's wings in Rio can affect the weather in Chicago (to paraphrase Edward Lorenz's metaphor). This state is active, dynamic, changing—like life. But it carries little or no information about its past or future; knowledge of the state of the weather today provides no information about what it will be in 5 years, and does not allow one to project back to conditions 5 years earlier. Life needs information in order to adapt to its environment. It must remember, for example, that certain units in its environment will eat it and that other units are good for it to eat. It must even remember that it needs to eat in order to survive.

The third state is in a narrow band just before the last few buttons are linked and the massive network emerges—between order and Chaos, at the Edge of Chaos. At this point, small networks exist that are tentatively linked with a limited number of other networks. The networks are sufficiently ordered to carry information about themselves, but close enough to Chaos that they experience its tug and are doing dynamic things. Here, biological networks are active enough to reproduce and sufficiently stable to have information that can be passed on to another generation. They remember that certain other units will do harm to them, and are active enough to act on that knowledge. They can explore new opportunities without forgetting where they came from—in case the new opportunities don't pan out. They are sufficiently isolated that they can act without disturbing other networks, but if they discover something useful, they are sufficiently linked that others can learn about it. Life can—and does—exist here.

Social Catalysts

We now ask: What catalyzes social behavior? What is it that motivates ants and wolves and humans to cooperate and live in groups? Our primary response is: selfish need. We cooperate because we animals pursue personal self-interests. We are motivated to survive and persist, and that motivation catalyzes us to unite.

At first glance it seems contradictory to claim that selfishness sparks cooperation, but on second glance it makes good sense. What better way to achieve ones' goals than to solicit the help of others, and what better way to avoid achieving ones' goals than to have others opposing us? An individual hyena could hardly bring down a large animal alone, but a pack of hyenas is a formidable force. A single human cannot build, let alone sail, a battleship, but a cooperating group of humans can. Even criminals tend to cooperate with one another—witness the success of organized crime.

Selfishness is a personal and local phenomenon. It is not conspiratorial; it needs no mandate; it is not imposed by some queen bee who coordinates the behavior of underlings. It is an individual trait and does not depend upon any external force. Similarly, cooperation is a product of that selfishness and needs no queen bee to emerge—it appears unbidden. Nobody is around in an ant colony board room putting together organizational charts and work manifests. Wolf packs do not have planning committees (which, of course, makes them more civilized than humans). Cooperation is a spontaneous outcome of individual-based, selfish rules.

Symbolic Catalysts

Humans are catalyzed by something else as well, something more cerebral. We respond to symbols, such as words, ideas, concepts, opinions, emotions, projections, and beliefs. We join social movements because of abstract beliefs, certain words can galvanize us to group action or involve us in mass hysteria, emotions motivate us to join mobs, we join discussion groups and academic classes to share ideas, we marry because of love, we create armies because of the fear of invasion, and we socialize because of friendship. We assign meaning to things that have no physical substance. These mental constructs interact with reality in such complex ways that some philosophers question whether our worlds are physical reality or cognitive illusions. Reality or not, they catalyze us to create complex webs of alliances that we call social structure.

Symbolic catalysts are at times difficult to differentiate from selfish needs catalysts. Do we, for example, marry because of emotions or because of the selfish need to procreate; are our armies the result of future projections or are they a survival strategy akin to the defensive strategies of many animals? Are some of these symbols little more than a flush of very physical hormones—love, for example? Such confusion, however, doesn't really matter, for the outcome is the same: Localized drives, whether needs based, symbolic, or hormonal, catalyze interactions that in turn cause social structures to emerge unbidden. The same general mechanisms that drive Kauffman's genetic networks are at work in human networks.

Social Solitons

John Scott Russell, an engineer and boat builder, was riding his horse beside an English canal in 1834 when he noticed something unusual. He wrote about this incident as follows:

> I was observing the motion of a boat which was rapidly drawn along a narrow channel by a pair of horses when the boat suddenly stopped—not so the mass of water in the channel which it had put in motion; it accumulated round the prow of the vessel in a state of violent agitation, then suddenly leaving it behind, rolled forward with great velocity, assuming the form of a large solitary elevation, a rounded, smooth and well-defined heap of water, which continued its course along the channel apparently without change of form or diminution of speed. I followed it on horseback, and overtook it still rolling on at a rate of some eight or nine miles an hour, preserving its original figure some thirty feet long and a foot to a foot and a half in height. Its height gradually diminished, and after a chase of one or two miles I lost it in the windings of the channel. (from Briggs & Peat, p. 120)

What's so unusual, you ask; he merely saw a large wave. In a sense that's true, but this wave was different. To start with, this was a solitary wave;

everyone knows that normal waves emerge as sets that move in concentric circles. Because of this feature, what he saw has been labeled a *soliton*. Second, normal waves travel a short distance then break up; this one traveled for miles without changing. Third, this wave was somewhat larger than expected. Russell subsequently experimented with this phenomenon and found that solitons extend to the bottom of the channel that carries them. Normal waves are small and ride the surface of water.

Waves are made up of smaller, individual waves, or frequencies. Typically such "wavelets" all do their own thing, thus they quickly break up and fade away. In solitons, the wavelets are coordinated in a nonlinear, or Chaotic, fashion. Each frequency is a small attractor, and each attractor correlates, or resonates, with its neighbors. That is, the attractors interact, and the interaction causes them to resonate in sync with one another. The dance is quite complex, and taken together the attractors describe a larger attractor—the soliton. Because of the interaction and resultant complex of correlated activities, the system behaves as a unitary whole that is distinctly more significant than the sum of its parts.

Solitons possess some interesting characteristics. The speed at which they move is related to their shape, thus tall thin solitons move more rapidly than short, squat ones. This in itself is not terribly interesting, except it means that, when two solitons intersect, things do get a bit interesting. When a faster soliton catches up with a slower one, it initially merges with the slower one and, for a short period, the two cannot be distinguished. But then the faster soliton reemerges ahead of the slower one, and continues to outpace it. The two solitons have maintained "memory" of who they are and what they are about; merging did not confuse them.

Adaptive systems behave in a similar manner. My favorite example of this is what I call the "highway rat pack"; I have also heard it called a pod. It is the pack of cars often seen traveling down interstate highways in a tight little group at 70 to 80 miles per hour. Everyone has seen them appear in their rearview mirror. Within a few minutes they are on you, and you may feel the urge to join them; if not, they quickly move past and disappear in the distance. Were you to join the pack, you would find that your driving behavior is controlled by your interaction with the other drivers. Everybody wants to be in front and nobody wants to be passed. Often drivers take turns leading the pack. Individuals are so intent on their "responsibilities" within the pack that it is difficult to break out of it. One must consciously take control of oneself and understand that what is happening is madness. But in a sense it is not; participants in a pack lose something of their individuality to what can only be termed a larger individuality. The pack is not so much a set of conscious agents as it is a corporate conscious agent. The individual drivers become part of something bigger—perhaps we could call it a social soliton.

These social solitons are everywhere. We see them in fads, rumors, cliques, mobs, riots, lynchings, social movements, clans, crowd behavior at sporting events (the phenomenon known as the "wave" is a good pun here), camaraderie within army platoons, political campaigns, and rock star concerts—any form of what sociologists call "collective behavior." When we see or experience solitons, we generally say that a "crowd mentality" has taken over. Often, subsidiary phenomena are at work—perhaps rumors, mass hysteria, or anger; at other times, solitons emerge because we become caught up in what we see happening around us. Solitons pose moral dilemmas of individual responsibility—do we, for example, hold John Ehrlichman responsibly for his role in the Watergate cover-up, or do we show compassion for a person who was swept up in events he couldn't control?

Both the soliton observed by John Russell in a canal and social solitons are a function of nonlinear dynamics. Further, both are stably dynamic, and they maintain memory of who they are and where they have been; that is, they possess characteristics we attribute to Complexity. Social solitons add a degree of adaptability—they change to adjust to their environments and to improve their effectiveness. Social movements, for example, respond to existing political contingencies. Social solitons are better able to map their environments, maintain information about their past, and project their futures. Social solitons can "reproduce" themselves; for example, social riots, like that which occurred at the Sorbonne in 1968, are rarely isolated events; rather they tend to be replicated in other locations.

Social solitons distinctly represent what we are calling Complex behavior. Chaotic physical systems can achieve stable coordinated behavior, as is demonstrated by Russell's soliton. Yet social solitons, unlike physical solitons, tend to be products of symbolic, rather than physical, communication. Even cellular automata communicate via the symbolic rules given them by humans rather than by physical contact. Further, communication among attractors in a social soliton is controlled in that each attractor has access to only a limited number of other attractors, and the attractors with which it can communicate can be at some distance. Attractors in physical solitons, by contrast, have direct access to any attractor within their physical proximity, but only to those in their proximity. Consequently the internal structure of a social system is typically far more ordered than is that of physical systems; that is, the internal structure of a physical system is Chaotic while that of a social system lies at the Edge of Chaos. The attractors that comprise social solitons likewise lie at the Edge, while those that comprise physical solitons are either stable or Chaotic.

CHAPTER

4

Shifting Historical Premises to the Edge of Chaos

▨ God of the Gaps

Modern organizational theory is wrapped in a legacy of old debates about teleology, causation, life force (*élan vital*), equilibrium, reductionism, and what it means to be alive. It reflects battles fought over the past few centuries to deny supernatural explanation, to substitute rationality for God. The battles, which were waged by thinkers like Sir Isaac Newton, Herbert Spencer, and Albert Einstein, have purged us of ideas that smack of mysticism, ideas such as teleology, and have led us on heady journeys into rationality. Despite the efforts of these and other thinkers, however, organizational theorists, whose science often mimics that of the physical sciences, have always had difficulty eluding teleology and similar "unscientific" thoughts. Even so, many of them have been caught up in the belief that they too will eventually ferret out nature's sociological secrets and bring rationality to organizational science.

In this chapter we will relate some of the old debates. As we develop the thoughts and perspectives of our philosophical forefathers, we will weave the Complexity theme into the discussion to show how some of the troublesome ideas with which they struggled are illuminated by Chaos and Complexity theories. We would like to establish underlying ideas that will be important as we develop a Complex Systems Theory of organization. We will question our culture's perspective on social dynamics. We will ask if Western thinkers have blinded themselves to important understanding in their zeal to remove God from the gaps in our understanding.

■ Pervasive Problems:
Order, Randomness, and Causality

Before the Western world "saw the rational light" during the Enlightenment period, people commonly attributed outcome to need. Horses had tails because they needed them for swatting flies, or government existed because human nature is selfish and people must be protected against their own brutishness (the Hobbesonian perspective). Much of nature and society were attributed to a divine creator who knew our needs. This is teleology. Then Newton came along with his heretical notion that all of nature can be attributed to some natural cause, Pasteur proved that life is not a product of divine spontaneous generation, and Darwin gave us tools for explaining life without evoking a deity. God's creativity was knocked off its position in center stage, physical explanations of nature and society replaced divine explanations based upon omniscient understanding of needs, and new perspectives on order and causality emerged.

Sir Isaac Newton was a particularly significant spokesman for the new scientific worldview. For instance, he articulated important ideas regarding causality—ideas that today pervade not only our understandings of scientific phenomena but that dominate the way we think about nearly everything. The core of those ideas is quite simple: event A causes event B; event B is proportionately related to A (i.e., small As cause small Bs); and any event can be attributed to something. The questions that we ask as a culture, whether scientific or offhand, reflect some variation of these themes. They betray an assumption that events can be linearly attributed to simple causes. The question, "Why did Grandmother die?" betrays a desire for meaning and rationality in life. "What drives people to riot?" implies a simple cause of social disorder. "Why is that boy such a discipline problem" betrays a belief that we could solve discipline problems if we could find the simple cause (today's solution is to chalk bad behavior up to physical problems and to treat children with Ritalin®). Each of these "causes" is likely implicated in the phenomenon it purports to represent, but it is not "the" causal agent of that event.

Actually, relatively few social events are the result of simple one-way causation; rather they result from complex interactions among a number of variables. It hasn't taken nonlinear theory to teach us this, for a number of recent social and organizational models make this argument. Loose coupling theorist Karl Weick, for example, is rather pointed about circular causality and multiple interactions.

It will take nonlinear theory, however, to force us to understand how dramatic this break from Newtonian logic is. Circular causation means more than confused or complicated, it means that order must be understood as the product of such interaction rather than the product of simple causality. One may be the source of information that leads to a rumor, but the social phenomenon that evolves about that information is an emergent, self-organizing entity. Rumors are fed by urban folkways, cultural fears, human biases, and imagination. The original information about which these forces emerge is really a minor actor in the process, a simple excuse for releasing the social dynamic, an interesting story that gives voice to something deep seated in the social psyche. Once the agent provides the trigger, he or she has no further influence, for emergence is the property of interaction, and the message becomes the servant of collective need. After a while, the messenger may even be hard-pressed to recognize the original message. To say that the agent caused the rumor is as naive as saying that the assassination of Archduke Ferdinand caused World War I; in both cases the purported causes were nothing more than pawns in a self-organizing process with pre-existing roots.

There is an even more dramatic break from Newton implicit in nonlinear theory. Not only are the traditional causal paths disrupted, but the very notion that every event has its predictable cause or causes is broken as well. At the very heart of traditional science is the assumption that all physical events can be understood, that there is, ultimately, a basic rationality to nature. God does not play dice with the universe, says Einstein. One may need to measure a thousand initial conditions simultaneously, but events will succumb to analysis. The outcome of even a coin toss can be determined if the precise state of every muscle in the arm, the state of convection currents, the mass of the coin, and the force of gravity are known. Nonlinear theorists say all this isn't so, that Lorenz's sensitive dependence and Poincaré's resonances lend a basic randomness to interactive events. Nature is not an automaton, predestined at the moment of the big bang; rather it is capable of free will, of creativity, of teleology. God cannot, after all, be banished from the gaps, for the gaps are axiomatic in nature.

Mathematical stability is closely related to this argument; like Newtonian causality, its assumptions seem to be burned into our cultural genes. As we discussed in Chapter 2, Newton identified two general categories of stability: the point attractor and the periodic attractor. That such stability exists is hardly disputable, but the fact that they exist so firmly in our psyche has blinded us to alternative perspectives of stability. To us, a phenomenon is either repetitive and stable or it is random and without pattern. We have little tolerance for disorder, and there seems little room for a middle ground. Nonlinear theory, however, teaches that randomness and unpredictability are givens, and that they can build order, albeit a rather complex one. Social stability exists; it is dynamic and somewhat disordered, but there needn't be an either/or perspective of order.

Finally, traditional Newtonian thought assumes that causality is time independent: That which works in one temporal direction will work in the other. If an event can be projected mathematically into the future, it can be reversed and projected into the past. If one only knows the current state of a system and knows the laws of its motion, one can determine where it is going and where it has been. Time travel is, hypothetically, possible. Chaos theory argues that these notions are largely inaccurate, at least in the interactive world of real events.

■ The First of Newton's Legacies: Social Physics

Perhaps the earliest theory of organization and society (other than philosophy) evolved shortly after Newton wrote *Principia,* during the infancy of the Industrial Revolution. Known as Social Physics, this theory compares society to a machine with its complex of different but interdependent parts. Just as machines require engines, cog wheels, and levers, a society requires governors, bankers, and police, and a factory requires leaders, line workers, and a sales force. The parts of such systems are held together by attraction and differentiated by repulsion. Social Physicists wrote of social space (analogous to phase space in physics), centrifugal forces, attraction and attractors, countervailing pressures, and social equilibrium.

Two ideas are introduced into organizational theory by Social Physics, one directly and the second indirectly. Both are important even today in one form or another. Equilibrium, which is directly introduced, resulted from observations of persistent structures in human affairs and from Newton's proposals about stability. The second notion, the one introduced by implica-tion, is that organizations are composed of units linked in a causal chain. In its simplest form, this refers to a system in which one component drives a second, which in turn drives a third, and so forth. Such a system is mortally dependent upon the well-being of all parts; if one component malfunctions, the machine's function is degraded by some degree and may even cease to operate. The modern computer program is structured like this; if even a semi-colon is left out of a program, it will likely crash. In today's parlance, such systems are called "brittle." This notion of systemic brittleness lurks behind many models of society and organizations. Science fiction authors tell tales of wildly disruptive time travelers, organizational theorists emphasize the critical importance of leadership decision making, and we worried about terrible things happening to the United States for the few leaderless hours after John Hinkley shot President Reagan. Some humorist once said, however, that if architects built buildings the way programmers create programs, the first termite that came along would bring our culture to its knees. The fact is we don't build buildings like that, and our societies are robust, not brittle.

Social equilibrium has been a rather troublesome notion for organiza-tional theorists. One observer can look at social systems and marvel at the persistence of society and family and organizations and cultures; another can observe the same systems and see only structures in constant states of flux. An individual is not the person he or she was 10 years ago, and neither is an organization. The person is more mature; the organization has perhaps adopted new product lines or changed the products it once produced, and surely many of the personnel have changed. Some systems may even have experienced dramatic change, as happened with AT&T® after divestiture. Systems that adapt, change. Yet structures do persist, and often with little apparent change. IBM® as a whole looks about the same as it did a decade ago despite the more modern appearance of its product line; similarly, public education hasn't changed much in the past 10 or 15 years despite the fickle-ness of public opinion. Things change in one sense, yet in another, they don't. Newton's model of stability doesn't help us resolve this contradiction; thus, in order to force social events into our worldview, social scientists have had to choose between an unstable (change) perspective and a stability perspective.

The debate over instability and stability models of social events is rather elegantly clarified by Chaos and Complexity theories. In Chapter 2 we discussed the similarities between Chaotic attractors and social dynamics—the fact that both are globally stable yet locally nonrepetitive. That is, adaptive systems are both changing and stable; they maintain cohesion and a link with their past while they drift about. Stability needn't exist at the expense of change, and vice versa. Much of this book is devoted to dissecting this notion; life and society and organizations are, we shall discover, unstable stabilities residing at the Edge of Chaos.

▓ Kant and Teleology

At about the same time that nascent sociologists were playing with their concepts of Social Physics—the middle to end of the 18th century—biologists and philosophers were focused on structural similarities among species. Darwinian notions of change and natural selection had not yet arrived (although a few radical French biologists, notably Jean-Baptiste Lamarck, were developing such ideas), so structure was considered fixed and unchanging. Further, biologists of that day argued that all life came from the omniscient and perfect God (i.e., a God that is rational and orderly—an argument that derived more from Newton than from God), thus biological structures are perfectly suited for their appointed tasks and there are logical patterns to structure. This movement, rationally, is known as Rational Morphology. Observations that would later lead Darwin to conclude that similar structures evolved because of common ancestry led biologists of the late 18th and early 19th centuries to conclude that organisms were variations on a few universal mechanisms. Their aim was "to find a kind of inherent necessity, the logic behind the apparent diversity" (Kauffman, 1993, p. 4).

To understand, imagine how we would react if it were discovered that natural selection plays no role in determining structural variations and that there has been no developmental history in biology. How would one explain variations and commonalties among organisms? Common ancestry could not be invoked, and we could no longer argue that structure responds to environmental sifting. Without evolution, how does one describe life? By demoting Darwin one gets a better appreciation and understanding of the questions asked by Rational Morphologists. Are there basic principles underlying structural differences and similarities in much the same way that differences and similarities in crystalline structure underline relationships among minerals?

The German philosopher Immanuel Kant, a leader in the Rational Morphology movement, expanded this perspective by considering the differences between animate and mechanical objects. As Stuart Kauffman observes:

For Kant, organisms were fundamentally self-reproducing, and therefore *self-organizing wholes*. In a mechanical device, the parts exist only *for* one another in that each is the condition of the others' functions toward a common functional end. In contrast, in an organism, the "parts" exist both for one another and *by means* of one another. For Kant, an organism "is that for which everything is both a means and end" (Webster & Goodwin, 1982). . . . Organisms are the mechanisms by which the whole is maintained, and the whole is the ordering such that the parts are maintained. (1993, pp. 4 and 643; italics in original)

Kant makes a rather revolutionary observation: Biological structure— eyes, ears, leaves, hips, legs—is a function of interactions. As Complexity theorist Brian Goodwin described it, Kant perceived organisms as "structural and functional unities resulting from a self-organizing, self-generating dynamic" (p. 197). This is Complexity theory almost 200 years ahead of time; that Kant understood it is extraordinary.

Complexity and Structure

Darwin hypothesized that common structure is the result of common ancestry and selection. This directly contradicts Rational Morphology's arguments that form is a function of necessity. According to Darwin's logic, a successful structure (say, a ball and socket hip) evolved millions of years ago because of natural selection—an accidental mutation produced the structure and viability was added to the animals that possessed it. The hip eventually dominated the species and, in the grand scheme of evolution, was subsequently passed on to species that derived from the original animal. That's why so many different animals today possess the ball and socket joint.

D'Arcy Thompson, in his literary treatise titled *On Growth and Form,* disagreed somewhat with the Darwinian notion of common ancestry, arguing that much of biological structure can be better accounted for by physical forces. He wrote in the introduction to his book:

Cell and tissue, shell and bone, leaf and flower, are so many portions of matter, and it is in obedience to the laws of physics that their particles have been moved, moulded and conformed. . . . Their problems of form are in the first instance mathematical problems, their problems of growth are essentially physical problems, and the morphologist is, *ipso facto,* a student of physical science. (pp. 7-8)

> We want to see how, in some cases at least, the form of living things, and of the parts of living things, can be explained by physical considerations, and to realize that in general no organic form exists save such as are in conformity with physical and mathematical laws. (p. 10)

This is where Rational Morphology might have taken us had not Darwinian logic come along, and Thompson is considered the last of the great Rational Morphologists. His book is filled with meticulous drawings of ink spills in water juxtaposed against jellyfish and men-of-war, photographs of a milk splash juxtaposed against hydroid polyps, pictures of artificial membranes formed by the diffusion of salt against the cells of a honeybee hive, the spiral of Archimedes against sea shells. His mathematics and his drawings make the point that the structures of living organisms aren't necessarily biological accident reinforced by natural selection, but the inexorable and inevitable result of the demands of physical law. Structural similarity across different species need not be attributed to common ancestry; rather similarities can be the simple result of physics—an "inherent necessity," as Kant put it.

These arguments bear significance for organizational theory as well as biology. "Inherent necessity" and self-organization challenge, for example, the close relationship that many theorists believe to exist between environmental pressure and organizational structure. Structural Contingency Theory, which is founded in the seminal work of James March and Herbert Simon, makes the underlying assumption that "a firm's efficiency is dependent on the relation between the state of the environment and the form of the organization" (Grandori, 1987, p. 1). Population Ecologists argue that, "Organizations exist in environments and are responsive to environmental forces" (McKelvey, 1982, p. 242), and "natural selection will turn out to be the best way to explain the relation of organizations to their environments" (p. 243; Population Ecology is a set of organizational theories based on the evolutionary principles of biology). The Kantian view, particularly in its more modern expressions, does not dispute that evolution is a force acting on structure, but suggests that many elements of structure may be better explained by physical forces or, as Kauffman argues, that structure is an interactive product of physical forces (particularly Complexity dynamics) and natural selection. One might argue, for example, that standard organizational forms (such as organizational departmentalization or hierarchical structuring) are as much or more products of the demands of inevitable necessity as they are products of common ancestry.

Organizational theory supports a specialty called systematics, which is concerned with categorizing social organizations in the same manner that biology is organized into phyla and species. Two broad perspectives can be identified in systematics: that which bases classification on evolutionary lineages or "family trees," and that which looks solely at current structural parallels regardless of lineage (an approach that Kant and Thompson would appreciate). Theorists commonly assume that both approaches will lead to similar conclusions but that ancestry will be the better predictor of structure. Systematist Bill McKelvey, however, has observed that there are many similarities among organizations that cannot be explained by common ancestry, leading one to wonder if there may not be more to structure than can be explained by selection. Thompson would certainly say yes, there is—there's physics and mathematics. Nonlinear dynamics would add that structure is also the product of the physics of interaction. Neither Thompson nor Chaos and Complexity theorists would argue that selection is unimportant, rather they point us to additional explanations of structure and behavior and life. Neither would choose to portray themselves as an alternative to evolutionary theory, rather they would choose to interact with Darwinism in explaining life's and society's wonders.

Teleology

Rational morphology and Darwinian logic have differing perceptions of causation. Teleological (or final) causation and efficient causation are largely opposite perceptions of cause-effect. Teleology would say, "This object exists in order to fulfill a certain goal," or "Drinking glasses are round to fit comfortably in the hand," or "Horses have tails to swat at flies." Efficient causation, to the contrary, would argue that, "This object is a function of forces with no intent," or "Glasses are round because the shape naturally emerges when molten glass is spun in a gravitational field."

Early notions of life favored the teleological perspective, while D'Arcy Thompson advocates efficient causation. Darwinian "survival of the fittest" is something of an amalgam of these opposites. Thompson explains:

> [With natural selection] . . . we have reached a teleology without a *telos*, . . . an "adaptation" without "design," a teleology in which the final cause becomes little more than the mere expression or resultant of a sifting out of the good from the bad, or the better from the worse, in short of a process of mechanism. (p. 4)

It is fair to say that Complexity theorists see causation from all three perspectives. The physics of Stu Kauffman's massive parallel systems, for example, generates order with decidedly nonpurposeful, physical interaction. Chris Langston's Edge of Chaos phenomenon emerged out of the activity of nonpurposeful cellular automata. These reflect a Kantian perspective and efficient causation. Even so, Complexity has room for systems of organisms moving myopically toward their own ends but aided by selective processes—the Darwinian ambivalence, of which Thompson wrote so eloquently. But for more complex systems (those that tend to be more highly differentiated, such as mammals or birds), the "myopic" behavior takes on an even greater sense of purposefulness that seems to transcend Darwin's blind sifting process. Within human systems many behaviors are unquestionably purposeful and teleological, as with the strategies of generals. We might argue with Darwin that, while intent is purposeful, our activities are nonetheless subject to vagaries and complexities well beyond our control, thus ultimately all activity is subject to blind selective forces. Undoubtedly our actions are subject to vagaries beyond our control, but blind outcome hardly explains the teleological success of the British in the Falklands or the American and UN forces in Iraq, where activity was clearly related to a desired outcome.

There is also the matter of acquired traits entering the genetic pool. Complexity theorists Norman Packard and Mark Bedau argue that learned behavior (such as climbing) can a priori favor certain types of structural change (such as the elongation of fingers and toes); thus purposeful behavior can itself predispose an organism to certain genetic changes. They call this mental teleology. This clearly violates Darwin's logic, and is more Lamarckian in nature. Lamarck developed an evolutionary theory 50 years before Darwin wrote of his adventures on the *Beagle*. Among Lamarck's contentions is the proposal that acquired characteristics can become inherited traits. Population Ecologists (Darwinian Theory applied to organizational theory) likewise argue that acquired traits are observable in social systems, where learned behavior is readily passed into the culture. Lamarck's argument regarding acquired traits, like those of Packard and Bedau, can only be labeled as teleological.

So just what is the role of teleology within the grand scheme of human and social evolution? Do humans control their present and their future, do they anticipate and mold that which is needed for survival, or do they mold what they think is needed in the hope that Darwin's whimsical gods will find favor with their work? Can we, after all, really master the complex interactions of social life sufficiently to know what we need and to control them to our own desires? We will struggle with this question on and off throughout the book, but ultimately we will conclude that life a complex dance involving teleological control, efficient causation, and Darwinian sifting. A theory of Complex behavior could hardly conclude otherwise.

▓ Darwin, Spencer, Social Darwinism

Darwin's natural selection is perhaps the most famous of the early assaults on teleology and vitalism. Darwinism allows scientists to explain structure without resorting to supernatural logic. It attributes structure to series of mutational accidents, the most effective of which survive. In a sense, natural selection is a sieve that screens out disorder and permits only the passing of order. A species that develops effective attributes can compete successfully, thus increasing the likelihood that its structure will survive.

Darwinian evolution is basically a random process. A popular debate among biologists revolves around the question, "If the biological clocks were set back 650 million years and evolution allowed to run its course again, would modern animals look much the same or be dramatically different?" A disciple of evolution through accident must conclude that a second history would yield completely different species, perhaps flying creatures that receive jet-like power assists similar to the "rocket" propulsion systems of squids, or tri-sexual rather than bi-sexual union. In fairness, Darwin recognized that the process of structural elaboration is not entirely random. Once an organism embarks on a given (accidentally selected) evolutionary path, certain other options are no longer available to it. For example, insects evolved exoskeletons, thus precluding development of endoskeletons and the attendant advantages of internal support systems. Further, the evolution of certain adaptive strategies tends to drag other adaptive strategies along related evolutionary paths. The opposable thumb, for example, probably affected the development of simian intelligence. Even so, the overall effect is one of accident; to paraphrase an earlier quote we used from Winston Churchill: History, and evolution, are just one damn thing after another.

Darwin also argued that evolution is a gradual, smoothly flowing process, with elaboration building on elaboration and species flowing smoothly into more elaborate species. Most biologists now argue that this is not true; rather, change is episodic, with periods of steady growth being punctuated by periods of sudden, dramatic change. Both positions pose problems, however. The gradualist must struggle with paleontological evidence of dramatic, episodic change, while the punctuated equilibrium advocate must explain how an organism's body structure (phenotype) can remain stable for millions of years while the constituting units (genotype) are constantly changing and occasionally manifesting in subpopulation phenotypes. One response to the punctuated equilibrium dilemma is that unchanging phenotypes are the result of stable environments: Natural selection favors the existing structure because it is better adapted to that environment than are mutated structures that might pop up in the population (see Kauffman, 1993, pp. 19-20).

Social Darwinism

The mid-19th-century social scientist Herbert Spencer adopted Darwin's theories for social explanation. Indeed, it was Spencer, not Darwin, who coined the famous phrase, "survival of the fittest."

Two different perspectives on social evolution can be identified in Spencer's writing. The first is called the "organismic" model and refers to his assertion that parts of social organization are like the interdependent organ's of a biological organism. Such units cooperate for their mutual benefit and support. Spencer's second perspective is called the "organic" model. This perspective compares social events to inter-species competition and is more in tune with Darwin's natural selection models than is the cooperation argument. Spencer favored this survival explanation of sociology and warned against incautious use of the organismic model.

These models lead one to radically different conclusions about organization. Advocates of the organismic model would conclude that society is consensual and mutually dependent; the metaphors are not unlike those presented by mechanistic models of Social Physicists, particularly their views about social equilibrium. Beneficiaries of the organismic perspective include Weber's Theory of Bureaucracy, Frederick Taylor's Scientific Management, and Talcott Parsons's Structural Functionalism. The organic model, on the other hand, is a competition model, and leads to conclusions about variety, divergence, and conflict in society and organization. This legacy can be observed in Ralf Dahrendorf's Social Conflict Model, Population Ecology, and the Process Model of the Chicago School.

Competition or Cooperation

I wish to focus here on Spencer's cooperation and competition proposals. There are other issues raised by evolution theory that can be addressed by nonlinear theory—punctuated equilibrium, for example, is important in Complexity Theory. Complexity also speaks to Darwin's assumptions regarding the random nature of evolution. These topics have already been alluded to as we have begun to explore nonlinear science, and will see fuller development in due time. For now we wish to ask whether society is conflictive or cooperative.

Spencer's organic model of social dynamics, the competition model, is probably more widely accepted among sociologists than is his organismic, or cooperation, model. Organizational structure, for example, is commonly interpreted in terms of power and struggle over scarce resources (Bauer & Cohen, 1983; Francis, 1983; Hannan & Freeman, 1977; Perrow, 1981; Pfeffer & Salancik, 1978, to name a few). Indeed, Walter Buckley's important sociological text on Social Systems Theory was quite definitive in its rejection of consensus (and the associated equilibrium) models of organization. Buckley and company were, however, influenced by misunderstanding about the nature of stability, which has traditionally been defined as periodic or repetitive behavior (Chaotic stability, as we have noted, is a recent insight). They were also influenced by a myopic view of biological and social cooperation.

Complexity Theory does not deny conflict and competition, but does argue that fitness is better described and served by cooperation. Evidence to support this is compelling. In biology, for example, Lynn Margulis and Dorion Sagan argue that a new organism emerged millions of years ago that produced a gaseous by-product devastatingly poisonous to all other life forms on Earth. One other organism learned to use this byproduct, however, thus launching a profitable symbiotic relationship between it and a poison-producing organism. The poison was oxygen, and the organism that learned to use it became what we today know as cellular mitochondria. Perhaps some would argue that this story illustrates evolution through survival of the fittest, but the fittest were those that cooperated, not those that competed. In this context, the phrase "survival of the fittest" seems contradictory; "emergence of the cooperative" seems a more apt phrase to rally about.

Such an example of cooperation is hardly isolated. Cities, for example, depend upon a complex network of cooperation and accommodation to provide services and resources to their inhabitants. Industries depend upon a network of suppliers, consumers, and related industries for fitness. The importance of cooperation is dramatically illustrated by Stuart Kauffman's simulations of coevolving systems. In his experiments with Boolean-controlled networks,[1] Kauffman created simulated species and programmed them so that he could control a variety of variables, such as the degree to which "species" impacted one another. He found that, when species interact at the Edge of Chaos, a dynamic equilibrium emerges in which each species is optimally fit at a level that does not disrupt the fitness of other organisms in the network. When Kauffman programmed one organism to accentuate its own fitness without concern for the fitness of other organisms, however, average fitness of all animals (including the selfish one) fell to dangerously low levels. Selfish competitive strategies, he concluded, are not viable survival strategies.

In the same manner, cooperation is important to social structure. Common sense tells us that it would be a sorry world indeed if no one could ever be trusted and if there were not some measure of predictability or dependability in relationships. Cooperation creates family structure, community, formal organization, and friendship. Very little of what we have accomplished as humans would be possible without cooperation.

Complexity theorist and biologist Brian Goodwin sums matters up rather bluntly: "The immensely complex network of relationships among organisms involves all imaginable patterns of interaction, and there is absolutely no point in focusing on competitive interactions, singling them out as the driving point in evolution" (pp. 180-181). Cooperation is indeed a far more powerful metaphor to explain social fitness than is the fierce competition of Spencer's organic world.

Two questions demand our attention at this point. First, if cooperation rather than "survival of the fittest" is the better metaphor for social fitness, then what provides motivation for elaboration and improvement? Second, one can hardly ignore the reality of conflict in social dynamics, so where does it fit in a collaboration model? The second of these questions should be addressed first. The boundary between conflict and cooperation is actually somewhat blurred. A football game, for example, is commonly considered competitive, yet it depends upon a considerable amount of cooperation— cooperation about schedules, the rules of the game, referees, how much to charge spectators, how profits will be distributed, and so forth. Without such agreement, the games could not occur. For 50 years following World War II, the free world and Communism were engaged in a cold war, a war that brought us to the brink of disaster at least once with the Cuban missile crisis. In retrospect, however, we can say that relationships between the superpowers brought stability to the world. Nations knew each other's capabilities and knew what would be or would not be acceptable to others. The USSR enforced stability on ethnically diverse and potentially unstable nations in Eastern Europe. Both sides had a great deal to lose from "breaking the rules" of relationship with their antagonists. Businesses can deal with organized strikes

Prisoner's Dilemma and Social Cooperation

The 1950s saw a great deal of anxiety about the possibility of nuclear warfare with the USSR. People built bunkers in their backyards to protect their families, school districts conducted evacuation drills to test logistics for getting children away from school and out of towns efficiently, and U.S. Senator Joe McCarthy built a career out of America's fear.

At first glance it may seem that discussing cooperation against an ambiance of fear, distrust, and opportunism doesn't make sense, but there is a logical and simple connection: when hostile factions cooperate on their nuclear strategies, there is little likelihood of war. Understanding the conditions under which cooperation occurs, then, was of vital interest to policy makers. Game theory emerged as an important tool for getting a handle on this important issue. The most famous game to emerge from this theory is called Prisoner's Dilemma. This game hypothesizes two prisoners being questioned separately by police for a crime they committed together. Each is told that sufficient evidence has been collected to bring minor charges, but that he could help himself by ratting on his friend. Specifically, if one tells, but the other doesn't, the defector (the one who abandons his compatriot by telling) gets off scot-free and the cooperator (the one who remains loyal) gets 5 years in prison. If neither prisoner tells on the other (i.e., both cooperate), both will spend 1 year in jail. If both defect by telling on the other, however, then both will get 3 years. Imagine the dilemma. If you tell, you could go free, but if your partner is as self-serving as you are, you could get 3 years. If you remain loyal to your partner and your partner remains loyal to you, then you get only 1 year; but you'll get 5 years for your loyalty if the partner turns on you. Imagine now that the game is modified for play with nuclear weapons, and you will understand why it was of such interest to policy makers in the early 1950s.

	Column Player Doesn't Talk	Column Player Talks
Row Player Doesn't Talk	1,1 Punishment when neither talks	0,5 Reward when column player talks and punishment when row player doesn't
Row Player Talks	5,0 Reward when row player talks and punishment when column player doesn't	3,3 Punishment when both talk

Prisoner's Dilemma is usually pictured as a 2 × 2 decision table as shown here. The payoff in the decision table can be modified for play as a game, in which case the prisoner's moderate "win" of 1 year in prison is worth 3 points, the moderate loss of 3 years in prison is worth 1 point, a big-time loss of 5 years in prison is worth 0 points, and a big-time win of no prison is worth 5 points. The less time you spend in prison, the more points you receive.

Early game theorists studied this game in single play mode—what decision should you make if you played the game only once (as an actual prisoner would)? Their studies showed that the best decision under such circumstance is to defect, to tell on your partner. The defector avoids the big loss and might even win it

(continued)

Prisoner's Dilemma and Social Cooperation (Continued)

all. But what if you play the game repeatedly? You will remember how the other player treated you in the last round and be aware that your adversaries may retaliate for maliciousness on your part.

In the late 1970s, Robert Axelrod, a political scientist at the University of Michigan, sponsored a Prisoner's Dilemma tournament. Computer routines representing strategies for repeated-play Prisoner's Dilemma were submitted by colleagues from all over the world. Programs played against each other and against a program that made random moves. Each game consisted of 200 rounds. The winner of this tournament—and of a subsequent tournament—was submitted by Professor Anatol Rapoport of the University of Toronto. The strategy used by Professor Rapoport is called TIT-FOR-TAT; his program cooperated on its first move, from there it mimicked its opponent's preceding move. The strategy usually "convinced" opponents that their best strategy was to cooperate, thus TIT-FOR-TAT is labeled a cooperating strategy. In general, programs based on cooperation performed significantly better than did those that were based on defection and self-serving behavior.

In the June 1995 edition of *Scientific American*, Martin Nowak and Robert May from the University of Oxford along with Karl Sigmund from the University of Vienna reported on two Prisoner Dilemma experiments they performed. In the first, they provided their computerized players with longer memories, a statistical (rather than absolute) propensity to cooperate or defect, and the ability to mutate their strategies. The players competed in repeated-play, round-robin tournaments as they had in Axelrod's tournament, and were tracked for millions of rounds. The researchers found that, as the rounds wore on, the trend was to cooperate. They also discovered that players would sometimes change their tendencies precipitously, moving from the propensity to cooperate to the propensity to defect (or vice versa) within just a few generations—a phenomenon suggestive of punctuated equilibrium.

Nowak, May, and Sigmund observed the emergence of the TIT-FOR-TAT strategy that had won Axelrod's tournament; they also observed a variation called Generous TIT-FOR-TAT in which a player occasionally failed to retaliate against defection. Generous TIT-FOR-TAT can encourage unconditional cooperation that, in the long run, is bad for society because exploiters can thrive in such cultures.

They observed yet another, more common strategy as well, one they called Pavlov. In this approach, a player repeats moves that provided it with rewards in the previous round and avoids moves for which it was punished. This, of course, is similar to the "stimulus-response" behavior that B. F. Skinner observed in animal behavior. The Pavlov strategy tended to work well if all players were Pavlovian, because such societies tend to foster cooperation and accidental defections launch only a single round of retaliation before cooperative peace is reestablished. Societies in which most players cooperate unconditionally (altruistic societies), however, encourage the Pavlovian players to become exploiters. Pavlov does not do well in a society of chronic defectors because, on every other move, it attempts cooperation and looses big time against its opponent's defection. A Pavlovian society is, nevertheless, able to protect itself against invasion by defectors.

Nowak, May, and Sigmund's second simulation functioned much like cellular automata. In this Prisoner's Dilemma simulation, competitors play against eight contiguous players in the same way that cellular automata units interact with their neighbors—and players interact regularly with the same individuals. After each round of play, cells are taken over by players who accumulate the most points.

The authors created two types of players: pure cooperators and pure defectors. They found that lone cooperators are exploited by neighboring defectors, but that four or more cooperators can hold their own in many situations. Lone defectors fare pretty well, but if a number of defectors clump together they work to their mutual detriment. After a number of generations, the relative number of cooperators and defectors stabilizes, thus mimicking the pattern of host and parasites, or prey and predators, in the biological world, or the mix of honest people and cheaters in social life.

---

more easily than wildcat strikes because, with the former, an organization is in control and is playing by a set of rules (however ill-defined they may be), while with the latter there are no rules and there is no one to negotiate with who can really control the strikers. The distinction between cooperation and competitive cooperation is blurred, both in definition and in effect. I argue, therefore, that much of what is called conflictive has the ultimate effect of creating the type of cooperation that Kauffman labeled dynamic equilibrium. Competition is part and parcel of cooperation.

The other question posed above is: What provides the motivation for elaboration and improvement if not "survival of the fittest" through conflict? To start with, systems can succeed or fail for reasons not related to competition. According to Javier Gimeno and several of his colleagues, the failure of small start-up businesses can be explained by such things as differences in the profit aspirations among different owners, differences in reasons for starting the business, and the availability or lack of availability of alternative work options for the entrepreneur. These reasons have little to do with selection and competition, and the list is far from inclusive. Most important, however, fitness accrues to those who are best able to garner resources and that ability goes to organizations that can create mutually supportive networks with other systems; it does not accrue to those whose sole goal is to serve self at the expense of others. The motivation to elaborate, then, could be as simple as survival, and cooperation is the best tool for achieving it.

▨ Structural Functionalism and Homeostasis

Talcott Parsons, the spokesman for the Structural Functionalist movement (second to third quarter of the 20th century), has argued convincingly for a stability perspective of society. A system, he wrote with coauthor Edward Shills, is composed of interdependent parts locked in deterministic relationships; that is, social groups are interrelated in stable and predictable patterns. These deterministic relationships represent order.

Social needs (teleology) is a cornerstone of Structural Functionalism. According to sociologist Walter Buckley, Functionalism "focuses from present to future event, and seeks to understand or explain a present phenomenon in terms of its consequences for the continuity, persistence, stability, or survival of the complex of which it is a part" (p. 76). At issue are purposiveness, social control, and goal orientation. Parsons argued that people and organizations cooperatively produce needed social structures that, under optimal conditions, function cooperatively for the common good. Society possesses given structures, then, because it *needs* them.

Parsons's critics replied that human causality results from a mixture of purposiveness and accident; and that people act first for their personal well-being rather than for that of the whole. They concluded that the future cannot control the present, thus causality must be efficient; purposiveness, they asserted, serves the same role as accident in the relentless march of efficient causation.

Both positions are correct in some measure; and their differences are more a matter of perspective than substance. Parsons's critics tended to see things from a micro- or detail level; they were like ants that observe society's day-to-day processing, the self-serving behavior, and the unintended consequences of decisions. Parsons, on the other hand, adopted a macro- or helicopter view; looking down on the system, he saw persistent social structures striving for their preservation and focused on need. The critics recognized that organization exists, but considered it to be secondary to process. Parsons understood that the system is driven by interactions among component parts, but his central themes were stability and need.

Parsons at times leaves one uncertain about just what he meant by stability. At points in his writings, his definitions seem to assume that stability is a dynamic concept that can flex and grow, and at other times his perspective seems more akin to Spencer's organismic (equilibrium) model. Clearly, he struggled with reconciling the dynamic nature of social existence with traditional, Newtonian definitions of stability and equilibrium. Parsons wasn't alone in this struggle, however. Sociologists of Parsons's day seemed to bring an either/or mentality to the table when it came to the nature of social structure: Society was either cooperative and in a state of equilibrium or competitive and constantly changing. Some philosophers, including Parsons, flirted with a middle ground, but couldn't quite light on it.

Parsons's flirtation is called "homeostatic." Equilibrium, he argued, was too inflexible and limiting; "homeostasis" was more flexible. This term (coined in 1938 by sociologist Walter Cannon) is derived from medical sciences, where it refers to the body's ability to regulate itself. Parsons used it to suggest that unhealthy trends in society are dynamically controlled by normative social structures. The goals of society, according to this perspective, needn't be fixed, but are allowed to flex with changing needs and environmental contingencies.

Homeostasis is a logical extension of a stability model of society, and it was yet another handle for critics to exploit. Homeostasis as Parsons perceived it is a normative concept; that is, it suggests there are certain functions that are good for the society (norms) and others that are not good. Opponents of normative theory purport that the norms that define what is right for the system are artificial. Normative theory requires that the observer assign value to different social functions. Critics prefer to speak of divergence and variety as neutral dynamics or even, in a sense, just as normal and necessary as is normative behavior. Without such divergent structures, they argue, a system would lack the mechanisms needed to elaborate itself.

Parsons called such divergent structures "deviant," which is consistent with his normative perception of stability. Deviance, he proposed, occurs because socialization must be learned, and some individuals fail in that learning process for whatever reason. Because of this, society must create mechanisms of control to prevent deviancy from damaging the system. If the control mechanisms fail in their duty, then the system must either change or disintegrate.

Complex Homeostasis

Ross Ashby, who wrote in 1960 on the brain and neural networks, provides an interesting mind-picture that will help us develop a definition of homeostasis that is a little more workable than is Parsons's. Imagine taking a crude, randomly wired autopilot, he suggested, place it in a flying plane, then by experimenting with one change at a time, making the autopilot function correctly. To work, the autopilot must hold a number of variables within acceptable bounds, including airspeed, rate of ascent or descent, pitch, yaw, and horizon. Any one of these variables could affect several others, thus rate of ascent affects airspeed, and pitch could affect yaw, airspeed, and horizon. There is, however, a range of acceptable states that each variable could safely assume; the plane would be OK within a rather wide range of speeds, for example.

Ashby's solution is a walk through parameter space in search of a combination of controls that maintain the various variables (parameters) within survivable ranges. Parameter space, which we discussed in Chapter 2, is an *N*-dimensional coordinate graph with each axis representing one of the variables (like airspeed or yaw) that can affect the state of the system (see Figure 2.3). Parameter space is divided into a number of relatively stable regions that are separated by bifurcation walls. Each region is internally self-similar, but contiguous regions can be dramatically different from one another. Ashby's autopilot is adjusted until a region of parameter space is found in which all pertinent variables are appropriately maintained.

Parameter space, and the attractors defined by it, have several characteristics that are important to our definition of homeostasis. First is the fact
that many regions of parameter space are fairly large and systems can wander
within them without experiencing significant change, thus airspeed can increase or decrease by certain amounts without disturbing the stability of our
airplane. Homeostasis for our purposes, then, is not a fixed state; rather it
drifts over a range of values without compromising the systems within it.
Alternatively, one could say that homeostasis can be perturbed without
causing dramatic change in the state of the system it represents.

Second, parameter space defines a set of attractors (see Figure 2.3). These
attractors expand and contract as they drift through a given region of parameter space, and they change dramatically when they cross a bifurcation wall
into a new region of parameter space. Different areas of a single region,
however, produce self-similar attractors. Homeostasis in organization and
society is represented as just such a stable attractor; like attractors, homeostasis gradually changes as it drifts through a region of parameter space.
Homeostasis is dynamic and changing, but different states can easily be
identified as being from the same "family."

Third, parameter space is divided into regions, each of which contains
different forms of attractors. A system that crosses a bifurcation wall will
exhibit different behavior, perhaps dramatically different behavior, than it did
in the prior region. If an attractor moves out of a given region of parameter
space, the system it represents destabilizes until it can find a new region that
will again maintain the structure within survivable parameters. If one were to
remove a wire from a working autopilot, for example, the system would have
to begin a new walk through parameter space in search of a new configuration
of the remaining wires that will maintain level flight. The sudden demise of
the USSR in 1989 left Eastern Europe, and the nations of the world, groping
for a new configuration of relationships that would allow the world to
reestablish relative security and that would provide the Eastern European
nations a measure of fiscal stability. The 1997 crisis in the economy of the
Far East left the world money markets struggling to return Eastern markets to
their original region of parameter space or to find a new configuration of
parameters that would again stabilize those markets.

Fourth, the size of homeostatic attractors that defines a given dynamic
can vary but should be appropriate to the needs of the system. An attractor
that fluctuates over too large a range of values is attempting to encompass too
wide a range of activities. Such activities should be divided up and allocated

to different attractors. Complexity Theory provides mechanisms for these different attractors to interact in a manner that contributes to the success of the broader system, as we shall see in the chapters on loose coupling and on change.

Fifth, the region of parameter space occupied by a system's attractor should be small enough to allow exploration of other parameter regions if needed but not so small that bifurcation walls are crossed too readily. A large region of parameter space may force a system to cover too large a range of values before a bifurcation wall is crossed, making it difficult to find new regions. Similarly, if the parameter region is too small, the system could cross a bifurcation wall with small parameter changes, making the region too unstable for most social dynamics. The proper size is large enough to permit reasonable stability but small enough to permit dramatic change when needed.

Sixth, and finally, the dimensionality of attractors should be balanced against the capabilities of the system to maintain homeostatic stability. If an attractor must juggle too many variables, a viable attractor may be difficult to find or may even be nonexistent. For example, Kauffman, in his analysis of coevolving Boolean systems, found that when the number of interdependencies among species increased beyond certain bounds, dynamic equilibrium (equivalent to our definition of homeostasis) did not evolve and the fitness of participating species fluctuated wildly. Put simply, there is a limit to the number of parameters that a system can juggle and still find homeostasis.

From these observations we derive the following definition:

- Social homeostasis refers to behavior that drifts over a range of parameters, but the various states of the system are self-similar; that is, the system is dynamically stable. By extension, homeostatic behavior is never repetitive, but neither is it unchanging.

- Homeostasis maintains a certain set of variables within specific value ranges required for survival and reproduction of the systems it represents.

- On occasion, certain factors may trigger dramatic (discontinuous) reformulation of homeostasis; in such cases the system may search for different patterns of behavior that serve its survival needs (new homeostasis) or it may find its way back to the initial homeostatic attractor.

- Homeostatic attractors are relatively small; that is, they encompass a limited range of behaviors. Various attractors interact with one another to produce more complex behavior.

- The range of parameters over which homeostasis ranges is sufficiently large to avoid frequent dramatic change but sufficiently small to permit the system to find a bifurcation wall if needed.

▦ The number of parameters simultaneously controlled by stable social systems is balanced against the ability of the system to find or achieve viable stability relative to those variables; that is, the homeostatic attractor is relatively focused in what it attempts to do.

Several general comments need to be made about this definition. It clearly addresses the debate regarding stability versus change that has been so pervasive in historical sociological literature. Stability advocates have been seemingly unable to get very far away from propositions that focus on lack of change in one form or another. Many organizational theorists define homeostasis with analogies to heat thermostats or regulation of body temperature, examples in which systems function to return some perturbed factor to a constant, unchanging state. Wayne Hoy and Cecil Miskel, for example, focus on "equilibrium," which they define as a state in which "the social and biological parts of the system maintain a constant relationship to each other so that no part changes its position or relation with respect to all other parts" (p. 30). The definition proposed in this book advocates a different sort of stability, one that is neither predictable nor repetitive, rather one that advocates unpredictable, constant change. This homeostasis is stable not for the usual reasons regarding change or lack thereof. It is stable because the system's actions, while unpredictable and never repetitive, are nonetheless confined to a certain range of relatively self-similar activities, and because its behaviors are not easily deflected from homeostasis. Finally, this definition includes allowances not just for change but for dramatic change as well.

Two types of change are referred to in our definition of homeostasis: continuous, nondisruptive change, and noncontinuous, disruptive change. The former refers to drift within a given region of parameter space and to the normal fluctuations that Chaotic and Complex attractors exhibit, while the latter refers to movement across a bifurcation wall. Our comments at this time are brief; however, one preliminary observation should be made. Change, whether continuous or noncontinuous, is a function of many factors, including environmental pressure, random behavioral fluctuations (random drift), mental teleology (deliberative behavior), and what for now can only be cryptically referred to as normal, dynamical behavior. Systems poised at the Edge of Chaos have a tendency "go crazy" on occasion; like the stock exchange (which is itself a system poised at the Edge of Chaos), they experience occasional wild and seemingly inexplicable fluctuations. The point will be explained more fully in the chapters on change.

It is easy to assume from what we have said thus far that the controlling parameters (environmental factors) are given and inert, that control is one-way, from parameter to system (or environment to organization). However, the system can do more than just search, it can influence the environment for its (the systems) own well-being. A system is not indiscriminately buffeted by environmental whim; rather it exerts some measure of control over that environment. An organization attempts to control uncertainty in acquisition of raw materials by, say, purchasing the company that provides those materials. A school system attempts to control disruptive behavior on the part of school board members by providing training and indoctrination workshops for newly elected members.

▩ Nonlinear History

It is useful to examine where we have been as organizational theorists. We often, for example, find things or ideas that, though important once, were thrown away when new toys came along, but that will help us understand problems in our present lives. Biologists cast aside notions of teleology and rational morphology and self-organization when Darwin came along, for example, but now we find these ideas have meaning again in Complexity and Chaos Theory. It is important to see how old debates create myopic worldviews, as did Newton's perceptions of causality and stability, for perceiving our myopia is the first step in broadening our view. It is important to examine how old ideas have emerged into their current form in order to see where we might go next, as we did with Parsons's homeostasis and Spencer's cooperation and competition models. And occasionally, when we reexamine our past critically, we find that it wasn't as primitive as we smugly like to imagine; the past was right, after all, about the intractability of the gaps.

CHAPTER

5

A Nonlinear Redaction
of Open Systems

The organizational theories of the last half of the 20th century are, in one fashion or another, variations of Open Systems Theory. Open Systems Theory, which became popular in the 1960s, made the then-revolutionary statement that organizational structure and behavior are heavily influenced by environmental factors. Theories before this had told us that leaders made the difference, that organizations were the logical product of rational behavior by the people who run the organizations. Machine theorists told managers early in the 20th century that productivity could be increased by controlling operating procedures, such as the length of time allowed for rest breaks or the way tasks were structured. They argued that superiors could assure efficiency by establishing goals, by carefully delineating responsibilities, and by structuring authority hierarchically. Human relations theorists from the 1930s and '40s preached motivation and human psychology, and sought ways to manipulate social activity in the organization. Machine Theory and human relations were closed theories; they assumed that everything of importance to the structure and success of an organization lay within its walls.

Systems Theory, by contrast, speaks of open structures. It argues that internal activities, such as leadership, technology, social behavior, motivation, and task structure, are more the products of external than internal factors.

Social expectations, laws, raw materials, society's technical sophistication, the behaviors of other systems, fiscal policies, competition, and buyers all shape, constrain, and dictate internal behavior. Leaders behave as they do because of notions they were taught by their culture, by the nature of the raw materials they process, by the degree of volatility in the competitive environment, by unions, and by legal constraints. Task structure is determined by learned behavior, the state of technology, and by the raw material the organization processes. Systems do not act in a vacuum, they do not control their own destinies. They are products of their environments.

Open systems can be defined as holistic, interactive, and cybernetic (they adjust using feedback). Each of these characteristics will be developed in the following sections. The intent, however, is not so much to tutor the reader in Open Systems Theory as to observe just how near systems theorists were to a theory of nonlinear dynamics, to see what Systems Theory can tell us about nonlinearity, and to observe how Systems Theory can be elaborated upon by Chaos and Complexity. Ultimately, the intent is to develop a nonlinear definition of systems upon which this book can build.

We begin by using Chaos Theory to explain an old puzzle in the Systems Theory literature, a rather dramatic and newsworthy puzzle that social and physical scientists debated back in the sixties and seventies but never resolved. We will then draw a framework from Systems Theory for understanding how complex systems interact with, or map, their environments, and will elaborate on this framework using Complexity Theory. We will look at what Complexity theorist Brian Arthur has to say about feedback and decreasing returns, which are key elements of Open Systems Theory. We will revisit another debate in the Systems Theory literature: the nature of life, and whether social systems are living entities. At the end of this chapter, we will pull this material, and that from the last chapter, together to formulate a theory of complex social systems. This theory will guide our subsequent observations about social systems in much the same way that Open Systems Theory guided theoretical observations during the last half of the 20th century.

■ Holistic Systems

Holism means that a system's capacity for action exceeds the individual or summed capabilities of its parts. The system as a whole comprehends more about its environment, can process vastly more information, has a broader repertoire of symbolic languages, has more advanced reproductive capabilities, possesses a more effective survival potential, and exerts greater control

Environment

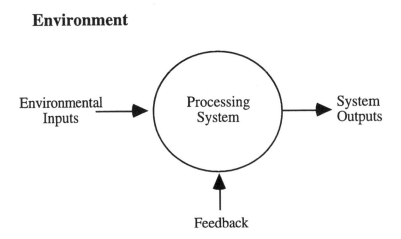

Figure 5.1. Generic Open Systems Theory Model.

over its environment than do its parts. One can readily understand this by mentally contrasting the effectiveness of 10 individuals acting alone with that of the same 10 people acting in concert.

The typical depiction of a Systems Theory model reflects this holism. There are a number of variations on the system's model theme, but they all have several things in common (see Figure 5.1). All, for instance, depict a system floating in an environmental sea, bombarded by environmental demands. The system selectively absorbs those demands, processes them, and returns some form of output into the environment. Open systems utilize feedback mechanisms to gauge the state of the environment and the environment's reaction to the system's output.

The primary forces motivating the system are environmental; the environment is its source of energy, the medium that determines internal structure and organizational functioning and that dictates change. Indeed a system that is not in one-to-one sync with environmental demands is not optimally fit. The feedback mechanisms enable homeostasis in that they provide information needed to adjust to environmental changes.

The system's relationship with the environment is not a whimsical one. The "membrane" that defines the system's boundary is semi-permeable; that is, it is capable of screening certain inputs. The membrane around the medical profession, for example, accepts only members who are certified to practice medicine. Similarly the membrane is selective in the information to which it responds, thus the system is not necessarily buffeted by environmental winds that have little to do with its interests.

Open Systems theorists derived a number of specific models of organization from this basic model. Harold Leavitt, for example, argued that the organizational system is a social entity dedicated to a certain technology, hence it is a sociotechnical system. A sociotechnical system is composed of four activities: tasks, structure, technology, and people. The task subsystem defines the processes that are performed within the system; the structure subsystem defines the way the system is organized and governed; the technological subsystem defines the type of equipment and knowledge a system must possess; and the human subsystem defines such things as the skills, attitudes, psychology, roles, and motivators of the people in the organization. These four subsystems, Leavitt continued, are interactive and interdependent; a change in one subsystem will reverberate with varying degrees of intensity throughout the system.

Daniel Katz and Robert Kahn focused more on the dynamics required to process environmental inputs than on the structures specifically associated with processing (Leavitt's focus). They identified five generic subsystems: the production or technical subsystems, supportive subsystems, maintenance subsystems, adaptive subsystems, and managerial subsystems. The production subsystems are concerned with the technology of production, thus they differ little from Leavitt's tasks and technologies subsystems. The managerial subsystems are concerned with organizing and governing organizational processes. The supportive subsystems interact with the environmental to ensure constant influx of energy (such as raw materials). The maintenance subsystems maintain the boundaries of the subsystem; basically they represent the forces of stability and status quo, or homeostasis. The adaptive subsystems provide checks and balances for the maintenance structures; they represent forces devoted to change in response to environmental pressures and environmental change. Like Leavitt and other Systems theorists, Katz and Kahn argued that the components of a system are highly interactive.

John Seiler's description of systems is a bit more complex. He envisioned systems composed of three broad, interdependent functions: internal inputs, activities, and internal outputs. Each of these functions is composed of its own set of subsystems. The subsystems of each function are interactive and interdependent within that function, and the three functions interact with each other.

Holistic Analysis of World Dynamics

There is a problem with the holistic perspective: It is not easily analyzed. The traditional reductionist approach in which phenomena are isolated for

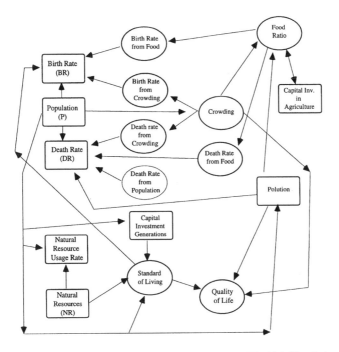

Figure 5.2. Elements of Forrester's Flow Diagram for the World 2 Simulation.

study violates the holistic principles that are key to Systems Theory. One of the more credible analyses by a Systems theorist is attributable to J. W. Forrester, whose studies in the late 1960s and early 1970s of world and urban dynamics were ambitious efforts to apply interactive principles, along with the power of computers, to prediction. Yet, as we shall see in a moment, his rather infamous analysis of system dynamics reveals yet another problem, one that will question the very assumptions underlying the way we frame theory in the social and physical sciences.

Forrester identified important elements of urban or world dynamics, then mathematically modeled the interactions of those dynamics (in the world model, for example, he examined such things as population, standard of living, pollution, natural resources, capital investment, and percentage investment in agriculture; see Figure 5.2). His models predicted a devastating collapse of world markets by A.D. 2050; this, predictably, generated considerable public discussion and consternation when it hit the press.

A group of scientists from MIT challenged his conclusions, noting that his model's formulas, when run in reverse to "predict" the past, produced some rather bizarre results (see B. P. Bloomfield's 1986 discussion). Population predictions, for example, began to grow exponentially in about 1895 and reached 3.9 billion by 1880 (remember, predictions are running back into time); this, of course, didn't happen in reality. If the models fail to work in reverse, the critics argued, how can one believe their predictions of the future? Forrester countered that the data on which the formulas depended (the initial conditions, or state of the variables at the beginning of the analysis) were improperly estimated. Forrester adjusted his initial population estimates to correct the 1880 anomaly, but the change caused strange results to emerge with other variables. He and his supporters suggested, among other things, that initial conditions are problematic and that difficulties with data hardly invalidated the importance of the models or of the general findings.

Forrester's retort got close to the truth when he focused upon initial conditions; indeed, system trajectories are highly sensitive to their initial conditions. Forrester—and his critics—would have expected, however, small initial differences to translate into small outcome differences, leading one to conclude that difficulty with reversal experiments is due to large initial errors (or inadequate models). Forrester failed to understand the real source of his problem, although the evidence was undoubtedly there in his data: Initial differences in complex, interactive systems diverge exponentially rather than converge stably. Edward Lorenz had seen the same phenomenon in his weather formulas and had deduced unpredictable Chaos; Forrester saw it in his world and urban models but stuck by the outcomes of his models.

We now also know that his models diverged because of Poincaré's resonance, or the release of potential energy through interaction (this was introduced in Chapter 2). Even had Forrester been able to measure his initial conditions accurately, his models would have failed him for this reason. His was a no-win proposition.

Forrester's critics likewise made an error of assumption, actually the same error he made. It was an error for which they can be forgiven, for it reflects the perspectives of some of the greatest thinkers of our time, thinkers like Albert Einstein, Stephen Hawkings, Simon Laplace, and Baruch Spinoza. This error is the assumption that time is bi-directional—an equation can describe a system's future and past with equal efficiency, a system's dynamics can be traced to its initial conditions, and system behavior can be reversed to its initial state. This assumption is at the very heart of predictability; to challenge it strikes at the root of rationality and science. The problem that concerns scientists lies in the alternative explanation: If time is not bi-directional, then nature is not predictable and science is not dependable; the future becomes a function of the random and the capricious.

There are critics of this scientific rationality of Einstein and Hawkings. Philosophers have argued that a world without uni-directional time is dehumanizing. Mankind is reduced to automata and God is relegated to mindless myth—human history is predetermined by cold equations and not by the free will of God or Man. Even the outcome of a coin flip is controlled by the precise state of muscles and nerves in one's hand.

Scientists have pointed to a troubling dualism in the traditional bi-directional perspective: Timeless predictability is forced to coexist in the scientific universe with irreversible, seemingly time-dependent processes of entropy. The two—predictability and entropy—are irreconcilably inconsistent unless entropy can, at least hypothetically, be reversed or otherwise explained. Or unless timeless predictability is wrong. Science has attempted to explain this dualism in a variety of ways. Many have argued that, although there are infinitely more ways for a system to be at entropic equilibrium than not, it is statistically possible for a system to reverse entropy. If one places hot and cold water in separate sides of a sealed chamber, the molecules will commingle until equilibrium is achieved; yet molecules are constantly on the move— thus, if one waits long enough, they could eventually move back to their respective corners. Quantum Theory argues that indeterminism is introduced by the very act of observation: A proton, for example, doesn't resolve as a wave or a particle until someone looks at it. Ludwig Boltzmann hypothesized an H-function, which is a value that dissipates as a system approaches equilibrium (hence its irreversibility; see Prigogine, 1996). Murray Gell-Mann attributes uncertainty to ignorance, the inability to measure all the minutia that must be measured to predict a complex system such as a volume of gas. Einstein himself struggled with this duality; as a result of those struggles he, along with Josiah Gibbs, introduced important applications of statistics to dynamic analysis.

Recently, Complexity theorist and Nobel laureate Ilya Prigogine has presented compelling arguments that we are misperceiving time, not entropy. Time, he maintains, is a uni-directional arrow, irreversibility is a fundamental law of physics unrelated to any approximations, and this arrow of time plays a fundamental constructive role in nature (that constructive role is the theme of the book you are now reading). His book, *The End of Uncertainty*, leaves one with the feeling that science is on the verge of revolutionary insight, change in its basic assumptions about causality and scientific function, change in the way it observes nature, and change in the very way we perceive ourselves. His theory bears the marvelous simplicity that characterizes scientific revolution (as when Copernicus simplified Ptolemy's overstuffed models of the universe or when Pasteur did away with the burdensome religious rationalizations surrounding spontaneous generation). It requires no meta-physical dead/live cat in a box (referring to Schrödinger's cat—a thought experiment from Quantum Theory) and no difficult-to-imagine merger of time and space. Prigogine's hypothesis validates what we sense around us: Time is real and it moves only in a forward direction.

Prigogine's hypothesis utilizes Einstein and Gibbs's statistical approach to analyze dynamical systems. He argues that exponential divergence attributable to sensitive dependence and to Poincaré's resonance/interaction dooms the individual trajectory to one-way, time-dependent evolution that can only be understood statistically. The details of this argument are available in Prigogine's quite readable book; the important point for our purposes is that interactive dynamics are neither predictable nor reversible. Both Forrester and his critics were wrong, Forrester for assuming that complex, interactive dynamics could be projected forward and the critics for assuming they could be projected backward. In effect, neither party proved anything except, perhaps, the fallacy of their assumptions.

■ Systems and Environment: Interaction and Energy Transfer

Despite difficulties with quantification, Systems Theory left an important legacy: It opened eyes to the reality of open, holistic systems interacting with, and dependent upon, their environments. The medium of such interaction is energy; thus interaction is the transfer of energy. When one billiard ball hits another, it passes energy to the second, enabling it, in turn, to roll across the billiard table. A hydra, during reproduction, passes life energy to its offspring.

Systems theorist Walter Buckley argued that systems assume one of three states based on the nature of energy transfer: organized simplicity, organized complexity, or chaos. Organized simplicity describes systems that coordinate activities by means of mechanical transfers of energy from organism to organism. Clocks, for example, transfer energy from the pendulum to a cog wheel, but only when the two are physically and properly contacting and aligned.

At the other extreme, "chaos" (presented in lower case to be distinguished from the "Chaos" of Chaos Theory) is a disorganized, random state in which the transmission of energy is a random process. Thus, according to Systems theorists, a turbulent river, with water molecules randomly bouncing against each other and against obstacles such as rocks, is chaotic.

Organized complexity lies in a broad band between these states. Systems that are characterized as organized complexities transmit at least some energy symbolically rather than physically, and the more highly complex an organism is, the more it depends on symbolic transmission. Language is the more readily understood example of symbolic energy, but it can include, among many other things, the wagging of a dog's tail, a bird's song, hormone messages, odors, temperature changes, and color changes. Symbolic energy is anything other than physical contact and that carries information that can be decoded by, and has meaning for, another entity (in some instances, symbolic information can be conveyed by physical contact also, as when one person hugs another).

To be useful, then, energy must not only shift from one entity to another, it must carry with it a message or information. Energy transfers must exhibit some measure of order to carry information. In a clock, for example, energy transfers are ordered in such a way that information about the passage of time can be transmitted from one component to another. At the opposite extreme, consider a box of "cocked" mouse traps, each balancing a Ping-Pong ball on its arm. Were one to toss a new ball into the box, a different sort of "system" would erupt. The transfer-of-energy phenomenon would be demonstrated quite dramatically, but any information the system might have contained would be quickly lost to lack of order.

Simple mechanical systems, like organized complexity systems, can be organized so that information can be passed from one entity to another. Simple systems are ordered *for* the transfer of energy, however, while complex systems *self-order because of* energy transfers (to paraphrase an explanation by Stu Kauffman of Immanuel Kant's philosophy about biological structure). Self-ordering is attributable to the capacity to "map" the energy of the environment; that is, the system possess mechanisms for imprinting environmental stimuli within itself and for referring to those imprints at future times. Newly hatched ducklings, for example, imprint images of their mother (or whoever is present) shortly after birth, and subsequently follow the lead of that mother-figure. Because of this ability to map the environment for future reference, persistent relationships can evolve, or self-organize.

Mapping is also related to the complex system's ability to order interaction patterns and, by extension, to categorize its environment. Consider, for example, an informal social group (a group that evolves naturally) within a formal social organization. Individuals create persistent relationships because the behaviors of certain other individuals are compatible with their own internal mappings (in plain English, those involved have something in common). The individuals of this resulting group remember their relationships and the patterns of their past behaviors. Such memories enable the group to maintain relationships over extended periods. Further, certain activities by other groups are incompatible with the focal informal group's internal maps and will be shunned or avoided. Individuals and groups, then, associate or disassociate, and categorize their environments, based on the state of their internal maps.

Mapping means memory, and it is the structures just described that permit memory. I argue that Complex (as opposed to Chaotic) attractors are the medium of mapping. They are sufficiently stable to retain memory; further, because of controlled interactions among attractors, sets of interacting attractors can likewise be sufficiently stable to permit memory. An attractor maps a piece of the environment by correlating, or vibrating in sync, with it. These, and similar, hypotheses will be developed over the following section and over the course of subsequent chapters.

Complexity Theory and Interaction

The perspective of Complexity Theory about environmental interaction and awareness is strikingly similar to that of Systems Theory. Systems Theory's three states—organized simplicity, organized complexity, and chaos—are almost carbon-copied by Stephen Wolfram's and Chris Langston's typologies: stability, Edge of Chaos, and Chaos. Even so, the definitions of Chaos and Edge of Chaos are far more richly developed than systems theorists ever imagined.

The core focus of Systems Theory differs somewhat from that of nonlinear dynamics. Open Systems Theory focuses largely on interaction with the environment, as well it should, for the environmental piece was missing from much of the previous theories of social behavior. Nonlinear analysis, Complexity Theory in particular, focuses on environment as well but is also sensitive to the internal dynamics of a system and how they relates to its external dynamics. Internal dynamics play a more important role in structural elaboration, change, and fitness than they do in Systems Theory, for example. Further, Complex structures are perceived as more resistant to environmental pressures than are the structures envisioned by Systems Theory. Environment certainly is important, but the relationship between system and environment is considered nonlinear or disjointed. Systems don't hop to every environmental wind, they often change in unpredictable spurts, and the relationship between environmental pressure and system response is typically loose.

Complexity Theory has a great deal to say about environmental mapping. Awareness, according to Open Systems Theory, is dependent upon the ability of a system to classify and assign meaning to events or objects. Complexity theorists would agree but are interested in understanding more about the internal dynamics of this mapping process. Complexity theorists observe, and Systems theorists imply, that some measure of stability is key to memory and mapping. Chaotic systems (whether spelled with an uppercase or lowercase "C") have little if any memory and are unsuitable for this task; any information they accrue is quickly lost to Lorenz's sensitive dependence and Poincaré's random resonances. Even so, a bit of Chaos is important to the mapping process, for without it memories are never acted upon. There is no adaptation, no reproduction, no creativity, no evolution. Life is a little bit stability, a little bit Chaos.

Complex attractors are sufficiently stable to maintain information for long periods of time, yet they are sufficiently vibrant to process that information. In addition, Complex attractors are relatively small, thus useful for categorizing information. Large, unitary attractors juggle too much diverse information to be helpful for this. Imagine a university composed of but one department. Every member of that department is responsible for expertise in all the academic disciplines in which the university engages, each member must understand all the nuances that arise in managing that university, and course schedules must avoid conflicts between any two courses. This is a large attractor, and one can readily appreciate the impossibility of dealing with all that must be mapped by such a system. Chaotic attractors are large; one need only examine Chris Langston's cellular automata in the Chaotic range to observe that. Stu Kauffman's simulations with Boolean networks produced rather large attractors in the stable range of behavior as well, although overstability rather than attractor size is the major problem here. It was only in the band between stability and Chaos that attractors assumed characteristics, including smallness, that were conducive to mapping.

Complex attractors communicate across the broader systemic network in a controlled manner. This is clearly seen in Kauffman's Boolean networks. Properly tuned between Chaos and stability, these networks form pockets of dynamic behavior separated by impenetrable barriers. Visualize a wall of lights governed by Kauffman's rules; there would be pockets of flashing lights separated by barriers of unchanging lights. These pockets are connected by corridors, although the number of pockets reachable from any given pocket (or attractor) is limited. If the wall of lights were tuned to the stable regime, the corridors would disappear and the attractors would be isolated; there would be no communication across the broader network. Were the lights tuned into the Chaotic regime, the walls would dissolve and every entity would communicate directly with every other entity. The controlled access available between these extremes permits stable exchanges of information and, as we shall discuss in subsequent chapters, permits the adaptation and evolution that Systems theorists attribute to mapping.

Mapping means memory: The stability observed in Complex attractors allows the retention of information, hence memory. But what mechanism accounts for the implanting, or mapping, of information into the attractor? I propose an answer that is actually quite simple: An attractor maps a part of the environment by resonating, or correlating, with it. A sales division resonates with that particular part of the market for which it is responsible, the physical chemistry division of a university's chemistry department resonates with the ideas in its field of expertise, and tax lawyers resonate with fiscal laws. By *resonation* or *correlation* I mean that attractors interact with a part of the environment, they become familiar with it; in a sense, they become a part of that environment both as observers and as actors. That is, a bit of the environment is made part of the organization.

Further, different attractors within a broader system, such as a manufacturing concern or a university, have controlled access to one another. This controlled access permits stability and memory within the broader system itself. Small networks of attractors emerge within the broader system. Each of the constituent attractors is responsible for a particular part of the environment, but their foci are interrelated. Hence the different divisions of a chemistry department are responsible for different specialties, but all are interrelated by the broader theme (chemistry). Each attractor is somewhat familiar with the focus of other attractors within its network (these attractors correlate with one another and with parts of each other's environment), but is primarily responsible for its own focus. These broader networks are what lend the system its holistic strength: Through interaction across networks, the system develops a knowledge and capability that far exceeds that of the individual attractors.

■ Feedback

One system is a source of feedback for others, and systems do work on each other's maps through the feedback of symbolic information. Feedback, according to Systems Theory, is important to any system that requires internal adjustments in order to remain in step with the environment. A thermostat maintains a constant temperature by adjusting its internal state in response to fluctuations it is able to sense in air temperature. The thermostat has a goal, say, to achieve and maintain an air temperature of 68°F. By selectively turning on the furnace when the air temperature is below 68°F and turning it off (or activating an air coolant system) when the temperature exceeds 68°, it can achieve its goal. Feedback, then, is a goal-directing process that dampens out deviation.

On this point, Systems Theory collides with discredited perceptions of homeostasis. Early writings about homeostasis argued a stasis closely akin to physical equilibrium, with fixed goals and stable states (like the thermostat that maintains a constant temperature). Systems theorists dealt with this issue by arguing that a system modifies its goals as it interacts with the environment, that goals and environmental stimuli are dynamically intertwined. Thus the system can change its goals on the fly in response to environmental fluctuations or demands, and is forever making adjustments to achieve those goals.

Negative Feedback

Feedback comes in two varieties: positive and negative. Negative feedback suggests that maturing systems eventually run out of steam; they reach a point in their development at which further effort provides negligible return, and they settle into an equilibrium state. Homeostasis, according to Systems Theory, derives from the damping of variation by negative feedback. Positive feedback sees maturation as a process of accruing resources like a rolling snowball accrues snow. Positive feedback does not lead to the type of homeostasis envisioned by Open Systems Theory.

Diminishing returns—the economic equivalent of negative feedback—argues that market demand stabilizes as need becomes saturated. The initial sales of a new car model stir up considerable market interest; subsequent sales generate increasingly less interest. At some point, the market for that car stabilizes. Apply a certain amount of torque to a ship's propeller and the vessel will cruise at, say, 10 knots. Double the torque and the ship may do 14 knots; triple it and you get to 15 knots, and so forth.

Negative feedback is similar; it refers to feedback that suppresses a certain activity. Peer pressure, for example, suppresses behaviors that peers consider deviant and directs the deviant toward stable, acceptable behavior. Feedback mechanisms on elevators suppress motion as a target floor is approached.

Negative feedback and diminishing returns favor no time, person, or place. They allow no particular advantage except that advantage that accrues to excellence. Diminishing returns corrals growth and prevents any given system from monopolizing environmental resources; thus there is plenty of opportunity to go around. With hard work and intelligence, any child who is born a citizen of the United States could become president, any Mom-and-Pop outfit could become a mega-corporation, and any town could become a Silicon Valley.

School vouchers, or "School Choice," popular in the United States during the Reagan and Bush eras, illustrates this. Choice allowed parents to decide which public school their children would attend. It was assumed that this would force schools to compete for students and that better schools would thrive while the less competent would be have to improve to survive. Diminishing returns favors only excellence, and deviations from excellence are either pulled to the norm or they don't survive. All schools, according to this free market assumption, have the same basic opportunity to pull themselves up. Opportunity for success is equivalently distributed across the "landscape" of schools; a school in the northern part of a district has the same opportunities as one in the south. The process is, to be sure, egalitarian.

Positive Feedback

Systems theorists spoke of positive feedback long before its recent popularization by economists and physicists. The idea was begrudgingly accepted by economists in the late 1980s. Resistance, particularly in the United States, was in part attributable to the fact that it challenged the premises underlying free market philosophy (negative feedback, the preferred economic paradigm, is democratic to a fault). Positive feedback, or "increasing returns" in economic language, refers to the deceptively simple ideas that are epitomized by a rolling snowball or microphone feedback: "Them that has, gets more," or, speaking Biblically, "To them that hath shall be given" (the rich get richer and the poor get poorer—we could go on for a while here). Positive feedback is deviation amplifying—feedback feeding on itself and pushing itself away from its current status. Systems theorists have flirted with these ideas from the early years of their movement. Magoroh Maruyama, writing in 1963, provided several examples. For example, he argued that the growth of a city on an agricultural plain begins when a farmer, for chance reasons, locates on that plain. His presence attracts other farmers, who in turn attract farming related industry, and so on.

Proponents of increasing returns would derive different conclusions about school choice, discussed a bit earlier, than do proponents of diminishing returns. Increasing returns suggests that initially advantaged schools, those with a brighter class of students, a better football team, and better organized parents, will be able to capitalize on that advantage at the expense of other schools, and that school choice would only exacerbate differences. Given a choice, more parents—in particular more parents who value education—would choose to have their children attend the advantaged school rather than the disadvantaged one. The advantaged school would benefit from an increasing population of concerned parents, and disadvantaged schools would suffer from their loss. This handicaps the latter in their efforts to attract the type of parent who can help pull them out of their doldrums; further, better teachers would seek employment at the advantaged school and tax money would flow to the better school because of its burgeoning enrollment. The disadvantaged school is locked in a vicious spiral of decreasing resources from which no amount of will power can save it. The advantaged school, by contrast, is locked in a spiral that feeds it ever increasing resources. Egalitarian excellence is not enabled by choice; rather, effectiveness is polarized into the haves and the have-nots. It's not free exchange and excellence that create Silicon Valleys and Japanese success and VHS dominance, it is initial advantage. Minor differences become exaggerated differences, and the lucky, rather than the best, rise to the top.

Efficiency and Increasing Returns

Complexity Theory comes down on the side of increasing returns. Brian Arthur, of the Santa Fe Institute for Study of Complexity, has applied the principles of Complexity Theory and increasing returns to economic systems. His proposals will help us develop a Complexity definition of systems.

Arthur argues that economic systems are self-reinforcing systems and can be better modeled by increasing returns than diminishing returns. Resources are not randomly distributed in a population, as traditional economics theory would have us believe; rather they condense about systems that already have a resource base. Factories are more likely to move to areas that already have resources from which they can draw than to locate in isolated areas. Silicon Valley begets more Silicon Valley, and Japanese success with electronics begets more Japanese success with electronics.

Arthur discussed four reasons for such behavior. First, the cost of setting up an operation commits an organization to continue performing in its current mode, even if more convenient opportunities subsequently present themselves. A corollary of this is that cost per unit decreases as an industry's output increases, thus making it difficult for a new upstart to challenge the existing industry. Second, proficiency with new technology typically comes at the expense of a long learning curve, one that can be avoided by sticking with the current technology. For example, the auto industry would naturally cringe at the thought of converting to battery powered cars because of the learning curve required to become as proficient as they are with gas driven autos. Third, Arthur argues that related industries stand to lose if a focal industry changes its technology and will consequently resist such change. Numerous manufacturers of microcomputer software are dependent upon the success of Microsoft's® operating system. Similarly, many different industries—such as oil distributors, repair shops, and filter producers—depend upon the gas engine standard and would resist changing that standard. There is far too much invested in certain industries to permit easy conversion to a different industry or technology. Finally, there often is an expectation or belief that the prevailing output will dominate the future, thus there is reluctance to try something different.

One other argument can be added to Arthur's four. This is something of a variation or Arthur's third point. We argue that the success of any given industry is dependent on the coordination of many different industries. VHS tapes are not a stand-alone success story; rather this industry's success is dependent upon the proliferation of VHS players, the use of VHS by the movie industry, VHS cameras, and so forth. The success of VHS is a story of interdependency and network: Each industry is crucially dependent on each of the others and the industry as a whole is dependent upon interaction. To switch to another standard—say, 8 mm—would require the dismantling of all these commitments to VHS and the creation of new interdependencies. The fitness of a given industry is in its networks, and changing a single industry is like chipping at the tip of an iceberg.

Organizational theorists call these barriers *inertia*. Population Ecology, a branch of organizational theory, argues that inertia leads to failure to adapt to environmental changes, thus contributing to deterioration in organizational fitness. Arthur, on the other hand, sees inertia as the source of market success. The difference is fundamental: Population Ecologists operate from the perspective of decreasing returns while Arthur's arguments are premised on increasing returns. Decreasing returns advocates see inertia as maladaptive resistance to change, while proponents of increasing returns focus on exponentially growing markets that are strengthened by inertia. That is, the very factors that contribute to inertia also contribute to strength and growth. One can hardly say that Silicon Valley, an epitome of success begetting success, is maladaptive because it cannot change its general strategy. It's doing just fine because its inertial strength allows it to choke off competitors, even those with better ideas.

Arthur contends that initial advantage is all-important; that is, markets are path dependent, or sensitive to the early history of market share. Further, the process that winnows out competing markets does not always discriminate between efficiency and inefficiency. The advantage, according to Arthur, goes to the event or system that accumulates the most resources early in its development (natural selection, by contrast, argues that the fittest will inevitably rise to the top). Beta video, for example, is slightly superior to VHS format, but VHS held an initially advantageous position in the video market and consequently grew to dominate that market. Late in the 19th century, both gas driven and steam driven engines competed for the automobile market. A cross-country race occurred around the turn of the century, however, that was won by a gas driven car; this catapulted the gas solution to national prominence and steam choked in the dust. We can argue from hindsight that VHS video or gas engines were the superior solutions for their respective markets; who can imagine, for example, that a steam powered engine could even begin to compete with a modern gas engine. But gas engines have been intensively developed for a century and steam has not. Perhaps if steam had captured the initial advantage, we would be saying the same things about steam as opposed to gas engines.

Once a solution is selected, the market tends to lock in on that solution. Locking in means that markets gravitate to certain "solutions," and once they have chosen a solution (whether it be the best or not), competing solutions find it difficult to break into those markets (the inertia phenomenon described above). Imagine, for example, how difficult it would be to break Microsoft's hegemony over computer operating systems, or to persuade Westerners to begin writing right to left instead of left to right.

▨ Living Social Systems

Systems theorists, like biologists, struggle with the definition of life—that which separates the animate from the inanimate, the living from the nonliving. Is it *élan vital,* the vital force that permeated the scientific thinking of earlier centuries, or can life be defined more rationally? Evolutionist John Maynard

Smith wrote that, "Life should be defined by the possession of those properties which are needed to ensure evolution by natural selection" (p. 7). Systems theorists say much the same thing, but say it in a slightly different way; and the way they say it leads us to a surprising conclusion.

Systems theorists argue that a living system is one that is open to environmental influence. Living systems sense, and interact with, their environment by means of symbolic messages. To accomplish this, they must be capable of mapping their world and of using that map to guide behavior. Thus a living system mediates its interaction with the environment by means of its world map; that is, it compares environmental stimuli with its map and responds, not in direct proportion to the stimuli, but according to the strategies suggested by the map.

From this one can deduce other crucial life characteristics. Life, for example, is complex in that its parts are interdependent and the whole transcends the capacities of these parts. Life can create replications of itself in remote sites and at remote times by the transmission of symbolic information. One can even argue that life is not of necessity carbon based. Biologically, life can just as logically be based on silicon as on carbon, for silicon possesses all the same life-enabling characteristics as carbon (there are, however, no known examples). In Systems Theory, life can be based on organizational structures that transcend the typically narrow view of carbon-based life, the view that defines life as a physical entity such as an insect or fish or human being. For example, one can usefully conclude that a mob or an organization or a family is a living entity that, although based on carbon forms, transcends carbon-based life. Such "super-social" structures possess the characteristics of life as defined by Systems Theory—they are sensitive to environmental stimuli and symbolic information, they use world-maps to mediate interaction with the environment, they reproduce themselves, are complexly interdependent, and are structured and ordered.

▓ A Model of Complex Systems

Organizational theories of the last half of the 20th century have been heavily influenced by the open systems model. In the following chapters we will examine how those theories might be reinterpreted with a Complex model of social systems. Open Systems Theory was the driving force in conventional theory; Complex Systems Theory will be the driving force in ours.

Complex systems, like open systems, are holistic: the total transcends the sum of the parts. A holistic system is composed of correlated resonances, referring to a synchronous state that emerges when entities interact. Social solitons, such as highway rat packs, fads, rumors, and mobs, emerge because of correlation. The behavioral trajectories of constituent entities are unpredictable and time-dependent (nonreversible), thus nonlinear; as Ilya Prigogine argued, it is because of this that creativity, self-determination, adaptability, life itself, exist. Since living entities pool their capabilities to create Complex systems, these systems possess similar, but accentuated, life characteristics. It is entirely possible that the correlated system will even add capabilities not available to constituent actors. Consequently, it is tempting to call the greater system, itself, living.

The depiction of the Systems Theory model in Figure 5.1 emphasizes interaction with the environment. A Complex model emphasizes internal dynamics. The Complex model does not deny environment and its role in organizational behavior, but fails to focus upon it for two reasons. First, environment in Complexity Theory is more than an undifferentiated state or one composed of generalized processes, as tends to be the perspective of open systems models. Rather, it is composed primarily of other systems that are loosely to moderately interactive with one another and with the target system. The structure and function of this network are similar to that of the networks that make up an individual system, although the parts in the larger structure may be less formally interrelated. Thus correlation exists at different hierarchies, and systems are embedded within systems that are in turn embedded within still larger systems. It is useful to isolate systems for analysis, but it is realistic to maintain the broader network perspective when doing so.

Second, Complex Systems Theory emphasizes the manner in which the system processes information, particularly that which is generated internally. In Systems Theory, the environment is all important: It provides energy and templates for behavior; it screens acceptable activity and structure from the unacceptable; it is the source of ambiguity and challenge. In Complex Systems Theory, the system is self-generating; it is not as dependent upon external judges and challenges; and it demands of the environment at least to the same extent that the environment demands of it.

We will refer to these systems as Complex adaptive systems (*CAS*), a convention adapted by the Santa Fe Institute to refer to adaptive, interactive networks of actors (the term is used interchangeably in a number of disciplines, which is testimony to the belief at the Institute that general principles govern all *CAS* behavior; see *Hidden Order* by John Holland). We will argue that Complex adaptive systems are structured by physics and teleology and are refined by selection. Physics refers to both an external and an internal process. External processes are those environmental forces that shape the structure; just as the form of a jellyfish is influenced by gravity, social structure and behavior are influenced by such things as the needs and limitations of the human animal and by the constraints of technology. Internal processes refers to the physics of interaction and network. Teleology is a product of the indeterminism of nonlinear systems. It allows the social entity to play important roles in its future. Selection, which is an environmental force, refines the order generated by interaction.

CAS are products of positive feedback and path dependence (sensitive dependence on initial conditions). The inertial system that emerges from interaction and positive feedback may not represent the best possible solution to the problems it addresses, but its accretion of resources make it fit nonetheless. As a system grows, it develops a network of related systems that support or are otherwise related to the target industry; this contributes even further to systemic fitness. Since fitness accrues to systems that can build support networks, *CAS* interaction is better described as cooperative than as competitive. *CAS* are homeostatic, not as Open Systems Theory defined it but as we defined it in the last chapter. That is, the Complex adaptive system is dynamically stable (possessing both Chaotic and stable characteristics), able to drift over a fairly wide range of structures and behaviors without threatening its relative stability, capable of changing dramatically if needed, inclusive of a limited range of behaviors, and focused in what it attempts to do. Homeostatic systems can be represented as Complex attractors in that they are relatively small, moderately coupled to other systems, and relatively isolated.

Finally, Complex Systems Theory identifies three states of behavior: stable, Edge of Chaos, and Chaotic. Neither stability nor Chaos is capable of exhibiting the characteristics associated with Complex systems; Complex behavior can exist only at the Edge of Chaos. Edge of Chaos attractors are sufficiently stable to maintain information about themselves and their environment, yet sufficiently vibrant to process that information. These attractors map their environments by resonating, or correlating, with them; that is, they interact with, and become a part of, their environment. Different attractors within a system resonate with one another, thus augmenting the capabilities of the broader organization.

We will elaborate considerably on this skeletal definition in the chapters that follow.

CHAPTER

6

Structural Contingency Theory

Differentiation and Awareness

For the next few chapters we will follow the legacies of Open Systems Theory, but will redefine, or redact, these legacies to reflect the perspective of Complex Systems Theory. In a sense, we will be looking at how organizational theories might have evolved had Complexity Theory emerged in the 1950s. These redefinitions will also provide a vehicle for further developing ideas underlying our new perspective of organizational behavior.

The legacy of Open Systems Theory tends to diverge in two directions. Some theorists argue that leaders steer their organizations through uncharted environments like ship captains navigate their ships through stormy seas. These theorists focus on prescriptions for effective leadership and consequently are called "prescriptive theorists." Two such theories will be examined: Structural Contingency Theory and Resource Dependency Theory. Structural Contingency Theory describes organizational strategies for dealing with environmental contingencies. Resource Dependency focuses on controlling environmental contingency with interorganizational associations. The second path taken by this legacy is known as "organic theory." These theorists argue that organizational activities and structure are determined more by the environment itself than by leaders. Two such perspectives will be examined.

The first, called Enacted Environment Theory, argues that unknowable environments interact with irrational leadership activity to produce haphazard organizational behavior. A second perspective, labeled Population Ecology Theory, is based upon Charles Darwin's selection theories.

Structural Contingency Theory (SCT), as we said, is a set of prescriptions for dealing with ambiguous environments. Its researchers have also studied relationships between environmental ambiguity and organizational structures such as organizational size and centralization of authority. SCT will provide opportunity to observe how several of the principles of our Complex systems model can be observed in organizational behavior. The mapping relationship between a Complex attractor and specific elements of the environment, for example, is readily evident in the SCT literature. An SCT principle called "organizational slack" has parallels in Complexity Theory that will help us gain insights into how organizations innovate. Finally, data generated by SCT theorists (and by some contemporaries of SCT in general sociology) will be examined to see if we can find footprints of Complex behavior.

■ Structural Contingency Theory

Structural Contingency Theory emerged at about the same time that Systems Theory did. Popular in the 1960s and 1970s, it argues that an efficient organization is one that has been properly tuned to environmental contingencies. As Anna Grandori states this idea, "A firm's efficiency is dependent on the relation between the state of the environment and the form of the organization" (1987, p. 1). Grandori carefully points out that SCT does not predict what specific organizational form will emerge under given environmental conditions, rather it predicts only that efficient organizations are correlated with their environments. She does not suggest, furthermore, that only one organizational form will emerge in a given environment. She does suggest that efficient forms will have received environmental tune-ups by their leaders.

Environmental uncertainty, then, is an important force here. If environments are stable, unchanging, and predictable, then leaders can put together a rather simple organizational structure, one run by a handful of straightforward rules and with minimal supervision. If the environment is unstable, however, organizational structure must be flexible—leaders and workers must be able to adapt on the fly and to make ad hoc decisions. Such environments are far too complex to be dealt with by a simple organizational structure; rather, environmental demands must be divided into smaller, more manageable tasks and assigned to different individuals or groups with different types of expertise. Put simply, tasks must be departmentalized. An organization that produces only bolts for a low-competition market can function with only a few departments representing a limited number of skills—perhaps manufacturing, marketing and delivery, and management. A computer electronics industry, on the other hand, operates in a highly competitive and rapidly changing environment and must depend upon many different departments representing many different skills.

Such *differentiation* creates a problem, however. When an organization splits into subdepartments with different responsibilities, the people in these subroles tend to develop differing perceptions of need, task relevance, status, priorities, goals, time, and responsibility. It's easy to understand why this happens; people's egos are tied up in their own roles, and they tend to feel that what they are doing is more important than what others are doing. Individuals in different parts of an organization are exposed to different pieces of the environment, thus they develop differing views of reality. A sales force, for example, deals with clients and their needs, while manufacturing personnel deal with suppliers and production processes. Each of these areas will have different ideas about what the organization's goals are, how long it should take to do things, which tasks are more important than others, who is in charge of what, and what roles the organization plays within its niche.

As differentiation increases, conflicts and miscommunications increase. This in turn calls for increased coordination, or *integration*. An organization can be integrated either by plan (rules, goals, standardized procedures, or outputs) or by feedback (communication, continual adaptation, or updating). If environmental demands are relatively stable, if outcomes can be predicted, then coordination by plan will suffice. Such environments demand little differentiation as well, thus contributing to the ability to coordinate with plans (large but stable organizations must differentiate extensively, of course, yet they do so because of size rather than environment). Highly differentiated organizations in volatile environments, by contrast, must be coordinated by feedback. When the environment is unstable, when contingencies and ambiguity would rip any plan or standardized procedure to shreds, coordination must occur spontaneously. Leaders must be close to the action and must be able to respond uniquely to unique problems; they must interact with the conditions that create problems; they must have the knowledge and the authority to make decisions that solve problems.

Yet another way to reduce the impact of an unstable environment (besides differentiation and integration) involves what is called organizational slack.

The most easily recognized example of slack is buffer inventory—the stock-pile of extra inventory that one might maintain to protect against unpre-dictable fluctuations in market demand. Slack is broader than just inventory, however; it is any reserve that is maintained to deal with contingency, uncertainty, and sudden opportunity. Slack is any stockpile of physical, human, structural, organizational, and managerial resources. Prudent manag-ers will not overschedule themselves but rather will allow themselves slack time for dealing with unanticipated problems and demands. Research and development represents resource slack devoted to future opportunity. Person-nel whose jobs are not fully specified have the slack needed to exploit opportu-nities. Slack can assume many forms; the common denominator among these forms, however, is the ability to explore new or unanticipated territory.

This basic outline of SCT is based in large part upon the 1967 research of two faculty members at the Harvard Business School, Paul Lawrence and Jay Lorsch. Lawrence and Lorsch examined three industries: a rapidly chang-ing and highly competitive plastics industry, a packaging industry experienc-ing moderate change and competition, and a stable container industry. They found that the plastics industry was the most differentiated of the three, followed in order by the packaging industry, then the container industry. These variations in organizational characteristics correspond to variations in the respective environments of those organizations (turbulent, moderately chang-ing, and stable).

Lawrence and Lorsch found that the most productive companies were also the most conflictive of the organizations studied! It would seem logical that just the opposite would occur, that effectiveness would be related to low levels of conflict. Indeed, Talcott Parsons and Structural Functionalism, which had dominated organizational theory in the decades before SCT, preached that organizations were composed of harmoniously fitted pieces and conflict was more a matter of deviance than of functional behavior. Conflict in well-oiled, effective organizations was illogical.

Given the whole situation, however, the conflict made sense to Lawrence and Lorsch. Dynamic environments offer great reward, hence the greater returns, but success and effectiveness amid ambiguity require that organiza-tions differentiate to divide that environment's demands into manageable pieces. It is quite reasonable to expect that individuals occupying the different roles this creates would assume different environmental perspectives and would consequently have different priorities. When people working under the same roof have different priorities, conflict is inevitable, and the more highly differentiated their roles are, the more conflictive they will be.

Slack at the Edge of Chaos

Complexity Theory looks at slack a bit differently than do SCT theorists. First, slack is a source of organizational robustness. Systems in which tasks are divided into specialties and performed sequentially may experience problems of failure because of brittleness. If one part of the system fails to perform its assignment, other systems may be unable to carry on as well. If, however, each part of a system can stockpile slack reserves, they can feed off those reserves when one section fails. Such systems are robust. Organizational slack reduces organizational brittleness by allowing some "give" in the organization.

Complexity Theory points to yet another function of organizational slack: It serves not only to promote stability but to promote change as well. To explain, I need to introduce a useful idea from Stu Kauffman's work with Complexity Theory. Kauffman envisioned fitness as a mountain range in which individual peaks represent a fitness strategy. Some of the peaks in the range are tall, thus highly fit, and others are short; some are rugged and others are gently rolling. The best peaks are those that are between smooth and rugged, for they tend to be taller; further, their degree of smoothness allows systems the option of exploring other peaks, while ruggedness isolates the peaks to the point that systems don't wander too readily. There are clouds, called neutral fitness shells, hovering some distance down these moderately smooth peaks; these clouds represent a range of activity about which a system can wander without experiencing significant change. These fitness shells are equivalent to the parameter spaces discussed in Chapter 2 and are related to our discussion of homeostasis in Chapter 4. They form below a peak's apex because of back mutations, or mutations that reduce a system's fitness (in organizations, back mutations include suboptimal decisions and compromises).

Picture a system as a clump of actors drifting within the cloud. A clump has dimension; that is, some of the actors are nearer the bottom of the clump than are others. Some actors are even somewhat detached from the rest of the clump. If the intensity of the back mutations is properly tuned—intense enough to drive the species down the peak to where interconnections with other peaks—ridges—can be found but not so intense that the entire species is driven to a low fitness level—some members of the species (likely the detached members, or those near the bottom of the clump) will be able to wander across those ridges and seek higher peaks. The wandering units are, in effect, fitness scouts, and they provide an important service for the species by exploring alternative solutions to organizational problems.

Scouts exist because of slack. They are the actors within the fitness cloud who are low in the clump, or who have even detached themselves from the clump. Later we shall associate these disassociated scouts with what are called gatekeepers, or individuals who are somewhat isolated from the main work group but who are in rather close contact with what is going on in the environment. For now, we associate scouts with individuals or departments that possess sufficient slack resources to explore alternate solutions to organizational problems. Such slack may be in the form of time or in resources that are not committed to the central function of the system. Fitness scouts are perhaps most obvious in a Research and Development (R&D) division of an organization. Slack resources must be allocated to create an R&D division—resources that are no longer available for the primary production processes of the organization and that are committed without a guarantee of return. These slack resources are set aside to search the fitness landscape for higher production peaks. Slack also allows the organization to capitalize on opportunities that may arise; uncommitted fiscal resources, for example, are available for investment opportunities, or slack time allows a teacher to plan special curricular initiatives. Again, slack resources are set aside to search for better ways of doing things. Such slack lies far enough below the fitness peak that it can search the fitness landscape, but the bulk of the organization remains high enough on the peak to pursue the primary task effectively. We suggest, as did Stu Kauffman, that the proper balance for this lies at the Edge of Chaos, where stable patterns (in the form of commitment to the primary function) just begin to melt into Chaos (represented here by organizational slack). At the Edge of Chaos the organization is sufficiently rigid to carry information about itself and to perform its core task adequately, but at the same time sufficiently Chaotic to allow it to use its information creatively, to explore new strategies for surviving, to change.

Structures created to control a contentious environment, to bring some order to organizations, can, then, create change. Slack both stabilizes and changes.

▨ Differentiation in Organizations

We need to elaborate somewhat on the notion of differentiation that was introduced earlier. Organizations can differentiate their structures horizontally, vertically, and spatially. Horizontal differentiation refers to the extent that, and manner in which, tasks are subdivided; vertical differentiation refers to the number of hierarchies in an organization; spatial differentiation refers to the geographical dispersion of an organization. We will use these notions shortly to develop a clearer perspective of mapping.

Horizontal Differentiation

Horizontal differentiation will be examined from two perspectives: The first examines how tasks are divided up, and the second examines the number of tasks required to perform a function.

Tasks can either be broken into small, easily mastered pieces or dealt with as one complex job with interrelated pieces. To build a car, one could either obtain the services of individuals who perform specific, well-defined tasks, or one could obtain the services of people who know how to build a car start to finish, who understand why things are done as they are, and who know how problems interrelate with one another. The first of these individuals is a specialist,[2] the second, a generalist.

Chair production deals with well-defined, clearly understood raw materials and processes, thus it is typically performed by specialists. Computer chip production requires high levels of training, but raw materials and procedures are still well-defined and can likewise be performed by specialists whose skills, while complex, are nonetheless specialized. Specialists, then, are appropriate for tasks that can be routinized.

Other professions, such as teaching, deal with raw materials and procedures so poorly specified that the job cannot be successfully routinized. These professions demand holistic knowledge. Teachers, for example, must understand effective instructional techniques, curriculum development, child growth and development, classroom management, and subject matter. They are called upon to deal with parents, public relations, governmental regulations, student health issues, and social welfare issues. All these skill areas overlap one another, so it would be impractical to divide them up among independent specialists. Rather, teaching is a job for generalists.

One can also differentiate tasks based upon the number of routines that must be performed. A job can be involved to the point that many different tasks are required—car production for example—or it can be uncomplicated thus requiring relatively few tasks—like chair production. The more differentiated jobs are those requiring the greatest number of tasks (see Figure 6.1).

A bit of a contradiction emerges at this point in our logic, however: Ambiguous tasks, the product of volatile environments, don't necessarily involve a larger number of distinct roles than less ambiguous ones, contrary

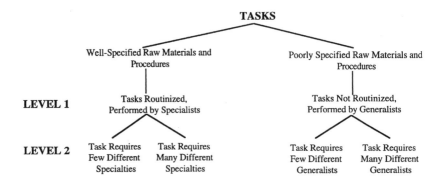

Figure 6.1. Two levels of horizontal differentiation as a function of test certainty to uncertainty.

to SCT logic. That is, ambiguous tasks, those requiring the services of generalists, may be in a sense less differentiated than unambiguous ones that require the services of specialists. The reasons have to do with interdependency.

Number of Roles and Interdependency

The schematic in Figure 6.1 suggests that both specialists and generalists may perform jobs with many tasks. Certainly, both can be embroiled in highly involved jobs that juggle numerous activities; nonetheless, equating differentiation in specialist and generalist organizations is somewhat misleading. The differences are in the nature of dependency and interdependency in the two types of systems.

Activities can be cleanly separated if there is little overlap in their respective responsibilities. In chair making, staining is only minimally related to cutting, and assembly can be isolated from wood selection; thus there can be separate, relatively independent departments for each function. For tasks involving more unpredictable raw materials and procedures, however, the picture is not always so clean. The responsibilities of medical personnel are not easily isolated, for example. Nurses work closely with physicians in the administration of medical treatment. Surgeons remove gall bladders but only in cooperation with anesthesiologists and surgical nurses. These roles are too interdependent to be neatly separated into isolated departments, and deciding whether physicians and nurses represent one or several roles is a matter of perspective.

We can get something of a handle on this by considering relationships among organizational parts as being either linear, independent, or interdependent. *Linear* relationships are those in which tasks are performed sequentially; that is, function "B" (e.g., chair staining) awaits completion of "A" (e.g., cutting), but staining is otherwise independent of cutting and cutting is minimally (if at all) dependent upon staining. If cutting were to be removed from this chain, then staining would be redundant, but the reverse is not necessarily true.

Independent separation refers to tasks that are totally unrelated. A factory, for example, may produce both microphones and speakers, each of which have little to do with the other. An organization can combine linear and independent structures, as when two independent activities linearly feed a third. Telephone production, for example, depends on the manufacture of speakers and microphones, but, as we've noted, speaker and microphone production are themselves independent functions.

Interdependence exists when different organizational roles are interrelated such that the parts form intricate networks of overlapping tasks. Were one part to be removed from the network, the remaining parts could absorb the loss and continue to function; that is, the system possesses built-in redundancy. Surgeons could operate without a scrub nurse; they would be shorthanded, but they have the knowledge to absorb that role. Nurses could even absorb many of the duties performed traditionally by physicians; midwifes, for example, have long performed in the physician's stead. Interdependent networks, then, are robust.

This is illustrated by a recent educational TV program in which a naturalist was demonstrating ecosystem fragility to a group of children. Each child was assigned a role as part of an ecosystem—rabbits, grass, foxes, and so on. The naturalist placed the children in a circle and had them hold a thin rope so that it passed back and forth across the circle in a web-like fashion. The children drew the web tight, then the naturalist cut a strand of the rope. The children all fell down, of course, and the naturalist told them that this represented the collapse of an ecosystem due to the destruction of any given part. This illustrates the linear forms of dependency described above.

The naturalist in this program stacked the illustration to favor her bias, however. Complexity theorists argue that ecosystems are more robust than her simulation allows. Such robustness can be illustrated by rerunning the naturalist's experiment using a longer rope, or even several ropes, and passing it (or them) through each child's hands several times. This represents an ecosystem in which the parts possess overlapping responsibilities and multiple interdependencies. Now when the rope is cut, nobody will fall. The network has built in redundancy that supports the system when individual pieces fail.

We have been struggling over the past few paragraphs with the question of whether an uncertain process represents few tasks or many tasks. Can the roles in interdependent dynamics be isolated and differentiated in the same fashion as those in linear or independent dynamics? The answer would seem obvious: They can't reasonably be isolated. From this perspective, the tasks performed by generalist are less differentiated than are those performed by specialists.

A specialist's role, then, can involve many tasks or few tasks, depending upon how involved the job is. Specialist's routines can be quite brittle, however, because the chain of events may be critically dependent upon each actor's performance. Generalists, on the other hand, tend to depend upon "differentiation-reducing," robust interdependency to deal with uncertainty, thus tend to have fewer distinct roles than do specialist organizations. One can differentiate between doctors and nurses, but their roles are so intermeshed that it's difficult to delineate their roles clearly.

The issue of interdependence has been examined by a number of SCT theorists. For example, in 1972, Jerald Hage and Michael Aiken defined *interdependence* in terms of participation in decision making (they argued that organizations that encourage participatory decision making do so because of the interdependent nature of their tasks). They found that both routinization and coordination by rules decreased as participation increased. In 1976, Andrew Van De Ven led a study in which he found that horizontal communications increased with task uncertainty.

Vertical Differentiation

Vertical differentiation refers to the number of authority levels in an organization. Vertical differentiation can be represented on a continuum that ranges from flat to steeply hierarchical. The simplest way to calculate the degree of vertical differentiation in an organization is to count the number of authority levels between the CEO and the lowest worker. This doesn't always work, however, because organizations may be divided into many different divisions, each with a different degree of vertical-ness. One solution is to count the number of authority levels in each division and calculate an average for the entire organization. This approach generally works, although it raises questions about whether divisions that have dramatically different structures, such as R&D and manufacturing, should be averaged together.

Vertical differentiation is related to horizontal differentiation in that both represent counts of a number of positions in an organization. The difference is simply that vertical differentiation counts the number of authority levels and horizontal differentiation counts the number of roles in a similar authority position.

Both vertical and horizontal differentiation have characteristics in common. Both are related to ambiguity in the environment, for example—but for different reasons. Horizontal differentiation exists to break tasks into manageable pieces, while vertical differentiation results from a need to coordinate the roles needed to deal with the environment (some organizational theorists argue that vertical differentiation may also be related to power issues). Both vertical and horizontal differentiation are also related to size, although the number of divisions as a percentage of total size tends to drop off as size increases.

Spatial Differentiation

An organization that is spatially differentiated has divisions or departments at different geographical locations. The reasons why an organization might disperse its operation are varied. If the needs of the clientele are so varied or ambiguous that service must be customized, then those services might best be placed close to the clientele. A state department of education operates in a complex environment, and coordination of the diverse needs of schools and their students may be better served by regional offices than by a centralized office. Alternatively, an organization whose raw materials are costly to transport may locate refining factories at diverse geographic locations that are closer to the sources of raw material. An industry whose market is unstable or dwindling (e.g., the tobacco industry) might diversify by purchasing different manufacturing operations at different geographical sites. An organization might spread out simply to take advantage of different taxing opportunities, or to place certain parts of its operations near populations that contain high percentages of workers with particular skills, or near money market centers such as New York. An R&D operation may want to locate near a university, for example, while manufacturing could best be placed in low tax areas and corporate offices would best be served near large cities with ample money markets.

Differentiation of Complex Systems

Complexity Theory describes differentiation from a somewhat different, yet related, perspective. In Chapter 5 we defined mapping as a process in which different organizational attractors (usually departments or divisions of a department) correlate with a given part of the environment. This is strikingly similar to SCT's claim that uncertain environments must be partitioned and assigned to different units of an organization. To wit, SCT is describing the same dynamics that Complex Systems Theory calls mapping. Differentiation, then, allows that an organization knows its environment, and the organization is a thinking, adaptive entity capable of processing information, categorizing it, using it.

John Holland presents a similar explanation of how complex adaptive systems build internal models of their environments. He refers to the differentiated units as building blocks. In isolation building blocks are of limited use, but they can be combined and recombined in tens of thousands of combinations, thus allowing the *CAS* to identify and adapt to unique situations. Holland illustrated by observing that if we see a red Saab with a flat tire by the road, we know how to respond. We may have never seen such a combination of events before, but we have the building blocks—red, car, tire, flat. We can put the pieces together and make sense of the situation.

Mapping in formal organizations operates essentially the same way. The system differentiates to map pieces of a complex environment. These pieces are building blocks and can be combined and recombined in numerous ways to allow the system to "know," and respond to, its environment.

SCT asserts that increased differentiation leads to conflict; that is, different organizational structures develop different worldviews that clash with one another. Such conflict, it continues, demand increased supervision. Differentiation, conflict, and supervisory control are evident in moderately large organizations with stable environments (that differentiate because of size and not because of environment), or in organizations with stable processes that require numerous steps to accomplish. In either case, numerous divisions create problems of conflicting constraints, and this increases the need for regulatory supervision. The conflicting constraints generated by differentiation in these stable environments cannot be tremendously complex, however, or managers alone simply could not deal with them. Complex environments require a different model of control.

According to Complexity Theory, organizations do differentiate more extensively for complex environments than for simple ones, and the network of conflicting constraints generated by uncertain environments may be too complex to resolve with supervision. Such complexity may characterize particularly large but stable organizations as well. SCT proposes that such organizations must be controlled by feedback and that they are prone to conflict and thus require more intense supervision. Complex Social Systems

Theory agrees with the differentiation proposal and with the claim of greater conflict, but argues that increased supervision is not always the answer. Such organizations are characterized by webs of constraints that are too complex to be resolved by deliberation. If the system is particularly complex, the constraints may defy any solution, and the system must reduce its complexity before it can ever expect to achieve fitness. Less complex systems still defy supervisory coordination but, according to Stu Kauffman, Complexity Theory provides a mechanism by which the constraints can be resolved.

Kauffman argues, simply, that Complex organizations must work out the conflicting constraints by adapting, evolving, and annealing (we'll have to wait until Chapter 14 to define this latter concept). To put this in SCT terminology, it is the conflict itself, that feature of differentiation that SCT seems to label as "bad," that ultimately leads to solution. The conflict is indicative of efforts by the divisions themselves to work out the constraints. If the system is not so highly differentiated that the web of conflicting constraints is intractable, nor so undifferentiated that large, individual units are frozen by their internal constraints, the system should achieve a state of dynamic equilibrium among its units, one in which the system continues to adjust and change, but in which the bulk of the constraints have been worked out. We tend to assume that this process occurs because of supervision, but supervision may play a far less important role than we think. The dynamics described by Kauffman suggest that managers could best utilize their time by enabling the process, by seeing that it doesn't degenerate into factionalism and personal attacks, that the conflict doesn't stagnate in defensive posturing—in short, by seeing that the process remains dynamic, positive, and focused on resolution.

The earlier discussion about interdependency is pertinent. Interdependency refers to a network of causality and is characteristic of organizations in uncertain environments. Those same causal links are used for communication and are ideal for making the sort of adjustments we are talking about here. Interdependency is not just ideal for dealing with complex problems, it is also ideal for dealing with the conflicting constraints that typify organizations in uncertain environments.

■ Formalization and Integration

Formalization is related to integration by rules. Formalization refers to the degree to which rules and procedures are imposed upon organizational functioning. If a delivery service carefully routinizes the delivery procedure, even to the point of gauging the precise time at which a pickup is made and specifying the amount of time allowed for that pickup, then that organization is formalized. Formalization is likewise evident when line supervision closely controls the activity of workers, when breaks are timed to the second, and when workers consult rules manuals for guidance in handling unusual situations. Research has shown, as expected, that formalization is high when environmental or task uncertainty is low, and vice versa (Hage & Aiken, 1972).

Centralization of Authority

The degree to which organizational control is centralized at the upper levels of the hierarchy would seem also to be logically related to uncertainty, and research has tended to support such a relationship. Jerald Hage and Michael Aiken, for example, concluded, in a study of social welfare agencies, that routine work is associated with centralization of decision making, increased formalization (standardization of procedures), and with a less professional staff.

Hage and Aiken also looked for a relationship between uncertainty and the number of rules that an organization creates (a measure of formalization). It seemed an obvious conclusion that organizations within stable environments would run their organizations via rules; other researchers had come to this conclusion, and their conclusion was consistent with SCT theory. Hage and Aiken's results surprised them: They found only a weak link between uncertainty and number of rules. Similarly, the important study of public personnel agencies by Peter Blau and Richard Schoenherr found only a weak relationship between formalization (rules regarding personnel regulations) and centralization of authority.

Blau and Schoenherr did not consider this contradictory, however. They observed that, in organizations where procedures foster the development of merit-based leadership, a highly trained cadre of leaders will emerge that is capable of decentralized decision making. This, Blau argued, accounts for the presence of decentralization among the formalized organizations in his study and explains the weak relationships he found between formalization and centralization. As he said in his 1970 study, "Rigidity in some cases may breed flexibility in others" (p. 160).

Given our discussion above about differentiation, conflict, and Complexity, we can certainly see why formalization and centralization could be higher in a stable than in an uncertain environment. Supervisory control is appropriate for resolving the modest network of conflicting constraints that can exist in more stable environments. But what about the seeming contradiction that Hage and Aiken discovered? They failed to find a predicted increase in rules among more stable organizations in their sample. Blau and Schoenherr attributed this to the emergence of a trained cadre of managers, and this hypothesis is logical. Complexity would add, without contradicting Blau and Schoenherr, that stable organizations can experience differentiation because of size or because their processes require numerous steps to accomplish. Such differentiation can produce a web of conflicting constraints that is just as difficult to resolve as those that exist in unstable organizations, thus increased formalization is not always the answer, even when the environment is predictable.

■ Criticisms of SCT

Anna Grandori provides a good summary of criticisms that have been leveled against Structural Contingency Theory. These critiques fall into one of four categories. First, SCT suggests a one-to-one correspondence between organizational structure and environment that cannot be supported. French theorists Michel Crozier and Erhard Friedberg argued in 1977 that American contingency theorists translated the pre-SCT assumption that there is one best way of organizing that serves in multiple situations into an assumption that there are many best ways with the choice among them dependent upon the nature of the environment. The metamorphosis is clearly an improvement over the classical model, but even so it ignores the fact that there may be a number of equally effective ways to deal with a given environment. Different organizations could approach a given environmental problem with any of a variety of strategies, and each of them could be successful. This is particularly true where the environment is forgiving—where there are ample resources upon which organizations can draw, for example, or where competition is low.

Second, SCT is criticized because it does not explain what happens if an organization fails to adapt to its environment. Organizations may not adapt because of organizational inertia or because of costs associated with change.

Third, SCT assumes that causation is essentially one-way, that environment drives organizational structure, rather than the alternative that organizations may affect environment. In fact, organizations control their environments by direct influence—attempting to control suppliers, clients, and so on—or by selecting less problematic environments through diversification.

Organizations may even select the environment in which they choose to operate, or they may choose to perceive only certain parts of the environment and ignore others—that is, they create their environment.

The notion that organizations might select their environments leads us to the fourth criticism found in the organizational theory literature: Environment is not an absolute, given entity. Two organizations may define the same market differently, thus approach it with different strategies, and both be successful. One firm, for example, may choose to build its fortunes on a quality, dependable product while another builds a reputation for innovation; such choices imply different approaches to the same environment or different perceptions of environmental problems.

Is, then, environment an objective reality or is it simply what we make it to be? SCT claims that environment determines organizational structure; an alternate school of thought claims that perceptions of environment determines structure. Some public schools for 10- through 13-year-old children, for example, perceive their environments as academic and downplay differences that exist among students, while others focus on academic and readiness differences among students of this age group. The former tend to respond to their perception of environment with structured, course-specific classes while the latter respond with an interdisciplinary team approach to teaching. Perception influences structure.

One more criticism can be added to Grandori's summary. SCT theory is prescriptive; that is, it assumes that effective managers can control their organizations' fates by finding optimal adaptations to environmental contingencies. The environment, according to SCT, may be ultimately unknowable and unpredictable, but strategies for dealing with such ambiguity can be found. SCT's approach, then, is focused on leadership behavior and on improving administrative decision making. This focus on prescriptive or control issues ascribes a potency to leadership that may be difficult to support, as we shall see in subsequent chapters.

CHAPTER

7

Footprints of Complexity

The Nature of Order

▨ Size and Structure at the Edge of Chaos

Although Structural Contingency Theory focuses primarily on the connection between environment and structure, a number of contingency theorists have turned their microscopes on other causes of organizational structure. In 1971, Blau and Schoenherr looked at whether the size of an organization affects its level of decentralization. Not surprisingly, they found that the number of organizational divisions (positions, hierarchical levels, sections per level, etc.) increases as the size of organizations increases. However, they also found that the rate of differentiation tapers off as size increases rather than expanding at a constant rate as one might think it would. Managers in large organizations supervise larger departments than do their counterparts in smaller organizations, thus larger systems have a smaller percentage of sections than do smaller ones. Blau and Schoenherr explained this by arguing that large organizations accrue a certain economy of scale that allows them to function with less administrative intensity and with larger departments than their smaller brethren.

This conclusion isn't entirely satisfactory, however. If, as SCT claims, increasing largeness creates increasing problems of coordination, there would seem to be a practical limit to how large a division can get in the name of scale economy. This doesn't seem the case in Blau and Schoenherr's data, for divisions tend to become large more readily than they become numerous as organizational size increases (see Figure 7.4, below, for example).

Complexity Theory provides an explanation that is certainly more interesting and perhaps even more convincing. An exponential relationship between order and size occurs naturally in Complex social networks (the tapering of, say, number of organizational levels with increasing size is an exponential relationship). It is related to reduction in the number of conflicting constraints in a system to make that system more manageable (we discussed this in the last chapter), and it occurs without outside force or motivation. Kauffman saw it occur in his Boolean networks, and he observed it in the ratio of cell types to genes among animals (the number of cell types drops off as the number of genes increases). In many ways, social systems aren't that different from genetic networks or neural networks or Boolean networks: They are complexly interdependent, adaptive systems of actors linked by communication and seeking local, often selfish, goals. Perhaps, then, social structures are subject to the same forces that shape any other adaptive network.

In this chapter we examine Stu Kauffman's self-ordering proposals, then reexamine data from SCT regarding the number of subdivisions within an organization. The goal will be to find clues suggesting that the natural physics of interactive systems can explain the phenomena that SCT theorists ascribe to the more prescriptive notion, economy of scale. We will support the findings with data from other disciplines in sociology.

■ Order From Disorder

Kauffman examined systems composed of units that interact with one another and form complex networks of interdependency. Units form networks, networks settle into attractors, and a network of attractors forms a system. Each unit within a system interacts with K other units, and Kauffman used Boolean rules to govern the relationships among his units. The OR rule in a $K = 2$ system (each entity in a system interacts with two others), for example, turns a unit "on" if one of the units with which it interacts is in an active ("on") state; the AND rule turns the unit on only if both inputs are active (see Figure 7.1). The number and characteristics of the attractors that emerge in such a system varies with K, and this fact leads to important observations.

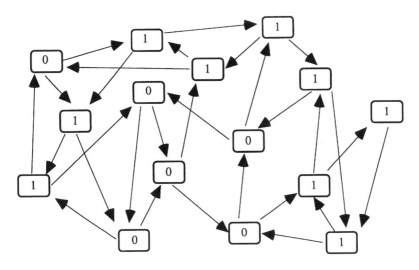

Figure 7.1. Kauffman's Network with $K = 2$ and $N = 15$.

Networks at Different Levels of K

When Kauffman turned his networked system loose in a computer, order (in the form of different attractors, or clusters of units) emerged—without the services of natural selection or economy of scale. When K was equal to N, the total number of units in the system (an extremely complex "wiring diagram," because every unit interacts with every other unit), the number of ordered states that emerged was equal to a little over one third of the total number of units (N). Thus for $N = 100,000$, the number of attractors would equal about 36,000. This is a lot of attractors. On top of that, they tended to be very large and tended to wander over much of parameter space. Most of them also drained rather small basins of attraction. A basin of attraction is a zone around an attractor; a point in phase space within such a zone but not on the attractor will be drawn to that attractor. A basin of attraction is also a buffer zone between attractors; a large basin assures that mutations in a given attractor usually flip it only as far away as its own basin, thus it returns to its original state. Small basins, however, leave attractors vulnerable to perturbation; they can easily change to a different type of attractor because they can easily jump beyond their basin. Further, the number of alternate attractors that could be reached from any given attractor in Kauffman's $K = N$ simulations was quite large; an attractor had the potential to become any other attractor in the system if mutated. Finally, perturbations (mutations) often had dramatic effect on these attractors—they were sensitive to initial conditions (a function of their small basins and close proximity).

For $K > 5$, the attractor size and the number of attractors remains quite large. The stability of the attractors was again low (small basins and sensitive dependence), and the number of other attractors that could be reached by any given attractor was large.

For $K = 1$, the attractors were fixed and unchanging. They were somewhat large and quite numerous. Each attractor was structurally isolated from the others, thus the dynamics of one attractor had no effect on the dynamics of others. Such isolation is called structural modularity.

When Kauffman set K to 2, order at the Edge of Chaos emerged. The number of attractors that evolved from this system was approximately the square root of N; thus for $N = 100,000$, about 316 attractors appeared. The length of attractors was likewise small; each attractor visited about $\sqrt{N}$ sites—that is, attractors had limited ranges of behavior. The attractors tended to drain large basins of attraction, and the system of attractors was interconnected with limited access to one another so that cascading damage was controlled and channeled. This was a reasonable number of attractors, and the system was sufficiently stable to maintain its form but sufficiently vibrant to change. In other words, $K = 2$ Boolean systems lie at the Edge of Chaos.

Order at the Edge

Random behavior diffuses across state space much as a gas spreads evenly throughout a box. There is no order: Energy does not organize itself, and delineable behavior does not emerge. Herbert Spencer argued that order, in the form of life, is separated from random disorder by survival of the fittest. The battle is an uphill one, however, and the struggle against disorder grows increasingly intense as life's complexity increases. Brian Goodwin compared this to the Calvinistic work ethic, in which hard work leads to the good life, and argued that this notion resonates deep within our cultural souls—hence the appeal of Darwinian evolution. Complexity theorists (particularly Stu Kauffman) argue that order is, instead, a natural phenomenon among interactive structures that does not depend upon outside work such as natural selection. Dynamical systems spontaneously box order into ordered life spaces. It's because of free interaction that order appears in Kauffman's $K = 2$ networks and not because of work by natural selection. In his experiments, natural selection is more a tuning knob helping order move around on fitness landscapes than a creator of order.

$K = 2$ systems function on a relatively correlated landscape, thus they have access to high fitness peaks and can move across relatively large areas of the landscape. These landscapes are at the same time somewhat rugged, hence are, to a degree, structurally modular (or confined in semi-isolated structures). Consequently, they avoid being spread across the undifferentiated lowlands of the landscape. At this Edge of Chaos state, fitness structures can take advantage of the best of two worlds—their correlated side allows them access to other parts of the landscape (they can change) while their rugged side allows them to consolidate their gains and achieve a measure of stability.

There is a related benefit. Since modular attractors are partitioned from one another, each has access to only a limited number of other attractors, thus change and cascading damage is confined or controlled.

Walling Off Attractors

$K = 2$ Boolean networks spontaneously create barriers between attractors—hence modularity. These partitions are composed of units that are permanently turned "on" or "off." They emerge in such a way that if you were to flip one of the units, the rules controlling it would immediately flip it back to its original state. Because they are forced to remain in one state or another, these partitions are called "forcing structures." Such frozen walls prevent a change in one attractor from migrating to another, or prevent the changed attractor from converting into something else (i.e., they foster stability). Consequently, change in the system is controlled; it can only migrate via openings in the forcing structures and only to a limited number of neighbors.

These notions can be visualized as a panel of lights (we discussed this illustration from Kauffman's book in Chapter 5). If the lights are wired so that the state of each influences the state of some number of other lights, we have a parallel network. When the wiring is set at $K = 2$, there will be pockets of flashing lights separated by walls of unchanging lights on the panel. The flashing lights represent attractors, and the unchanging lights are barriers, or forcing structures. The number of pockets equals approximately the square root of the total number of lights on the board. Further, there are holes in the walls where changes in one attractor can breach to one or more other nearby attractors. If K is decreased, these breaches disappear, and the size of the attractors increases rather dramatically; if K increases, the barriers shrink or dissolve and the attractors increase in number and size.

Another Path to Order

By now, the reader who is considering applications of this material to social events should be concerned about the requirement that K be limited to 2 inputs before useful order emerges. In actual social and organizational behavior people are dependent upon many other people, departments are dependent on at least several other departments, organizations are dependent upon a number of other organizations; to wit, K in social life is typically much larger than 2. Fortunately, controlling K is not the only way to tune interactions and produce order. Bias in favor of certain types of interconnections (referred to by Kauffman as P) can also tune order, and where P is used to create order, variable K can be higher than it otherwise would be.

Homogeneous Clusters

The order that emerges by tuning P utilizes fixed barriers just as K does, but the barriers are dependent upon the nature of interaction rather than the number of interconnections. P in binary (on/off) networks refers to Boolean bias in favor of one binary state over another. Typically, one would expect half the conditions in a network to favor that "on" state and half to favor the "off" state. If 60% of the rules (or combinations of rules) favored the "on" state, then we would say that $P = 0.60$. For a given level of K relative to N, there is a critical value of P (referred to as P_c) beyond which fixed structures will emerge. If, for example, $P_c = 0.80$, then P greater than 0.80 favors order, and P less than 0.80 favors Chaos. The value of P that marks the onset of fixed structures and order varies with K; specifically, P_c increases as K increases.

Kauffman labeled the fixed structures that emerge when $P > P_c$, "homogeneous clusters." Such clusters differ from the barriers that emerge from forcing structures. At $K = 2$, networks create fixed structures by forcing individual units to a 1 or 0 state. Homogeneous clusters, on the other hand, are typically held in place by the activity of several inputs rather than just one input; thus unit D may be held in place by the joint activity of A, B, and C rather than by the activity of any one unit. That is, the unit is held in place by the activity of other units with which it interacts: It is held in place by interdependency.

What, then, is P for social systems? The clue to this answer is that units are held in place by interdependency, thus P is related to stability that arises from interdependency. It refers to any restraints that different actors in a network exert upon one another; it may also refer to the strength of relationships among units. Examples in social life include culture, mores, belief structures, norms, licensure, rules and regulations, emotional attraction such as love or friendship, and social inertia. I propose that a combination of such biasing structures (P) and controlled numbers of actors with which a given actor is interdependent (K) acts to partition social systems into a set of relatively stable substructures.

▨ Social Systems and the Square Root Principle

Complexity Theory predicts that systems left to their own devices naturally and spontaneously seek order. Kauffman has found that Complex systems controlled by Boolean rules obey the square root principle, and argues that the universal nature of the phenomenon is evidence for a dynamic more powerful than natural selection. That is, if selection is the random process that evolutionists argue, it should create biota with any number of substructures. That such a universal feature exists, a feature that is independent of selection dynamics, is evidence of a more potent dynamic. It is, Kauffman argues, evidence of the potency of Complexity dynamics. Similarly, if the exponential function is found to be descriptive of social systems, we lend credence to the argument that Complexity dynamics, more than human determinism, influences social structure. We will accept Kauffman's implicit assumption that the square root principle may extend beyond simple Boolean networks.

On the basis of these assertions, we can propose the following hypothesis:

> The number of groups that emerge in a social system is a square root, exponential function of the number of people in that system.

I recently experimented with this informally with a group of 25 students in a qualitative research class. Two related doctoral programs were represented, and most students had been in their respective program a year or more. Interaction among the students was encouraged, and no effort was made to contrive any subgroups. Interestingly, four clear subgroups emerged and there was one additional "sorta" group that never completely jelled. If there were indeed five groups, as is suspected, then the square root principle is supported.

Had this been a serious study, in-depth interviews would have been conducted and detailed field notes collected to confirm and elaborate on the observations. Even so, this quasi-analysis illustrates the type of experimentation available to social scientists.

In Chapter 15 I report on a similar experiment in which principal components analysis is used to cluster respondents to a questionnaire. The assumption behind the analysis is that opinions about the subject measured by the questionnaire will be the products of interactive dynamics. Again the analyses revealed clear grouping according to the square root principle.

Blau and Schoenherr's cluster data can also be represented as a root function of population size. The data used for these analyses had to be replicated from XY plots presented by Blau and Schoenherr in their book, *The Structure of Organizations;* the original data were not available. The process was admittedly prone to error—each coordinate point had to be traced back to an X and a Y axis to determine the value of the data that created that coordinate point. However, the basic shape of the resulting plot of points was close to that provided by the original authors. That is, the curve that was fitted to our replicated data would not be terribly different from that which would fit the original data. I would expect an accuracy to within a few tenths of a unit.

Once the data on the size and number of divisions were replicated, root curves were determined by trial and error. Data were first generated by guessing at the exponent that might describe a curve for the data (I usually started with $X^{0.5}$, which represents the square root function (X represents organizational size). Each datum thusly generated was then subtracted from the corresponding datum for number of divisions, then summed. Extreme, singular cases at the high end of size were excluded because of their possible lack of representativeness, but this made little difference. From that point, the exponent of X was adjusted up or down until the smallest summed deviation was obtained. The process is similar to that used with least square analysis in statistics, and can be represented with the following equation:

$$Z = \sum_{1 \rightarrow N} (Y - X^a)^2$$

Y represents the number of divisions observed by Blau and Schoenherr for each organization in the study; X is the size in number of employees of each organization. X^a is the estimation of Y from X. The exponent a in this equation is adjusted until Z is minimal.

Size by Position

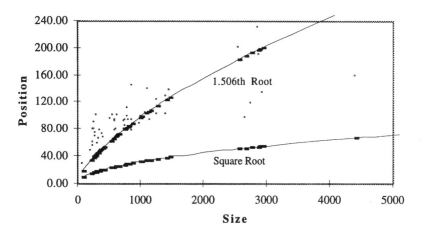

Figure 7.2. Plot of organizational size by number of positions, with exponential curve overlays. Data derived from Blau and Schoenherr's study of public personnel agencies in Canada.

Figure 7.2 is a plot with an exponential curve overlay of Blau and Schoenherr's data for organizational sizes against the number of formally identified positions per organization (different job titles) in 52 public personnel agencies in Canada. That best-fit curve is the 1.51st root of organizational size ($\sqrt[1.51]{Size}$), thus there are many more positions in Blau and Schoenherr's data than would be predicted by our square root hypothesis. The only way to obtain this number of clusters with Kauffman's Boolean simulations would be to set K to about 12; this is far greater than $K = 2$, which produces Edge of Chaos order. This is not surprising, however, for the number of formally identified positions does not necessarily represent the number of identifiable clusters in a system.

Blau and Schoenherr also provided plots for the number or hierarchical levels in each organization; this is presented in Figure 7.3. The curve that best fit these data was calculated by raising X to the 3.62th power. As can be seen in Figure 7.3, this is much flatter than a square root function would be.

The authors provided data on the average number of sections per level for the organizations they examined. The total number of sections per organization was calculated by multiplying sections per level times number of levels, and used to produce the plot in Figure 7.4. This plot can be fit by a line representing the 2.4th root of X, which is a reasonably good fit for the square

Size by Number of Levels

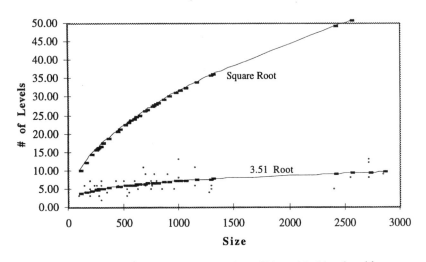

Figure 7.3. Plot of organizational size by number of hierarchical levels, with exponential curve overlays. Data derived from Blau and Schoenherr's study of public personnel agencies in Canada.

Size by Number of Sections

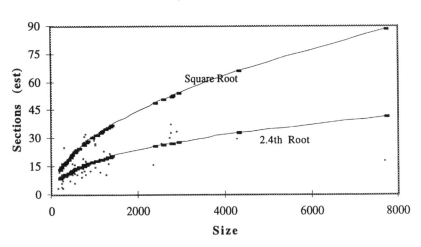

Figure 7.4. Plot of organizational size by number of sections, with exponential curve overlays. Data derived from Blau and Schoenherr's study of public personnel agencies in Canada.

root curve. The number of sections per organization, then, represents the clusters we have been seeking.

This finding suggests (I use the word in its fullest sense of the tentative) that the number of sections in an organization emerges out of an interactive, nonpurposive ambiance, and that interactive dynamics influence purposive behavior. For example, a group of individuals and roles can formally split off from a larger section because roles and personalities have swirled together within the parent section and have defined a niche that demands formalization. A group of scientists within an R&D department can draw together because of common research interests; later the research agenda of that group develops to the point that it is made formally independent of the original group. This process is a function of interactive dynamics, and such dynamics gravitate toward the square root principle. As Brian Goodwin argued, this Edge of Chaos site is an attractor that draws behavior to it—and Adam Smith might add, as if by an invisible hand. New sections are created, then, when the dynamic needs them to maintain its balance on the Edge.

I fully realize that science demands a more rational explanation than this mildly mystical one (although interactive dynamics do at times appear mystical), and one is certainly available. One can argue that the number of formal clusters within an organization are related to problems associated with conflicting constraints. If there are too many sections, the system will be unable to work out the web of conflicting constraints among the systems. Breaking a system into small "manageable" pieces does not necessarily make the system as a whole more manageable. Too few sections, by contrast, simply shift conflicting constraints within a few large sections. A given section can change only by simultaneously satisfying all the constraints it is attempting to juggle within itself. The first scenario, too many sections, is constantly in a state of flux because of sections jockeying for positions they can never achieve (so to speak); the second tends to freeze because the sections cannot resolve their internal constraints in order to change. Obviously a compromise is required; one that produces sections large enough to produce stability yet sufficiently small that conflicting constraints can be broken up and worked through by the jockeying process (Kauffman refers to the process of jockeying as "patches"; this will be developed more fully in Chapter 14).

Support for the Square Root Principle From Other Sources

There is a fair body of research that can help support or reject the exponential hypothesis. Some of the most interesting data come from researchers

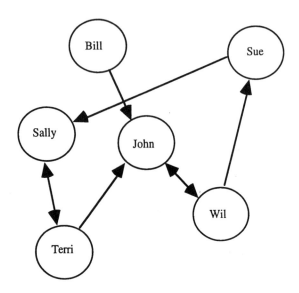

Figure 7.5. What a simple sociogram might look like. Single-headed arrows indicate one-way choice, double-headed indicate that the pair chose each other.

who call their work "sociometry." Sociometry was briefly popular in the 1960s and has since evolved into a study of social networks. It refers to an analysis of the way people group themselves, and to whom people look for such things as leadership and prestige. Its primary tool was something called the sociogram. Subjects were asked questions like, "What person in your class would you most like to invite to a party?" Or: "Who in your village, outside your immediate family, do you most enjoy socializing with?" When the data were collected, responses were coded on graphs composed of concentric circles. The individual most often cited was placed in the center of the target, and subsequent circles indicated the number of connections among the remaining individuals in the analysis (see Figure 7.5). Procedures were developed for identifying subgroups from such data.

A number of studies of this sort can be found in a 1960 book edited by J. L. Moreno, titled *The Sociometry Reader*. Charles Loomis, for example, analyzed the 25 families in a stable, family-centered community in El Cerrito, Mexico, and identified five groupings from his sociograms. Robert Weiss and Eugene Jacobson, using a procedure called matrix analysis, identified 27 groups among 196 employees in a complex governmental organization. Elaine Forsyth and Leo Katz did a similar matrix analysis of 25 teenagers from a cottage in the New York State Training School for Girls and found five clusters (or perhaps six clusters—one group could possibly be resolved into two groups). John Gullahorn found five groups within an office of 29 women employed by a large Eastern corporation. Like the last two studies, Gullahorn employed matrix analysis, but he collected data by observing who was talking with whom at regularly measured intervals. Finally, Charles Proctor analyzed two villages in Mexico. In a village called San Juan Sur, he examined 75 households and identified nine clusters among those households. In the second village, a place called Atirro, he found seven clusters among 77 households (the 2.23rd root). San Juan was the more stable community and Atirro was split geographically; these facts may help explain the differing results. Interestingly, Proctor utilized principal components analysis to identify his clusters; others have also suggested using such procedures to analyze complex structure in interactive networks (a good but somewhat technical description of the procedure can be found in Simon Haykin's book, *Neural Networks*).

In nearly all of these analyses, the number of clusters identified was very close to, if not exactly, the square root of the total population size. There are a couple of small exceptions. In Proctor's analysis of the Central American village of Atirro, the number of clusters was the 2.23rd root of the total population size, but that finding may be due to the fact that the community was split geographically. In Weiss and Jacobson's analysis of 196 employees in a governmental organization, 27 groups were identified, which is the 1.76th root of 196. There is a possible explanation for this discrepancy. Five of the groups were administrators and the remaining 22 were workers. Like Atirro in Proctor's study, these two subsets of the population were largely isolated from each other: Only a single connection linked them in the organizational chart. Weiss and Jacobson did not report the number of individuals in each of these two subsets, so we cannot analyze them further.

Supporting the Hypothesis

The data that I found all supported our earlier hypothesis, and much of the support was rather dramatic. Is this sufficient to "reject the null"? I would like to leave the jury out on that one, for further study is needed. The null is certainly not yet accepted, at any rate. We can at least tentatively suggest that the square root principle may be universal in social life. If so, then one can discount alternative explanations such as economy of scales, for, as Kauffman said about biology, there is no reason why such alternatives should provide a universal pattern rather than many different patterns.

CHAPTER

8

Resource Dependency

The Emergence of Order

▨ Organizations and Daisies

In his popular best-selling book, *Complexity: Life at the Edge of Chaos,* Roger Lewin tells of visiting the unconventional biologist Jim Lovelock at his home in St. Giles on the Heath, England. Lovelock is noted for his argument that life controls its physical environments. Instead of the one-way street in which the physical world—temperature, sunlight, moisture, atmosphere—influence life's possibilities, Lovelock contends that life influences these variables in return.

To explore his hypothesis, Lovelock created a computer simulation of a world with no biota—one in which the principles of physics alone ruled. Temperature in that world began rather low but increased steadily over the course of time; on a graph of time against temperature, temperature plotted as a 45° line rising from left to right. Lovelock then added some electronic daisies to the silicon world, some white daisies and some black daisies. When the program was rerun, the black daisies initially proliferated—they were naturally selected because the world was cold and their color absorbed and held heat. The temperature graph line rose sharply for about a third the distance it had when there were no daisies, then leveled off to a shallow incline

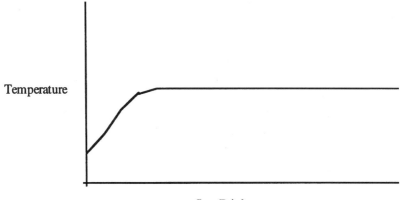

Figure 8.1. Plot of sun brightness against temperature in Lovelock's Daisyworld.

(Figure 8.1). White daisies began to appear when the temperature got a bit warmer, because they were able to reflect heat and keep temperature at moderate levels. Without external control, without a "queen bee" calling the shots, adaptive organisms acting in their own self-interest and responding to environmental conditions were controlling environmental conditions! Biology was not passively accepting what the physical world dished out. Lovelock called his simulation Daisyworld.

Lovelock had more complex versions of Daisyworld; there were simulations with different colored flowers, or with animals—predators and prey dancing together in a struggle for survival. But the results were always the same. Nature evolved and survived; and its actors achieved environmentally stable states (ESS—a state of balance among actors) not only among themselves but between biota and physics.

Lovelock referred to this as the Gaia hypothesis after the Greek goddess, Mother Earth. The Gaia hypothesis was controversial to say the least. For one thing, it was not reductionist; it didn't dissect nature into small pieces for study, but looked instead at nature from a holistic perspective, and modern biology is about reductionism. Further, traditional biology is unable to accept the suggestion that something besides natural selection might be at work in nature. Noted evolutionist Richard Dawkins argued, for example, that the Gaia hypothesis was fatally flawed because there were no worlds competing for survival in the model. The term *Gaia* itself suggested New Age philosophy, which certainly did nothing to ease the concerns of scientists. Perhaps Lovelock's biggest offense, however, was his insinuation that evolution is teleological, that nature creates its environment based upon need. Teleology is a curse word to most biologists.

Organizational theorists, and social theorists in general, don't share biology's consternation over conventional teleology. We embrace it for a number of reasons, one of which is because we want to feel in control of our organizations. There are entire models of organization built around the assumption that leaders determine the destiny of their firms and institutions, the most notorious being Machine Theory from the early part of the 20th century. Yet Lovelock, and Complexity Theory, speak of an unconventional brand of teleology, one with which even we may not be entirely comfortable. Lovelock's teleology is bottom-up, not top-down. Machine Theory is top-down teleology—the boss controls and manipulates. This is teleology we understand. With bottom-up teleology, nobody is in control. Actors, behaving according to local rules and for self-interest, generate order, and do so without board rooms and 5-year plans.

This is teleology yet it's not teleology. It is teleology because the system manipulates its environment, but it is not teleology because the process occurs without plan. The emergence of structure is a product of interaction, of physics, of need, and of accident and natural selection. It is nonpurposive teleology that is driven by interactive forces.

Neither the word *teleology* nor the word *evolution* serve us here. For one thing, each carries preclusive baggage. We need instead a word that reflects interaction, nonpurposive teleology, physics, and, of course, natural selection. Packard and Bedau used the term *telic waves* to get at these notions, but that suggests something pulsating, and it ignores the broader dynamic. John Holland calls it aggregation, referring to the emergence of *CAS* from the aggregate activity of subunits; biologist Robert Wesson, focusing upon a more purposeful side of evolution, called it "positive evolution." Of the two, Holland's notion of aggregation refers to the fuller sense of the idea we're trying to name, but the words themselves don't convey that. I propose, instead, the term *Complex Natural Teleology*. It is obliquely suggestive of natural selection, it emphasizes a nonpurposive teleology, and it acknowledges complex interactive forces. It, better than any of the other terms, describes the gist of the dynamic we are exploring.

Complex Natural Teleology is the dynamic that causes networks of interactive units to form. It is, as Lovelock argues, a two-way affair between system and environment, but environment must be understood as other networks and as physical forces. The dynamic is also heavily influenced by events internal to the network. All this will be sorted out by this chapter.

Resource Dependency (RD), the focus theory for this chapter, deals with strategies used by organizations to manipulate their social environments in order to assure their supply of physical resources. The focus of other theories, such as Structural Contingency Theory, is on how to use resources; the focus of RD is on how to acquire them. It is about how managers go about enhancing their organizations' survival and how they manage the demands of interest groups from whom they receive resources and support (thus RD is labeled prescriptive theory). It is about the nature of interaction among different environmental actors, and it's about humans controlling their environments and environment controlling its humans.

▥ Controlling the Organizational Environment

Resource Dependency (RD) theorists argue that organizations depend upon transactions with their environments for survival, and that the level of certainty in those environments shapes the nature of organizational interactions. Jeffrey Pfeffer and Gerald Salancik, gurus of RD, premise their hypotheses on the observation that organizations seek to control uncertain dependencies. Such dependency exists when a needed resource is dominated by relatively few suppliers or when an organization must compete with numerous other organizations for scarce resources.

Structural Contingency Theory, the subject of the last chapter, proposed that organizations reduce their difficulties with uncertain environments by adjusting their internal structure (they accumulate slack resources, for example). Resource Dependency theorists argue that organizations reduce uncertainty by adjusting relationships with their environments. Thus RD theorists talk about influence and power and role expectations, and about informal cooperation, social pressure, association, cartels, interlocking directorates, and joint ventures.

Interacting With Environment: Conflicting Constraints

Organizations have different preferences—different needs, wants, or perceptions; some seek profits, some prestige, some growth or power. The preferences of different organizations may be incompatible, such that satisfaction of one preference precludes satisfaction of another. When a college math department teaches differential equations in a manner that is incompatible with the way they are presented by the physics department, it frustrates

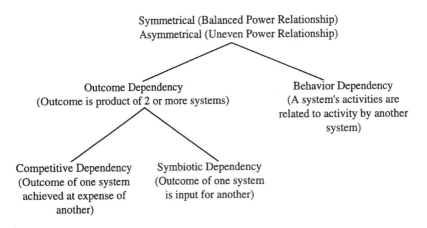

Figure 8.2. Pfeffer and Salancik's categories of interdependence.

the preferences of physics; when the courts rule in favor of divestiture, they frustrate the preferences of large organizations; the preferences of ecologists are often incompatible with those of loggers. Stu Kauffman observed the same incompatibility phenomenon with his Boolean simulations. He noted that order emerges only slowly, if at all, in high K systems (systems with many interdependencies), and the structures that do emerge are Chaotic. He attributed this to conflicting constraints; this is the same term used by Pfeffer and Salancik to explain the incompatible preferences they observed. Conflicting constraints, Kauffman observed, increase rapidly as the number of interdependencies among actors increases. Uncertainty, even Chaos, then, is the product of such constraints, and it is the resolution of this that RD attempts to understand.

Different Ways to Interact With an Environment

Pfeffer and Salancik identified several categories of interdependency (Figure 8.2). They distinguished between outcome interdependence and behavior interdependence, for example. Outcome interdependence exists when an organization's activity is dependent upon the activity of some other organization. It comes in two forms: competitive and symbiotic. Competitive outcome interdependence exists when the outcome achieved by one organization can be higher only if the outcome achieved by another is lower—that is, when two organizations are competing for the same resource. This is a zero sum game, the type described by Prisoner's Dilemma (see Sidebar in Chapter 4).

Symbiotic outcome interdependence, by contrast, exists when the output of one actor is input for another, or when two systems are mutually dependent upon each other's output.

With behavior interdependence, an actor's activities are dependent on the actions of another social actor. For example, a baseball team can compete only if an opposing team agrees to appear.

Interdependencies can also be symmetric or asymmetric. They are symmetric when the players all have about the same power, or access to resources. They are asymmetric when one actor holds all the cards—when one actor is much more powerful than other actors in the environment and can exert its will over other actors. If one or two organizations had a monopoly over a particular raw material, they could demand about any price they liked for the raw material. This is asymmetrical interdependency.

These distinctions help us understand why organizations structure their environments as they do. If a system is on the short end of an asymmetric relationship, for example, its best strategy is to buy out its environment—to purchase a source of raw material, for example. It might also ally itself with systems that produce something different than they do, thus creating countervailing power. More on this in a bit.

Reducing Dependency With Alliances

Organizations control uncertainty by forging alliances. Alliances are founded upon formal or informal—or even "understood"—agreements among firms to cooperate with one another. Alliance represents a restructuring of exchange relationships in a way that creates permissive environments, as opposed to restrictive ones. Through alliances organizations increase mutual control over one another's activities for their mutual benefit. Once established, it is to the participants' advantage to continue the patterns of interaction, at least until conditions change and the alliance is no longer useful.

The mere fact that one actor is dependent upon another does not in and of itself constitute a problem necessitating an alliance. Bakeries are dependent upon wheat farmers, for example, but there is plenty of grain on the market, so bread-makers need not get into the farming business. Pfeffer and Salancik argue that problematic relationships are related to four issues: the magnitude of dependence on a resource, or the degree to which an organization uses a resource; the criticality or importance of the resource (some resources, like electricity for lighting, have low magnitude but high power); the degree to which one group has discretion over the resource needed by another group; and the degree to which resource control is concentrated.

Avoiding and Offsetting Dependency

Dependency is not a problem for organizations that can find ways either to offset the control of another system or to evade its stranglehold. Evasion is typically the less satisfactory of these two solutions because it requires that the system compromise itself in some way. A system may, for example, evade by lowering its aspirations or by trying to please too many constituencies. In neither case are underlying problems resolved.

According to Pfeffer and Salancik, avoidance comes in several varieties. A system may avoid problems by finding ways to finesse or juggle conflicting constraints. It may, alternatively, seek to influence or manage the demands of other systems. Third, it may seek to neutralize demand altogether.

Daniel Katz and Robert Kahn called the problem of conflicting demands "information overload" and proposed several strategies for dealing with it. One may attack problems on a first-come, first-serve basis—that is, by queuing the demands; this, however, can cause difficulty if an important demand isn't dealt with on a timely basis. A better strategy is to prioritize the demands according to importance. This, however, may run afoul of a different sort of problem: Satisfying one demand may constrain one's latitude in satisfying another demand. Pfeffer and Salancik add that conflicting demands are less intense if one actor doesn't know what is being done for other actors. If company B doesn't realize that it can demand a higher price for its raw material like company C does, then user company A will be just that much less at the mercy of its suppliers. Alternatively, one actor can be played against another. If, for example, beef producers can convince their market that the high cost of beef is due to grain feed costs, they take pressure off themselves and may influence the price of their feed in the process.

The second of Pfeffer and Salancik's avoidance strategies involves managing the conditions of a demand. One can do this by putting the system in a position of determining when a demand has been satisfied; physicians, for example, can determine when a patient has received all the treatment he or she needs. A system could attempt to control the formation of demands by involving itself in efforts to establish standards or by manipulating demand through advertising. Systems can avoid demand by building slack inventory, as when nations reduce their dependence on oil producers by building strategic reserves of oil. Mobsters in the 1920s controlled the rules of exchange themselves by intimidating their suppliers. Actors can take control of organizations that provide needed resources or markets, as when a commodity manufacturer purchases a shipping line. A system might attempt to restructure its needs; during World War II the Axis nations attempted to reduce their dependence on oil-producing nations by manufacturing synthetic oils, for example. Diversification is an important and common variation of demand restructuring. Here, an organization diversifies its product line so that it will no longer be so highly dependent upon a single supplier or a single market. A system may even try to break up the asymmetrical demand by resorting to such things as antitrust suits and co-optation.

Finally, a system can avoid demands altogether by selecting the markets it will serve and those it will not serve. Auto insurance companies, for example, can avoid serving high-risk markets by pricing themselves out of those markets.

Manipulating the Environment With Mergers

Manipulating a problematic environment is more satisfying and permanent than is avoiding a problem, and much of the Resource Dependency literature focuses on this strategy. A system manipulates its environment in order to control the resources or markets that are important to it.

The most direct way of doing this is to buy out the environment; this is called merger. If a system purchases a company that differs from itself but that supplies it with raw materials or purchases its products, it integrates vertically. If the organization purchases its competitors, it integrates horizontally. Vertical or horizontal mergers occur when the level of trade among different industries is high. Diversification is a third type of merger; it involves producers with differing products that may—but probably don't—trade with one another.

Horizontal Integration

Anna Grandori argues that horizontal mergers are likely to occur in competitive interdependent situations. Competitive interdependence, it will be remembered, exists when the outcome of one organization can increase only at the expense of another; that is, it occurs when two organizations are competing for the same resource.

Competitive interdependence, she continues, is related to the number of firms in an industry—more firms, more competition. The relationship between competitive interdependence and number of firms is mediated, however, by the degree to which the resources used by competing organizations is concentrated. If there are lots of firms and relatively little resource, then competition is high. If there are lots of firms and low concentration, by contrast, firms don't have much over which to compete. Impact and uncertainty, then, increase with concentration.

If concentration is particularly severe, however, uncertainty eventually decreases because fierce competition forces horizontal mergers; only a few large firms emerge from the fray, and they learn to cooperate with each other.

Vertical Integration

Vertical mergers are related to the degree of symbiotic interdependencies among systems. Symbiotic interdependence exists when the output of one actor is input for another, or the two systems are mutually dependent upon each other's output. Firms merge with the source of their resources or buyers of their products if relationships with those buyers or sellers are uncertain. As was the case with horizontal integration, the motive is to reduce dependency.

Diversification

Diversification likewise aims at reducing dependency among systems, but its approach is somewhat different. It is useful when integration is not possible, when a firm within a symbiotic environment cannot buy its suppliers or purchasers, and when a system within a competitive environment cannot absorb its competition. With diversification, organizations control their difficulties not by dominating the problematic firms (suppliers, buyers, or competitors) but by expanding their own interests to reduce dependence on uncertain relationships. Tobacco farmers may devote acreage to cotton and soy beans because conditions in the tobacco industry are uncertain, for example. Hanes Hosiery's® merger with Sara Lee® helped it survive competition with foreign producers. Diversification makes organizations less dependent upon a whimsical, single market.

Manipulating the Environment With Interfirm Coordination

Interfirm coordination is more common than merger; it includes such things as co-optation, trade associations, cartels, and informal agreements. It represents a way to stabilize interdependencies and is particularly useful when coordination is needed only occasionally or when a market is so volatile that merger would constrain flexibility. Coordination is more flexible than merger because relationships can be changed as needed. According to Grandori, however, this can be somewhat problematic because there is no authoritative, central control.

If organizations are in an asymmetrical relationship, the dominant system may be in a position to demand the cooperation of the other, and may even be able to impose complex, bureaucratic controls over the relationship. General Motors can demand certain price structures from many of its suppliers and can even force them to submit to audit to ensure they don't make excessive profit.

Coordination is preferable to merger in highly volatile markets, markets in which technology or markets change rapidly. Large, computer technology firms, for example, use a number of small, specialized producers. They ally themselves with these producers rather than merging with them because computer technology changes so rapidly and mergers could become obsolete overnight. The small producers benefit because they can make a lot of profit quickly, and the large firm benefits because it doesn't have to carry inventory on expensive and transient operations.

■ Complex Alliances

Alliance formation is a common, indeed necessary, behavior among Complex adaptive systems (*CAS*), and the emergence of alliances can be attributed to more than just the prescriptive deliberation proposed by RD theorists. Rather, they result from the full range of dynamics implicit in the term *Complex Natural Teleology*, which was developed earlier in this chapter. The next few paragraphs are intended to describe more fully how Complex Natural Teleology fosters the emergence and development of networks.

Resource Dependency theorists argue that organizational leaders deal with environmental uncertainty by forging alliances with other organizations. Environment is defined relative to resource allocation, and problems with allocation manifest as conflicting needs and preferences among organizations. Alliances emerge from agreements to interact according to certain rules, thus they structure preferences in a way that makes relationships predictable and stable. This process is deliberate and teleological; it represents a rational approach to dealing with contingent environments.

Complexity theorists contend that alliances, or rather, networks, are necessary with or without unstable environments, that they are a function of systemic interaction under any circumstance. The alliances to which we now refer are more inclusive than those described by RD theory. Complex alliances refer to networks of systems that depend upon one another for their fitness; this includes resource providers, to be sure, but is not limited to them. It includes any system that nourishes and enables, or is otherwise related to, the product or function of a given industry. Automobile producers are not viable without the support of oil refineries, gasoline outlets, repair shops, highway construction firms, and traffic control agencies, for example. None of these industries supply or consume the product of the automotive industry (except in limited ways, such as purchasing parts), yet automotives is intimately dependent upon them. VCRs would be of little use, even impossible, without home cameras, iron oxide production, retail outlets, and the movie industry. Networks do more than provide resources for a particular organization and stabilize its environment, they make an industry possible, they give it fitness regardless of the environment. Moreover, many of the pieces of these networks come together not by design or prescription, but simply because there is a niche for them in the developing network.

This "coming together" process is implicit in the term Complex Natural Teleology. Earlier we identified four processes that define the term: autocatalytic interaction, physics, need, and natural selection. The heart of the process is autocatalytic interaction, referring to a dynamic in which parts of a system catalyze one another. Autocatalytic interaction, according to Stu Kauffman, creates order; it is useful in describing how individual industries evolve and is useful for describing how our networks emerge. Initially, in its infancy, pieces of the incipient network emerge and find one another. Thus in the late 1800s oil refinery found engine technology and a marriage emerged. Engines found an outlet in personal transportation, personal transportation stimulated the development of oil refinement and led to gas stations. Maintenance shops emerged, as did parts stores. The cost of the new technology spawned the development of specialties in financial institutions and insurance companies. The rubber industry was boosted by the need for smooth rides, as was highway development. Financial institutes made it easier for everyone to own a car, and paved highways and networks of gas stations made the automobile a comfortable and convenient mode of transportation. Widespread use created a need for traffic control, thus police forces were expanded, traffic laws proliferated, traffic lights and radar guns were invented. Increased use also boosted the fortunes of body shops and insurance companies. And so on.

Industries beget industries beget industries, and each reinforces and strengthens each other. The network grows like a snowball—Brian Arthur's increasing returns. This is autocatalytic interaction.

There is another piece to autocatalytic interaction, something that goes on beneath the surface as networks emerge and grow. We referred to this process earlier in the book as correlation. When elements interact, their individual "resonances" begin to coordinate, to harmonize. This dynamic is crucial to the network. The actors in a network must develop something of a common worldview, a sense of common purpose, a common understanding of how problems are to be solved, an understanding of each other's needs. They must be sensitized to one another so that they respond more or less together. They must feel some sense of common identity, have a common focus. This doesn't mean that all the parts are reading from the same page. Each maintains its identity and is focused on its own well-being, but the parts of a network have changed their individual identities to the extent needed to accommodate one another. Compromises have been made, roles have been identified, a sense of network has emerged. This is what is meant by correlation.

John Holland uses terms like *aggregation* and *tag* to describes these same processes, but from a slightly different perspective. Aggregation "concerns the emergence of complex large-scale behaviors from the aggregate interactions of less complex agents" (p. 11). He illustrates with an ant hill. An individual ant, he notes, has fixed behavior and will usually die if circumstances don't fit that behavior. A colony of ants, by contrast, is capable of highly complex, adaptive behavior that has amazing capacity for survival. Holland goes on to observe that aggregates thusly formed can themselves form higher level meta-aggregates, and that these can combine to form meta-meta-aggregates. Individual actors, then, are building blocks that can be combined and recombined in myriad ways. Applied to cognition, this, Holland argues, allows us to make sense of unique situations using only a relative handful of building blocks.

The aggregation dynamic is facilitated by what Holland calls tagging. Tags are rallying points, symbols or actors or behaviors that serve to delineate a given aggregate from an undifferentiated background or from other aggregates. Social tags include strong, articulate leaders; product names; and professional identity. Tags permit an aggregate to select among agents that would be otherwise indistinguishable, thus "providing a basis for filtering, specialization, and cooperation. This in turn leads to the emergence of meta agents and organizations that persist even though their components are continually changing" (p. 15).

The physics side of Complex Natural Teleology comes in several forms. There is a "physics" to autocatalytic interaction. Networks can't juggle too many participants, for example, for too many participants mean too many conflicting constraints to accommodate. The internal structures of organizations cannot be so rigid that they can't flex to accommodate others. The size of networks may be restrained by environmental carrying capacity, or their form may be restrained by human laws. The network may be restrained by the state of technology; computer chips didn't become a part of the automotive network until nearly a century after its inception, and there are certainly pieces that will join the network in the future as technology develops.

Need likewise expresses itself in various dimensions. Deliberate teleology, which is described by RD's prescriptions, represents one dimension of need. Here the actors perceive their needs and work deliberately to satisfy them. There is, however, something of a bottom-up teleology in network emergence, the same sort of bottom-up teleology we saw in Lovelock's Daisyworld. There is an element of things happening naturally, happening simply because they find expression in the network. However, the "happening" is driven by the unexpressed need to survive and increase fitness. Computer chips were a natural for the automotive industry; granted someone had to make a deliberate decision to incorporate them, but it didn't take a genius to see the potential. Computer chips and cars were an inevitable marriage that increased the fitness of both. Same thing with the union of plastics and automobiles; it was a natural thing to happen. Likewise, the system "naturally" manages to control its environment, to generate demand for its products, to suppress problematic laws, to generate economic flow (in the form of jobs) that help make it possible for people to buy cars. No one necessarily sat in a board room and decided to invent plastic so that cars could use it; that would be top-down teleology. This union, and many others, just emerged; needs were met by bottom-up dynamics.

Finally, natural selection refines the process; it assures that the network is maximally fit. Note that Complex Natural Teleology does not see selection as the cause of order, rather selection modifies the structure to improve its fit within the environment. Selection is not the sole source of fitness, for that is assured by exponential growth in the network, by the sheer strength of multiple industries focused together, by the power of inertia. Rather, selection keeps an eye on the market and assures that the network responds to that market. Its role is crucial, for an industry that consistently refuses to adapt will eventually suffer.

Network Fitness

In 1956, sociologist Lewis Coser wrote a counter-intuitive little book titled *The Functions of Social Conflict*. In it, he argued the benefits that derive from the cross-cutting conflicts within a society. Such interdependency creates social cohesion, he maintained, in much the same way that woven thread creates strong fabric. This also is the argument of Complexity Theory, except that it sees no reason to focus only on conflict. The accommodations that make up the compromised social state create systems that are both viable and stable.

Complexity theorists propose that order emerges, and is able to resist disruption (is fit), because of interactions and interdependencies that exist inside and outside of the system. The famous Hawthorne study by Elton Mayo in the 1930s found that informal groups, which result from social interaction and interdependency, are more potent at controlling productivity than are the formal expectations and demands of management—not to mention being resistant to the will of researchers (Mayo had predicted incorrectly that he could control productivity by altering work conditions—the social group responded, but not as he expected). The same principle applies to industries; the automotive industry, for example, is strong because of its interdependent networks of auto manufacturers, service stations, the plastics industry, the highway industry, oil producers, and steel producers. Strength derives from interdependency, and interdependency is a naturally emerging phenomenon.

More particularly, fit, dynamic, stable systems result from interaction and accommodation among the participants in a system—the dynamics we call Complex Natural Teleology. Emerging *CAS* work out their conflicting constraints and their relative roles such that their mature relationships are stable and the system is fit. Because their components work out a relationship, the systems are noninvadable; that is, they resist outside manipulation, and they at least somewhat control conditions under which new members become part of the group. Similarly, actors within the network are discouraged from abandoning the alliance because to do so would deny them the significant benefit of group membership. Even extinction of individual actors is resisted because of the strength actors accrue from network membership. When actors do leave a network, the alliance either accommodates the loss with internal alterations or it finds a new actor to replace the lost roles.

Deliberate alteration of such systems is not a simple process. Because stability and order are products of emergent interdependencies, any given actor in the network is sufficiently established, and fit, to resist change. Further, any given agent has allies—the agents in the rest of the network. Imagine how difficult it would be to switch from gas fueled cars to electric powered autos—the infrastructure for gas cars would have to be dismantled at great expense and disruption, and a whole new network of support constructed for electric cars. Stable, complexly interactive organizations create functional interdependencies that can be realigned only at the risk of significant disruption to the network and, consequently, to its fitness and the fitness of the environment it serves.

The following itemizes some of the network dynamics that make change difficult. These dynamics are variations, in one form or another, on the notion of inertia that Brian Arthur and others have proposed.

• To change an existing *CAS,* significant investments of resources in the structure must be dismantled, reallocated, or even lost (equipment must be replaced, for example, and expertise loses its efficacy).

• Emerging *CAS* have myriad choices, but as they develop and make commitments to certain choices, the further choices available to them begin to dwindle. If, for example, an emerging university creates a college of agriculture on its campus, that college is eligible for federally funded public service money that supports a wide variety of activities. Such a commitment, however, restricts the university's ability to spin off separately administered colleges from agriculture because the divisions that are transferred to a new college may very well lose their public service support and have to be funded with local money. More important, spin-off is resisted because of the interdependencies that emerge around the common focus provided by the public service money.

• Learned patterns of behavior and problem solving that have evolved over time may have to be restructured at considerable cost to the organization.

• Organizational structure and fitness are built on complex interpersonal and inter-group dependencies; restructuring may disrupt these interdependencies, thus forcing the organization into a disorganized and relatively unproductive period of recovery.

• Power relations emerge in organizations and resist changes that may threaten that power.

In short, complex adaptive systems are not like a room full of furniture that can be rearranged, added to, or deleted from at will. Rather, organizations are akin to an ecological web in that the whole is defined by the interactions, interdependencies, and inter-commitments among the parts. This is the nature of fitness, however. Resistance to change does not necessarily mean that a system has stultified; it may instead mean that the system is quite fit, good at doing what it is supposed to do.

Interfirm Coordination in Japan

The Japanese economic system provides particularly good examples of networking and of the strength that derives from networks. This fitness was particularly evident in the 1980s when dramatic economic changes were forcing an unprecedented number of mergers and leveraged buyouts in the Western nations. This frenzy of activity was accompanied by an equally frenzied spate of joint ventures as organizations scrambled to increase profits and avoid hostile takeovers. In Japan, during the same period, mergers were rare and takeovers unheard of. There were a number of strong business alliances in Japan, and these undoubtedly were a large part of the reason that mergers and takeovers didn't occur.

Japanese alliances are typically centered around banks and are called *kinyu keiretsu* (financial lineage) or *kigyo shudan* (enterprise group). These are informal alliances of capital suppliers and trading partners that are knit together by trading agreements, intercommunication, and common owner-ship. Michael Gerlach, an organizational theorist, undertook an intensive, 3-year analysis of these business alliances while living in Japan during the 1980s. He wrote that this nation has six major enterprise groups. Three are descendants of prewar holding companies; they are the Mitsubishi, Mitsui, and Sumitomo groups. The other three were formed more recently around the commercial banks of Fuji, Sanwa, and Dai-Iche Kangyo. Gerlach identifies three mechanisms that bond these alliances:

> high-level executive councils which symbolically identify group members and the boundaries of the social unit, as well as provide a forum for interaction among group firms; exchange networks—specifically debt, equity, director-ship, and trade networks—that define the position of individual firms in the group and establish group-wide constraints on behavior, and group-wide industrial and public relations projects which affirm the existence of the *kigyo shudan* as a coherent social unit. (p. 129)

Enterprise groups are centered around banks because of manufacturing's unusually heavy dependence upon loan capital and because of heavy bank

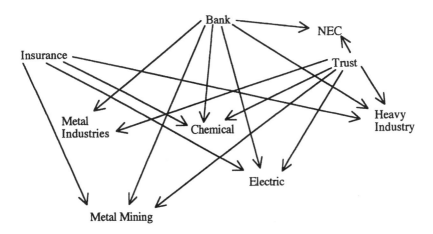

Figure 8.3. Representative interdependencies in an enterprise group in Japan.

investment in companies' equity shares (a practice that is illegal in the United States). The "main bank" for an enterprise group not only provides the bulk of its firms' revenues, but looks after the firms in the group in a variety of ways. It affirms the commercial health of constituent firms, thus helping them obtain loans from other banks. The main bank helps its firms find business customers, it comes to the rescue when its companies experience financial difficulty, and it gives lending preference to its firms. Figure 8.3 depicts fiscal relationships among firms in a typical group.

Ownership of companies in these enterprise groups is quite different from ownership in Western society. Stockholders are the legal owners of companies—true whether one is in Japan or Germany. In the West, more stock is owned by individuals than by corporations, and, at any rate, stockholding is a neutral enterprise engaged in for its financial returns. In Japan, more stock is owned by institutions than by individuals, and a firm's major stockholders are companies within its enterprise group—companies that have a vested interest in the firm.

Consequently, firms in an enterprise group own one another and the group as a whole owns itself. Banks take active roles in the management of client firms, particularly clients that are experiencing financial difficulty. Intergroup trading is stable, thus providing financial constancy to the firms in a group. If a firm's stock price increases dramatically, its trading partners don't rush to cash in on the windfall since the strength of the one firm benefits all firms in the group.

Interlocking ownership is called *kabushiki mochiai,* which means "to hold mutually" but that carries connotations of helping one another, shared interdependence, and stability. Gerlach reports that cross-holding within groups accounts for a third to three fourths of the stock holdings of Japanese enterprises; by contrast, less than 8% of stocks in the United States are held by other corporations.

In a short-ranged perspective, this network of self-canceling ownership makes no sense. Why should a company borrow heavily to own stock in a company that has likewise borrowed heavily to invest in it? It's like gift exchange; the materialistic thing to do is to invest money in one's own well-being rather than investing in self-canceling gifts. Similarly, Japanese firms could do better in the short run to invest in their own growth rather than "exchanging" stock purchases.

Gerlach argues that the benefit should be understood from its broader perspective, however. The practice removes stock from public trade, thus discouraging takeover and lending financial stability to firms and to their enterprise groups. The practice represents the tangible glue that links firms in the enterprise. It forms mutually beneficial, stable relationships among trading partners, controls environmental uncertainty, and makes the enterprise group a formidable force.

■ Complex Natural Teleology and Deliberate Behavior

In this chapter, we have used RD theory to develop an understanding of social catalysis, one of the four elements of Complex Natural Teleology. We will now use its prescriptive nature as a springboard to discuss the teleological side of Complex Natural Teleology.

Organizational theorists have long debated whether social structure is determined by complex social forces or by leadership decisions. Do market forces and natural selection decide which organizational forms are successful, or do wise and insightful leaders manipulate the environment to their benefit? Resource Dependency theorists quite clearly side with the prescriptive argument that leadership manipulates the environment, but Enacted Environment theorists and Population Ecologists, whom we will study in subsequent chapters, beg to differ. Who is right—or are they all right? Two questions fall out of this debate and are addressed in the following material: First, can humans control their collective dynamics with deliberate behavior, and second, can humans control their future? The answers have tended to polarize opinions among organizational theorists, but Complexity Theory suggests that there is merit in both sides of the story, that reality is actually the product of a dynamic tension between the two.

A Two-Way Evolutionary Street

Biologists have rather adamantly maintained over the past 150 years that environment and structure do not create genetic activity—the causal flow is not from structure to gene, rather it is from gene to structure. There are recent fascinating challenges to this assumption; biologist and Complexity theorist Robert Wesson, in his book *Beyond Natural Selection,* provides numerous examples in which the reverse can be observed. Regardless, the argument regarding uni-direction causality in biological structure is for the most part true. Social scientists are far less certain about their related question: Can deliberate behavior affect social structure? Even those who model their thinking after that of biological evolutionary theory must deal with obvious triumphs of human will. We will address this question by couching the issues in terms that a biologist can relate to: the genetic model. Specifically, we will develop a model of social genetics and will ask whether social structure is the product of one-way or two-way dynamics between social genes and social structure.

The genetic system is a portfolio of templates, general models of how a biological system is to be structured. Noted biologist Richard Dawkins argues that social structure possesses a parallel structure, which he calls the "meme." Biological structure is the product of genetic blueprint; similarly, social behavior is the product of cultural content, or a common understanding of how things should be and how reality is to be defined. Culture, then, is society's gene, or "meme."

Systematist Bill McKelvey (systematics is a specialization in organizational theory that studies organizational typologies) focused on a more organizational manifestation of Dawkins's meme. He argued that industries are based upon a core technology, a dominant competence—comp, for short. He defined this as how a system arranges its affairs so as to compete and survive. The core competence of the university is related to teaching and research; that of phone companies is related to telecommunications. Comps, which are the more specific, organizational equivalent of memes, are the templates that dictate the structure of formal organizations.

Biologists have identified mechanisms by which the genetic blueprint is translated into form; similarly, organizational theorists have identified mechanisms by which the blueprint on cultural memes is translated into social structure and behavior. Arthur Stinchcombe wrote back in 1965 that organizational form results from a process he called *imprinting*. Organizations, he observed, imprint and retain characteristics they were born with; they are products of the philosophy of their founders and the beliefs and constraints that existed at the time they were conceived. Extending this to Dawkins and McKelvey, organizations imprint the memes and comps of their parent culture as they develop and mature—that is, they learn. The transference process isn't physical as it is with genes; memes don't split and bond with "remes," or anything of that sort. Rather the information within memes is transferred through mimicry, interaction (correlation), and teaching.

Memetics—culture and imprinting (if I may coin a variation of Dawkins's "meme")—is a simple and intuitive concept that could arguably represent a step forward in biological evolution. Genetics depends upon physical, biochemical mechanisms and hardwired behavior (instincts). The process is effective but it is typically slow; changes can take tens of thousands, even millions, of years to show up in a species. Memetics, by contrast, is a function of learning and culture, both of which are vigorously dynamic. Major, novel changes can appear in memes, full blown and ready for transference to the culture's young, within a single generation. Memetics, then, is a more vigorous way for life to adapt and evolve. We needn't wait on nature to take its course, we can "have our cake" today.

Memetics gives rise to possible new definitions of what constitutes species. Ideas, for example, scientific theories, religious beliefs, political ideologies, emerge and interact within a Complex environment, thus they qualify as social species. Social structures, such as fads, rumors, families, communities, cliques, political parties, and formal organizations, all can be considered memetic species or subspecies. Unlike genetic species, there can be significant cross-fertilization and cross-cutting ties among these species. A person can hold membership in a number of cultural species; he or she can belong to a family, a friendship clique, a political party, a religious belief system, and a formal organization. Information, then, isn't passed around only within the memetic structure of a single species as it is with genetics; rather, different species influence and mold one another in very complex ways. This contributes to the vigorously dynamic nature of memetics.

Now we return to our original question: Can information pass from the environment and from deliberate behavior to the meme, or is an immutable meme the sole source of cultural blueprint? That is, do humans control their destinies? This is one of those satisfying situations in which an answer is obvious from the mere fact the question was formulated. Memetics is a two-way process, with information passing from the meme to the social and vice versa. Behavior is the product of cultural memes, and memes are influenced by intentional behavior. Our mothers and grandmothers were housewives; that was the memetic message of the 1950s. Today, after the feminist movement of the 1960s, 1970s, and 1980s, and after dramatic changes in the economic goals and abilities of our society during the same period, women are expected to work, and housewives are even looked down on in some quarters. The environment and deliberative behavior have conspired to change this meme. The key characteristic of memetics is flexibility, and two-way, teleological information exchange is very much a part of that flexibility.

Even so, the tenets of Complexity Theory would suggest that interactive forces are by far the more powerful and pervasive actors in this teleological show. Indeed, these forces probably run all shows, controlling even what powerful leaders and powerful movements can accomplish. Where interactive forces and deliberate behavior compete, the deliberate behavior will have a long uphill battle, for consensus, when the product of strong interdependency, is a powerful force. Thus cultural content is malleable but it is not fickle, and memes, like genes, have an enduring quality about them. Culture is stable despite, and because of, its interactive nature; it protects its own integrity and it lends that stability to the society that emerges from it. Social structures do respond to social activity, and consequently culture can be dynamic and alive; yet it responds sluggishly, thus it possesses constancy.

Both dynamic and stable characteristics are important. Memetics is powerful because of its dynamic nature, but its power derives from stability as well. Stability allows learning gains to be consolidated and it allows systems to increase in fitness. A system in a constant state of flux is doomed to crawl forever across the lowlands of its fitness landscape. Had the early microcomputer industry never settled on certain standards, such as those regarding storage peripherals, it would still be experimenting with undeveloped technologies. Contrary to popular assumption, fitness isn't always the property of those who change.

My argument, then, is that deliberative behavior does influence memetics; indeed it is this that makes memetics so much more dynamic and powerful than genetics. Yet the process is interactive; memes have a lot to say about the impact of intention, and they choose which behaviors will influence social structure. I would betray the core theme of Complexity Theory to argue otherwise—memetics is a complex, interdependent dance between powerful forces of stability and forces for change—some of which are purposeful.

Controlling the Future

The second question posed earlier—can humans control their future, based on anticipated needs—is strongly teleological. It has seen little circulation in biology for 150 years but is clearly embraced by many management practitioners: Effective leaders are seen as those individuals who can evaluate future needs and adjust their structure accordingly. The prescriptive-organic debate in organizational theory revolves about whether we can succeed at such effort, given the complexities of social life.

We have argued that deliberative effort affects cultural content, but have also cautioned that deliberative activity is heavily influenced by larger, more impersonal forces. These forces are the product of the day-to-day, person-by-person interactions that go on in a social structure, interactions that lead to shared beliefs and common understandings. Culture is more a bottom-up phenomenon than a top-down, purposeful one, and it is complexly, overwhelmingly complexly, interactive. Leaders don't so much control social behavior as they take credit for its accomplishments by dint of their positions, they focus its activities and keep it on task, and sometimes they manage to manipulate it but often only within broad pre-established parameters. Social movements likewise function within an already established milieu. The women's movement of the last half of the 20th century, for example, is the manifestation of a movement that began a century earlier, and it thrives because of a culture whose awareness of social justice has been heightened by a complex of historical and current events. Movements and leaders can rarely be separated from the impersonal cultural forces within which they survive. We must be careful, then, about advocating a teleology of deliberate, anticipatory control. By the same token, given the very definition of interaction and interdependency, we would be foolish to discount totally its role in the dynamics of memetics.

Within such constraints, however, can we deliberately manage our future? Part of the answer lies in whether we can foresee our future, and the answer to that is obvious: The future is cloudy at best. Who can predict whether the leader who supports the current perception of the future will be replaced with a new leader with a different agenda? Who can anticipate where technology will take us—10 years ago, computer-based drill and practice was a hot topic upon which education founded its pedagogical planning; today this is anachronistic because technology has changed so dramatically. Who can predict when our vision of the future will be disrupted by economic change, the loss of allies, or by drifting cultural interests? We shape a cloudy, tenuous future, and that alone is a significant compromise for teleology.

Even so, humans do relate to their future and have some success in molding it. We shape it rather well when our environment is stable, but then our efforts typically focus upon maintaining that stability, the status quo, rather than changing it. When we have sufficient power, we can force our will upon the future; powerful leaders focus less on anticipating the future and more on creating it. Informal associations among organizations, the type described by Resource Dependency, will occur naturally from interactive dynamics, but they occur much more readily when directed by deliberative powers. Deliberation can forge associations where they don't occur naturally, and formal association is almost always (though not entirely) the product of leadership behavior. So yes, we do possess the capacity to build our own future, and our cultures have many marvelous stories of that occurring.

Regardless, we must be cautious lest we hurt ourselves trying to pat our deliberative backs. Structure, form, and behavior are still the result of complex interactions among multiple actors, and deliberate behavior is strongly influenced by natural and memetic forces. Deliberate activity, as we've said numerous times now, typically occurs within the context of interactive forces over which we have limited control. In a mere 7 years following the teleological military success over Iraq in 1991, American diplomacy had difficulty reuniting the forces it commanded earlier for a renewed assault on Iraq. Futures have a way of getting away from us because they are the products of so many forces.

▓ Intermission

It is easy to become so involved in the details of an argument that one loses track of the emergent picture, so allow me to pause to clarify the story line that is developing and to focus on where we will go from here. In Chapters 4 and 5 we developed a general model of Complex social systems and suggested that the principles underlying this model should guide the development of further, more specific theories of nonlinear social systems in the same way the principles underlying Open Systems Theory guided subsequent organizational theories from the 1950s forward. The notion of Complex adaptive systems (*CAS*) was presented as the general model of Complex systems (analogous to the open systems model of that theory). *CAS* are characterized by such things as interaction among constituent parts, by homeostasis, by the ability to map their environments, and by positive feedback. Chapters 6 and 7 focused upon differentiation within Complex adaptive systems; here we argued that *CAS* are composed of a limited number of moderately interacting substructures and that such differentiation allows a system to map, and process information about, its environment. Chapter 8, the current chapter, focused upon the autocatalytic and teleological dynamics of Complex Natural Teleology, processes that shape organization.

From here we will examine the logic behind traditional Western perspectives of causality, how that has blinded us to the emergent phenomena described by nonlinear theory, and how irrationality and resulting creativity are the very source of social order. We will take a closer look at the nature and form of interaction among subunits in a Complex adaptive system in Chapter 10, and in Chapters 11 and 12 will look at natural selection and how it nudges *CAS* to the Edge of Chaos. Chapters 13 and 14 will examine organizational change, which is much of what nonlinear dynamics is about. In Chapter 14, we will examine sudden change (among other things); this gets at the heart of Einstein's Island, the thought experiment from Chapter 1. Chapter 15 will develop procedures for studying Chaotic and Complex systems, and in Chapter 16 we will bring matters together relative to the Einstein's Island mind experiment.

Organizations in Wonderland

Enacted Environment

he belief that organizations and environments can be controlled, that structure derives from leadership, is deeply ingrained in prescriptive theory and, indeed, in Western society. We are so sure of the power of authority that we don't think twice when leaders attack daunting tasks with the abandon and naïveté of a Don Quixote—when, for example, a politician promises to corral runaway deficit (or drugs, or violence), or when a college president aspires to single-handedly streamline a complexly interactive university. We assume that if one has the authority to deal with a problem, the ability to do so is a matter only of desire and personal skill.

The organic theories in this, and subsequent, chapters are a reality check that sharply debunk this belief. The first set of proposals to be discussed, Enacted Environment Theory (EE theory), claims that causation is too complex to be controlled, that we take credit for change after the fact (like the pet cat that falls from a cabinet then looks at you as if to say, "I meant to do that"), and that environment is less a constant and more what we make it to be. The second set of proposals, called Population Ecology of Organizations (PEO), says that leaders may muck around with structure if they can, but they have little control over the success or failure of their efforts. Such control falls to environmental forces, and success goes to those structures that are fitter within the unknowable environment.

Organizational structure, according to both these theories, is rarely a one-to-one expression of simple causes and is not always under our control. In the extreme, leaders and organizations are like flotsam in a river, buffeted by forces of which they are a part but over which they have little control. EE theory adds a new layer of understanding to Complex Systems Theory. Complexity theorists such as John Holland and Stu Kauffman leave us with the impression that interactions among elemental units in a complex adaptive system are logical; Holland, for example, describes elemental interactions among individual actors in terms of simple stimulus-response. This is understandable because their observations are based upon computer simulations, and simulations require some set of basic rules governing unit behavior. EE theory will show that such interactions are every bit as unpredictable and capricious as is the behavior of the systems they create—at least among humans.

■ Organizations in Wonderland

Enacted Environment is the Alice in Wonderland of organizational theory: It tells us that what we believe or think may not be what is. It defines a world in which reality and logic—at least as we define logic—are not to be confused. We congratulate ourselves, for example, for our successes when in actuality success is often just presented to us. We believe that we objectively evaluate situations and find optimal solutions for problems, that we control the future with goals, and that we make rational decisions, when in reality those situations, problems, and futures control us. We believe deeply at an almost primal level that events in our world result from simple, direct cause, while the truth is that causation is exceedingly complex.

The way humans relate to success and failure is particularly interesting. We have a rather basic inner need to feel in control of situations, to feel that we can cause things to happen by wit and by willpower (hence the siren songs of Stephen Covey, Zig Ziegler, and Norman Vincent Peale). This drive is so deeply ingrained that hindsight almost automatically attributes experiences to foresight. Thus an angry outburst may later be rationalized as mere playacting intended to influence matters toward a desired outcome (a mental conversion of blind passion into logical deliberation—I do this often with my teenager). When painful things happen, we tend to blame ourselves, as if we could have been in control of the situation that created the pain. School principals give glowing "take credit" speeches when the school board pats them on the back for high test scores, while somewhere in the back of their brains—the honest parts—they wonder how the hell it all happened. Lest the non-educators smirk, I should point out that CEOs do the same thing when profits are up. Such reactions are not entirely dishonest, however: It is hard for humans to understand that events may not be the result of simple and deliberate intervention.

Except when we fail. Because we commit to the belief that events can be controlled, defeat assaults our pride and presents a mental dilemma. Psychologists call this dilemma "cognitive dissonance," referring to those moments when things do not happen the way we said they would or the way we willed them. People invest their egos and their efforts in the belief that they can make things happen, and if their goal eludes them, their self-esteem is assaulted. This causes defense mechanisms to kick in to buffer the ego. Individuals may, for example, shift the blame for failure—convince themselves that perfectly good plans have been sabotaged by malicious events or people (success may be due to simple causation, but failure isn't). An even more interesting reaction is the very human practice of throwing symbolic acts at failures to make them look like successes. Such symbolism lends a veneer of accomplishment, and we humans have no difficulty converting veneers into accolades. Thus problems are dealt with by firing CEOs, by implementing shallow legislation (e.g., "no pass, no play"), or by shuffling people and positions. In each of these examples, the basic dynamics underlying the original problem are scarcely touched, yet we convince ourselves that our difficulties have been vanquished, that we are successful when actually we have failed. Such behavior protects our pride, but, through a dervish-like twist, it also protects us from learning from our failures.

Doomsday prophets offer a classic example of this phenomenon. These prophets are fairly common, and include such notorieties as David Koresh and Jim Jones. One interesting class of doomsday prophets convinces their followers that the world will end on a specific date and time (hence the term *doomsday*). These groups have been known to sell their possessions, quit their jobs, and wait on a mountain top, in a commune, or in the jungles of South America, for the fateful day. Cognitive dissonance is the black mood that sets in when the doomsday comes and goes without incident. One would expect the followers to feel angry and betrayed, but that would require them to admit mindless gullibility. Their leader, who is likewise experiencing dissonance (not to mention a bit of pressure), typically salvages matters; he or she may, for example, claim that God has seen their faithfulness, and, unlike ancient Sodom where a few good men could not be found, the faith of this modern group has been sufficient to save the world. Everybody's ego is salvaged and their actions rationalized.

Misguided Decision Making

Yet another target of Enacted Environment is our belief that optimal decisions can be made by careful planning and rational logic. The famous educator John Dewey proposed a decision-making model that illustrates this mind-set. The model was originally intended to guide children in exploring their environment, but it has been adapted as a model for administrative decision making. The adaptation proposes the following steps for approaching a problem:

1. A problem is identified and carefully analyzed so the decision maker is thoroughly aware of the scope and causes of the problem.
2. The decision maker, or preferably a group of decision makers, brainstorms possible solutions to the problem; no analysis or value judgment is made about solutions at this time.
3. Once all possible solutions are on the table, each is analyzed to ascertain its potential effect on the problem.
4. The optimal solution from the pool of possible solutions is selected and implemented.
5. The effect of the solution is evaluated; if new problems arise, then the process loops again.

When I present this model to my graduate students, the inevitable reaction is, "Who the heck has the time for that!" There is obvious insight in this reaction: Administrators make hundreds of decisions daily and rarely have the luxury to analyze even the most crucial in any depth. This model can be critiqued in other ways, however, ways that shed further light on human nature and, by extension, on Enacted Environment.

Perhaps the more pervasive assumption of the model is that decision makers have access to perfect information and, similarly, that they perfectly understand the rules of social cause and effect. The first step in Dewey's model calls upon the decision maker to understand the nature of a problem. If subordinates are dissatisfied, what specifically is the source of that dissatisfaction (official pronouncements by worker organizations often simply restate the symptom or substitute desired solutions, such as salary increase, for the cause of the problem)? If a mandated change is not being implemented, what are the actual barriers, rhetoric aside? What is the source of declining sales? What experiences motivate a problem child's behavior at school?

It's rare, however, that one has access to all the information needed to understand problems because most problems that administrators face are attributable to a complex of interactive events with rich histories. Discipline problems, for example, often begin in utero—ask any parent, children are born with personalities. Matters begin to snowball within hours of birth: The demanding child frazzles an exhausted mother; the father moves quickly into the fray; other people (such as siblings) soon join this developmental process; contextual variables, such as poverty or permissiveness, become important; institutions like church or day care interact with the situation; and so forth. A complex infrastructure that we call personality is constructed from the interaction of thousands of inherited and environmental factors, and the teacher who attempts to identify specific, local causes of the discipline problem is naive.

Related to this is the model's assumption that events are attributable to simple, one-way causes. One of the intellectual founders of Enacted Environment, Karl Weick, said about managers that their problems persist because they "continue to believe there are such things as unilateral causation, independent and dependent variables, origins, and terminations." Weick continues, "Examples are everywhere: leadership style affects productivity, parents socialize children, stimuli affect responses, ends affect means, desires affect actions" (1979, p. 86). Simple causes are indeed common in the physical sciences; chemists know, for example, that water causes sodium to burst into flames, and physicists know that an action causes an equal and opposite reaction. There are few simple causes in human behavior, however. Pain *usually* causes people to recoil, but its effect on behavior is generally idiosyncratic. The thought of good food *usually* causes people to become hungry, but the relationship between the mind and eating habits is poorly understood. Workers are *almost always* receptive of pay raises, but the relationship between salary and motivation is fraught with complexity. We can speak of a statistical tendency for people to respond in certain ways to stimuli, but even probable relations often involve numerous variables interacting in complex ways. To make matters even more problematic, causation is usually a two-way street. Thus while parents socialize children, children also affect the behaviors of parents; and while leadership style may affect productivity, productivity also affects leadership style.

The Dewey model assumes further that human organizations are capable of rational or logical decision making. Rationality, of course, is a moot issue when causality is poorly understood. Yet even if this were not a problem, our decisions are rarely logical; rather they are tainted by personal biases, external pressures, and inaccessibility. Imagine, for example, what happens if one person in a decision-making group is intensely wedded to one of the proposed solutions, another is mentally unable to grasp anything but a direct approach, and a third is the boss, who coincidentally has just come out of a board meeting in which the very issues under consideration were discussed. Assume also that no one present has technical expertise about the problem. Biases and outside pressures are on the table, most participants are probably trying to second-guess the boss, and the solutions to which the group has access are limited by the lack of technical expertise. Logic will likely have little to do with the ultimate decision—at least not the type of logic one would hope for.

To make matters worse, decisions are often made before the problems they address arrive on the scene! This seems a curious statement, but we all do it. People buy computers with little more than a rationalization for the purchase (it'll be good for the kid's schoolwork, or, I can do some of my work at home) rather than purchasing the machine to address a definitive need. We stumble across a good quotation in our reading and later try to manipulate a conversation so that we can use the quote, or we hear a good repartee and ache for an argument in which to apply it. Hypochondriacs learn of symptoms and look for opportunities to experience them. And it is not unusual for decision makers to stumble across a good solution to something and then to look for a problem to which the solution can be applied. As EE theorists have put it: Give a small boy a hammer, and he'll find all sorts of things that need hammering. Technology (or restructuring, or motivational speakers, or grants) is the answer, what is the question? Decisions are not necessarily tailored to problems as Dewey's model suggests; indeed, problems may be "enacted" simply to fit a preconceived decision.

Finally, the Dewey model suggests that our problems are real problems and not merely created issues that address certain needs or biases; that is, problems are independent, concrete entities created by an independent, concrete environment. The nature of environment is key here: Does it create us or do we create it—or do we create each other? Enacted Environment asserts that there is circularity in the relationship between organization and environment; thus we create each other—both are products of their relationship with each other. Organizations shape environments and environments shape organizations. The problems we solve, then, are a product of that relationship and not the product of an inert environment. Likewise, decision-making structures are more an element of problems than a solver of them—they simultaneously respond to, and help create, the challenges an organization faces. Decision making is not a one-way street, it is an interactive process.

■ Interaction and Causality

It seems that wherever we turn and whatever we discuss, whether it be evolution, attractors, Complex Systems Theory, prescriptive theory, or, now, Enacted Environment Theory, we bump into causality. We have laid more than sufficient foundation for a Complexity definition of causality, and it's time to tackle the task.

> Effect within Complex social systems is the product of deterministic, capricious, nonlinear histories of relationships among multiple actors. The resulting network behavior is stable, somewhat (but only somewhat) sensitive to initial conditions, and bounded in scope.

This definition is designed to contrast with traditional notions of causality and with probabilistic definitions of adaptive behavior, both of which tend to emphasize simple, linear relationships between causal agent and outcome. Traditional causality can be short-handed as:

$$X_{(i)} \xrightarrow{n} Y \qquad [9.1]$$

where one or more events $X_{(i)}$ deterministically cause a predictable n amount of outcome in Y. The Complexity definition is similarly deterministic but possesses two additional characteristics:

■ It suggests that numerous variables interact deterministically in highly recursive and nonlinear, but somewhat capricious, relationships; thus it is redundant to identify X and Y (independent and dependent) variables—Figure 9.1 illustrates. Note, however, that this is a tentative representation; we will make an important modification to it in the next chapter.

■ For traditional causality, relationships between variables are regular in that a change in one causes a smooth, predictable change in the other. In the Complexity definition, relationships between *and among* variables can be either smooth or discontinuous. This can significantly complicate prediction.

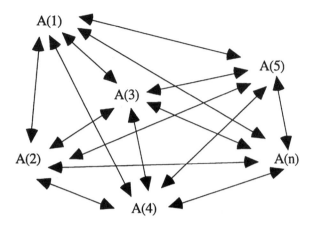

Figure 9.1. Representation of complexity causality. Variables $A(1)$ through $A(n)$ are recursively interactive.

Earlier we quoted a founder of Enacted Environment, Karl Weick: "Examples [of traditional belief in unilateral causality] are everywhere: leadership style affects productivity, parents socialize children, stimuli affect responses, ends affect means, desires affect actions" (p. 86). Weick was moving toward what he called a "circular" perspective of causality, one that is similar to this Complexity version. Leadership is as much, if not more, affected by productivity as vice versa; parents and children socialize each other; responses affect stimuli, means affect ends, and actions affect desires.

Statistics and Causality

Statistical models are little more than traditional deterministic models except that the variables we study are composites, or averages, of measurements across numerous cases, thus the data fluctuate over a range of values. For example, a statistician could measure the reading achievements of a large number of children or the life spans of a sample of light bulbs. The data could be used to determine whether increased funding of education causes improved reading performance, or to what degree different filaments affect the life spans of light bulbs.

Graphically, a statistical variable can be pictured as a line that rises from a baseline then drops back down, thus from the side it looks like a bell (the normal, or bell, curve). Each point on the line represents the number of cases that exhibit a given level of functioning—in our examples, different areas

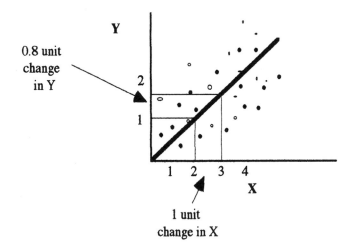

Figure 9.2. Traditional depiction of causality in statistics.

under the curve represent a number of individual reading achievement scores or the life spans of individual light bulbs. The point along the line where it rises farthest from the plane represents the predominant behavior of the persons or things that provided the data. This is the average or mean value for the data, and the range of values about the mean represents the data's variation.

Two variables, X and Y, are statistically different from each other if the curves that represent them overlap on their peripheries with a specified distance between the respective means. One might, for example, use this method to test the difference between light bulbs with filament A and bulbs with filament B. If the mean value for the life of bulbs with filament B lies well into the upper tail of the curve for filament A, we might conclude that filament B has a significantly longer life than filament A.

Alternatively, a researcher could determine whether two variables are related to one another by plotting the X variable against the Y variable on a coordinate graph, thus yielding a cloud of coordinate pairs (see Figure 9.2). Variable X can be said to vary with, or predict, variable Y if the cloud of coordinate pairs approximates a straight line. A researcher could use this method to see if, say, reading achievement scores go up as educational funding increases. The degree of vertical-ness in the approximated line indicates *how much* variable X affects, or causes, variable Y. Imagine a plot of two variables that yields a somewhat flat or horizontal cloud of coordinate points such that a line drawn through the cloud has a rise of only 0.10 units for every 1.0 unit change in X—interpret this just as you would if the stairs on your porch gradually rose 1 inch per foot. Thus for every 1 unit of run along the X variable (like 1 foot of run along the ground under your stairs), there is a 0.10 unit rise or increase in the Y variable. With such a flat cloud of points (and assuming the study were properly designed), the researcher might conclude that a 1 unit increase in X "causes" only a 0.10 unit change in Y. If the line were fairly steep, however (say 0.80 rise per 1 unit of run), one would conclude that a unit increase in X "causes" a 0.80 unit increase in Y.

$$X \overset{0.80}{\rightarrow} Y \qquad\qquad [9.2]$$

If X causes an 0.80 unit increase in Y, we can do some deep mathematical magic (square 0.80) and determine that variation in X accounts for 64% of the variation in Y. If Y represents the heights of trees in a grove and X is the ages of those trees, we would conclude that age accounts for 64% of the differences in heights among the trees. But age still leaves variation unaccounted for—10-year-old trees, for example, aren't all the same size. What then might account for the remaining 36% of the variation? Differences in soil characteristics is a likely candidate, so let's say we find that soil characteristics account for another 12% of the variation in tree heights. That puts us up to 76% of the variation accounted for. Other variables, such as sunlight and moisture content of soil, can be added to explain even more variation. Added variables are going to account for less and less additional variation, however, because the effect of each new variable overlaps with all variables already in the equation. We get up to, say, 85% of the variation in height accounted for and find that anything else we add only accounts for percentages of a percentage, with each percentage of a percentage less than the last; at this point, further effort is fruitless.

So what accounts for the remaining 14% to 15% of the variation in heights of trees?

Statisticians would conclude that the rest is due to unspecified events—perhaps one tree was stunted because it was shaded by a rock during early development, some variance is due to genetics, some trees were damaged by deer and suffered subsequent insect infestation, and so on. Carried to the ultimate, this logic is little more than Newtonian causality in disguise. If we only knew all the hundreds or thousands of events that contribute to the error term, we could perfectly determine the heights of trees. Similarly, if we only knew the precise state of every muscle, every tendon, every nerve of an arm while releasing a flipped coin, we could precisely determine the result, heads or tails, of the flip. Uncertainty or probability is nothing more than ignorance, the result of what we don't know. This is Laplace's demon who observes every jot and tittle of the universe and predicts its future. Once initial conditions are fully specified, the rest is fully known.

Complexity Theory and an Ancient Debate

This discussion revolves around an issue that is strewn all over the landscape of philosophy, and that has a pedigree that traces back to the ancient Greek philosophers. Epicurus, a follower of Democritus, defined nature in terms of a deterministic, orderly world of atoms, and he struggled over just how human freedom fit into this world. He argued that, to maintain our freedom, it would be better for us to believe in gods rather than physicists, for the latter bring only inviolable necessity. That is, the physicist traces all behavior, thought, action to atomistic, mechanical causes that were set in motion with the big bang; thus our destinies are determined long before we even are born. Nobel laureate and Complexity theorist Ilya Prigogine summarized the dilemma thusly:

> How contemporary this quotation [from Epicurus] sounds! Again and again, the greatest thinkers in Western tradition, such as Immanuel Kant, Alfred North Whitehead, and Martin Heidegger, felt that they had to make a tragic choice between an alienating science or an antiscientific philosophy. They attempted to find some compromise, but none proved to be satisfactory. (1996, p. 10)

Prigogine's book, *The End of Certainty,* provides an excellent review of this debate.

Prigogine argues that compromise between science and philosophy is not needed, that uncertainty is a natural element of interactive systems. This is heretical; it flies in the face of traditional science, which has sought for centuries to deny indeterminacy or to attribute it either to ignorance or to error introduced by the act of observing (the quantum physics perspective). According to Prigogine, indeterminacy can be attributed to two characteristics of nonlinear systems: (a) sensitive dependence on initial conditions, and (b) potential energy and resonance. Both of these have been defined in earlier chapters. Sensitive dependence refers to the tendency of nonlinear systems to magnify minor errors of estimation in initial conditions. Importantly, such errors are not the result of inaccurate measurement, for such inability would be tantamount to ignorance of initial conditions. This puts us right back where we started—the traditional explanation that there is no indeterminism, there is only ignorance. Rather our measurement problems are an inherent necessity, a basic property of the systems being measured.

Prigogine argues that the second reason for indeterminacy, resonance, is even more compelling than sensitive dependence. Henri Poincaré, who observed that particles in motion posses both kinetic and potential energy, first proposed this argument. If a particle is isolated, potential energy plays no role in its dynamics and the trajectory can be determined. If, by contrast, the particle interacts with numerous other entities, potential energy is absorbed and dispersed in random fashion and the particle's dynamic cannot be determined. The reason, according to Poincaré, is resonance. Resonance is what a spring does when it is displaced, then released. Resonance has different values at different locations in phase space. The interaction of particles with random states of resonance is related to the amount of potential energy in those particles, hence their unpredictable dynamics.

Returning now to the regression problem developed in the last section, the Complexity theorist sees the grove of trees and all its components—tree height, soil, animals, sunlight, and more—as a network of interacting, randomly resonating parts with a sensitively dependent history. During the developmental stages of the grove, the component parts interact in complex, intrinsically random ways. As trees increase in height, shade increases and sunlight decreases, and as the amount of sunlight changes, the heights of subsequent trees are affected. For some trees, the shade will come during crucial growth periods, for others it won't—and the difference is a matter of whimsy. Furthermore, soil is affected by sunlight and interacts with age of trees (which both fertilize and deplete the soil), animal life is attracted by the grove and participates in the interactive process (they feed on foliage, pollination flowers, etc.), and so it goes. As one variable increases, another might decrease, thus affecting in turn the state of the first; a third variable is depressed by changes in the first variable but increased by changes in the second—variables interact and change over time because of interaction. Pieces of the system ebb and flow in an idiosyncratic dance, and the tree heights one observes at any given point in time are, in part, a product of that dance.

Receding Histories and Disappearing Futures

The variation observed in the heights of our trees is, then, a function of the fluctuating interactions over the history of the grove, and that history is locked within the current state of the forest. Scientists can read only part of that history, however. They cannot read the entire history because of the indeterminism we've just discussed: If a system cannot be predicted into the future, it cannot be traced into the past.

Interestingly, one can calculate how much of a Chaotic history can be read before the past is lost with something called the Lyapunov exponent (named for A. M. Lyapunov, the Russian mathematician who derived it).[3] The Lyapunov exponent is calculated from the history of a given phenomenon, such as the stock market. If data yield an exponent of, say, 0.024, one can expect to lose 0.024 units of information monthly and can expect to lose all information within about 1/0.024 = 42 months into the future (the interested reader can find more information in John Casti's very readable book, *Complexification*).

So it's small wonder that statisticians can't explain all the variation in tree heights. The variables that affect height have not been steady over time, they have fluctuated. Things like soil characteristics measured today are somewhat different from soil characteristics 20 years ago; indeed, part of the reason they have changed is that the trees the soil spawned have dropped leaves that have enriched that soil! The key to causality is interaction and history, both of which are difficult or impossible to reconstruct.

How, then, is prediction of any sort possible? Several answers are suggested by our discussion. First, prediction is possible because causation is deterministic: Events cause other events to occur. Further, Complex behavior often does possess dominant tendencies and in such cases it is the lesser differences in detail that are attributable to Complex dynamics. Prediction is possible within a limited time span before information is lost by the magnification of measurement error. Prediction is possible because of the stable relationship that emerges among a set of interacting variables in a Complex (as opposed to Chaotic) network. One can predict, for example, about how long it will take to make a car because of the stable relationships with raw material suppliers, workers (predictable absenteeism rates, work rate, etc.), stable relationships with consumers (without stable demand, production rate would attempt to follow the market, with unpredictable results), and stable market share. Prediction is possible because the behavior of attractors is bounded; weather, for example, may not be predictable in its detail, but we can predict with absolute assurance that we will not awake tomorrow to 200° temperatures (Fahrenheit, Celsius, or Kelvin)—the scope of the weather attractor is bounded. This is even more true of Complex attractors, which tend to be much smaller, thus more bounded, than Chaotic attractors. The possibility, for example, that a very shy person will wake up tomorrow even a little less shy is remote.

▨ Irrational Humans and Complex Structures

This chapter has been about human irrationality, and our discussions have underscored—even contributed to—insights in Chaos and Complexity theories. As we noted earlier, a number of Complexity theorists assume that local rules controlling individual behaviors are essentially rational. This is certainly not true of human behavior and is probably not true, or at least not entirely true, in much of the biological realm. How, then, can anything faintly resembling order emerge from basic irrationality or randomness?

Part of the answer is simply that order emerges because of interaction; it doesn't matter whether the behaviors of the interaction are always optimally logical (actually we will argue later that fitness peak climbing is best served if they aren't). For the moment, however, we will focus on another part of the answer. The very nature of irrationality and randomness itself enables the evolution of order and structure. Our technologies, our inventions, our science, our organizations, movements, and passions all exist because of the dynamic, unpredictable side of the Edge of Chaos equation (the other side is the very stability we now critique; despite the arguments of the next few paragraphs, that balance is critical). Without irrationality, form would have stagnated eons ago into the simple, uninspired creations of uncreative physical laws. There would be worlds but no people, rocks but no smelters, seas without boats or fish, mountains without hiking trails or trees. Prigogine and Heidegger and Democritus and Whitehead and Popper all struggled with the tyranny of science and Newtonian physics; Chaos and Complexity theories have given voice to their struggles: Irrationality is God's creative spark.

Irrational behavior destroys that arrow of time so cherished by traditional physics. Irrationality is the social equivalent of Poincaré's unpredictable resonances. It is the characteristic that makes life a nonlinear journey. It frees us from the controls imposed on our activities by Newton, the controls that, Laplace argued, make us slaves to the state of the universe at its creation. It is this inventiveness that allowed nature to create life and allows humans to create organization.

When I lose my keys, I tend to look in places I think they will be. In all likelihood, the keys are lost because they got placed somewhere I don't expect them to be. The first strategy provides no information I don't already have, the second, looking in the unsuspected nooks, provides new information. Creativity is the second strategy: It is doing the novel, the unexpected. Obedience to initial conditions, the time-reversal paradigm, creates only that which is available in those initial conditions; disobedience of those conditions, the random and the irrational behavior, produces marvelous new inventions of life and organization.

Ilya Prigogine argues that Einstein's insight was a turn of the irrational that certainly would have been lost to us had Einstein never existed. I disagree: Relativity was an inevitable product of insights that were challenging traditional Newtonian thought with or without Einstein. Einstein was unarguably creative and brilliant, but creativity is the property and product of our social *CAS* and is not monopolized by one individual. Prigogine further argued, quoting Alfred North Whitehead, that the world we know has "slipped through the meshes of the scientific net" (quoted in Prigogine, 1996, p. 189). This I most certainly agree with. The wonderfully diverse and often surprising order we experience in our biological and our social worlds does not exist because we march lockstep to finite laws of a deterministic science; rather, it exists because life takes unexpected turns at every crossroad.

CHAPTER

10

Coupling at the Edge

▦ Loose Coupling at the Edge

Prior to the 1970s, theories of organization tended to assume, by omission or commission, that different parts of an organization influenced one another to a rather significant degree. Systems theorists, for example, contended that change in one element of a system forced adjustments by other elements. Enacted Environment theorists argue that, in many organizations, quite the opposite is true; that component parts are not tightly coupled, rather they are loosely coupled.

The elements of loosely coupled systems have little effect on one another. The degree of coupling between any two parts can be determined by the number of activities they commonly influence, the amount of time it takes for events in one part to be felt in the other, and the level of determinism linking the two (relationships in which a 1-unit change in one part causes a change of 0.10 in the other might be called loosely coupled, while those in which a 0.80 unit change is felt might be called tightly coupled). Earlier we discussed a system of Ping-Pong balls on cocked mousetraps. Toss a loose ball into the system and you get a good example of a tightly coupled system. Isolate subsets of the system with walls, however, and loose coupling becomes evident.

Tightly coupled social systems are Chaotic. With apologies to Edward Lorenz and "sensitive dependence on initial conditions," one could say that the flapping of a clerk's arms in a Chaotic system can affect organizational decisions hundreds of departments away. Loosely coupled systems, by contrast, are stable—units are largely isolated from one another, thus change in one part of the system tends to be contained.

In this chapter, we propose that fit systems are neither tightly coupled nor loosely coupled, rather they exist at an in-between level of coupling. That is, they exist at the Edge of Chaos.

Loosely Coupled Attractors

Organizations and other Complex social systems can be defined as collections of subunits, and it is the relationships among those units—their degree of coupling—that draws our attention. Obviously, these subunits include departments or work details. Subunits may also be defined as areas of specialization within an organization, as informal groups, or as power alliances. Subunits may or may not overlap formally defined positions, for organizational charts often fail to reflect actual operating structure.

If social systems are neither too tightly nor too loosely coupled, if they are coupled at the Edge as we have hypothesized, they should possess characteristics of Complex attractors. An attractor is a self-contained set of interacting entities. A Complex attractor

- mixes characteristics of strange and periodic attractors, thus it is nonrepetitively repetitive
- drains a relatively large basin of attraction
- is small (involving a limited range of behaviors)
- is partitioned from other attractors by structures that are difficult to cross
- has access to a limited number of other attractors
- is stable to perturbation
- is not terribly sensitive to initial conditions

The first point defines Complex attractors relative to physical equilibrium and to random change; behavior in one sense is repetitive and predictable, but in another sense, every day is different and subject to surprises. The last definition of Complex attractors, their relative lack of sensitivity to initial conditions, is related to this first. It argues that two closely aligned behaviors tend to remain closely aligned much longer than they do in Chaotic systems.[4] Taken together, we see that a Complex attractor is largely stable—capable of carrying information—yet mildly unstable—permitting dynamic use of its information. Social attractors (subunits) are likewise stable and unstable, capable of carrying information yet also capable of transmitting information to other units, of passing it to offspring, of accumulating new information, and of using the information to solve problems.

The remaining characteristics of Complex attractors can be similarly applied to social behavior. For example, a work unit's responsibilities may be sufficiently generalizable that a fairly large set of related tasks can be assigned to it, or the work tasks may be sufficiently routinized that the unit can draw workers from a rather broad skill pool (i.e., *complex attractors drain fairly large basins of attraction*). The range of work unit behaviors is typically limited—the workers in, say, a car assembly paint department do not usually become involved in product sales (i.e., *complex attractors are small*). Work units are separated by physical distance; by physical barriers; by rules and regulations; by social, educational, or skill barriers; by intervening attractors such as administrative units; and by mores, customs, and taboos (i.e., *complex attractors are partitioned by fixed barriers*). There are breaches in the barriers, but access across the barriers is limited; often the breaches occur between individuals who are called "gatekeepers" (i.e., *complex attractors have limited access to one another*). Work units are robust in that they are not deflected by minor perturbation, such as change in personnel or disruption of work flow (i.e., *complex attractors are stable to perturbation*). Finally, different inputs (different worker personalities or skills, varying raw materials, turnover in managers) can all serve the same end; that is, the differences are not typically magnified (i.e., *complex attractors are not terribly sensitive to initial conditions*).

The imagery of coupling and of Complexity Theory is illustrated in Figure 10.1 (note that this is the promised modification of Figure 9.1). Units 1 through 4 are moderately coupled with one another and, to a lesser extent, have moderately coupled internal structures (we shall argue in this chapter that *CAS* are moderately, rather than loosely or tightly, coupled). Unit 1 is somewhat strongly tied to unit 3: there is a strong, two-way link between them (solid-line two-headed arrow) suggesting that their relative tasks are interactive. Further, there are informal links (dotted line) between individual A(4) in unit 1 and A(5) in unit 2, and from A(2) in unit 1 to A(9) in unit 3. Consequently, a change in the structure of unit 1 has a fair probability of affecting unit 3. The chance of a change in unit 1 migrating to unit 2 is less probable because of the weak link between those units. The likelihood that unit 1 changes would migrate to 4 is even slimmer because of the distance between them and the weakness of the intervening links (unit 1 is not directly linked to 4).

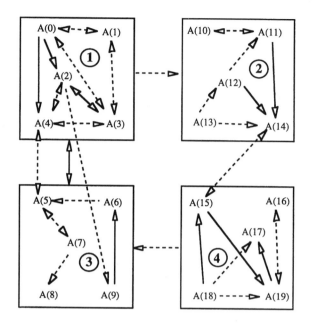

Figure 10.1. Special interaction as loosely coupled systems.

The Seven Deadly Benefits of Loose Coupling

In 1976, Karl Weick published an article in *Administrative Science Quarterly* in which he discussed loose coupling in educational organizations. In this article he argued that there are seven pros, and corresponding cons, that accrue from loose coupling (what I refer to facetiously as the seven deadly benefits—although "deadly" is a bit strong). First, loose coupling allows portions of an organization to persist and evolve independently. Change, he argued, occurs more readily when the organization develops small, independent chunks and then coordinates them rather than forcing the entire system to come together simultaneously. The downside of this, he continued, is that units in a loosely coupled system aren't pressured to discontinue non-productive practices. Second, small, loosely coupled units are more sensitive to environmental demands than are monolithic, tightly coupled systems; however, this characteristic may subject the system to the whim of energy-draining fads.

Third, loose coupling allows local adaptation to local environmental conditions when change of the entire system would be a problem, but it may hinder the diffusion of local changes that could benefit the entire system.

Fourth, the loosely coupled organization can permit isolated units to experiment with novel structures or procedures without committing the entire system, but loose coupling may inhibit the diffusion of experiments that are productive. Fifth, loose coupling can isolate problems or breakdowns, but the isolated structure may receive little assistance from other units in correcting its problems. Sixth, self-determination is encouraged by loose coupling (thus it is akin to "slack" in Structural Contingency Theory); this permits more flexible response to uncertain environments. However, it also means that individuals or units may be on their own in hostile situations. Finally, it may be cheaper to run a loosely coupled system than to provide the expensive coordinating systems needed for a tight structure; the trade-off here is loss of control.

That Which Limits Change Also Enables It

The characteristics of Complex attractors that were outlined at the beginning of this chapter are similar to those Weick proposed for loosely coupled systems, but Complexity approaches matters from different perspectives. Complexity Theory is more insightful about the nature of coupling and about the dynamics that characterize different coupling patterns.

An obvious contribution by Complexity Theory is that properly coupled units—sets of attractors in Complexity Theory—are capable of change but are largely protected from cascading damage; that is, a change in one attractor is unlikely to spread to many other attractors. This differs from Weick's focus on the avoidance of systemic change (e.g., portions of the system can persist or evolve independently; local units can adapt to local conditions without affecting other units; individual units can experiment without involving the system; breakdowns are isolated). Stuart Kauffman's simulations of units interacting at the Edge of Chaos show largely impenetrable walls isolating different attractors. These walls are composed of stable entities; in social systems they are composed of such things as traditions (I envision a culturally active Paris during the Renaissance surrounded by tradition-bound rural cultures), rules and regulations, taboos, and licensure restrictions. Overly stable systems, those with the weak connections that loose coupling implies, are composed of attractors that are completely or almost completely isolated from one another; highly coupled (thus Chaotic) systems possess few barriers; these systems can be rather volatile (alternatively, as we shall see, they may freeze their activities to protect themselves from volatility). Moderately coupled attractors are connected by a limited set of corridors, hence change can spread through the system but tends to do so in a controlled fashion. These systems are at the Edge of Chaos; here, cascades are not avoided as they are in more loosely coupled systems, nor is change typically volatile, as it could be in tightly coupled systems.

Complexity theorists have found that cascading change occurs in varying levels of intensity—from that involving a limited number of units to that which engulfs the entire system—but that this widespread change occurs much less frequently than does limited change. EE theorists have argued that loose coupling prevents cascading damage, and leave us with the impression that major damage is possible only in tightly coupled systems. However, the only way a system can keep all its changes small would be for it to completely, or almost completely, isolate its subunits—to be loosely coupled in the fullest sense of the word *loose*. Systems poised at the Edge of Chaos are partially connected (as opposed to tightly coupled); thus they are entirely capable of change and major damage, though relatively rare, is quite possible. As we shall see later, systems assume the risk of cascading damage because of the optimal fitness found at the Edge of Chaos. The stock market is an excellent example of hierarchy in cascading damage. Most fluctuations in the market are small, some are of moderate intensity, and on occasion—for no apparent reason—fluctuations will be alarmingly large.

When major cascading damage occurs, we often look for outside causal forces, or we attribute the damage to simple causal events. According to Complexity Theory, cascading damage is more often the result of normal internal dynamics that, for no particular reason, just happen to get out of hand. Meteors evidently caused several extinctions on Earth, but the overwhelming majority of such events (and there were many of them) can hardly be attributed to heavenly visitors. The unrest of the 1960s was undoubtedly attributable to the Vietnam War, but it was also due to natural interactive dynamics—the youthful society, a generation gap, prosperity, a youthful president replaced by an old president, racial unrest. Many changes just happen, a streak of bad luck at the biological or social roulette table. Nothing substantive can account for the dramatic drop in the stock market in 1987 and again in 1997, or the vast majority of biological extinctions that have occurred over Earth's history, or the sudden demise of the USSR. It is the nature of Complex systems that change spontaneously engulfs the system on occasion.

Complexity theorists also argue that systems control change and growth by means of localized cascades. Just as change typically spreads to only a limited number of attractors, the attractors of a developing system typically spawn only a limited class of new attractors. A variation in the cells lining the esophageal tube of an embryo may generate a stomach but is not likely to create a brain. Similarly, the maturation of manufacturing procedures in a developing organization is more likely to spawn specialized manufacturing departments than it is to spawn service departments.

From all this, three hypotheses can be derived: (a) social change comes in varying intensities, but most changes are relatively limited; (b) moderate coupling permits organizational growth and elaboration to proceed in an incremental, controlled fashion; and (c) change is often a natural consequence of interaction, and the process does not require an external perturbation to explain it.

Environmental Sensitivity

We will elaborate on several of Weick's seven pros and cons in later chapters on change. For now, we will expand on the second of Weick's "deadly benefits," the one regarding the greater environmental sensitivity of loosely coupled systems, and its corollary that heightened sensitivity may subject the system to the whim of energy-draining fads. According to Complexity Theory, sensitivity and whimsy may be a bit more involved than Weick gives them credit for being.

Sensitivity is related not only to the nature of coupling, but to the fitness of a system and to the severity of environmental change as well. Fit systems are better able to resist environmental pressure than are less fit systems. Further, fit systems tend to respond differently to different levels of perturbation. These three characteristics, coupling, fitness, and environment, are tightly intertwined with one another, however, and it is difficult to discuss one without discussing the others.

Before expanding on these observations, we need to clarify the definition of *coupling* a bit. As noted earlier, the existing organizational literature defines coupling relative to the strength of relationship among units, or the extent to which behaviors in one unit affect those in another. Kauffman defined coupling from several perspectives, two of which are pertinent here. The definition he used most frequently referred to the number of links between units (he labeled this K); he also defined coupling relative to the nature of the interdependencies among units (labeled P). P can refer to the strength of relationships among interdependent entities or to any similar restraint on behavior. At times he mixed the two definitions, noting for example that a large K could be offset by adjusting P. We will define coupling similarly: Coupling refers to the number of links among the units of a system (like Kauffman, we will label this K), or it refers to the nature—including the strength—of relationships between units (which we will label P). A system is tightly coupled if either K is high or P is conducive to exchange (as is the case with strong links); a tightly coupled system with high K, however, can be "loosened" with a low index of P, and vice versa.

Kauffman also described coupling between systems and referred to S, the number of systems in a niche, and C, the degree to which different systems affect one another. In this chapter we will focus only upon internal couplings (K and P) and will discuss external dynamics in the chapters on change.

Sensitivity and Coupling

Stu Kauffman studied the adaptive behavior of highly interconnected systems (high K systems in which constituent units affect many other constituent units) vis-à-vis that of less interconnected, or low K, systems (the same general principles will apply to high versus low P systems). A system evolves or matures by altering pieces of its structure. Developing embryos alter esophageal cells to create stomachs and intestines; the sales division in a developing organization may mutate into a home sales division and a corporate sales division. In a highly connected, thus Chaotic, system, contiguous states may be quite different from one another. In our earlier discussion of the convoluted regions of parameter space we saw that small steps in any direction can cross bifurcation walls. Applying the metaphor of fitness landscapes, Chaotic systems exist on a rugged landscape where a single step can carry a system a long distance up or down its current peak. Changes that occur on correlated landscapes (or in the larger regions of parameter space), by contrast, are not particularly disruptive because nearby states are not all that different from one another.

Mature systems usually adapt on somewhat correlated (i.e., moderately coupled) landscapes, thus change does not significantly affect their structures. Immature systems adapt on rugged (tightly coupled) landscapes. This enables rapid growth and adaptation during the developmental stage. Further, the climb up the rugged peak is both productive and rapid because emerging systems have numerous fitter states ahead of them. A mature system on a rugged landscape, however, will likely be unfit because such systems have exhausted most of their fitter options and have many unfit options they can visit (backward mutation). Mature systems on rugged landscapes, then, can ill afford to change, while developing systems benefit tremendously from changing.

Highly interdependent systems are ripe for disruption not only because nearby states are so dissimilar, but because perturbations can easily cascade across the numerous linkages between them causing system-wide damage. Thus a perturbation in one department of a high K, or tightly coupled, organization disrupts that department and in turn forces collateral, disruptive changes in many other departments. One protection against cascading damage is rigid stability, but that could leave the organization defenseless in volatile environments. Another, more robust, strategy (as we shall see shortly) is to back away from tight coupling and loosen the structure somewhat.

Perhaps all this could be better understood if we were to identify concrete examples of highly interdependent social systems. The family is a good example of such systems; changes in one member of a family can significantly affect other members. Other possible examples include armed forces platoons in combat situations, a tightly knit work group whose responsibility requires that every member perform effectively (the hot processing division of a metal plant, for example), sports teams, and consensus-based normative systems such as the church. In each example, the failure or the improvement of any given group member, or a change in given aspects of the group's dynamics, could dramatically affect the system. If, for example, the breadwinner or -winners in a family failed to produce financial support, the family could find itself homeless or even dissolved, with parents separated or children in foster homes. If a cult's doomsday prediction fails to occur, the cult could be thrown into disarray. If the weaponry of an army platoon were changed, the way the platoon performs or the way it structures itself could be dramatically altered.

Our first lesson about sensitivity and whimsy, then, is that tightly coupled systems, or systems on rugged landscapes, are potentially more sensitive to change than are loosely coupled systems, or those on correlated landscapes. Weick's argument would seem to directly contradict this; he felt that small, loosely coupled units would be more sensitive to environmental demands than would monolithic, tightly coupled systems.

This discrepancy is attributable to Weick's failure to define his perspective clearly. Actually, Enacted Environment theorists have never quite pinned themselves down on this issue. At times, their attitude has been that tightly coupled systems are unstable and that any perturbation entering such a system would quickly engulf every element of that system. They also have argued that highly connected systems throw up constraints to change (see Pfeffer & Salancik, for example)—an argument that somewhat contradicts the claim that tightly coupled systems are unstable. Then Weick confuses matters a bit more by arguing that loosely coupled structures are more adaptive than tightly coupled ones. All these arguments are correct in their own way, but EE theorists never quite get around to sorting out the differences.

The differences are explicable. Small loosely coupled structures are sufficiently flexible to respond to local conditions because they don't have to deal with conflicting constraints to the extent that a more tightly system does. Tightly coupled systems, however, when not protected by rigidity or by other defensive mechanisms (such as size), can be devilishly sensitive to environmental demands. To understand, we must explore more about coupling and the way it relates to an organization's ability to control perturbation. It all has to do with organizational fitness.

Organizational Fitness

Following is a six-part definition of fitness from a Complexity perspective:

- A fit system is one that is integrated into, and supported by, a significant number of environmental resources; secondary to this (and almost inevitably because of it), fit systems have accumulated significant amounts of internal resources.
- Fit systems are part of a network of interdependent systems (what Holland called meta-aggregates).
- The component parts of fit systems are interrelated in ways that allow them to dissipate the impact of perturbations—each component can absorb and neutralize small pieces of an original change because of the nature of the relationships among units (e.g., redundancy, overlap) and because the individual units have excess resources. Remember the Ping-Pong balls on cocked mouse traps that we described in Chapter 5 (perturb one trap and all hell breaks loose)? Imagine instead a box of cocked mouse traps loaded with blobs of Jell-O®; such a system should quickly absorb and dampen any perturbation.
- A system may be fit because it is so large or complex that changes that would be significant to other systems are barely noticed by it. A negligence suit would be far more devastating to Mom's Diner than to IBM® (the large N phenomenon described by Kauffman).
- A system is fit when it operates at the Edge of Chaos; that is, when it is at a certain point between tightly coupled and loosely coupled.
- Finally, fitness is a function of environmental change.

The first three of these definitions refer to networks. Systems can resist cascading change if they have supporting resources to help them absorb the change, and they generate those resources largely through interaction with other systems. Thus a family that loses income may receive support from extended family members or from community groups such as their church. Assaults on fitness can be resisted when a number of systems are dependent upon each other's welfare. The trucking industry is fit because of truck stops, the existence of interstate highways, a pool of potential laborers who are road savvy, the ready availability of maps, and governmental regulations that structure and standardize driving procedures. Changes may be absorbed by fit organizations because of cooperative interrelationships among components possessing excess or redundant resources. An army platoon that loses a key operator (say a rocket technician) can continue pretty much as before if the training of other technicians overlaps that of the rocket technician's. It's all in the interrelationships.

The fourth element of the definition, organizational size, is actually an extension of the third point. Large organizations will typically have gotten large because they have accumulated significant resources and have allied themselves with other systems. Such resources allow a complex or large organization to dampen cascading change before it spreads very far. Change in small, less mature organizations with limited networks and resources, by contrast, may affect the whole system before the change can be brought under control.

Fitness at the Edge of Organization

The fifth definition of fitness refers to what Kauffman calls "a bold hypothesis": Adaptive systems are maximally fit when they evolve to the Edge of Chaos. A mature system on a steeply rugged landscape is likely to be trapped on a low fitness peak because the majority of peaks on its landscape are low. The cascading damage characteristic of rugged systems can knock it off its peak, but that usually does little more than send the system to a valley or to another low fitness peak. A rugged terrain is so vast that the probability of finding optimal fitness when perturbed is remote.

A system on a smooth landscape, by contrast, can "peak-hop" so easily that the likelihood of its getting a coherent act together is remote. High peaks are reasonably easy to find, but back mutations pull it down the peak to rather low fitness levels. In extreme cases the landscape can be so smooth that system behavior is undifferentiated—it simply spreads across a bland landscape in which one peak looks pretty much like another.

The argument here is compelling in its simplicity: Organizations that are too loose cannot coordinate and differentiate, while those that are too tight are either unstable or are frozen into global behavior. Optimal behavior is somewhere between the extremes—tight enough to coordinate activity and share resources, but loose enough to enable creativity and change. Systems appropriately located between the extremes absorb perturbation because of the resources they derive from network membership and because their network couplings are loose enough to dampen the spread of damage.

A system can adjust its fitness terrain by adjusting its degree of coupling. Such adjustments may be accomplished by changing the number of linkages (K) among component parts. They can also be accomplished by changing the nature of interactions (P) among parts. P is a function of interdependencies, and we have discussed the benefits of such interrelationships rather extensively; P may also be related to the strength of relationships, but strength of relationship is merely a variation upon interdependency.

Amazingly, much of this adjusting occurs without conscious input by human architects; as the famous economist Adam Smith put it, the adjustments occur as if moved by an invisible hand. "Edge of Chaos" is not part of the lexicon of organizational theory, thus managers and leaders would not know to move their systems to the Edge. Even if they were aware of the notion, they would not know where the Edge is for their systems, thus deliberative effort would be a rough approximation at best. Ultimately, a system must find its optimal landscape by trial and error in response to the pressures of natural selection. Managers participate in the process less by design, although rough approximation may speed up the process, and more by allowing the process to occur. Organizations must seek their level, and leaders can sometimes serve their systems best by getting out of the way of the search and by making sure that other factors do not interfere.

Fitness and Environment

Fitness is also a function of the state of the environment, and much of what we have just developed assumes a relatively stable environment. When, however, the environment changes significantly, fitness can be compromised. If, for example, there were no longer sufficient crude oil to support widespread use of the automobile, then dramatic things would happen to that industry. An altered environment would alter the fitness of the industry and force changes. Fitness landscapes are not static phenomena—they shift and deform when their environments change. Yet fit systems are not so sensitive to environment that they sway mindlessly or helplessly to every environmental breeze. Complexity lends stability to organizations, and response to environmental pressure is a function of the way a system is coupled.

TABLE 10.1 General Effect of Environmental Change on System Change

	World Changes Often But Only Slightly	*World Changes Often and Dramatically*	*World Changes Radically But Only Occasionally*
High	Essentially frozen		
The number of other sites affected by unit		All units likely to change, but those influencing few other sites change more often.	Fitness drops dramatically and high influence sites are more likely to change initially; as fitness increase, lower influence sites change.
Low	Essentially unfrozen		

NOTE: High influence units are likely to change only at low fitness; low influence units are more likely to change than high influence units, but change occurs in smaller steps than for tightly coupled systems.

Kauffman examined three types of changing environments: those that change often but gradually (like the retail merchant environment), those that change often and dramatically (like the electronics industry's environment), and those that change radically but only occasionally (like the transportation industry's environment over the past two centuries; see Table 10.1). Kauffman's computer simulations suggested that, when the environment changes slowly, highly interdependent structures are less likely to change than are sites with lower levels of interdependence. That is, organizations with extensive networks can resist perturbation better than systems with poorly developed networks. When the environment changes often and dramatically, all units are likely to change, but those influencing few other sites change more often than those affecting many sites. Finally, when the environment changes radically but only occasionally, the fitness of all systems drops dramatically. Tightly coupled systems are affected immediately by radical change—any slack resources they may have depended upon before to buffer them are simply overwhelmed by the enormity of the perturbation, and change passes through their highly connected networks rapidly. The example above of an automobile industry without crude oil illustrates; or witness the impact that the trucking industry had on the railway system. Less interdependent systems, by contrast, respond more sluggishly because of their more isolated substructures, but do respond nonetheless. Such sluggishness may, however, buy the larger system time for recovery.

This leads us to an important observation: Systems are rarely—if ever—just tightly coupled, just loosely coupled, or just coupled to the Edge; rather, they are better described as possessing a range of coupling patterns. Families, for example, may be tightly coupled financially but moderately coupled in the outside interests of family members and loosely coupled in their tastes for clothing. Likewise, an organization is composed of tightly coupled sites and loosely coupled sites—and everything in between. Such patterns of coupling are advantageous in several ways. For example, such systems are able to diversify their fitness strategies, basing fitness in some cases upon a set of closely cooperating activities and in other cases upon partial autonomy. Thus the system can encourage such things as innovation with its loose structures and can establish stability with its tighter structures. Further, the diversified system is better able to deal with whatever the environment may throw at it. When its world changes gradually, it can easily adapt by changing loosely couple structures. It can flex when the world changes more dramatically, for some of its structures will keep up with the environment and others will be able to react more cautiously. Finally, when the world changes radically, the diversified system just may be able to hold itself together with its loosely coupled structures while it waits out the difficult times or does major surgery on its tightly coupled networks.

We can illustrate with the automotive industry. The various parts of that system—automobile assembly, metalwork, plastics, retailing, computer chip production, and the such—are dependent upon one another, but not totally dependent. If the plastics' industry changed the way it molded plastic, the auto assembly industry would probably see little impact and the computer chip industry might see no impact—in this regard, these elements are loosely coupled. The computer chip industry makes a good living from sales to car makers; they could survive without these sales, but not quite as opulently—in this regard they are moderately tight with the auto industry. The steel industries could likewise survive without the car industry, but their link to that industry is even stronger than is that of the computer industry, and they would be quite disinclined to lose the market. Other industries, notably oil refining, are intimately linked with the production of cars and would be seriously impacted if tomorrow the world woke up to, say, laws requiring conversion to all electric cars. Tight linkages, such as that with the fuel industry, resist change and devote significant resources to avoiding it (such as lobbying to prevent stricter laws regarding pollution control). Looser linkages, such as those involving the computer industry, allow innovation and change because chips don't dance to only the tune played by automobiles. The automotive industry as a whole is poised at the Edge of Chaos but is buffered with both tightly and loosely coupled relationships.

Loose Coupling and Change Agents

Jeffrey Pfeffer and Gerald Salancik, authors of *The External Control of Organizations,* argued that

> the greater the level of system connectedness, the more uncertain and unstable the environment for given organizations.

They continue,

> Changes can come from anywhere without notice and produce consequences unanticipated by those initiating the changes and those experiencing the consequences. . . . [In a fully connected system], any disturbance entering the system at any point would quickly affect every element. (p. 69)

We have labeled this sort of system Chaotic, with its large attractors and sensitive dependence on initial conditions. Pfeffer and Salancik go on to note that loosely coupled systems are more difficult to change than are tightly coupled systems because they absorb perturbations.

We, of course, have added significantly to this rather simplistic perspective, but I would like to trace these assumptions to a natural conclusion about leadership and change.

Because loosely coupled systems can be sluggish in response to manipulation, the argument goes, managers see them as problematic and tend to devote energy to reducing the sluggishness. Loose coupling is particularly problematic when leadership is attempting to introduce change into a system— loosely coupled systems devour change agents. According to Pfeffer and Salancik, organizations can employ a variety of strategies to reduce sluggishness, including reorganization and stabilization of exchange relationships. Such actions increase interconnectedness by reducing internal and external variability. Tighter coupling leaves the organization more amenable to change.

But this, in turn, presents managers with a new set of unanticipated problems. If Pfeffer and Salancik's assumptions are correct, the altered, more

changeable system will be less able to resist unanticipated, potentially destructive perturbation—and, since the system is more tightly coupled, such
perturbations will have access to larger portions of the system. Further, the
environment is also likely to make unanticipated adjustments to reduce the
uncertainty it experiences because of the organization's actions. The net result
is that, for the sake of short-term changeability, the organization may ultimately suffer increased instability and experience unanticipated changes.

Pfeffer and Salancik told a story about the Nixon era that illustrates.
Prices and wages were frozen by President Nixon during the early 1970s in
an attempt to curb runaway inflation. During the freeze, the managers of a
certain organization that retailed primarily in the northeastern United States
were accused of overcharging for their goods and were required to roll back
their prices. At that time the managers of that organization were attempting
to open markets in the southeastern United States. They decided to accommodate the federal requirements by cutting prices in those southern markets
rather than cutting them in the Northeast, thus they obtained a competitive
advantage over their southern competitors and drove several small organizations out of business. Nixon's effort not only failed to control the prices that
had originally precipitated his actions, but it increased market interconnectedness (an action in the Northeast had ramifications a thousand miles away
in the South), resulting in market instability at that distant site and the
resultant demise of several organizations.

The logic of Complexity Theory suggests that Enacted Environment
ascribes too much potency to leadership in this chain of proposals. Organizations are protected against the whims of management by the interactive
robustness of their networks of interdependencies. A robust system has
numerous channels by which tasks can be performed, so if some channels are
closed off, others fill the voids. An army platoon in which soldiers are so
occupied with their own responsibilities that they have no time to pick up
pieces of a void left by the loss of a rocket technician is tightly coupled. The
loss of a single component—like the loss of the horseshoe nail in Tennyson's
famous poem—can reverberate through the system and lose the war. The
networks in a robust system absorb such perturbation and are consequently
resilient to change.

Social systems at the Edge of Chaos are robust; further, they derive
strength from their interdependent relationships. They resist efforts to introduce change and are quickly able to repair damage to their networks. Imagine
trying to disrupt the network of manufacturers, mining firms, video stores,

consumer and film industry commitments, and electronics markets that support the VHS video format. Perhaps the greatest inroad on this network in recent years has come from 8 mm formats, but even that attack has experienced only limited success. The cigarette industry has historically managed to isolate and largely neutralize assaults on its markets through an extensive network of politicians, farmers, addicts, and advertising. One of its more serious recent challenges was launched by California, where laws provided cigarette tax funds for initially quite effective anti-smoking campaigns. Through its networks with politicians and, oddly enough, physicians, the industry managed to divert much of the campaign's money to research, thus diluting the anti-smoking message. The video and tobacco industries, like all viable industries, are robust systems, thus they resist change and repair damage.

Administrators who wish to tighten their organizations to make them more amenable to change must deal with robustness and networks. As we've noted, tight organizations in which components are highly dependent upon one another are subject to cascading change and are less viable than Edge of Chaos robustness. If change agents could actually succeed in tightening their systems, they would unwittingly reduce organizational fitness. Fortunately, robust networks are quite effective at resisting such efforts. For every element of the organization that a manager tightens, there are a hundred (give or take something) that remain at the Edge of Chaos and a few units that are as far to the loose side of the Edge as the manipulated element is to the tight side. The system, then, is buffered to absorb any impact the manager's actions may have.

I tell my students not to worry that bad administrative decisions will bring their organization down around their ears—they won't. In doing so, I'm not denigrating the importance of good leadership or endorsing lackadaisical behavior, I'm simply reassuring them that social life is sufficiently robust to survive human frailties. Systems have a way of returning naturally to the Edge of Chaos—that optimally fit location between loose and tight coupling.

Loose Coupling Spin-Down

Returning to the theme of causality from the last chapter, we can now conclude that social causation is not a simple cause-effect phenomenon, nor is it fully interactive as Figure 9.1 would seem to suggest. Rather, social causation is the product of measured interaction—interaction that is sufficiently tight to allow the emergence of stable structures but sufficiently loose to allow flexibility and change. It is coupled at the Edge of Chaos where it risks dramatic cascading damage but reaps the benefit of maximum fitness in taking that risk.

Thus far in this discourse on Enacted Environment we have discussed misperceptions people have about the potency of leadership and the control people have over their worlds, we have attempted to clarify these misperceptions in part by defining social causality, and we have explored various notions about loose coupling. Now we look at what all this means for decision making.

▓ Decisions in a Garbage Can

Enacted Environment has observed a phenomenon that nonlinear dynamics theorists have failed to observe: Not only can order emerge out of local rules, the local rules need not of necessity be rational. Complexity theorists like John Holland and Stuart Kauffman have assumed a logical stimulus-response type of behavior among interactive actors, yet EE theory suggests that interactive behavior can instead be quite irrational. EE has not observed, but we will argue, that such irrationality is a source of creativity in a system, one that hastens the climb up fitness peaks. EE calls these observations the Garbage Can Model of Decision Making.

Karl Weick began his article on decision making in educational organizations with provocative imagery:

> Imagine that you're either the referee, coach, or spectator at an unconventional soccer match: the field for the game is round; there are several goals scattered haphazardly around the circular field; people can enter and leave the game whenever they want to; they can say "that's my goal" whenever they want to, for as many goals as they want to; the entire game takes place on a sloped field; and the game is played as if it makes sense. (p. 1)

Soccer games, of course, are not fought under such conditions, but, Weick asserts, organizational "games" very often are—contrary to common belief. We impose upon sporting events the rationality we believe exists in organizations. In reality, organizational participants wander on and off the decision-making field, rules of engagement change on a whim, players fabricate opportunities to "make goals," and everyone is of the opinion that it all makes sense. The discrepancy between our perceptions of social organization and its reality is at the heart of the Garbage Can Model of Decision Making.

Michael Cohen, James March, and Johan Olsen defined organizational garbage cans with the following rather famous statement in their 1972 article:

> Organizations can be viewed for some purposes as collections of choices looking for problems, issues and feelings looking for decisions in which they might be aired, solutions looking for issues to which they might be answered, and decision makers looking for work. (p. 1)

Four streams swirl within this organizational garbage can: fluid participants, choice opportunities, problems, and solutions. The fluidity of participants can be viewed from two perspectives. The first involves the difficulty of defining organizational boundaries. Participants in a public school organization certainly include the staff and students—the latter being the raw material that the educational system processes. But students, in another sense, are clients who are served by the organization, and if they are included within the organization's boundaries, should we not also include other clients such as parents? Likewise, the school's community is served by the school and has a significant stake in its goals, thus it also could be considered a participant. In a manufacturing concern, should stockholders and clients and governmental regulators be defined as participants in the organization? Organizational boundaries are difficult to define, thus organizational participants are a matter of perspective. Second, and more to the heart of the garbage can hypothesis, decision making often entangles accidental or unsuspecting participants. The employee who walks into the boss's office at just the wrong time may find him- or herself suddenly caught up in the boss's problem of the day—the decision maker reaches into the organizational garbage can and pulls out the participant, who just happens to have swirled to the top of the can at that moment.

Choice opportunities are situations in which choices must or can be made. Organizational participants have variable access to problems requiring decisions—those to which a supervisor is privy may differ from those to which a line worker has access. Furthermore, choice opportunities, like participants, swirl in and out of the decision maker's focus in seemingly arbitrary fashion. This is due in large part to the arbitrary way in which the environment generates choices and in part to the decision maker's definition of environment. On this latter point, humans tend to select their environments (or their view of reality) based on their personal preferences, biases, and knowledge. Wherever possible, we choose to deal with, or focus our awareness on, choices in which we are interested or for which we have skills in solving.

Choice opportunities, however, can be quite literally invisible to us simply because we do not have the knowledge to define them. When we lose something, such as our keys, it is our nature to search where we think the keys are and to ignore sites we think are unlikely candidates. On the surface this would seem logical, but often an article is "lost" because it has been placed in a non-routine location. Yet the non-routine location is invisible to us. Similarly, decision makers not only are unable to resolve issues they don't understand, they often are unable even to perceive that choice opportunities about such issues are available. An important variation on this might be called the "group conspiracy" hypothesis. A groups, an organization, any Complex social system, defines reality for its members and enforces its perceptions through interaction, feedback, and, if necessary, sanction or exclusion. In the early 1970s we laughed at elephant jokes (How can you tell if an elephant has been in your refrigerator? You'll find footprints in the Jell-O.). Today we wonder if that era was quite sane, but those jokes were funny because the culture of the day decided they should be. Similarly, Newtonian physics defined the scientific reality (Thomas Kuhn called it a paradigm) of the 19th century, and problems that lay outside that reality were ignored—scientists literally could not see them because they could not be defined relative to the prevailing reality. Likewise, decision makers focus on problems that can be defined by the paradigm of the day. In the 1950s, for example, sexual harassment, at least in its more subtle forms, was largely invisible to us because of the accepted definition of male-female relationships. During those same years we didn't miss the capabilities of Xerox® machines because we didn't envision their possibilities. Sometimes we define choice opportunities for ourselves that are virtually impossible to resolve (politicians promise to do something about crime, stock brokers aspire to predict the market) because the prevailing paradigm of organizational theory reinforces an unrealistic perspective of leader potency. Choice opportunities are a function of how we define our environment, which in turn defines what is visible to us.

Solutions and problems also move in and out of the decision maker's field of vision in an arbitrary manner, and the two are often unrelated to one another until someone decides to link them. Decision makers have at their disposal a set of solutions and a set of problems, and neither necessarily precedes the other. People pick up solutions over the course of time without having problems to which they can be applied; they do so in anticipation of an applicable problem or simply because the solution is attractive to them. This allows any of several possible scenarios. When problems do arise, we might sort through our available solutions until one is found that seems appropriate (if we have time, the search may approximate rationality, limited only by the scope of available solutions). Alternatively, we may reach into our garbage can and grab the solution that is most accessible to us at the moment; like participants, solutions often are linked to problems because they just happened to be available. Or the solutions we have at our disposal may define the problems we focus on and may even lead us to create problems in order to have a forum for our solutions.

▓ Organizational Learning

The perspectives presented by EE theory would seem to suggest that organizations, particularly those exhibiting the characteristics of organized anarchies, are like flotsam drifting in a river, with no obtainable goals and with little if any control of the stream down which they are floating. Such a conclusion is not entirely unreasonable, but neither is it entirely true. EE theory, like Complexity Theory, argues that order or meaning does emerge out of local decisions, whether irrational or not.

The conclusion about flotsam is not entirely unreasonable because the EE perspective is grounded in flotsam metaphor. Organizations faced with complex environments will indeed often respond with what can only be characterized as random behavior. Stu Kauffman stated the rationale for random decision making rather nicely, even if he is a biologist rather than an organizational theorist:

> Despite the fact that human crafting of artifacts is guided by intent and intelligence, both processes often confront problems of conflicting constraints. . . . I suspect that much of technological evolution results from tinkering with little real understanding ahead of time of the consequences. . . . [W]hen problems are very hard, thinking may not help that much. We may be relatively blind watchmakers. (1995, p. 202)

So men and women tinker blindly, like the blind watchmaker that, according to biologist Richard Dawkins, guides evolution. EE theory even suggests that they often tinker without much thinking at all. As they tinker, however, they begin to sense certain patterns, and these patterns organize their perceptions and understanding of events around them. The flotsam begins to fight back and organize itself. They tinker, they observe, they restructure. Their observations influence their tinkering and their structuring influences observation and tinkering. Actors expand the repertoire of their garbage cans, and learn to use their garbage with some degree of intelligence. All this changes the environment, and the environment, in return, influences their emerging perceptions. Eventually the organization—and the tinkerers that comprise it—comes to an "understanding" with its environment, it develops the ability to anticipate, however vaguely, certain classes of contingency, and it learns to deal reasonably effectively with environmental situations. Organizations don't plan their environments, for environments are too complex; they simply learn to thrive within them. Like prides of lions, they hunt prey and drive off enemies, and often do so with impressive intelligence and guile, but opportunities and problems and consequences are largely beyond their control. They organize their experiences; a network of survival strategies emerges out of interaction with the environment and among decisions themselves. This is autocatalytic interaction supported by physics, need, and selection—what we have called Complex Natural Teleology.

McPherson, Crowson, and Pitner refer to this as "problem finding" rather than "problem solving." Experienced leaders should have an intuitive sense of just what he meant by this. New administrators often spend a lot of time rushing from one fire to another. It seems they can never get to their planned routine because so many surprise problems pop up. As they mature into the job, however, they find that they can structure their activities to neutralize many of these problems before they happen. They may do this with rules; they may do it by learning to see problems before they arrive; they may do it by establishing certain expectations of subordinates. Whatever their strategies (and the strategies are multifaceted), these administrators become problem finders, and their lives become much calmer as a result. They may even believe they are in control, and in a sense they are. But a complex environment, ultimately, is never controlled; our administrators have more properly only learned to thrive within those environments.

Organizational learning is analogous to searching a fitness landscape. Systems on extremely rugged landscapes are unable to benefit from learning because such landscapes are so vast that it is virtually impossible to stumble across optimal peaks. Thus truly monolithic, high K organizations would experience significant difficulty finding a mix of interacting parts that makes them fit. At the opposite end of the continuum, systems on smooth landscapes are so uncoordinated that, again, learning is of little service. Their fragmented agendas spread across the landscape, thus they are unable to get their acts together and search for global optima. It is only at the Edge of Chaos that organizations are capable of searching fitness landscapes and finding optimal fitness peaks. Here the terrains are small enough that optimal peaks are find-able and rugged enough that aimless behavior can be avoided. On the Edge, systems are sufficiently coordinated to permit mutually beneficial interaction, yet sufficiently loose to avoid immobilization from conflicting constraints. There is stability yet enough vibrancy and interrelationship to allow change (Weick was somewhat correct when he argued that loose coupling prevents innovation from spreading, but he failed to see the consequent need for some level of coupling). Fit organizations are neither loosely coupled nor tightly coupled; rather, they are coupled at the Edge of Chaos where searching—or learning—is maximally effective. Thus the process of learning involves not only developing strategies for dealing with the environment, it requires that learners develop their networks of relationships and their repertoire of garbage to the Edge.

Some research on organizational learning has been less than conclusive in support of the learning hypothesis. The problem, according to these studies, is that people aren't always good at learning from their mistakes. The supervisor who "triggers" on grooming, for example, will unswervingly select the three-piece-suited applicant for a new position despite a checkered history of success with this strategy. Anna Grandori's literature review of what she called "human judgment bias" (1987, p. 99) discusses this class of phenomenon, calling it error due to overconfidence, insensitivity to prior probability, self-serving bias, insensitivity to negative evidence, illusory correlation, and narrow-minded conclusions about causality.

But no one has said that learning is a perfect process. Learning occurs because we are irrational, not because we are rational. If we were rational, we would climb quickly to a peak that, in all likelihood, would not be highly fit. Why? Because perfect decision makers do not necessarily search. They begin their journey within the basin of attraction of a given peak and move unerringly, one logical decision after another, to the top of that peak. Most peaks are low, however, thus they inevitably wind up on a local, rather than a global, optimum.

Imperfect decision makers search; they bounce from mistake to mistake and peak to peak. There may be little hope for some, such as the three-piece-suit aficionado, but even their mistakes are useful, for they distort the peaks of others who are searching, forcing colleagues to find new peaks. The stupid in our midst are more than a little aggravating, but thank God for them. They are, after all, part of the larger irrational structure that brings us to the Edge of Chaos and, in doing so, makes us fit.

Darwin and Organizations, Goats and Monkeys

erbert Spencer, with a rare flash of eloquence, wrote in 1851 that, "Progress . . . is not an accident, but a necessity. Instead of civilization being artificial, it is a part of nature; all of a piece with the development of the embryo or the unfolding of a flower" (quoted in Lewin, 1992, p. 147). This is the essence of the Spencerian insight: Social structure is not an artificial construct apart from the rest of nature, rather it is very much a part of that nature and subject to its laws. Spencer attributed cultural and technological progression to social mutations, the most effective of which survive. He argued that natural selection is a sieve acting on social mutation to screen randomness from order. Spencer even coined that famous catch phrase of Darwinian logic, "survival of the fittest."

A more consistently eloquent writer, William Shakespeare, had his dark character Othello say to Lodovico, "You are welcome, sir, to Cyprus.—Goats and monkeys" (Act IV, Scene 1). I first read this when I was an idiosyncratic teenager and it struck my fancy. With slight modification I use it here: "Welcome to PEO.—Goats and monkeys." (PEO, or Population Ecology of Organizations, is the modern expression of evolution theory.) It is the mixed metaphors in Othello's greeting, more than the sarcasm, that appeal. These metaphors intertwine the affairs of humans with those of animals. Spencer

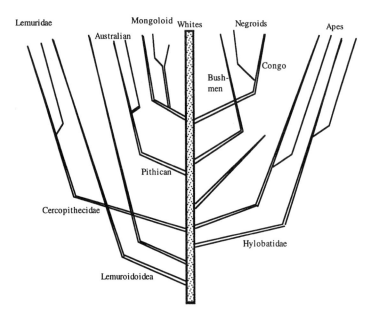

Figure 11.1. An evolutionary family tree based on Earnest Hooten's 1946
characterization.

speaks of similar metaphors, except that, where Othello sought to highlight
the lowliness of human behavior, Spencer seeks to define humans within the
context of broader forces. This is the essence of Spencer's claim that civilization is a "part of nature; all of a piece with the development of the embryo
or the unfolding of a flower."

Earlier we discussed the fact that Spencerian theorists made at least two
major mistakes: They bought into an assumption that fitness is hierarchical
with man at the top of the heap, and they allowed their theories to be
politicized. The notion of a fitness hierarchy turned out to be difficult to
support; after all, who's to say that a shark is less fit than a monkey, at least
for the environment it occupies, or that a roach is less fit than man when that
particular insect has been around millions of years longer than have *Homo
Sapiens*. Further, the hierarchical view of fitness fed one of mankind's darker
sides—racism. This racism is clearly illustrated in Figure 11.1, an evolutionary "family tree" derived from one published by biologist Earnest Hooton in
1946. Here, the Caucasian race is depicted on the peak of the tree's main trunk
while other races and peoples are shown on side branches; the implications
are clear and need no elaboration. When this superiority thesis became

politicized—the second of the Spencerian errors—the results were devastating, and nowhere more evident than in Nazi Germany.

Nazism was the death of Spencer's brand of Social Darwinism; his theories had "evolved" into something that civilized mankind could no longer tolerate. The death was not merely ideological, however; Spencer's logic simply could not support the superiority thesis—superiority could not even be defined without a long list of caveats and exceptions (e.g., "given its particular niche," "depending on how you define 'better,' " "increasingly complex brains have a significant impact in nature, but the second largest impact is exerted by the eminently un-complex bacterium," "greater complexity is good in one sense, but more complex systems are easier to break"; for an excellent discussion of these problems, see chapter 7 of Roger Lewin's book, *Complexity: Life at the Edge of Chaos*). On top of this, 20th-century theorists grew interested in a less global perspective of life, one in which human volition plays a more prominent role than it does in Social Darwinism. Organizational theory in particular turned its attention to prescriptive theories of leadership and organization, theories in which people control structure and guide the organization's future.

But the core ideas in the social evolution perspective will not die. Stripped of its rhetoric, speculation, and interpretation, Darwinism is, after all, neutral on the issue of progression; it states merely that natural selection will favor organisms that are best able to survive in a given environment. As Roger Lewin observes, Darwin himself vacillated on the subject. Darwin wrote in a letter to an American friend, Alpheus Hiatt, "After long reflection I cannot avoid the conviction that no innate tendency to progressive evolution exists"; yet toward the end of his book *On the Origins of Nature* he also wrote, "And as natural selection works solely by and for the good of each being, all corporeal and mental endowments will tend to progress toward perfection."

The core ideas—Spencer and Darwin without political overtones and progression—emerged again in the late 1970s under the name Population Ecology of Organizations; some of its principal advocates have been Michael Hannan and John Freeman, Jack Brittain, and Bill McKelvey. What this resurrected theory can say about the development and character of complex adaptive systems is the subject of the next two chapters. This chapter focuses upon the role of natural selection in the dynamic we have labeled Complex Natural Teleology. The next chapter develops several equations of population growth with an eye to demonstrating in Chapter 15 how these equations, which describe orderly growth dynamics from the conventional

PEO perspective, can also describe Chaotic behavior. Before looking at our first objective, however, we need to develop a brief overview of PEO theory.

▓ PEO and Environment

The basic and most widely known law of evolution is that, in a dangerous, unforgiving environment, the fittest survive. Population Ecology Theory likewise emphasizes the importance of environment in determining organizational structure. It argues that effective organizations will be "in sync" with diversity in their environments, and that unsuccessful organizations will be replaced by more successful ones. Structural Contingency Theory and Resource Dependency, the prescriptive theories discussed in earlier chapters, are also concerned with environment, but their focus is on how leaders can deal with those environments. They don't have a lot to say about the nature of environment or how environment deals with organizations. PEO switches the emphasis: It is the environment, more than leadership, that dictates the shape of organizations, thus environment bears close scrutiny. Environment isn't merely a rough sea to be navigated by a wise ship's captain, environment is the captain.

An organization, according to PEO, exists within a niche that contains an assortment of resources needed by the organization. Organizational structure is not just static form on an organizational chart, rather it is a dynamic set of activities for exploiting resources within a niche. Environmental niches affect organizations and their structures by withholding or providing resources, and organizations vary in their ability to wrestle resources from the niche.

Fred Emery and Eric Trist have organized environments into four categories. Their first environmental type is stable but dispersed (see Figure 11.2). This environment is unchanging, which seemingly would encourage development of older, more formalized organizations (older because stability permits a selection bias in favor of learning). This advantage for age is lost to dispersion, however; there is nothing to learn in a Type I environment—what is true in one situation is not true in another. Large organizations might be able to survive, at least for a while, in this environment because they could draw on internal resources, but any other type of organization would have a rough time.

Complexity Theory puts this a bit more simply: Viable order emerges because of interaction over resources, and systems in a dispersed environment do not interact so viable order is not likely to emerge. Emery and Trist argue

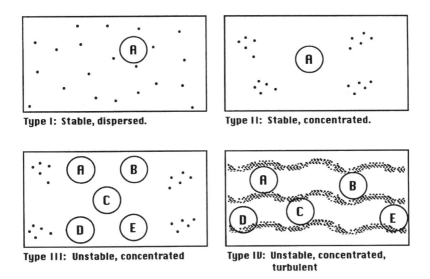

Figure 11.2. Emery and Trist's four categories of environment. Image derived from similar drawings by authors.

that there is no information in a dispersed environment; according to Complexity Theory, unchanging systems are full of information because of their stability, and such stability allows them to maintain information over time. They don't change, thus they maintain a complete record of who they have been and who they will become. Lack of information, then, is not the problem; the problem is that the information is unusable. There is so much variety it's ungeneralizable, thus unlearnable (i.e., every situation is different), and there are no mechanisms in the system for changing or sharing or even using the information. The environment envisioned by Emery and Trist is all information and no dynamics—it's in the frozen, stable area of parameter space described by Stu Kauffman.

Emery and Trist's Type II environment is stable and concentrated. Order exists because units or resources are clumped into groups, and each group is stable, unchanging. PEO theorist Howard Aldrich focuses on the importance of learning and strategy in such an environment. In biology, an organism with the capacity to learn can return to those parts of the environment with concentrated resources more readily than can less bright competitors. In the competitive world of social organization, it is the system with the most effective strategy (plan, behavioral complexity) that will most effectively exploit the Type II environment. Organizations in this environment tend to be isomorphic with the environment; that is, their development is driven to environmental conformity.

The Type III environment is likewise concentrated, but it is unstable rather than stable because of increased competition. Strategy, which was useful in Type II environments, is no longer sufficient: Successful organizations must embark on campaigns (Aldrich calls them operations) and must possess power. In warfare language, a strategy is what one does to keep the troops fed, or the procedures one uses to respond to enemy fire; a campaign is the invasion of Normandy. Strategy, in a sense, is standardized procedure, while a campaign coordinates strategies and adds a series of tactical maneuvers along with a plan for dealing with possible enemy reactions. Further, organizations that can increase their power relative to that of their competitors will be advantaged; an obvious source of such power is size, so Type III environments favor largeness. Aldrich continued that if no organization is able to dominate in this environment, then all competitors should evolve very similar structures, which is a form of isomorphism.

Type IV environments are unstable, concentrated, and turbulent. In these environments the rules of resource acquisition deteriorate to the point that they are obscure. Turbulence, Aldrich argued, is likely due to intense competition in which actors become good at surprise maneuvers.

Stu Kauffman's simulation of coevolving organisms gives a different slant to the Type IV profile. He found that selfish move strategies (such as surprise maneuvers) disturb the stable balance that exists among actors in a niche thus jeopardizing, rather than improving, the fitness of the self-serving mover while depressing the fitness of the entire ecosystem. This would suggest that some sort of agreement among organizations not viciously to exploit situations at the expense of others is advantageous to all. Such an agreement would reestablish a Type III rather than a Type IV environment.

Aldrich argued that if any organization were to survive in this environment, it would be one that had even a slight advantage in its ability to read the environment and predict the strategies of competitors, a fact that, he argued, explains corporate espionage. We argue that the advantage will go to organizations that learn to cooperate.

■ Natural Selection

The second law of classical thermodynamics states that energy is entropic—it runs down, dissipates; thus heat seeps out of a warm body and disappears into the universe, the universe itself is running down, and order inexorably disintegrates. In 1871, James Clerk Maxwell challenged this assumption, arguing that entropy is statistically more probable (by a long shot) than order, but probability always allows the possibility that a system can buck the odds. To illustrate, he envisioned a two-chambered box with both sides containing equal numbers of hot and cold molecules randomly distributed throughout each chamber; this represents maximum entropy. A demon stands at a trap door that is built into the partition between the chambers. The demon permits cold molecules from one chamber to pass through the trap door to the other side and allows hot molecules to pass the other direction. The cold side, then, gets colder and the hot side, hotter.

Maxwell's principle has not been observed in physics, and Maxwell didn't expect that it would—he only wanted to demonstrate the potential, however remote, that entropy could be reversed. But, according to evolutionary theory, Maxwell's demon does exist in nature; it's called "natural selection." Like Maxwell's demon, natural selection is a sieve that sorts order from chaos (defined here as a random state). Natural selection permits fit structures to pass from the "cold" side of the box to the "hot," and moves unfit structures out of the "hot" side. Natural selection sorts order from disorder. In nature and in society, natural selection causes species to emerge and organizations to evolve.

Natural selection is a force that is external to, separate from, the organization on which it acts, thus its effect is independent of the organization and, more to the point, is independent of the behaviors, understandings, and efforts of participants and decision makers within the organization. This tends to grate on administrators, who prefer theories that tell them they are in control of their organizations. Administrative egos don't care to believe that they are mere flotsam in a stream. But PEO does not claim that administrators are impotent any more than Darwin would claimed that the jungle cat is impotent against the jackal and the monkey. Administrators do make decisions that affect their organizations and influence their environments. Rather, natural selection is like an external judge that evaluates what occurs in the organization—including administrative activity—and determines whether the activity (or, more accurately, the accumulated effects of activities) leaves the organization sufficiently fit to survive. Natural selection rewards those structures and forms that successfully exploit resources, and it sanctions those that are less successful. It evaluates based on the nature of contingencies in the environment and the behaviors of other organizations and forms.

Natural selection *affects* organizational form by modifying existing forms or by eliminating old ones (Anna Grandori defines *form* as specific configurations of organizational goals, boundaries, and activities). It *acts* on form by means of almost anything—deliberate decisions, accidents, knee-jerk reactions, new products, or idiosyncratic personalities. One might imagine the organization as a cauldron of activity experimenting with forms; natural selection allows only the more successful experiments to pass into permanent form. The process of selecting organizational form, then, is largely random, for the activities that natural selection screen are themselves random. Any of a number of different forms could emerge from this process; the winner is simply lucky enough to pop up in the right place at the right time. Because of the "luck angle," were the history of an organization to be rerun, the forms that emerge would likely be different from those that currently exist. This is the old Darwinian logic that we discussed earlier in this book: Were the history of the natural world rerun from the Cambrian period, life would likely look entirely different than it does today. In principle, the process is democratic; no one behavior has any more chance of passing its "genes" into organizational form than any other. In reality, of course, certain structural commitments favor behaviors that spawn complementary structures—an assembly line is more likely to give birth to further automation than to an artisan culture. Even so, the basic, democratic, principle remains: Within the confines of the trends, natural selection chooses blindly from a set of randomly occurring behaviors. Anything else smacks of teleology.

▨ The Three Sides of Evolution

Aldrich identified three stages through which evolution passes: variation, selection, and retention. Variation provides the impetus for change, and it must exist for evolution to occur. Selection is the process by which fit variations are separated from the less fit. Retention is a mechanism by which selected structures stabilize and maintain themselves.

Variation

Variation is the foundation upon which evolution is constructed. In a uniform world, one in which everyone thought and acted identically, there would be no incentive for change (unless some people got tired of the uniformity—but that attitude would constitute variety). Further, PEO doesn't care where variety comes from; it might be naturally occurring or it might be deliberately created, as when a leader makes a decision or takes initiative. The deliberate brand of variety, however, illustrates an important difference between prescriptive theories and nonprescriptive theories such as PEO. Decision makers perceive their efforts as future-controlling and teleological—current behavior is dictated by desired future outcomes. Darwin and PEO maintain that such efforts are not teleological, they are merely another source of variation that is cut from the same cloth as accident or mutation. Natural selection acts on deliberate behavior with the same indifference it accords the accident. The random forces of natural selection are in the organizational driver's seat; leaders may provide fuel for the ride, but they are, nonetheless, in the backseat.

Aldrich identifies three types of variation: that which exists between organizations, variation within an organization, and variation over time. Variation between organizations refers to differences among organizations in form and in strategies for accumulating resources. Internal variation refers to such things as organizational modification, turnover in leadership, and variety of function and structure. Time-related variation refers to changes over time in the way organizations look or act.

Variation over time is called random drift by biologists. Aldrich argues that drift occurs because tasks are not performed exactly the same from one situation to the next, thus random errors are accumulated that allow the organization to drift into uncharted regions and possibly lead to deteriorating fitness. Innovative organizations may deliberately introduce such variation, or it may be introduced in an attempt to imitate successful organizations. We argued in Chapter 6 that the region of drift promotes exploration and innovation.

Innovation as a Source of Variation

According to economist A. Alchian, innovation is "adaptive variation leading to new organizational forms . . . an ability to abandon old forms at the right time." Those who fail at innovation are called reckless; those who succeed, brilliant. There is, however, a certain hit-or-miss quality about innovation that mollifies the failures and mutes the successes.

Innovation is, in evolutionary terms, a long-jump strategy. Biological long jumps occur when several characteristics of an organization mutate simultaneously; metaphorically, the system jumps from its current fitness peak to one some distance away—one that may even be beyond the horizon. Yet peaks beyond the horizon cannot be seen—the organism cannot know whether it will wind up on a better or a worse peak. That's not a problem in biology; after all, an entire species doesn't jump at once, just a few individuals. If it works, fine, if not, then the more conservative of the species carry on. When an organization innovates, however, it often carries the entire system with it, thus the organization is at risk.

Selection

Selection, natural selection, is the heart of Darwinian evolution and of PEO; it is the presumed force that single-handedly creates order out of chaos. It is, according to advocates, an inexorable force, thus change cannot be avoided; it is driven by accident, thus humanity rather than God is the motivational engine; it is egalitarian, thus rich and poor alike have an opportunity to succeed; and it is founded on competition, thus free market philosophy is validated (Marx and Lenin, however, used the same natural selection to argue that the free market will fail and communism will prevail). Natural selection favors those who are better at acquiring resources as opposed to those who are best; Darwinians now side-step the hazards of a science of superiority. Selection draws strength from environmental constraints; those who better accommodate those constraints are positively selected.

Selection does not function independently of variation and retention, the other two topics under discussion. Variation stimulates behaviors upon which selection can act; those that are successful are positively selected. However, bias in favor of successful activity is useless if there are no mechanisms for retaining the better-fit behavior. This means, among other things, that successful variation must also be adopted by a broader system. If a single tiger were to develop bigger teeth and more powerful claws, then it would probably dominate its environment—it is selected to succeed and live a long life because of its heightened fitness. If, however, the advantage isn't diffused to other tigers, the advantage will pass into oblivion with the favored tiger's death, and the species will be no better than before.

Diffusion among animals occurs because advantaged individuals are more successful at mating; since they live longer they mate more often, thus their genes tend to dominate heredity. Within social systems, diffusion occurs because selection favors imitation of successful strategies. In the 1980s, Apple® experienced success with the 3½-inch floppy disk and other companies imitated that success; in the 1990s, Eastern Europe attempted to imitate Western success with a free market; selection favors the imitators and sanctions those who fail to imitate success.

Retention

Retention is the third of Howard Aldrich's triad, following variation and selection. Retention occurs when a selected trait becomes a regular part of the way things are done. Retention enables stability in structure and behavior. Retained traits tend to become part of an organization's culture and are taught to new recruits as the proper role to act.

Two questions about retention seem to beg our attention: First, what does retention have to do with the evolutionary process, and second, what forces cause it to occur? Aldrich tells a story that he calls Hora and Tempus, which will help answer the first of these questions:

There were once two watchmakers, Hora and Tempus, who went about their jobs in dramatically different ways. Hora built his watches piece by piece, with each new piece bringing the watch nearer completion but adding to the complexity of the watch on which he was working. Hora found that as the watch grew, it became more and more difficult to handle; pieces would fall out of the watch and it became increasingly difficult to get each new piece in place without dislodging other pieces. He just didn't have enough hands to do the job, and often it took weeks to complete a single watch. Further, if the watch were very complex, he simply was not able to get it together, thus he had to stick with simple jobs.

Tempus was smarter. He assembled his watches in modules and then put the modules together to make a complete watch. Each module was a self-contained unit composed of a few manageable pieces, thus Tempus could whip out several watches each day. Furthermore, Tempus had no problem whatsoever with complex watches. They took a little longer because there were more modules to assemble, but simple or complex, the modules were the same.

The message is simple: Change in which one attempts to assemble all the pieces simultaneously is difficult if not impossible. When one changes by putting together independent pieces or modules (i.e., stopping in between periods of construction) and then assembling the modules, the process is simpler and proceeds at a much faster rate.

As suggested by the Hora and Tempus story, retention pauses the evolutionary process after each gain, thus breaking it into manageable chunks. Consequently a system can construct a segment of an evolving system, then take time to consolidate the gain before launching into construction of another piece. Retention enables the accumulation of knowledge and complexity; without it, improvements would vaporize at every new fad, and the system would never be able to move any distance from a random state. Evolution without retention is like Maxwell's gas box without the demon to control the trap door. The door allows Maxwell's gases to accumulate gains. Selection without retention is nothing but useless change, for the system never consolidates its gains.

Regarding the second question posed earlier, the mechanism of retention is inertia. Inertia is attributable to such things as the cost of change, inability to foresee the need for change, and vested interest in the status quo (we have discussed this in earlier chapters). Some theorists argue that inertia is negatively reinforced by natural selection (it characterizes a system that is not keeping up with the environment) while others, including Aldrich, argue that retention promotes the survival of a system.

The reasons for these different interpretations of the value of inertia lie in the assumptions that motivate the respective assertions. Those who see inertia as debilitating, for example, assume that the environments of organizations fluctuate constantly and that systems can maintain fitness only by matching those changes. Those who, like Aldrich, see retention as positive, argue that retention allows organizations to consolidate their gains. Complexity Theory introduces yet another perspective: Inertia allows organizations to control or dominate their environments. The stable states that inertia promotes so overpower environmental pressures that alternative, even better fit, structures have no opportunity to emerge or to displace the existing stability.

I recently heard a rather popular futurist extol the virtues of a bi-cheeked bicycle seat he had invented; he claimed that his bicycle seat was a better idea, certainly a more comfortable one, and could consequently be the paradigm of the future. In actuality his general idea for a more comfortable bike saddle has been around a long time. In 1925, the U.S. patent office patented a bicycle and motor bike seat that, the inventor claimed, enhanced the riding comfort of either sex (the patent description is humorously explicit on this point). The seat had a key-hole shaped slot, with the large hole in the center of the seat and the narrow slot running from this to the narrow front peak of the saddle. The futurist's saddle had a less suggestive slot running lengthwise through it, and the two cheeks slanted upward a bit. The 1925 saddle was undoubtedly a "better idea," but it failed to unseat the prevailing solution (forgive the pun), and it's doubtful the futurist's version will either. The entrenchment of the classical bicycle seat precludes a toe-hold by new, even better fit, ideas. (The obsessive reader might look up U.S. patent number 1,538,542; the interested reader may want to track down a humorous book by A. E. Brown and H. A.

Jeffcott titled *Absolutely Mad Inventions,* published in 1960 by Dover Publications in New York.)

▧ Refining the Order

That is the PEO perspective on the evolution of order. The perspective that we've developed in this book is one of aggregation or autocatalysis supported by physics, teleology, and natural selection. We turn now to a discussion of how natural selection participates in the process we have called Complex Natural Teleology. The PEO perspective is not so much usurped by this Complexity perspective as it is re-rendered; selections dynamics are still operant, but they assume a somewhat different role.

We've said that order emerges out of autocatalysis. Unlike survival of the fittest, autocatalysis requires no outside work, it just happens. Darwinism is an uphill battle against the forces of entropy, or the tendency of any system to run down. As a system increases in order, the forces of entropy strengthen and Darwin's battle becomes increasingly fierce. Complexity Theory projects no such struggle; order requires no energy (outside of raw materials). Order is inevitable rather than improbable.

Natural selection has a different role, one that is more realistic. It helps refine the order that interaction creates; it helps order increase in fitness and helps it adapt to environmental contingencies. Yet even in this it is aided by Complexity. Life is fittest at the Edge of Chaos, and movement toward the Edge is natural and free. Darwinism and Complexity interact in complex ways to make systems fit.

To understand how this happens, we need to learn a bit about a concept that the noted biologist and statistician Sewall Wright introduced in the early 1930s. This concept is called the "fitness landscape." Wright drew mental pictures of evolving life forms struggling up fitness peaks. Certain catastrophes occur on these landscapes, catastrophes that conspire against the emergence of life and social order. Life tumbles off the hills, or fails to muster enough strength to get up them, or the hills themselves shrink from under the struggling systems. Wright's pictures are very Darwinian, but his imagery is useful for our purposes. Fitness landscapes were briefly introduced in earlier chapters, and will be developed more fully here.

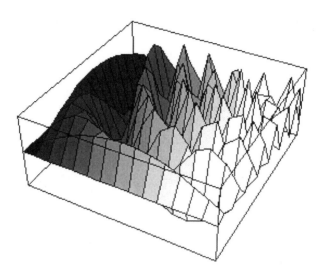

Figure 11.3. How a fitness landscape, with tall, short, rugged, and smooth peaks, might be visualized. Peaks in the rugged regions would have high values of K; those in the smooth regions would have low values of K.

Fitness Landscapes

Imagine an evolving system as a rubber sheet. There are bumps, or peaks, on this sheet, some of which are sharply angular while others are gently rolling. Some are tall, others are short, the remainder are everything in between (see Figure 11.3). The hills on a sheet represent fitness choices for a given system. A particular sheet might represent the competitive strategies that are available in a given market, with the tall hills representing strategies that produce more profits for the organization than do shorter hills. Evolution is a process in which a system searches such "fitness landscapes" for higher and higher fitness peaks.

The peaks on a fitness landscape vary not only in height, but in ruggedness as well. Some are quite angular; a step in any direction could carry a system a considerable distance from its original location (i.e., the system could change significantly). Others are gently rolling; a step in either direction leaves the system pretty much where it was before.

Degree of ruggedness is related to several characteristics. It's related, for example, to the number of actors within a system that directly affect one another. In a manufacturing plant, it's related to the number of departments that are directly dependent upon the products of any one department. In a social organization, it's related to the number of members who are directly affected by the behavior of any one member. The greater the number of direct interdependencies, the more rugged the landscape.

Kauffman labeled a system's level of interdependency, K. If any one department in a manufacturing plant is directly linked to two others, then $K = 2$; if a department is linked to 10 other departments, then $K = 10$. We have discussed the dynamics of such interdependent networks in earlier chapters, and will try to add to those discussions rather than rehash them (except to summarize some of the points).

The fitness of an individual unit within an interacting cluster is dependent not only on its own state, but on the state of each unit to which it is linked. The fitness of production department A, for example, may depend upon its own effectiveness and on that of departments B and C. If one unit in a cluster changes, the fitness of all other units in the cluster changes with it.

At $K = 0$ (clusters are made up of only one unit and there is no coordination among units), a collection of units is maximally fit when each of its members is fit. As K increases, matters become more complex, however. A given unit's effectiveness becomes dependent upon the states of other units in a system. You might think that, again, the system is fit when everyone in the system is fit, but unfortunately it's not that simple. What is good for one unit in a cluster of linked units may not be good for another. Maximum efficiency in manufacturing may play havoc in sales; the comfort of a patient sometimes spells inconvenience for the physician; the way math is presented in a high school math class may lead to confusion in a physics class. Such incompatibilities are called *conflicting constraints,* a term we defined in the Resource Dependency chapter; the level of such conflict measures the system's *internal complexity.*

Clusters are themselves interconnected in a vast network, and large networks are less affected by changes in individual clusters than are small networks. The idea here is that an individual fish (i.e., cluster) has less influence in a large aquarium than in a small aquarium. Consequently, the ruggedness of fitness landscapes is a function of the total number of units (N) in a given system. Take two systems; in both, units interact 8 at a time ($K = 7$), but one system is composed of 25 units, the other of 2,500. Obviously, a mutation in one of the clusters of the smaller system would change that system more than would a mutation in a cluster of the larger system. Since rugged landscapes are those in which mutations create significant change, high N systems are less rugged than low N systems (other things, like K, being equal).

Given a constant N, systems in which every unit affects every other unit are subject to violent change. The pattern of interaction in this large K system (with its resultant, convoluted pattern of conflicting constraints) is so complex that there is no way to predict the cumulative impact of such cascading change. In other words, the fitness of every unit in the system changes to some random and unpredictable value as conflicting units change, re-change, and re-re-change in a complex, cascading dance, and the fitness of a network after a single mutation is uncorrelated with its premutation state. This is what adaptation on a rugged landscape is about: A single mutation moves the entire system to a new, unpredictable level of fitness. Different states of highly rugged landscapes are uncorrelated with one another.

If ultimate ruggedness occurs when every unit in a system is dependent upon every other, ultimate smoothness must occur at $K = 0$. On this smooth landscape, any given change affects only the unit that did the changing, and the overall impact on the system is nil. That is, when $K = 0$, a "mutated" system's behavior or structure is little different from—or highly correlated with—what it was before mutation.

Searching the Landscape

Evolution can be represented as a search of the fitness landscape for optimal fitness peaks. The system walks about, step by step, mutating its component units one at a time. If the "mutation" is beneficial, it is retained and the system has moved one step up the particular peak it is on. If the mutation is dysfunctional, the system rejects the move.

The journey up a peak may lead the system up a side peak, one that lies off the main peak and is not as tall as the main peak. These are called "local optima." A local optimum is an adaptive strategy that represents, so to speak, a dead end. The higher a system of clusters climbs on a local peak, the greater the commitment to the adaptive strategy that peak represents. Climbing down from such a peak requires that a system dismantle and reverse its structural commitments; that is, the cluster must devolve before it can move to another fitness strategy.

Something similar happens in Brian Arthur's economy, which we discussed earlier. Arthur argues that stable technologies are the product of numerous interactions among varied actors. These interactions or interdependencies include all the support structures and spin-off industries related to a given technology. Consequently, once an economy commits to a certain technology or market strategy, it becomes difficult to retreat from that commitment and to change directions. The rational, indeed necessary, choice then is for the market simply to stay where it is—at its local optimum—even if a more productive technology looms on the horizon.

Behavior on Rugged Landscapes:
The Complexity Catastrophe

In his book *The Origins of Order,* Kauffman speaks of certain behaviors on rugged landscapes as "surprising." He was possibly a bit exuberant in his assessment, but the features he observed are at least interesting and do contribute to the theme being developed.

First, the more rugged a landscape, the more optima there are to choose from. As K increases, the number of optima increases rapidly, and the probability that a system of interacting clusters will be trapped at an optimum short of maximum fitness becomes increasingly inevitable. Further, high K spawns a large number of short peaks, thus the overwhelming probability is that any given system will be trapped on a low fitness peak when the landscape it is searching is rugged.

We observed earlier that as K increases, the number of conflicting constraints among units increases. Maximum fitness for the manufacturing department may conflict with maximum fitness for sales; the best strategy for presenting concepts in a high school math class may pose difficulties for physics teachers. The more conflicts a system has to deal with, the fewer good (fit) compromises it has. As a result, highly rugged landscapes look more like bean hills than the Rocky Mountains. Kauffman called this the "complexity catastrophe." Highly complex systems have a large number of low fitness peaks and very few, if any, highly fit ones.

Smooth Landscapes Backwards and Forwards:
The Error Catastrophe

On rugged landscapes, mutations cause significant change in a system's structure, so natural selection has a lot to work with. Although systems on rugged landscapes tend to freeze on small peaks, selection remains potent up until the time it reaches its peak.

Matters are a bit different on smoother landscapes. As a low K population begins to climb a fitness peak, many of its mutations will be advantageous to survival and will be favored by selection. Some mutations work in reverse, however—they move in the direction of reduced fitness. Initially this is not a problem; so many fitter states are available that selection and mutation can pull the organism up the fitness slope. But the steps taken on a correlated landscape are small, and selection never has dramatic change to work with. Furthermore, as optima are approached, the number of potential forward mutations decreases but the number of backward mutations remains fairly constant or even increases. At some point short of optima, selection is no longer able to overcome the force of backward mutations. The system reaches a balance point where selection and forward mutations fail to offset the strength of back mutations, and the population stabilizes. We discussed this balance point in Chapter 6, where we called it a neutral fitness shell. In that discussion, we compared the neutral shell to a cloud hovering somewhere below a fitness peak, and we discussed random drift within the shell and movement across ridges from one shell to another. The current discussion draws attention to how a shell arrives at a given point on a fitness peak.

Kauffman refers to the tendency for a system to slide down correlated peaks as "error catastrophe." Error catastrophe is influenced by two factors: the degree of correlation on the landscape (the distance a system slides increases with correlation) and the mutation rate (if forward mutation rate is high, the backward rate is also high). There is irony in this latter point: The very notion to which we have traditionally ascribed the forward march of nature can actually serve to retard it!

Moderately Correlated Landscapes

Low K (correlated) systems, particularly those experiencing strong mutation rates, are driven so far off their peaks that they tend to drift across low fitness valleys and, because they are forever wandering, to experience difficulty organizing a coherent structure. High K systems, by contrast, tend to freeze on low, rugged peaks. In between these extremes of ruggedness is a point at which a system's complexity (K) and mutation rates are tuned such that structures just begin to melt off their peaks. These intermediary systems, like their more rugged cousins, are stable enough for coherent structure to emerge; they can maintain information about themselves; and they can build on their past. At the same time they are sufficiently correlated to be able to search across the landscape for fitter peaks. Further, moderately correlated landscapes contain a number of rather tall peaks (a general characteristic of smooth landscapes). These characteristics represent optimal conditions for system fitness; not coincidentally, this compromised state is at the Edge of Chaos. Natural selection helps physics and teleology (the other actors in

Cmplex Natural Teleology) find this Edge state, and takes over the process of searching the Edge of Chaos landscape for optimally fit peaks.

■ PEO and Complexity

Howard Aldrich and other population ecologists argue that variation and selection and retention are the source of order and innovation in organizations. We have now argued that selection is probably not the major determinant of order but that its role, instead, is to help refine order that is created by autocatalysis (or the expanded dynamic that we earlier labeled Complex Natural Teleology). Fitness is the product of a search across a fitness landscape for high peaks; this process is fired by external pressure (selection) and by interaction dynamics (Complexity). We shall see a bit later that the process involves even more—it involves interaction among landscapes, the evolution of coevolution.

CHAPTER

12

Pushing the Envelope

Limiting Organizational Expansion

One of biology's many "interests" revolves about the limits that environment places on population size. How many mosquitoes can a given environment support, for example (everyone's first answer, "too many," is not sufficiently precise), and how does the presence of, say, bats, limit the mosquito population? Population Ecologists ask similar questions: How large can a given industry become, and how do competitors affect each other's growth?

Bear in mind that the following discussion is about organizational populations rather than individual organizations—unless a given organization is the only one of its type (like AT&T® in the long-distance phone niche prior to the mid-1980s). To keep definitions clean, we will borrow Bill McKelvey's definition of organizational species from his work in organizational systematics (*systematics* is the organizational equivalent of a biological taxonomy). An "organizational species," he argued, is the dominant competency of an industry, and "the total pool of comps making up the dominant competencies of all members of an organizational population" (p. 196). McKelvey labeled the dominant competency a "comp" and called the pool of competencies "compools." From this we can define a given "organizational species" as a set of organizations that share the same compool. It is prudent to refine McKelvey's definition a bit, however, to permit focusing only on organizations within a given niche, all of which share the same compool. This allows us to describe, say, the canning industry in northeastern North America as opposed to the canning industry worldwide. Such limit is based on the assumption that the carrying capacity of an environment may vary from niche to niche—the Southern United States, for example, can support a much larger compool of grits producers than can the Pacific Northwest.

We'll be getting into some math over the next few paragraphs, but math-phobic readers are encouraged to stick with it. The discussion will be kept as conceptual and simple as possible, and what we are about to discuss is an important component of Population Ecology Theory. More important, we will extend this discussion in Chapter 15 to show how traditional PEO mathematics can become Chaotic.

▨ Organizational Growth

The degree to which an organizational population can expand within its niche is determined by at least two factors: the carrying capacity of the environment and the growth rate of the organization. The same limits apply in biology: The expansion of a population of mosquitoes, for example, is a function of the carrying capacity of the environment (the amount of available blood, for example) and the rate at which mosquitoes can produce offspring. It should surprise no one, then, that the mathematical formulas used to describe population growth in biology are the same as those used to describe organizational growth.

There are two general versions of the formula: the difficult version and the easy version; to quickly ease the reader's alarm, we will concentrate on the latter. The more difficult class of growth formulae can be represented as:

$$dX/dt = rX(1 - X) \qquad\qquad [12.1]$$

Growth formulas in this form are called differential equations. They describe the moment-by-moment growth of a given species, thus they can be used to plot growth on a piece of graph paper as a smoothly flowing line.

In most cases, however, one can "get by" knowing only how large a population is periodically—say every 3 months or once a year. In that case, we can simplify the formula significantly (even though it may not appear very different at first glance). The new formula is:

$$X_{new} = rX_{old} (1 - X_{old})$$ [12.2]

The thing that makes Equation 12.2 easier is that most people can solve it using no more knowledge than what they remember from their first algebra class; solving Equation 12.1, on the other hand, would require a brushup on college calculus.

So let's attack Equation 12.2. As is true of all math, the letters in this formula represent real events in the world. X represents the size of an organization as a percentage of the environment's carrying capacity; thus if X is 0.60, the population being described is at 60% of the environment's capacity. The variable r is nothing more than growth rate (if we're talking about organizations) or birthrate (if we're talking about mosquitoes). In Equation 12.2, this variable can range from 0 (such a species won't last long) to 4. Anything beyond 4 is too much for a species; it's like humans having 20 babies every 9 months—that would kill anyone. Besides that, it fills and depletes the niche, thus the species starves. After you understand how this all works, get out your calculator and solve the equation with r set to 4.1 and see what happens.

Now, it makes sense that you would multiply birthrate (r) times existing population size (X_{old}) to get the size of the next generation. If the birthrate is 0.5 (one offspring for every two parents), for example, then the next generation will be half of the present generation (0.5 times the current generation size equals half the current generation); if the birthrate is 2 (two babies born for every organism that currently exists), then the next generation will be twice the current one.

If r is even slightly over 1.0 and there are no restraints on growth, you can imagine what will happen before long—the world will be overflowing with this population. Environments, of course just can't carry an unlimited number of any given species and that's where $1 - X_{old}$ in the equation comes in; it represents the limit (in the form of starvation, discouragement of new growth, etc.) that environment places on population growth. If a population has filled only 10% of an environment's capacity, then obviously there're plenty of resources left to support further growth. But if the population is at 80% of an environment's carrying capacity, resources are becoming scarce and further expansion is resisted by environmental pressure. The closer a population's size approaches an environment's capacity, the more the

Using a Spreadsheet to Solve the Logistic Equations

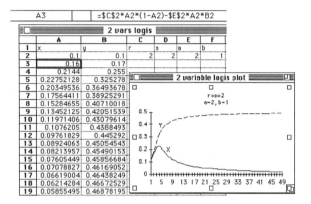

The logistic formulas with which we are working can be set up on any computer spreadsheet program. This example was created on Microsoft Excel,® but translating the instructions to other spreadsheets should be easy. The illustration uses the two equation logistic model (Equation 12.4).

Assign a column for the X variable and one for the Y, as shown above. Single cells are needed for each of the remaining variables—r, s, a, and b, as shown. Enter initial values in row 2 beneath the respective labels; in our example the initial values are $X = Y = 0.1$, $r = s = 2$, $a = 2$, and $b = 1$. All these variables are explained in the main text. In row 3 of column A (the column for the X variable), enter the equation for calculating X as follows:

$$=\$C\$2 * A2 * (1-A2)-\$E\$2 * A2 * B2$$

A2 refers to the value in cell A2, C2 refers to the value in cell C2, and so forth. The $ symbol in the second of these references makes that cell fixed—no matter where on the spreadsheet this calculation is being performed, C2 will always refer to cell C2. If the dollar sign is absent, the formula references a moving (relative) site.

In column 2, row B, enter the equation for calculating the variable Y:

$$=\$D\$2 * B2 * (1-B2)-\$F\$2 * A2 * B2$$

This equation calculates the second values of X and Y (after the initial values). However, the equation must be calculated repeatedly. To accomplish this with Microsoft Excel® simply point to cell A3 with the mouse, click and drag to cell B3, then drag down (without releasing the mouse button) about 100 rows. All the cells dragged across should be highlighted, including A3 and B3. Now, on a Macintosh, hold down the Command key and press the "D" key to copy your formulas into all the highlighted cells (check your spreadsheet program's manual for IBM or for other spreadsheet brands). The equation will be entered repeatedly, as required.

Most spreadsheet programs will plot an XY coordinate graph, which is the appropriate way to illustrate your results. Consult your manual for instructions.

Now that you've set up your spreadsheet, you can experiment with different initial values of X, Y, r, s, a, and b by simply changing the value in the appropriate cell in row 2. The program will automatically recalculate the equations based on your new initial values.

environment will discourage further growth (at 80%, for example, a lot of mosquitoes die off because they can't find food). In $1 - X$, then, 1 represents 100% of the environment's carrying capacity. By subtracting X_{old} from 1 and multiplying the result times rX_{old}, we are limiting the rate of growth that a species experiences. If X_{old} is 100%, then $1 - X_{old}$ is 0, and 0 times rX is 0—the population is stopped in its tracks. If X_{old} is 1%, then 1 minus X_{old} is 99% and 99% times rX hardly depresses the growth rate at all. It may be mathematical, but if you think about the whole thing conceptually, it makes perfect sense.

We use this equation to determine what happens to population growth over time, and to achieve that, the formula must be recalculated repeatedly, with the most recent output (X_{new}) being used as input (X_{old}) in the next calculation. Lets say that the population of industries in a rapidly growing new market is at 10% of market capacity, and that the growth rate for new industries is 2. Plugging these figures into Equation 12.2 we get:

$$X_{new} = r \, X_{old} \, (1 - X_{old}) \qquad [12.2]$$
$$X_{new} = 2.0 \cdot 0.10 \, (1 - 0.10)$$
$$X_{new} = 0.18$$

The next time we look at the population, then, it should be at 18% of environmental carrying capacity. To see what comes next, we substitute 0.18 for X_{old} in the equation; the growth rate remains the same at 2.0:

$$X_{new} = 2.0 \cdot 0.18 \, (1 - 0.18)$$
$$X_{new} = 0.2952$$

The population has grown from 10% capacity to 18%, then to almost 30%. On the next cycle, the population will jump to 42% capacity, then to 48%, then to 49% where it will grow slowly for two more cycles until it reaches, and stabilizes at, 50% of environmental carrying capacity. In only eight cycles, the population reaches an equilibrium with its environment. If we start with a growth rate less than 1.0, the population will get smaller every cycle until eventually it is infinitesimally small—for all practical purposes it ceases to exist. If the birthrate is between 3.57 and 4, the population size will not stabilize at all—it is, instead, Chaotic (with an uppercase "C").

For growth rates between 1.2 and about 2.8, populations multiply in an interesting and, it turns out, important way. This pattern of growth is illustrated in Figure 12.1. The straight portion at the top of the curve in this figure represents equilibrium, what we would get when populations stabilize. The

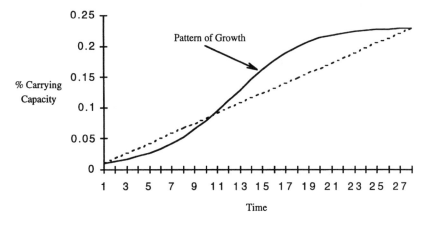

Figure 12.1. Growth of a population from 0.1 to equilibrium for $r = 2.0$.

curved line plots the first 29 cycles of growth we get from our equation when $r = 2.0$. Note that population growth begins rather sluggishly—growth is nearly linear—but by the sixth cycle it is beginning to pick up steam, and for the next 13 cycles or so the population grows rather quickly. Eventually it runs out of steam, levels off, and approaches equilibrium. We can describe what is going on conceptually. For the first few cycles, the population is gathering resources, building mass so to speak. Each new resource (or member of the population) will, in turn, generate two new resources (or population members—remember, $r = 2$); once sufficient momentum is accumulated we see explosive growth. The environment, however, is able to support only a certain amount of growth in the population, thus after a while constraints slow things down and the population approaches equilibrium with that environment—a balance between growth pressures and environmental constraint.

Biologists call this sort of plot a logistic, or S-shaped, curve (likewise, the formula we're using to generate the graph is called a logistic equation). Logistic growth is quite common. Cesaré Marchetti, a faculty member at the International Institute for Applied Systems Analysis in Austria, has found it in all sorts of places where we wouldn't expect to find it. The cumulative production of Mozart's work over time, for example, can be plotted as a logistic curve, as can the growth of mainframe computers in Japan, construction of Gothic cathedrals in Europe, and the worldwide volume of airline traffic. It is as if adaptive systems are driven by an internal, subconscious program that controls human productivity.

Organizational Growth: Competition Model

Building on our equation, we can add one more term to represent the impact that a second, competing population would exert on the first. That second term is $aX_{old}Y$, and the new, modified equation is:

$$X_{new} = rX_{old}(1 - X_{old}) - aX_{old}Y \qquad [12.3]$$

In the extra term, Y represents the size of the second population expressed as a percentage of carrying capacity, and a represents the success of the second population in frustrating the efforts of the first (a high value of a, for example, might suggest that Y is outbidding X for market sales). To represent the degree to which the two populations fill their common niche (thus the likelihood that they will clash over resources), the new term multiplies X_{old} by Y; if X and Y are large, the probability they will come in contact with one another is high.

In this model, the size of population X is dependent upon the relative sizes of r and a. Generally, if population Y increases its competitive edge over X (variable a gets larger), then X must increase its growth rate in order to offset Y's advantage. For example, if we start with both populations at 30% capacity and set Y's competitiveness (a) at 2.0, then equilibrium can be achieved with growth rates ranging from 1.58 to 3.5. Within this range, population X can occupy up to 54% of the market niche. If competitiveness, a, increases to 4, the range of growth rates r required for equilibrium is 2.2 to 4.1 and the population can occupy up to 46% of the niche. X has had to increase its growth rate to capture a smaller part of the niche. This trend becomes increasingly evident the more Y's competitiveness increases.

Organizational Growth: Interacting Organizations Model

In a quest for ever-increasing realism, we can expand our growth equation one more time. This time we will not change the equation itself so there is nothing new to learn in that regard; instead we will add a second equation. The second is exactly like the first except that it calculates the growth of a second population (labeled Y). In this equation, variable s is the growth rate of population Y (like r is the growth rate for X), and variable b represents the competitive advantage of X over Y (see Equation 12.4). This linked pair of equations is easy to solve; simply solve the first equation for X_{new} and plug the solution into the second equation in place of X (you'll find it in the last expression—bXY_{old}). Then solve for Y_{new} and substitute that solution into the last expression of the equation for X (of course you will substitute X_{new} from the first cycle for X_{old}). Continue this back-and-forth process until equilibrium is achieved (or until it becomes evident that equilibrium is unachievable).

$$X_{new} = rX_{old} (1 - X_{old}) - aX_{old}Y \qquad [12.4]$$
$$Y_{new} = sY_{old} (1 - Y_{old}) - bXY_{old}$$

In testing this equation we found that growth rate is an important determinant of market share; as one might expect, the percentage of captured carrying capacity (equilibrium) increases with growth rate. With two populations, not only do the equilibrium points increase with growth rate, the population with the higher rate will experience the higher equilibrium point—again as one might expect. This will be true even if we give the population with the smaller growth rate something of a competitive advantage. Thus if we start with both populations at 10% of niche carrying capacity, and if we give Y a slight competitive advantage over X ($a = 0.6$ and $b = 0.4$) but give X the higher growth rate by setting $r = 2$ and $s = 1.2$, then population X stabilizes at 50% carrying capacity and Y is driven out of its niche (i.e., it stabilizes at $Y = 0.0$). Population Y, despite a competitive advantage, just does not have a sufficient growth rate to compete. To offset X's advantage and to survive, Y would need to pump up its competitive edge from 0.6 to 6.0 (compared to X's 0.4). At this point, Y would manage to eke out 11% of niche and X would stabilize at 16.6% (see Figures 12.2a and 12.2b). One might say that, although X is producing more "babies" than Y (remember, $r = 2$), Y is ravishing them to assure its own survival; alternatively, one might argue that organization X is growing faster than Y but Y is out-bidding X for customers.

Population Y could also survive if its growth rate were increased to a level closer to that of X. If we set its rate s to 1.8, with $r = 2$ like before (Y still has the competitive advantage—$a = 0.6$, $b = 0.4$—and the initial values of X and Y are 0.1), then X will stabilize at 40% of its niche and Y stabilizes at 36% (see Figure 12.2c).

If we increase growth rates r and s without changing the competition variables (a and b), the equilibrium points of the two populations will *increase*. If, however, we set $r = s$ and progressively increase the levels of competition (with a approximately equal to b at each increase), the equilibrium points of the two systems *decrease*. Increased competition is detrimen-

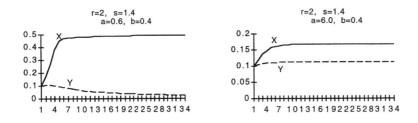

Figures 12.2a and 12.2b. Offsetting differences in growth rate with a competitive advantage. Derived from Equation 12.4. For all plots, number of generations is on the X axis, percentage of niche is on the Y axis.

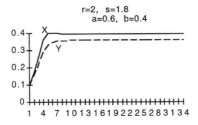

Figure 12.2c. Offsetting difference in competition by increasing growth rate. Derived from Equation 12.4.

tal to both actors because it cuts into the percentage of niche that each exploits.

At increased growth rates, something else interesting begins to happen: The pace set by the more successful population seems to drive the behavior of the less successful population. Let's set s for population Y at a constant 2.5 and see what happens by gradually increasing the growth rate of population X. Normally, a growth rate in Y of 2.5 will produce a stable equilibrium in population Y, but when r, the growth rate for population X, gets to 3.4, both populations begin to fluctuate—X fluctuates between 0.50 to 0.68, and Y jumps between 0.48 and 0.53 (this is called period 2 fluctuation). The curious fact is not that X experiences period 2 fluctuation—this is a common phenomenon that we'll explore later in the book; rather, the curious point is that Y is forced into period 2 fluctuation by X. At $r = 3.75$, we get period 4

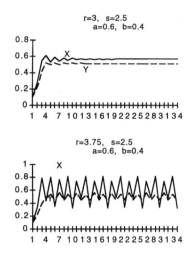

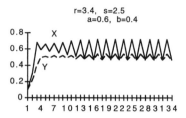

Figures 12.3a, 12.3b, and 12.3c. Growth rate of one population drives the behavior of the other. As *r* increases from 3.0 to 3.4 and then 3.75 (*s* is constant at 2.5), the population shifts from period 1 to period 2 to period 4 fluctuations.

fluctuation, meaning that *X* cycles repeatedly through 4 values; population *Y*, despite its growth rate remaining at 2.5, likewise cycles across 4 values (see Figures 12.3a-12.3c). Period 8 occurs at about 3.77, followed shortly by period 16, period 32, and so forth. Obviously something is about to happen: that something is Chaos, but that's Chapter 15's story.

Let's see if we can summarize our findings from experimenting with these growth formulas:

- ▓ A population's share of its niche increases as its growth rate increases, but too high a growth rate can overwhelm the environment and destroy the population.
- ▓ Population growth often follows a logistic, or s-shaped, pattern.
- ▓ A population's point of equilibrium with its environment decreases as competition from another population increases.
- ▓ Achieving equilibrium among highly competitive populations requires higher than usual growth rates.
- ▓ A competitor's high growth rate can be offset by a very large competitive advantage or by narrowing the difference in growth rates.
- ▓ When two populations compete for resources, the pattern of equilibrium (whether period 2, period 4, etc.) established by the population with the higher growth rate determines the pattern for the other population.

Math ∩ Reality

Does math intersect reality? Actually, this is a redundant question because math is the language of reality. A better question would be: Do our equations properly capture the essence of reality? Have we spoken the language properly?

François Nielsen, a sociologist and mathematician, has done a fair amount of work on just this question, and in 1977 he teamed up with Michael T. Hannan to determine whether the logistic formula could describe real-world events. Their conclusions were published by the *American Sociological Review* in an article titled "The Expansion of National Educational Systems: Tests of a Population Ecology Model."

Nielsen and Hannan examined the enrollment growth of national educational systems between 1950 and 1970. They measured growth rate (r) as the speed at which the size of an organizational population adjusted to environmental carrying capacity. Environmental carrying capacity was defined as available resources, such as money and number of potential students. The study looked at elementary, secondary, and higher education schools in both rich and poor national environments. Their conclusions supported their growth model—the equations did indeed describe the realities they examined. They also found that more complex schools, those with greater diversification of labor (higher education schools were the most complex, followed by high schools, then elementary schools) responded more sluggishly relative to changes in carrying capacity than did less complex organizations. Stu Kauffman, it will be remembered, came to similar conclusions about high K systems (K refers to internal complexity). Likewise they found that resource-intensive institutions exhibit higher levels of inertia in responding to environmental change (like complexity, this variable—resource intensiveness—increases from elementary to secondary then higher education). Putting it all together, colleges and universities, which are highly complex and require large amounts of resources to transform students, respond slowly to environmental changes and take longer to achieve equilibrium, while elementary schools, which are less complex and use fewer resources, respond more rapidly.

More recently, organizational theorist Stephen Guastello has demonstrated that the number of employees in small construction firms can likewise be described with the logistic equation. In Guastello's study, hiring rate was the growth parameter. He concluded that organizations that hire only as positions arise are at a disadvantage against firms with more dynamic hiring policies.

■ **Carrying Capacity and Structure:**
   Generalists Versus Specialists

Environmental carrying capacity (X in the above equations) is not a constant commodity—it changes and fluctuates with market conditions, product demand, number of potential clients, availability of raw materials, and countless other environmental variables. It makes sense to argue, then, that different organizations adopt different strategies for dealing with these fluctuations. Population Ecologists identify two general approaches to adaptability: the generalist approach and the specialist approach. The generalist organization performs a lot of functions, but it performs each only well enough to get by. The latter type of organization—the specialist—performs only a few tasks, but it concentrates on doing them with a flair.

The generalist organization concentrates on maintaining flexibility so that it can respond to differing environmental demands. Flexibility comes from the accumulation of slack resources to carry it through the rainy days and to help it explore alternative activities. An organization is flexible when it "feeds" on a variety of resources and generates different products from those resources. Truck farms, which produce a diversity of crops, are generalists, as are mutual funds, department stores, and large, diversified hospitals. The specialist organization, by contrast, does not concern itself with embracing varied outlets, for flexibility is not a major concern. It seeks merely to gorge itself on a few resources, usually with the intent of accumulating enough fat to carry it through draught periods when those resources aren't in abundance. Cotton farms are specialists, as are theme-oriented radio stations (oldies stations, for example), resort motels in seasonal markets, stock portfolios with little diversity, and specialist trade schools.

If the environment is uncertain, the generalist organization will obviously do better than the specialist; if one of its products isn't producing much return, for example, there are others to pick up the slack. The specialist organization will not do so well in a fluctuating environment; it will make money only when the environment decides to cater to its specialty, thus it goes through periods of low productivity. A motel in a nonseasonal market (generalist) does reasonably well year 'round because it attracts different types of clientele, while resort hotels in seasonal markets (specialist) do very well during (but only during) their season.

In a stable environment, however, a specialist organization will run circles around a generalist, thus a specialist radio station will typically outperform one that attempts to cater to a diversity of tastes as long as the demand for the specialty music is consistent. In a stable environment, the generalist's slack resources become an expensive liability while the specialist runs lean and fast.

The advantages that accrue in stable or unstable markets aren't all that clean-cut, however; there are other determinants that affect adaptation. If the lengths of time over which the market fluctuates in an uncertain environment are short, for example, specialist organizations can make it quite well across the lean times and may, in balance, outperform their generalist counterparts. This is particularly true when the good times are really good, as they would be for motels in seasonal markets such as at the beach. If, on the other hand, the lean times are particularly long, then specialist organizations are less likely to survive and the generalist will be the winner.

Success is also dependent upon the severity of environmental fluctuations. If the fluctuations don't cover too broad a range, the generalist will probably do better; if fluctuations are dramatic, then the specialist probably has the advantage. Most generalists are unable to diversify enough to keep up with dramatic fluctuations, and without the ability to survive in all situations, their advantage evaporates. The specialist doesn't waste energy trying.

If the durations are long and the fluctuations are dramatic, then neither the specialist nor the generalist can survive. In this case, a third type of organization is favored. This third type might be considered a super variety of the generalist; Population Ecologists call it the *polymorph*. The polymorph is actually several different organizations that are either under one administrative roof or linked in a federation of organizations—RJ Reynolds Tobacco Company®, for example, combines cigarette production with cereal production and at one time included maritime shipping. The different "suborganizations" in the poly allow the mega-organization to weather a variety of quite diverse conditions; there's always some product that can carry the others through their lean times.

Given all these restrictions, according to Anna Grandori, "adaptation becomes a game of chance in which a firm chooses a strategy (specialist or generalist) and environment chooses an outcome (say by flipping a coin)" (p. 110). This, of course, is the essence of Population Ecology and survival of the fittest.

All this is summarized in Table 12.1, which is based upon a similar table in Grandori's book. "Coarse grain" and "fine grain" refer to the duration between states of the environment, with coarse referring to long periods between states.

r-Strategists and k-Strategists

The reader may be a bit out of breath after trying to keep up with all the "if-thens" in the last few paragraphs, but hang in there because we are going

TABLE 12.1 Effects of Duration Across Environmental Change and
Degree of Fluctuation on Organizational Form

Frequency of Change	Compatibility Between	Superior Organizational Forms Among Several Competing Populations
Fine-grained (short duration)	Compatible (similar) environmental states	Generalist
	Incompatible (dissimilar) environmental states	Specialist
Coarse-grained (long duration)	Compatible (similar) environmental states	Generalist
	Incompatible (dissimilar) environmental states	Generalist or polymorphic

NOTE: Based on representation by Anna Grandori

to press this theme forward a little farther. Remember growth rate, r, in the logistic formula? Some organizations concentrate on growth strategies for survival, thus they are called r-strategy organizations. There is also a variable labeled k in the logistic formula; by simplifying the equations we managed to omit it in our earlier discussion. k is nothing more than the numerical carrying capacity of an environment (in the earlier logistic equations, we by-passed population size k and went straight to *percentage* of carrying capacity, which we labeled X). k is suggestive of market saturation, and k-strategy organizations focus on survival in a stable, densely populated environment, one that is at equilibrium relative to environmental carrying capacity.

r-strategy organizations are cheap and easy to set up; they concentrate on minimizing start-up costs and on simple structures. This gives them the ability to move quickly into a burgeoning market and to get out of a failing market with minimum losses. k-strategy organizations make significant investments in their plants and equipment, and have more elaborate organizational structures than do r-strategists. k-strategists plan to stay in business for a long time. Predictably, you would expect to find r-strategists in uncertain markets, in markets that thrive on innovation, or in newly opened markets. By contrast, one would find k-strategists in mature, competitive markets with relatively little uncertainty. Theme-oriented radio stations are r-strategists; they may play golden oldies today, but if Reggae music is the fad tomorrow, they have the flexibility to make a quick transition. AT&T, on the other hand, has made significant commitments to phone lines, communication satellites, radio transmitters, and similar equipment; it isn't expecting the communications market to dry up, or change radically, in the near future, nor is it planning to move whimsically on to other interests. AT&T clearly is a k-strategist.

Changing Complex Organizations

▩ *Star Trek* and Change

One particular episode from the original *Star Trek* series had the *Enterprise* caught in a time warp and carried back to the early 1930s. Captain Kirk, Spock, and the ship's doctor, Bones, beamed down to Earth where Kirk fell in love with a young social worker. Spock, meanwhile, managed to link with the *Enterprise's* computers and discovered that the social worker would soon be hit by an automobile and die. He further discovered that if for some reason she were not to die, her pacifist influence would grow, and her movement would prevent President Roosevelt from entering World War II until after it was too late to stop Hitler. Captain Kirk, of course, found himself in a position to save the young lady, thus changing history in a massive and devastating way.

The movie *Back to the Future II* had a similar plot. In this case, a sports almanac was brought back from the future to the 1950s, and the world of the 1980s was dramatically changed as a result. Marty McFly, the hero played by Michael J. Fox, had some edge-of-seat adventures recovering the almanac and reversing its damage.

This is a common theme in science fiction: A character visits the past and some minor event forever alters the future. This theme assumes that history is brittle and is easily perturbed by minor events. A similar assumption is often made by neophyte social Chaologists about the implications of Lorenz's butterfly effect, or sensitive dependence on initial conditions. If the flapping of a butterfly's wings in Texas can dramatically change weather patterns in Chicago, then the flapping of one's mouth, or seemingly innocuous decisions, or random behaviors, can dramatically affect an organization's future.

Indeed? Can history and social systems be altered by minor events? Did Rosa Park's sore feet and racial indigestion change race relations that day in 1955 on a city bus in Montgomery, Alabama? Did the death of young Adolph Hitler's father precipitate World War II? Did Bill Clinton's boyhood handshake with John F. Kennedy lead to his own run at the presidency of the United States? Did Robert Frost's traveler in "The Road Not Taken" dramatically alter his life by his single choice of paths ("Two roads diverged in a wood, and I—/ I took the one less traveled by,/ And that has made all the difference")?

The answer is yes . . . and no. Actually more no than yes. Obviously this begs explanation, and the following two chapters on Complexity Theory and organizational change will do just that. We will revisit the issue at the end of that explanation.

▓ From Paint Jobs to Core Technology

There are several ways to categorize change, and we will examine a number of them in this chapter. We begin by describing change in relation to its degree or type of effect on a system. The least obtrusive (but most common) is called a paint job; next is technological change, then structural change—or perhaps the order should be reversed for it is debatable as to which of these latter two is more potent.

Paint Jobs and Rain Dances

The paint job, or the rain dance (a term suggested by political scientist Murray Edelman), is probably the most common form of change. Paint jobs project an image of doing something, but they leave the basic structure of the target problem unchanged. We see paint jobs when a board fires its CEO for poor profits, leaving the basic problems that created the losses untouched; or when parents of university students feel more secure after the provost writes a scathing indictment of student drinking in the alumni newsletter. The imagery conveyed by the term rain dance is similar, but emphasizes a slightly different perspective. This suggests that something occurs that makes us feel that we are doing something about a problem, makes us feel that we are in control, when in reality our actions have little to do with the underlying problems. Rain dances leave us feeling good. If something does change following the rain dance, we are quick to credit our efforts; if nothing happens, we often ignore the fact as we plan our next dance.

Early in the 1990s, West Virginia passed a law that revoked the driving licenses of students who dropped out of school. The law had minimal impact on dropout rates, but people felt good because they thought they had done something about an embarrassing problem. State lotteries implemented to benefit education can likewise be considered public rain dances. Lotteries typically add 1% to 3% to a school system's budget, although even this is often drained by legislative cuts in general allocations. Voters, however, are lulled into believing they have taken care of education with their lottery; consequently, general tax increases for education become difficult to obtain.

Technological Change

Technological changes affect the central activity of an organization, what Glenn Carroll and Michael Hannan have called the core technology and Bill McKelvey has called comps. Comps or core technologies are the basic competencies required to produce a firm's products. In a chemical plant the core technology is chemistry; in a law firm, it is law; in a school, it is instruction. For elementary schools to cease teaching ability grouped reading lessons and instead to individualize instruction would require technological change. Shifts from hand-crafted production to automated production in manufacturing industries is technological change.

This is the most substantive of the change strategies. In many cases it is the most complex to implement because of the many collateral and supportive activities that must also be changed. Individualized instruction in public school classrooms would require, among other things, revised textbooks; retraining programs for teachers; revised strategies for managing classrooms; attitudinal acceptance by teachers, administrators, and parents; revisions in teacher training programs; alterations in financial support structures; and alterations in physical facilities. Technology is not a single event, rather it is a complex of interactive events.

This latter point regarding the interactive nature of structure epitomizes a central point of this book and of Complexity Theory. Unfortunately, it is often misunderstood or ignored by change agents. Technological change cannot be isolated to a few organizational functions. School principals proudly roll new computers into classrooms, give the teachers a few lessons, then leave them to their own designs. They assume that a new technology and a few lessons constitute change, but they don't. Teachers must learn to integrate that technology into their existing curriculum, to make it a part of the broader pedagogical process, but we rarely teach them how to do that. Classroom computing requires significant technical support, ongoing training, and investment in software and in new innovations, but schools too often fail to make those investments. Teachers need to restructure their approach to instruction, to make students more active participants in the learning process, but we fail to convey this need to them. Computer-based instruction requires trade-offs in a district's budgeting process, requires the formulation of new policy (to control pirating of software or to protect the integrity of networks, for example), requires long-range planning for technological improvement, and requires that networks with vendors and other educational users be nurtured. Computer-based instruction is not as simple as pushing a computer into a classroom, yet all too often we treat it that way. Change, particularly technological change (in the broader sense of that word), implicates complex interdependencies and multiple actors, yet change agents often approach change as if it were a simple linear process. Everyone has witnessed failed change efforts; undoubtedly a little reflection can attribute the failures to simplistic assumptions about the nature of the change process.

Organizational Change

Organizational change is an alteration it the way social systems are structured. Most restructuring efforts are organizational change: CEOs are replaced, positions are reclassified or shifted around, responsibilities are redefined, roles are done away with and new ones are created. Organizational change is more extensive than are rain dances and paint jobs, but like its more simplistic cousins, it often serves as proxy for more substantive technological change.

Organizational change can unwittingly trigger technological change, however. University restructuring is usually initiated to shift resources to the classroom or to research; this, of course, is a deliberate effort to aid the organization's technology. But were that organizational change to eliminate middle-level administrators responsible for such things as budgeting and scheduling, extra responsibility would likely fall on the professoriate and would inadvertently hinder instruction and research (a technological change). Technological changes are often problematic under the best of circumstances for they involve a complex of interactive interdependencies, they can evoke troublesome unanticipated consequences, and they may require long learning curves during which organizational fitness is depressed. When they occur as uncontrolled and unanticipated consequences of organizational change, they are even more problematic. One loses the benefit of any anticipatory planning, and ego investment on the part of change agents may lead them to ignore the problems for significant lengths of time. This is why it was implied a bit earlier that organizational change could be more potent than technological change.

▓ Do We Change Events or Do Events Change Us?

This section will address two broad perspectives on change: that which sees change as deliberately instigated and under the control of its human authors, and that which sees it as organic, the product of interactive dynamics. These perspectives mirror one of the large debates in organizational theory: whether organizational behavior is prescribed and controlled by leaders or organically related to environmental ambiguities. Early theorists, particularly Machine theorists, leaned completely to the prescriptive side of the debate; they mirrored the very human need to be in control. The intervening years have seen us struggle with the rather painful realization that we control less than we would like. Contingency and Resource Dependency theorists sought ways to "finesse" the uncertainty; Enacted Environmentalists analyzed the uncertainty; and Population Ecologists have largely ignored the human element.

But still the control mystique persists, despite the rambling of theorists. Matters need to be put into perspective.

When People Change Events

Deliberate change is, obviously, change that we as humans set out to accomplish. We have it within our power to place computers within public school classrooms, restructure our organizations, throw people out of office, pass laws that affect the way we do things, force people to be accommodating of those who are deprived or handicapped, and change the way teachers teach. Organizations can take over other organizations, fire their employees, and revise their organizational philosophies. We can organize projects for predetermined ends. All of this constitutes deliberate change.

These examples, however, betray one-dimensional perspectives of change. They betray, for example, a presumption that simple acts, such as placing computers in schools, are sufficient to create deep-level change. They reflect a belief that the appearance of change (such as restructuring) is an appropriate substitute for substantive change. They presume that we control the future, or that change and improvement are synonymous. They assume that change is the property of the change agent and ignore the power of history and interactive dynamics. They make the basic assumption that human control is the prevailing reality, thus all change events are interpreted within the context of that reality.

Such assumptions are misguided, of course, but not entirely wrong. Humans are the major actors in the change process, and sometimes our deliberate efforts have significant effect. Nonetheless, nearly all change must be interpreted within the context of broader historical and interactive events.

The Heroic Leader

Perhaps the most cherished belief about change in Western society is that it emanates from charismatic leaders. The stories of Lincoln, King, Churchill, Meir, Kennedy, DeGaulle, or Henry Ford are cherished because they are about people who fought epic battles and created significant change in their societies. They are about people who dominated, and humans like to dominate. The notion taps a primal human urge, and we want to be like them.

Yet charismatic leaders may not be quite all they are stacked up to be. Ronald Corwin argued that, while visionary and intelligent leadership is certainly important, innovation is a complex process that involves more than good leadership. It involves, for example, timing. Charismatic leadership is potent when the timing is right—it is doubtful, for example, that Martin Luther King would have made much impression 50 years before his time. Oskar Schindler (of *Schindler's List*) was highly successful before and during World War II, but he was not successful after the war. It's in the timing.

Change requires, Corwin continued, significant support from subordinates and stakeholders—George Bush, for example, was successful in the Gulf War because of broad support from world leaders and public opinion. Further, charismatic leaders may have skills needed for one stage of a change process but not another. They may be excellent visionaries and communicators but lack the managing skills needed to see a task through, or their skills may be suited for one set of conditions but not for subsequent conditions. Kennedy was undoubtedly good at stimulating revolution in American politics, but it took someone of Lyndon Johnson's abilities to exact cooperation on social legislation from the U.S. Congress. George Patton was highly effective during World War II, but his warring hostility toward the USSR would likely have been a liability during the cold war.

More important, charismatic leaders rarely accomplish their feats alone, and sometimes they are even credited for success that essentially happened to them. The integration movement in the United States can trace its roots to court cases in the 1850s, and certainly to cases that were heard in the 1930s and 1940s. Martin Luther King did not originate the movement, he inherited it. Eisenhower was surrounded by competent leaders and massive resources during World War II. Anti-slavery sentiment and support was firmly rooted long before Lincoln wrote the Emancipation Proclamation. Churchill was an inspiring speaker and able leader, but it was young pilots—bolstered by failure of Goering's Luftwaffe to press crucial advantages—who won the battle over Great Britain. Charisma often succeeds only because interactive events allow it.

So, we might ask, what is the role of leadership? Does Complexity Theory relegate it to the back pages of our theory books? Actually, the leader's role is crucial. Perhaps the civil rights movement would have happened without King, or the Battle of Britain would have been won without Churchill, but undoubtedly someone would have taken their place. Leadership serves, among other things, a role that John Holland has called the "tag." A tag is some symbolic or physical structure that labels a complex adaptive system. In biology, pheromones serve as a label in insect reproduction, and coloration serves to label gender among certain birds. Humans "tag" themselves with the jewelry or clothes they wear; youths, for example, go to some length to differentiate themselves from adults. Businesses label themselves with logos, advertisements, and reputations. Politicians tag themselves with political postures. Professions tag themselves with licensure. A tag is anything that separates a *CAS* from its undifferentiated background. Tags create identity; they are rally points about which a *CAS* can coalesce. A nation's flag and its nationalistic rhetoric rallies patriotic identity. Symbols such as Rodney King rally violent outbursts.

Heroic leaders are tags in two senses. They rally unified behavior, and they serve as symbols of the cause. One does not think of the Battle of Britain without thinking of Winston Churchill, and one cannot begin to measure the impact of his speeches upon British resolve. Leaders don't usually fight the battles—our presidents don't fight aliens on Independence Day—rather they symbolize the battles. They are the battle cry that rallies resolve and the battle flag about which soldiers come together. It is largely because they symbolize the larger movement, however, that they are potent. They derive strength and resources from that movement. They negotiate for the *CAS*, they solicit support for it, they focus its efforts, they even guide it within broad parameters. Yet they are also products of the *CAS*, they are nothing without it. Their influence on and for the *CAS* cannot be separated from their relationship with it. In a very real sense, their activities are the activities of the *CAS* itself, and not merely the activity of a strong personality. Their effect is the effect of the whole, their identity is the identity of all, they are an element of the super-entity.

Strategic Planning

Strategic planning and reorganization are rather popular change strategies because of their emphasis on rational, proactive leadership. The process involves analysis of current conditions and identification of structural and organizational problems; formulation of strategies for addressing the problems; and implementation of those strategies. In Chapter 9 we discussed Dewey's decision-making algorithm; strategic planning is little more than that algorithm in modern clothing.

Strategic planning has been the darling of organizations in the last decade of the 20th century for a variety of apparent reasons, some of which serve perceptual and psychological, rather than rational, needs.

• In a time when budgets are tight, when organizations are preparing for "re-birth" in the 21st century, and when firms want to project a "meaner, leaner" image, strategic planning is a public relations coup—to use an idea championed by commentator Rush Limbaugh, it is a "feel-good" strategy. It portrays the organization as being in control of its present and its future; it leaves the impression among managers, stockholders, and the public that something has been done about "the problem"; it wins brownie points with fiscally conservative legislatures. In short, it is a paint job. (In deference to Mr. Limbaugh, incidentally, I must admit to misrepresenting his application of the "feel-good" terminology. When I heard him use it, he was lambasting the foolishness of liberal politicians and public school officials; I have never heard him use it to address the foolishness of big business.)

• Organizations may implement strategic planning with less than compelling rationale. The organization may be structurally quite sound, resources may be sufficient, and profits may be stable, but still it reorganizes. The managers of such organizations are apparently caught up in the faddishness of the movement, which promises protection against imagined future, and unseen present, problems. There may also be a broader, unspoken agenda in this variation of the rain dance, however: Strategic planning can provide leadership with an opportunity to reinforce its position in the pecking order. It is a statement that says management—like the shaman at primitive rain dances—is potent and in control.

• As a fad, strategic planning projects an image of modernity, of being in sync with the times. It is a statement that the stultification of old has been cast aside, and 21st-century clothing is put on. From this perspective it is, again, an image-enhancing rain dance. I should hasten to add, however, before I am dismissed as a cynic, that society needs its rain dances. They renew our spirit and give us faith in the future—even if they do tend to be shallow.

• Strategic planning is a tool for making organizations more efficient— the 1990's buzzword here is *downsizing*—and it lends a mien of the rational to that effort. This strategy usually involves organizational-level change; positions are eliminated and roles are consolidated. It is based upon the assumption that there is deadwood in the organizational structure; if true, then strategic planning can be quite useful. There is a danger, however. In a zealous desire to be modern and lean, managers may cut into technological meat and leave the system less effective and questionably efficient. Change of the magnitude often witnessed in strategic planning and reorganization typically upsets existing networks of accommodation and forces an extended period of readjustment. From the Complexity perspective, fitness is disrupted and the system must re-climb its fitness peak. Lower productivity offsets gains from personnel cutbacks, morale is assaulted, and overall effectiveness is compromised.

• The usual goal of strategic planning is efficiency, but leaders may aspire to effectiveness as well. That is, strategic goals may include improvements in the quality of production. The most obvious tool for this is innovation. Robotics may be introduced into a manufacturing process, microcomputers or distance learning may be injected into classrooms, new accounting procedures may be introduced into a payroll department. This is technology-level change. Such strategy may, of course, serve efficiency goals as well. The degree to which technological change is accepted by workers depends upon whether it is perceived as threatening or supportive. In 1977, Michael Moch and Edward Morse evaluated the impact of 12 technological innovations in approximately one thousand hospitals. They found that those that were designed to facilitate diagnosis and treatment were accepted by the staff while those perceived as extending the control of administration, such as efforts to better monitor expenses, were less acceptable.

Corwin has argued that strategic planning assumes change "can be controlled by opportunistic managers who are wise enough to find the right strategies" (p. 204). As Philip Selznick put it in his book *Leadership in Administration,* "Leadership reconciles internal strivings and external pressures, paying close attention to the way adaptive behaviors bring about changes in organizational character" (p. 162). Such assumptions are prescriptive in that they prescribe effective behavior among leaders; they are strategies for dealing with internal and external contingencies, and they assume a close relationship between administrative behavior and organizational outcome.

There are several conceptual difficulties associated with strategic planning. It assumes, for example, that leaders posses sufficient knowledge and wisdom to evaluate present conditions adequately, and enough foresight to project future conditions. Such omnipotence is unlikely in any but the more stable situations, but even if it were possible, people would disagree about the nature of problems and about needed solutions. In fairness, leaders can often base their plans upon the often supportable assumption that current conditions will prevail into the future. Markets won't change substantially, political conditions won't deteriorate support, and public opinion won't turn against the system. Insurance agents can assume, for instance, that demand will be constant in the foreseeable future and can therefore base planning upon judgments about shortcomings in their ability to profit from their markets. Such plans might include expansion of the sales force or diversification of the product line. Even so, there is no one best way to enhance profits, thus different sales managers will see the solution differently. Further, there may not be agreement on the nature of an organization's shortcomings. One partner in an insurance company, for example, might argue that the market is being exploited as efficiently as is possible and that problems with profits lie in the way current resources are allocated. This person might conclude that claims criteria should be tightened up. Another partner might disagree about market exploitation and argue that a more aggressive sales force is needed. The point is that it is quite difficult to effectively evaluate the nature of problems facing an organization. Leaders often must decide on a course of action and pray that they've called it correctly. In this regard, strategic planning is merely a way to make ones' guesses look credible and authoritative.

Strategic planning assumes simple linear relationships between leadership behavior and organizational outcome. In reality, organizational structure and behavior are the products of complex, interactive dynamics, and relationships between cause and effect are often nonlinear and recursive. Things change suddenly rather than gradually; events cause each other; phenomena result from convoluted, interactive networks of cause and effect.

Change often sparks realignment of power structures; this can generate unanticipated resistance that strategic plans rarely anticipate. Unanticipated consequences can be a problem even when power is not directly implicated. Leaders may, for example, "field-test" a change in a certain department, but the attention and influence experienced by that department as a result of their favored status may create dissension and resentment in other departments. The realignment of power that accompanies reorganization may likewise create morale problems. Professors in a reorganized university may have administrative burdens dumped in their laps that drain energy from teaching and research. Change invites unanticipated problems; for strategic planning, which emphasizes control and predictability, this is a problem.

Psychological Change

Humans seem to have an innate belief that others around them are rational. We see ourselves as logical, and it is logical to assume that others will respond to our brand of logic. Thus, to generate change, we need only overwhelm others with our compelling logic.

There are several obvious problems here. One is the assumption that we are brilliant and compelling, and that one can fall on its own merits. Second is the assumption that we all see things the same way, that there is one constant reality and we (personally) have mastered it. In reality, reality is a matter of perception and focus; we all experience different environments in our lives, and we interpret events in the same environments differently. The things to which we ascribe importance differ from person to person, thus each of us has different perceptions of our environments and corresponding different brands of logic. One of the more interesting human phenomena is the way our different perceptions interact and the degree of energy we put into changing each others' perceptions of reality. Politicians devote much money, effort, and time into convincing us that their perceptions of social needs are the right perceptions. Advertisers make a science out of convincing us to alter our patterns of wants and needs. Parents socialize children by maneuvering their perceptions of propriety and reality. Leaders could be defined, in part, as individuals who are good at manipulating the perceptions of others. The political correctness movement is premised in part on efforts to change our worldviews through manipulation of our language. Such, however, is the dynamic that generates culture, common effort, fads, rumors, riots, and formal organization. Society fosters common perceptions of at least the general parameters of reality, because individual perceptions interact and adjust to one another.

But all this is not the problem I most wish to focus upon. The focal problem is the assumption that the source of a problem lies within—is the property of—the miscreant. There is no doubt that there are difficult people among us; there are the arrogant, the self-serving, the noncooperative, the lazy and indolent, the saboteurs, the nay-sayers, the ineffective, the bitter—somebody stop me. We assume that the root of organizational change lies within these people (and we are partially right), and that by appealing to their better sides, their problems can be corrected (and here we are mostly wrong). When we fail, we blame the failure on the individual. Perhaps that is the best we can do under the circumstance.

Organizational theorists Daniel Katz and Robert Kahn wrote that, in the 1960s, it became faddish among organizations to send workers to t-group workshops. T-group analysis attempted to change individuals, to reconstruct them from the inside out and return them to their organizations as more productive and effective workers. The strategy made several potentially fatal assumptions. It assumed that the individual can be changed, that the changes will become permanent parts of the individual's personality, that the individual will carry the change with him or her back to the work place, that the worker's colleagues will accept and respond to the changed personality, that the colleagues will make collateral changes themselves, and that the organizational pressures that helped create the original personality and the pattern of interactions with colleagues that fed the defect will no longer be potent forces. This is brittle logic, and it doesn't take but one broken link to disrupt it.

Personality is the product of complex interactions with complex histories; consequently, it is not easily changed and certainly is intractable to efforts that ignore the social context of personality. Managers have an obligation to improve conditions that feed personality defects and to be tolerant of idiosyncrasy; leadership efforts can significantly improve unhealthy social environments; and sometimes a problem with deviancy may require exorcism (firing, lateral promotion, or the such). Change is not an individual process, however, it is a group processes.

Power-Coercive Planned Change

Robert Chin coined the term *power coercive planned change* to refer to change that is enforced by power elites and by sanctions. This strategy is commonly used by governmental agencies and accounts for the success of a number of programs aimed at public education, such as programs for exceptional children and federal remediation programs. These strategies do not depend upon co-optation and cooperation; they do not depend upon buy-in by those affected. Typically they generate significant resentment in the initial stages, but a sufficiently powerful elite can prevail. In time the targets will buy into the program, despite the heavy-handed implementation strategy. Resentments don't last, and people move on to be replaced by others who know nothing of the imperious behavior that generated the programs. Despite their roots, such programs do gain acceptance.

When Events Change Us

Stu Kauffman argued that human endeavors are often beyond the control of their agents. He was quoted in Chapter 10 on this issue, and that quote is repeated here:

> Despite the fact that human crafting of artifacts is guided by intent and intelligence, both processes often confront problems of conflicting constraints. . . . I suspect that much of technological evolution results from tinkering with little real understanding ahead of time of the consequences. . . . [W]hen problems are very hard, thinking may not help that much. We may be relatively blind watchmakers. (1995, p. 202)

Perhaps this insight derives from the fact that human endeavors are not so different from the activities observable in general biology, which is Kauffman's forte. Whatever the source of his inspiration, he fairly summarizes the essence of the organic perspective of organization. His work in general so obviously relates to findings of Enacted Environment and Population Ecology theorists—even after accounting for the a priori relationship between biology and Population Ecology—that the task of synthesizing and applying Complexity Theory for organizational analysis has not been all that difficult.

Organic theorists likewise propose that social organization and behavior is a product of forces that are bigger than the individuals who craft them. Causation, they argue either by direction or indirection, is nonlinear and recursive rather than simple and linear. Many organizations have fluid rules, unstable environments, and poorly specified goals and objectives. Decision making in such organizations is more a matter of happenstance than rationality. Organizational units are loosely coupled, thus only somewhat responsive to one another. Structure is more a product of natural selection than rational planning and is sensitively dependent upon environmental conditions and the availability of resources. Humans may act purposively, but their actions are judged by the whims of selection and are accorded no more, or less, respect than the basest accident. Growth in organizations is a product of growth rate and the carrying capacity of the environment, thus some organizations emerge that take advantage of growth opportunities while others emerge that have learned to exploit stable markets. And finally, social order is complexly interactive, stable, and difficult to change.

Four perspectives of organizational change are embedded within these definitions of organic theory. The first perspective comes from Enacted Environment Theory and is called "learning." The second relates to Population Ecology's arguments about Darwinian adaptation. The third perspective is derived from the notion of organization as culture. The fourth perspective belongs to Complexity Theory. We will discuss the first three perspectives below, then devote the next chapter to our Complexity definition of change.

Learning Theory and Loose Coupling

Learning Theory begins with the very organic proposal that men and women tinker blindly with the activities of their social organizations; like blind watchmakers, they are never quite sure of what they are doing. As they tinker, however, they begin to sense certain patterns, and these patterns organize the tinkerers' understanding of events around them. They tinker, they observe, they restructure their tinkering. They are influenced by their environments, but their environments are conversely influenced by their tinkering. Eventually the organization—and the tinkerers within it—comes to an "understanding" with its environment, it develops the ability to anticipate, however vaguely, certain classes of contingency, and it learns to deal reasonably effectively with environmental situations. The organization, and its tinkerers, learn how to survive and thrive. Like a pride of lions, it hunts prey and drives off enemies, and often does so with impressive intelligence and guile. Even so, opportunities and problems and consequences are still largely beyond its control.

From this perspective, change is the process an organization undergoes as its tinkerers learn their environment. Learning is quite similar to adaptation in Population Ecology; both are a process of elaboration guided by experience. Learning and adaptation both come in two forms: drift (change attributable to selectively neutral environmental meandering) and selectively active fitness evolution (peak climbing or peak hopping). We'll discuss these in more detail in the next chapter.

Learning Theory focuses on the roles of individuals and the learning they undergo to make their organizations effective and to increase personal resource-gathering potential. Learning also occurs on a broader plane of which organizational participants are less aware. The organization itself must adjust its degree of coupling in order to adapt effectively, to produce innovative behavior, to increase overall organizational fitness. The proper level of coupling is learned rather than intelligently derived, and this learning effort is the job of the *CAS* as a whole. Organizations must learn to couple themselves at the Edge of Chaos. This observation isn't just now being introduced; it has been a theme of this book and will be developed intensely through the next chapter.

Loose coupling assumes that organizations and organizational components are often only weakly interactive. Karl Weick derived seven observations from these assumptions (see Chapter 10). Four of these observations deal directly with change. First, loose coupling allows units within an organization to persist and evolve independently. Change occurs more readily when the organization develops small, independent chunks and then coordinates them, rather than forcing the entire system to adapt simultaneously. The downside of this, according to Weick, is that units in a loosely coupled system aren't pressured to discontinue nonproductive practices. Second, small, loosely coupled units are more sensitive to environmental demands than are monolithic, tightly coupled systems; however, this characteristic may subject the system to the whim of energy-draining fads.

Third, loose coupling allows local adaptation to local environmental conditions when change of the entire system would be a problem; but it may hinder the diffusion of local changes that could benefit the entire system. Fourth, the loosely coupled organization can permit isolated units to experiment with novel structures or procedures without committing the entire system, but loose coupling may inhibit the diffusion of experiments that are productive.

We dealt rather thoroughly with the second of these observations, that regarding sensitivity to the environment, in Chapter 10 and won't repeat that discussion here.

Weick's first observation proposes that change is most likely when units evolve independently. The thrust of this argument is quite logical: It's easier to juggle small, independent units than it is to juggle everything at once. The story of the watchmakers Hora and Tempus from Chapter 11 captures the gist of this reasoning. Complexity theorist Stu Kauffman argues similarly that high K systems (what EE theory calls tightly coupled) must deal with so many conflicting constraints that it's difficult to achieve fitness.

But just how independent can adaptive units be? In Conway's Game of Life (see p. 25 in Chapter 3), a single, isolated unit will not survive; it dies from isolation. A network of units must exist before survival becomes possible. Likewise, a single individual is essentially nonviable; at best, isolated individuals will live out their lives, but their lineages will not be continued. Even at that, survival will be difficult—imagine trying to live in a world without access to grocery stores, hospitals, farmers, police and fire protection, neighbors, family—the products of a society.

A completely isolated organizational unit suffers similar difficulties: It would have neither access to resources nor outlet for its products. The absurdity is self-evident. The issue that loose coupling should address is not isolation but the balance between isolation and inter-relationship required for effective survival.

It's not just survival at stake here; change itself depends upon interaction. Isolated systems have little incentive to change; they achieve local optimum, and freeze. The Utopian religion known as the Shakers exemplifies; their brand of birth control (abstinence) left them on a shaky (sorry) fitness peak. They didn't produce replacement members, and converts to a sexless society have got to be hard to come by. Sex versus nice furniture is not a tough choice for most people. Their rather severe "tags" isolated them on a rather low (improperly coupled—my apologies once again) fitness peak, unable to get off because to do so would have required the dismantling of the essence of Shakerism.

Tightly coupled systems, by contrast, are in irreconcilable states of flux, for every whimsical wind batters the network, allowing it no semblance of order. If a unit were to find a high fitness peak (which is unlikely because of the astronomically large number of low peaks in such systems), that peak would be deformed in the next round of changes. Their problem is they change too much. They can, of course, protect themselves by freezing their dynamics, but that defeats change altogether.

Interaction is a necessary prerequisite for change. Change (like fitness) is related to degree of isolation/interaction. Interactive groups distort each other's fitness landscapes. The "selfish" adaptive moves of one group compromise the fitness of another group, forcing it to change. That adjustment in turn perturbs other groups, and so it goes. Left alone and isolated, systems are not likely to change, but placed in a network of interacting units, they are forced to change. The trick for the *CAS* is to find (or learn) the level of coupling at which this can occur without being so tight that every wind devastates the system.

Young markets are tightly coupled, thus they are characterized by dramatic change. The microcomputer market was in a such a volatile state of change during the 1970s and early 1980s; numerous players flashed onto the playing field with their own brand of hardware and operating system, and just as quickly flashed off the field. The first marketed microcomputer was the Altair®; that company lasted only a few years. The TRS-80®, the Texas Instrument®, Commodore®, Heath®, Ohio Scientific®, Digital®, NCR®, IBM®, NEC®, Wang®, Xerox®, and Apple®, to name a few, made their bids, each with their own architecture, operating systems, and marketing ploy. The Commodore was inexpensive, Apple introduced an architecture called MOS 6502® and developed the first floppy drive, Tandy's TRS® utilized its patented TRS-DOS® operating system, and IBM went with the Intel® architecture and IBM-DOS® operating system. There were many other systems and architectures, including Z80®, Motorola M6800®, CP/M®, and Unix® (Phillip Anderson has published an excellent review of all this; we will review his findings more thoroughly in the next chapter). Each new entry perturbed the landscape and forced change in the network of manufacturers. The landscape was tightly coupled and rugged, and change was rampant.

This is ideal for developing technologies because it allows them to rapidly explore their fitness landscape, but matters must eventually settle because good fitness peaks are difficult to find or hold onto in tightly coupled systems. If unique operating systems and architectures could perturb a market forever, the technology would remain forever in an experimental, low fitness state, trying new things for a while then discarding them for a new experiment. To achieve high levels of fitness, a network must settle on one or two technological solutions and develop them.

Networks settle when they become less interactive. The actors shouldn't be isolated from one another, for they will have little incentive for change, but they shouldn't be so tightly interactive that they experience no stability. The actors should be able to perturb each other's landscapes, but not to destroy them. If network interactions are properly tuned (it should come as no surprise that proper balance occurs at the Edge of Chaos), networks will eventually achieve dynamic Nash equilibrium, or environmental stable state (ESS; in Game Theory, Nash is the choice among conflicting choices that leads to fewer losses in the long run; like ESS, it represents stable a relationship among actors in a niche). Once the microcomputer industry settled, the time between innovations lengthened and the microcomputing field became rather stable and rather highly fit. Actors were, however, still sufficiently interactive that perturbations occasionally occurred, as witnessed when Apple sales plummeted in 1996 because of product delivery problems. The big two (MS-DOS and Apple DOS) still compete with style, service, and bells and whistles, thus they still keep each other on their toes, but the landscape is nothing like it was in the late 1970s. Change occurs, but it is controlled. The landscape is sufficiently rugged that changes are possible, but sufficiently stable that high peaks are obtainable.

Loose Coupling and Innovation

Weick's third and fourth observations about loosely coupled structures deal with dissemination of innovation. The third proposes that loose coupling permits local adaptation, and the fourth argues that loose coupling permits experimentation without disruption of the entire network. The downside of both these benefits, according to Weick, is that dissemination is discouraged.

Dissemination refers to the natural movement of innovation through a population. Paul Mort was one of the earliest and most influential dissemination theorists. Mort focused on dissemination in public education. In the late 1950s, he reported that invention initially spreads very slowly in education. Once an invention has spread to about 3% of the population it speeds up, but even so it takes about 20 years to saturate a population. The *NEA Bulletin* reported in 1969 that kindergartens were offered in only 46% of the school districts in America—94 years after their introduction to this country.

Invention can spread more rapidly than this, however. An innovative physics curriculum developed by J. R. Zacharias of MIT in 1956 was rather thoroughly disseminated among public high schools within a decade. This was attributable to a prepackaged program and aggressive training initiatives. Agricultural dissemination models, which include research at land grant universities, agricultural experimentation stations, and agricultural extension programs, are able to spread innovation much more rapidly than are educational networks.

Several researchers have tried to understand why some organizations adapt innovation more rapidly than others. Everett Rogers and Rekha Rogers reported that opinion leaders, people who are influential in getting innovation adapted, tend to be young, educated, cosmopolitan, and of high social status. They are also often viewed as deviants (using Parsons's definition) by their peers. One particular type of opinion leader is called the gatekeeper by Rogers and Rogers. Gatekeepers communicate extensively with people outside and inside the organization. They receive information from outside the organization, filter it, and pass it to colleagues inside the organization.

Richard Carlson studied the nature of innovative school superintendents in the United States during the 1950s. He concluded that the rate of dissemination in a given (geopolitical) state was related to friendship patterns among superintendents. Early adapters tended to be young, were close to relatively few of their peers, received high ratings of professionalism, and sought out administrators outside their geographical state—that is, they fit the profile of gatekeepers. Superintendents with extensive friendship connections in their state were usually late in adapting innovation.

In the chapter on Structural Contingency Theory, we argued that organizational slack permitted "scouts," who are somewhat disconnected from organizational goals, to explore alternative fitness peaks. Scouts are lower in the fitness shell than are other actors and are more likely to have access to "ridges" that connect to other fitness peaks. They are consequently more likely than their colleagues to explore alternative fitness strategies. Gatekeepers serve the same purpose. Like scouts with slack resources, they are not well integrated into the organizational structure. They are a bit less fit, which likely means they are not well supported by internal networks or hampered by internal commitments. They are therefore prone to explore alternate fitness peaks and to provide information and opinions about what they find.

Returning to Mort's findings, does any of this help explain why innovation spreads so sluggishly in some systems but so rapidly in others? Carlson reported that superintendents who were well connected within a system and poorly connected outside their system were slow to change; that is, high internal complexity with its delicate balance of conflicting constraints (high K) and low external complexity (low C, or degree to which systems influence one another) resists innovation. We have also argued that loosely coupled systems—referring to "loose" in the full meaning of that word (low K and low C)—also resist change. Here there is no incentive for change, nor are there channels for the dissemination of change. Rapid dissemination seems characteristic of moderately integrated networks (moderate C) with relatively few internal complexities (moderate K), such as agricultural networks of farmers, extension agents, researchers, and experimental stations. Internal complexity is not so complex that change must be discouraged nor is it so loose that change has no incentive nor outlet for dissemination.

Likewise, external complexity (C) is high enough that the exchange of ideas (mutual perturbation) is encouraged yet low enough that innovation is neither rampant and Chaotic nor stymied by a morass of conflicting constraints.

Darwinian Organizations

Population Ecology Theory argues that change is Darwinian, that the environment judges organizational events, rewarding those that improve organizational survivability and sanctioning those that don't. Much of the work in Population Ecology has looked at just how organizations adapt to different environments.

In 1980, Paul Lawrence and Davis Dyer circulated a working paper in which they reviewed their research on the changes that organizations encounter during their life cycles. Lawrence and Dyer argued that organizations tend to begin their life cycles in markets that are relatively uncluttered by competition and in which entry and adaptation is relatively cheap and easy. Not many organizations can begin life in an industry with prohibitive start-up costs, particularly if the technology will change dramatically as the organization matures. Instead, new organizations first emerge in inexpensive markets, those that require relatively little investment in resources. These sorts of industries can change readily as the market matures because of their low overhead investment. Further, success in these markets typically goes to those organizations that move quickly and grasp fresh opportunities—the first-movers—a tactic that requires fluid, easily modified structure. Population Ecology calls this the r-strategy, or growth strategy, from their work with population growth and the logistic equation (remember $y = rx(1 - x)$, in which r represents growth?).

As markets mature, resources dwindle and environments become more competitive. A maturing market, then, is more dog-eat-dog than are less mature markets, thus it demands more robust forms of structure. In this stage, the strongest competitors are those that can capture resources and use them efficiently. The market is no longer oriented toward the r-strategy; rather, its environment favors a k-strategy (k, in some forms of the logistic equation, refers to absolute population size). Organizations employing this strategy achieve efficiency through greater investment in plant and equipment, increased size and slack, and more elaborate organizational structure. They have traded the ability to change rapidly and capture the first-mover advantage for efficiency and stability.

In the next stage of life, markets are more stable, partially because the environment is dominated by a few large organizations whose relationship with one another is predictable, and partially because the technology has matured to the point that it doesn't change much. Such markets accept few new competitors because the firms that are in the environment dominate. Markets are largely saturated, thus growth is no longer dependent upon competitive advantage; rather expansion requires diversification. Organizations must seek different markets to increase their assets and to avoid loss from environmental perturbation (diversification in the tobacco industry comes to mind). They may do this by expanding to international markets or by diversifying their product lines.

In extreme conditions, when resources and markets are unusually scarce, the environment may favor what Lawrence and Dyer have labeled s-strategy, for stress. Successful organizations develop a tolerance to the stress of arid environments by becoming highly efficient. They typically occupy marginal resource niches and often have almost monopolistic control over resources. To achieve high productivity at low cost, these systems must be highly formal (centralized control) and highly integrated (requiring little supervision). The steel industry or certain parts of the food industry can be found here.

The evolution of nonmanufacturing industries, such as hospitals, research institutes, and universities, is somewhat different. They typically start out as small systems but are pressured toward greater differentiation by technological advances, and finally toward a niche with high uncertainty and relatively few resources by governmental regulation and intervention. In this final stage, they are loosely coupled, organized anarchies.

Cultural Change

Culture has lurked in the wings of modern organizational thought since the 1920s when Elton Mayo conducted his famous experiments at the Bell Wire Operating Room of the Western Electric® plant in Hawthorne, Illinois. In these experiments, Mayo discovered that the level of lighting in the work room—any level of lighting, high or low—improved the productivity of workers. That was counterintuitive for social scientists of that day; increased lighting, they argued, should encourage productivity and low lighting should discourage it. The organizational model in the 1920s maintained that humans were extensions of a larger mechanical process and would behave in direct proportion to appropriate input variables. Mayo's major conclusion from the series of studies surrounding this "illogical" finding was that human attitudes and perceptions—the culture of the work group—are more powerful determinants of organizational behavior than are externally manipulated variables.

Other noted theorists have alluded to culture over the years, but always within the context of their studies of the "harder" sciences of decision making, management strategies, and the such. In the 1930s, Chester Barnard defined *culture* as a social fiction that gives meaning to work and life. In the 1940s, Phillip Selznick defined *institution* relative to meaning, solidarity, and commitment. In the 1960s, Andrew Halpin and Don Croft popularized the notion of organizational climate.

According to Robert Owens, culture was catapulted to the center stage of organizational theory in the early 1980s by two books. The first was William Ouchi's *Theory Z: How American Business Can Meet the Japanese Challenge;* the second was *In Search of Excellence: Lessons From America's Best Run Companies,* by Thomas Peters and Robert Waterman. Ouchi argued that Japanese firms were outperforming American counterparts because of the focus of the Japanese on humanization in the workforce. Peters and Waterman observed that culture and values are the glues that energize successful organizations.

Culture is variously defined, but the thread running through all definitions deals with common perceptions and definitions of reality. Terrence Deal, for example, defines it as "a learned pattern of unconscious (or semiconscious) thought, reflected and reinforced by behavior, that silently and powerfully shapes the experiences of a people." This "provides stability, fosters certainty, solidifies order and predictability, and creates meaning" (p. 301). Edgar Schein defines culture as patterns of basic assumptions that serve the system well enough to be taught to new members as the correct way to perceive, think, and feel in relation to common organizational problems. The perspective of organization derived from Complexity Theory is similar in that it focuses on interactive dynamics and the order that naturally emerges from spontaneously coordinated behavioral "resonance."

Studies of culture and change focus on the complex mix of attitudes, beliefs, perceptions, management activities, technologies, organizational structures, histories, rituals, and symbols that make up a given system. This mix is stable and enduring, thus difficult to maneuver. Successful change agents must adapt a long-term perspective, must be adept at perceiving and manipulating a complex network of symbols and events, and must not be deterred by what might be called "organizational mushiness," or sluggish and unpredictable response (like pushing a massive blob of gelatin).

Richard Snyder, of the University of California in Berkeley, has written about cultural change in the aircraft industry. In 1966, Lockheed® aircraft decided to manufacturer a wide-bodied medium-range passenger jet, the L-1011 TriStar®. The project was immediately beset by setbacks and scandal, however. The first was the bankruptcy of its engine supplier, the Rolls Royce® Company. This led to a financial crisis that was averted only when Congress intervened with a bailout, and that required massive layoffs at Lockheed. Then in 1975, Lockheed was involved in an international scandal in Japan; some questionable payments from Lockheed caused the downfall of Japan's prime minister. All this was financially disastrous for the company and led to a "bloody competitive war" with McDonnell Douglas®. Lockheed lost over $2 billion in that battle.

Throughout, the Lockheed plant at Palmdale, California, which was responsible for the L-1011, was also plagued with problems. It had trouble keeping production on schedule and was significantly over budget, it had expensive problems with product quality, and had suffered a long series of management changes. The plant was well known in the company for the autocratic and demeaning leadership style of its managers. Workers wrote letters to the president of the company complaining about excessive work, dictatorial leadership, and public humiliation from managers. Morale in the plant was low and there were serious hostilities between departments. People were afraid to report accurately on the status of projects, fearing they would be chewed out or even fired.

In 1979, Dale Daniels, a respected engineer and manager with Lockheed, was given responsibility for the L-1011 plant at Palmdale. Daniels made a practice of finding people he could trust and of delegating authority and responsibility to them. He espoused philosophical principles by which he lived ("Don't sell your integrity—it's the only thing that can't be bought"; "You may be better at something than someone else, but you are not better than they are"; "Attack the problem, not the person"; "You don't have to make people do things your way to get performance"; and "When things go wrong, don't shoot the messenger"). Within a week of assuming responsibilities at Palmdale, Daniels distributed a memo outlining his philosophy to everyone in the plant.

Daniels believed in management by walking around; he wanted to get to know the people in the plant, to understand the problems of production, and to tap into the "deep level" of plant dynamics. Initially, workers at the plant were skeptical; they had heard similar stories before. Managers talk a good talk but often fail to live up to their words. Daniels reported that when he first began to walk about the plant, people would avoid him. They were afraid of humiliation or accusations. At times, Daniels had to chase workers down to talk to them. Further, they didn't believe his philosophy, thinking it wouldn't work or that it was simply rhetoric.

Daniels's goal was to turn things around, to change the culture of the plant. He realized that if he were to accomplish those goals, he would first have to dispel the cynical attitudes. Consequently, he put his philosophy into action and insisted that the managers under him do the same. He encouraged workers to report their problems accurately by not sanctioning their failures; he did not allow people to shift responsibilities for problems to others, requiring them instead to deal forthrightly with solutions; he did not belittle employees and refused to let his management team do so. He required that his management team walk the floor, to tap into the deep level of the organization. He got rid of managers who could not adjust to his philosophy.

Second, Daniels realized he would have to build teamwork at the plant. He bought blazers for his management team with L-1011 emblems emblazoned on them; the managers wore them proudly. Daniels and his team of managers initiated a number of production strategies aimed at increasing productivity and controlling costs; the team became quite proud of their results. Daniels realized that positive morale depended not only on good human relations programs, but on effective task behavior as well.

The results were impressive. The attacks between departments, the employee harassment, and the difficulty obtaining accurate information, ceased. Manufacturing hours dropped significantly, costs came down, and the production schedule improved. The plant developed an excellent reputation in the Lockheed industry, and its employees were proud of their association with it.

Daniels changed the culture of the Palmdale plant because he was sensitive to the attitudes, the tasks, the perceptions, and the behaviors that constitute effective culture, and because he understood how to turn culture around. At the L-1011 facility, he did this by clearly articulating his philosophy and by living that philosophy, by assuring that his philosophy was consistently applied by his management team, by modeling desired behavior, by building a team that imbued the desired practices, by monitoring the culture's "deep structure" on the floor of the plant, and by removing technical barriers to production.

CHAPTER 14

Stability and Change at the Edge

▓ The Wild Side of Change

Jon Krakauer, author of the popular non-fiction *Into the Wild,* writes of an eccentric named Gene Rosellini. Rosellini's story is not the thematic tale in Krakauer's book, but the story well illustrates a thematic tale in this book. Rosellini believed that mankind has devolved rather than evolved over the millennia since we first appeared on this planet, that civilization has softened us. He wondered whether modern humans could again live as they had in pre-history, or if we have moved too far from our roots to survive without modern artifacts. Over the decade following his 1977 arrival in Cordova, Alaska, Rosellini tested his hypothesis by living off berries, roots, and seaweed, and by hunting game with spears and snares made from wood and stone. He built the hovel in which he lived by sawing logs with sharp-edged rocks. He endured bitter winters with only the resources at hand. He used nothing produced by society, no metal tools, no store-bought food. He lived as he perceived Cro-Magnon people had lived.

His experiment failed; he couldn't do it. In a letter to a friend he wrote, "I learned that it is not possible for human beings as we know them to live off the land" (p. 75). He decided to embark on a new adventure: he would walk around the world. Before this new experiment began, however, Rosellini committed suicide for reasons we may never know.

Rosellini missed an important point. His inability to keep at his wilderness existence did *not* prove that mankind is unable to return to its roots, for there are too many alternative explanations for what happened to him. One likely candidate for alternative hypothesis emerges from Complexity Theory: Humans are unable to survive a wilderness existence, or any existence, *without the support of other humans*. We've all seen stories in *National Geographic* of present-day primitive tribes living off the wild—it can be done—but I suspect we'll rarely see stories about primitive individuals existing without support from other people. There is little reason to believe that a tribe of New Yorkers or Londoners or Muscovites could not learn to live as primitive people lived, but, as Rosellini's experience suggests, there is reason to suspect that a single New Yorker or Londoner or Muscovite would find it quite difficult.

The difference is networks. People need support from other people; they need to pool their efforts to produce artifacts required for survival; they need backup in case things go wrong; they need to divvy up the various tasks required for survival; they need to hunt in packs to bring down the big game that will provide enough food for the winter; they need spouses to produce offspring and, to paraphrase Hillary Clinton, they need a tribe to protect those offspring. Moreover, for long-term survival they need more: Networks need to interact with other networks—people need to form a network of networks—in order to keep the gene pool vibrant, to learn new, better strategies for survival, and to weather dramatic environmental changes.

These last two points involve innovation and the way it emerges and spreads. The dynamics of innovation require a commerce of ideas among a number of networks. Innovation rarely occurs in isolation, the brainchild of one person's fertile imagination, and even if it were to arise spontaneously, it would require a network of networks to disseminate. As we shall argue in this chapter, typical innovation involves the "implosion" of a variety of separate events. Innovations that emerge in different networks bump into each other because of interaction among those networks, and eventually someone sees how the separate events can be pulled together into major innovation. Complexity Theory—and this chapter—is about networks and about how the dynamics of networks produce fitness and innovation and change.

■ Change That Doesn't Change and Change That Does

Change is one of those things that one can metaphorically pick up in one's hand and turn about to observe its various facets and perspectives. We do just that over the next few paragraphs. We look first at change as random drift, then will define it in its more dramatic forms.

Drifting Stability

Traditional organizational theory is a science of stable systems, but it has never really been comfortable with stability. We've had something of a love/hate relationship with Talcott Parsons's equilibrium model of structure; it appeals to our intuition about the basic stability of social systems, yet we sense that systems are in constant states of flux as well. Open Systems Theory compromises between stability and change by portraying social stability as homeostatic—a moving stability in which systems adjust their internal accommodations to adapt to changing environmental demands. Structural Contingency Theory teaches us how to maintain some sense of stability in a contingent, unpredictably changing world, and Enacted Environment more or less abandoned any notion of stability in organized anarchies. Perhaps it is the either/or mind-set bequeathed to Western society by Aristotle (if A, then not B) that gets in the way of reconciling this issue, for our expectations of change and of stability are unforgiving. We expect systems either to change or not to change, and it's difficult for us to conceive of middle ground.

In our earlier definition of homeostasis for Complex Systems Theory, we argued that stability is actually quite dynamic in a neutral sort of way. We argued in Chapter 6 that a system's range of behavioral options can be pictured as a cloud hovering just below a fitness peak. At any given time a given system's fitness lies somewhere within that cloud, and over time it drifts about the cloud. Biologists call this cloud a stationary fitness shell, and they call movement within the shell, random drift. In the biological time frame, drift within a shell could go on for millions of years; the same drift can be observed in social organizations as well, but the time frame is a bit shorter. Automobiles change more or less gradually, year by year, to accommodate changing technologies or consumer tastes. Preferences in music evolve gradually, responding to whimsical consumer tastes and social mores. Such phenomena can, and do, change radically from time to time—as when rock and roll blew big band and country swing off the music charts in the mid-1950s—but between explosions, they drift.

Humans often assume a deliberative role in this process. They decipher— or attempt to decipher—environmental trends and purposively focus the organization on those trends. The leader's role in random drift is to interpret trends for followers, to help colleagues and subordinates accept and adjust to changes, to coordinate the various elements of change, and to help the system maintain its focus and identity as it drifts. In general, the leader holds the organizational clump together within the fitness cloud and helps it move about within that cloud.

It typically doesn't matter too terribly much where the organization goes within the cloud, for the stationary shell is selectively neutral. Jellyfish would logically become shorter and less sinuous if their environment became more viscous (the Rational Morphology perspective from Chapter 4), but they would likely survive just fine if their structure didn't change or even became more sinuous. Fitness hill climbing is not an issue with drift, thus position within a shell is not crucial. That is, there is not a critical relationship between environment and organizational structure within stationary shells, and organizations that are not crisply in tune with their environments can survive quite well. Were this not the case, systems would have difficulty surviving at all. Firms competing within an environment that demands expensive production procedures, like auto manufacturers, simply could not afford to replace existing technology with every innovation that blew their way. If churches had to accommodate every social flap that came along, they would cease to function as protectors of moral stability and would become trendy country clubs instead. If survival pressures were to force all humans to develop identical academic and performance skills, there would be no Einsteins.

Drift does have a dynamic, fitness-related side to it. Forty-year-olds would find it difficult to survive using strategies that served them 20 years earlier, for example, because shells themselves drift about on their fitness peaks. Consequently, a survival strategy that once lay within the neutral range can drift outside it. Even so, the shell is relatively large, and a system has considerable latitude within which it can drift despite shell drift. Thus one's religious beliefs or a factory's manufacturing procedures often need not change over time.

Stability, then, is what happens within a stationary shell. Stability is not equilibrium, for, unlike equilibrium, stability is somewhat insensitive to the parameters that define it. Equilibrium precisely balances its constituent forces; Complex stability does so only grossly. Complex adaptive systems must have breathing room, they must change. Stability in no way represents lack of change, rather it represents drifting change. It provides that survival latitude that the *CAS* require, and it also provides the connection with the past that is required for learning, analysis, and reproduction.

Drifting stability differs from the homeostasis of Open Systems Theory in that it allows random motion while open systems are supposedly in sync with changing environments. Creativity and innovation emerge from some-what unstructured, idiosyncratic behavior, and the homeostasis of Systems Theory offers only slave dynamics. Neither equilibrium nor traditional homeostasis serves complex adaptive systems, but, at the other extreme, neither does random, unstructured change. Complex adaptive systems thrive in moderately unstructured states of slow change. That's what drifting stability is.

Changing Fitness

Catastrophic change occurs when a system leaves its fitness shell and migrates to another. Catastrophic does not necessarily mean devastating, although devastating is certainly included; rather it refers to any substantive change in structure, behavior, or level of fitness. Catastrophic certainly means technological-level change and may mean organizational-level change. Catastrophic change occurs when systems elaborate their structure, which they do as they mature, or when they change what they do or how they do it. The Coca-Cola Company® experienced catastrophic change when it changed the taste of its soft drink in the 1980s. Sears Roebuck® experienced catastrophic change when it dropped its catalog division in the early 1990s. AT&T® experienced such change when it broke its operations into smaller corporations in the mid-1990s.

Catastrophic change need not be so dramatic, however. Ford Motor Company®, for example, introduced a new body style for its Taurus® in 1996; that change altered its fitness by tapping into a new, sportier market; this qualifies as catastrophic change. When companies diversify their operations, when they expand into new markets, when they alter their technology (as when the microcomputer industry introduces a new generation of chips), when companies change the way they produce their products, they experience catastrophic change.

The metaphors we have used for random drift—stationary fitness shells and parameter space bubbles—help explain. Catastrophic change occurs when a system leaves the shell it is in and moves to another shell on a different fitness peak. In parameter space, catastrophic change happens when a system crosses a parameter wall and enters a new niche.

Catastrophic change occurs readily in Chaotic systems and rarely in stable ones. A Chaotic system is in an area of parameter space where regions are intricately intertwined about one another, where even a small change in parameters might move the system across a bifurcation wall and into a new region. Alternately, Chaotic systems exist on rugged landscapes where a single step can carry the system to dramatically new fitness levels. Public education, which floats in an environment of fickle and impatient public attitudes, can be considered somewhat Chaotic. Highly stable systems, by contrast, exist in large regions of parameter space and can drift for "miles" and "years" without ever reaching a bifurcation wall. Such systems fail to innovate and change (outside of drifting). The American automobile industry existed in such a region during the 1970s, thus they were unable to respond quickly to the Japanese auto invasion. The optimal state is between Chaotic and stable, a state in which parameter regions are sufficiently large to allow relative stability but small enough to permit occasional catastrophic change.

The difference between random drift and catastrophic change is not clean, and it would be a disservice to try to make it clean. Some changes are clearly one or the other—the onset of mob behavior or the decline of the USSR is obviously catastrophic, for example. Others, particularly small changes, may be considered catastrophic from one perspective and drift from another. Taurus's body change, for example, might be defined as drift within the context of broad market forces but be considered catastrophic to the plants that produce that automobile. It depends upon the scale with which one is evaluating.

▓ The Mechanics of Change: Complexity in a Sandbox

In 1989, physicists Per Bak, Chao Tang, and Kurt Wiesenfeld published the results of an elegant and simple little experiment they had concocted. They put together a mechanism that dropped sand, a grain at a time, onto the platform of a sensitive weight scale. As the sand was dropped onto the plate and the pile formed, avalanches would occasionally occur. When the plate was full, the avalanches spilled over the side and could be measured. There were many small avalanches, a few medium sized avalanches, and occasionally there would be a very large avalanche. Bak and his colleagues found that the size of these avalanches plotted as a power law distribution.

Social scientists are familiar with a different sort of distribution, the normal distribution. All sorts of social phenomena are normally distributed— human weight and height, student achievement, IQ, employee attitudes about change, socioeconomic status in a population. With normal distributions, most units in a phenomenon exist at a middle value (the mean) and frequency tapers off as units move away from the mean; the results describe a bell-

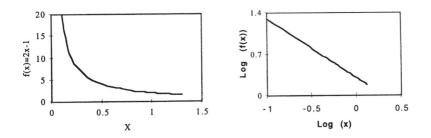

Figures 14.1a and 14.1b. Plot of the power law equation, $f(x) = 2x^{-1}$. The plot on the left (14.1a) was created with raw data results; that on the right (14.1b) was generated by converting raw data to logarithmic equivalents.

shaped curve. The power law distribution is another type of distribution, one that social scientists know little about even though it is descriptive of many social events. This one describes the distribution of art museums according to city size (see Blau, 1995); it describes the size and frequency of cities themselves, it describes the relationship between absolute and perceived noise levels, the extinction of species over the past 600 million years (Raup, 1991), the physical size of species by their frequency, the pattern of intervals in Bach's "Brandenburg Concertos," the nature of aesthetics, the distribution of wealth by individual or of authors by number of books they publish, the frequency of specific words in a novel, and the diameter of trees (see Schroeder, 1991, and West, 1996).

Such distributions are characterized by many small values and few large values. If size of events is plotted against number of events at each size level, you get a line that starts high, drops precipitously, then levels off. Figure 14.1a plots the power law distribution described by the simple equation, $f(x) = 2x^{-1}$. If x in this equation were the size of intervals between the notes in Bach's *Brandenburg Concerto,* and y were the number of times a given interval size is observed, then the plot would indicate that there are a lot of small intervals and few large intervals. Actually there's no "if" about it; this equation does indeed describe the interval sizes in Bach's work. Figure 14.1b is the same plot, but with data on the X and Y axes converted to their logarithmic equivalents. The result is a characteristic straight line.

The presence of a power law distribution suggests something lurking in the background that brings order to events—Adam Smith's invisible hand, or Complexity's (not so?) blind watchmaker. With Bach's "Brandenburg Concerto," that force is the human sense of aesthetics, the fact that we resonate to self-replicating patterns on many different scales but prefer that most of them be small. The distribution of exponentially large numbers of art museums in large cities like Washington, D.C., and Paris is not a function of cultural enlightenment (Washington is surely proof of that), rather it is a function of the explosion of resources—inhabitants, money, tourists, cultural reputation—that accrue to such cities (if this sounds like Brian Arthur's increasing returns, it's because it is).

Change is also described by a power law distribution. The traditional explanation for change is very Newtonian: It is the product of outside force and simple causes. The dinosaurs disappeared because a meteor collided with Earth, public school curriculum changes because researchers discover better ways to teach, and organizations disappear because they are driven out by competition. Actually, dinosaurs probably did respond to a meteor off the Yucatan peninsula; however, my experience suggests that it would take more than a meteor to make school boards respond to educational research. But that's just the point. Few animal extinctions can be explained by outside forces, few policy decisions can be traced to some singular event (Sputniks don't come along all that often), and organizational extinction can be as whimsical as the stock market, particularly among emerging industries.

Bak and colleagues bring a different perspective to the issue of change. First, they suggest that, while the occurrence of change is a random, often unpredictable event, its intensity distribution is not random; rather there is a power law order to the process. If the intensity of change were random, large events would have the same probability of occurring as small ones. Instead, something is reorganizing matters in a non-random fashion, which brings us to the second point to be derived from Bak: Change is controlled by complex interactive forces. A particle of sand in Bak's sandbox is held in place by the particles around it, which in turn are held in place by the particles (including our original particle) around them. That is, there is a network of particles that support one another. A newly dropped grain will probably slide a short distance down the slope of the pile before it is caught by the network. In all likelihood, it will dislodge a few other particles before it comes to rest, and they too must be caught by the network. Most cascades will be caught before damage spreads very far, some cascades will spread a bit before they are caught, and a very few will be quite catastrophic. To some extent, the small cascades even help prevent large cascades, for they redistribute tension before it becomes critical.

The third point that Bak's work suggests is that the magnitude of change is not necessarily related to the magnitude of perturbation. A single grain of sand might start a small landslide or a large one. The size of a slide depends somewhat on the amount of tension that has built up in the system (particles on the edge of going), but major slides can occur when little tension exists. Results are sensitively dependent on initial conditions. Put more simply, it depends on where the particle hits and how the network is connected at the point and time of perturbation.

But this is sand and people are people, so one might ask what this has to do with social change. I propose that social networks possess the same dynamics as Bak's sand, and will spend much of the chapter explaining.

Moderately Coupled Sandboxes

Many of the dynamics that make Per Bak's sand do what it does have been observed in biological ecology by scientists such as Stu Kauffman, John Holland, and Murray Gell-Mann; these scientists have also argued that similar dynamics exist in social systems. The step from animal ecology to human ecology is not a particularly long one. Social systems, like the networks in biology, are moderately coupled (as opposed to loosely coupled). Moderately coupled systems, like grains of sand, interact with one another and affect one another's behavior. The parallels between sand and social behavior aren't clean, of course; grains of sand interact through simple contact, for example, while interaction in social structures is mediated by individual personalities, by policies and procedures, by any of a number of idiosyncratic events. Yet whatever the details in how sandpiles and human systems behave, the broader dynamics are too similar to ignore. Like sandpiles, social systems are vast networks; any given social unit in the network is linked to a limited number of other units; and activity in one social unit can affect behavior in others. Social systems, like the sandpile, experience many small and few large landslides of change. Anyone who has observed fluctuations in the stock market, the behavior of crowds, the dynamics of fads and rumors—anyone who has observed changing social structures has seen the social equivalent of Bak's sandpile.

Moderately Coupled NKCS Systems and Cotillions

In the earlier chapters on loose coupling we related social systems to Kauffman's fitness landscapes in order to refine our perceptions of loosely coupled systems. For example, we discussed the difference between loose and tight coupling, and concluded that systems aren't loose in the sense implied by traditional Loose Coupling Theory (largely absent of interaction), but rather that fit systems are more likely coupled somewhere between loose and tight (moderately coupled). We argued that "civilized," or controlled, organizational change is dependent upon existence at this middling position, and that change is either difficult to achieve or is uncontrolled at the extremes of coupling. We will now expand these notions a bit, but I promise to tie them to Bak's proposals when we are through. What we will see is that Bak's observations are very much related to the dynamics of networks.

Key principles used thus far to guide our hypotheses about coupled systems and fitness landscapes have been based largely upon Kauffman's study of NK systems, or systems of N actors linked K at a time. That model does not account for other species, however—competitors in the environment. In real life, species coevolve, they create environments for one another, they dance together on coupled landscapes. One species' fitness landscape is not determined by that species' evolutionary strategy alone, and its landscape is not fixed. Rather a species' landscape is deformed by activity on other landscapes with which it interacts. If a species of frog develops a stickier tongue, then the landscapes of the insects upon which it preys is deformed—in this case, they shrink to lower fitness levels. If the insects develop "Teflon" feet, the favor is returned.

Prior to Complexity Theory, two hypotheses on interacting, or coevolving, relationships predominated. The first was the "Red Queen" hypothesis, after the namesake in Alice's Wonderland, that suggests that species are in a constant arms race with none ultimately gaining on the others but with everyone running furiously. The other is ESS (also called Nash equilibrium), which argues that species can only race so far and must eventually compromise and stabilize. After all, how sticky can the tongue get before nature runs out of tricks?

To explore all this, Kauffman expanded his network to include S number of species with C links among them. C is a measure of interdependence among species, thus it is similar to Kauffman's P; high C is assigned to species Kauffman wanted to be highly interdependent, and vice versa. That is, C measured the number of characteristics in one species that respond to changes in another species. What he found from his experiments with these networks is that fit systems exist in between Red Queen and ESS at a point one might refer to as dynamic ESS or dynamic Nash, but which we know more generically as the Edge of Chaos.

Kauffman's studies revealed that, unlike NK systems where high internal complexity, K, led to Chaos, coevolving systems can be Chaotic (exhibit Red

TABLE 14.1 State of Systems When *K*, *S*, and *C* Are Varied

		Internal Complexity, K	
Competition, C		*Low*	*High*
and	*High*	Chaotic	Mixed
# Species, S	*Low*	Mixed	Stable

Queen behavior) at *low K*. That's because *C* is now in the driver's seat. If *C* is high, a small change in one species likely deforms, or destabilizes, the landscape of the species to which it is linked. Low internal complexity simply greases the way to instability because conflicting internal constraints, which can hinder change, are removed. High *S*, particularly in combination with high *C* and low *K*, can also generate Red Queen behavior because large numbers of interacting species have difficulty finding stable compromises with one another, and because there are many species to be deformed (see Table 14.1). By contrast, the opposite combination of variables—high internal complexity (*K*) in combination with low interdependence (*C*) and few species (*S*)—is conducive to stability, or traditional ESS.

Dancing and Emergence

Kauffman used his *NKCS* simulations to study the emergence of networks, such as biological niches or communities. In this book, we are interested in the emergence of social communities, of cultures, cliques, and cartels. Kauffman's conclusions spoke of biological species; we speak of the organizational equivalent called comps, from Bill McKelvey's work in organizational semantics (roughly, a comp is an internally consistent, identifiable technology, such as electronic retailing or engineering). We speak also, however, of sub-comps, such as departments in an organization or specializations within a profession. Kauffman asked what happens when actors—species—move in or out of a developing biological niche; we ask what happens when actors—comps or sub-comps—move in and out of a developing social niche. Kauffman had biology in mind when he developed his simulations; we have social structure in mind as we analyze his findings.

Networks, whether biological or social, emerge naturally out of *NKCS* interaction. John Holland introduced his book *Hidden Order* by observing that in any given city there is a vast, interdependent network of grocery stores, clothing stores, banks, service stations, schools, restaurants, malls, factories, transportation services, and repair shops, all dedicated to supporting the inhabitants of the city. Amazingly, these networks, with all their complex intricacies, with their unbelievable levels of efficiency and effectiveness, emerge naturally. There are no committees coordinating the process, deciding what services are required, putting out requests for bids on the various roles, constructing massive Gantt charts (planning flow charts), making sure all the pieces fit together. Actually, one can be rather sure that the best way to ensure that it won't get done is to assign the task to a committee. Our computers would likely burn out attempting to work out the complexities of assembling a modern city, one that can deliver smoked herring and automobiles and espresso on demand, yet cities emerge naturally as if moved by an invisible hand. They emerge from the bottom up, through the interaction of component parts, rather than top down, through the coordination of a central planning committee. How that happens is what Complexity, and this book, is ultimately all about.

Kauffman found that emergence is a process of adjusting, what Enacted Environment theorists call "learning." Ultimately, the outcome of emergence is Nash equilibrium (or ESS in biology), but during the emergence stage, species—or comps—engage in what is called a pre-Nash dance in which they compete for position in the network. One comp in the dance evolves and other comps respond; the responses perturb still other comps, who make adjustments of their own. Change ebbs and flows and reverberates through the immature, emerging network as it struggles to define itself.

Kauffman found that the waiting time before Nash equilibrium occurs is short when the internal complexity of individual players (K) is high relative to the amount of effect comps have on one another (C). Conversely, when internal complexity is less than inter-comp competition $(K < C)$ Nash arrives much more slowly. We noted earlier that high K and low C networks tend to be stable, so emergence under these conditions would logically achieve Nash rapidly; similarly, low K high C networks tend to be Chaotic and the time to Nash under these conditions would logically be very long.

Kauffman also found that players with high internal complexity (K) did better in competitive (high C) dances than did less complex players, but that the low K players benefited from competition with more complex players. After Nash is achieved, less complex players do better, so the best overall strategy in emergent competition is to adopt a low K structure, dance against a high K player, then dominate in the end game.

Kauffman last examined the effect of varying S, the number of comps in a network. He found that the waiting time for equilibrium increased as S increased, and reached a point at which Nash could not be obtained. There were simply too many comps for such a network to find a fit, mutually beneficial Nash. Further, as *S* increases, the mean fitness of the organisms in the network decreases. For particularly large values of *S*, the negative effect on fitness is quite dramatic and can cause the fitness of the various organisms to fluctuate wildly. Under these conditions, some networks, or comps within a network, will visit fitness levels below mean fitness; at this level, a comp is in danger of extinction.

Coevolution: The Emergence of Networks of Networks

Actors enter a dance with raw levels of internal complexity and of competitive overlap with other actors in an emerging network; that is, their initial states are untempered by network membership. Further, the number of actors at the emergent table is usually quite large (there were, for example, a large number of operating systems vying for position during the early development of microcomputers). During this pre-Nash period the network is not very fit: *S* is too large, levels of *K* among the various actors are incompatible with one another, and *C* is random and productive of unstable relationships. Because interdependencies among actors are not evolved and stable, new players can enter the niche without difficulty, and actors can leave the niche without their passing having been noticed. This will change as the system matures.

Notice our focus in these observations about emergence is upon the fitness of the network and not just that of individual comps. Complexity Theory is characterized by its focus upon interdependency and network. These parameters, *K*, *C*, and *S*, are adjusted during the pre-Nash dance to values that maximize the fitness of the network (but that may or may not maximize the fitness of individual actors). The number of actors is culled, species (social or biological) adjust their internal complexity, and the degree of competition among actors is increased or decreased, as needed. If the network starts out Chaotic, it becomes less so; if it starts out deep in the stable regime, it becomes more dynamic. Actors in highly competitive situations will likely become more complex (increase *K*) to resist change; low *K* actors will likely seek out competition against high *K* competitors. Prey will seek to decrease *C* and predators will seek to increase it. They do all this because it is to their myopic advantage to do so. They do it because natural selection presses them to do so. The outcome does *not* necessarily maximize individual fitness, rather it maximizes their fitness in relationship to the network. This is more than evolution; it is, as Kauffman put it, the evolution of coevolution.

When this process of niche building first begins, the particular mix of comps that comes together is not particularly important, and actors enter or leave the mix easily. In the early stages of development the network is readily invaded, for the fitness of the network is little different from that of the ambiance from which it is emerging. Because network fitness is low, most members are threatened by invasion in some manner, and large avalanches of change are common. As the network matures, invasion becomes more difficult. At maturity, invading comps have difficulty surviving in the niche, and most avalanches are quite small. Network fitness is at its peak and outsiders don't "fit in"; on top of that, the system is sufficiently robust—possessing many redundant couplings—that even successful invasion (or extinction) has little effect on the network.

According to Kauffman, the evolution of coevolution can be visualized from yet another perspective. Envision the fitness landscape turned upside down; now instead of peaks there are holes. What you get is called a potential energy landscape by physicists. Physical systems run down, they don't run up like biological or social systems. Hot water loses heat, molecules in a space dissipate, universes run down. Instead of climbing peaks to fitness highs, physical systems descend to low energy states, hence the holes in the potential energy landscape. Other than that, many of the principles that apply to fitness landscapes apply to potential landscapes: The number of holes varies with the complexity of the system, and there are shallow holes and there are deep holes. Systems exist initially on the surface of this landscape, then wind their way downward into the holes. If the landscape is complex, or rugged, the system may very well get trapped in shallow local minima (the opposite of optima) because complex systems are characterized by very many shallow holes and very few deep holes. If the landscape is not at all complex (if it is smooth), the holes are moderately deep but the walls between them are shallow, thus the system wanders readily from hole to hole, doomed never to get a coherent act together.

In a coevolving system of potential energy landscapes, actors perturb each other's landscapes and knock each other out of their holes. Imagine marbles on a vibrating potential surface. Typically they will pop in and out of holes, but as they work their way into ever deeper holes it gets increasingly difficult to pop them out. Eventually marbles find a hole so deep that the vibrations no longer dislodge them. Similarly, actors on coevolving landscapes are not allowed to rest on their laurels. They perturb one another; new actors enter the stage and existing ones leave it; and in the process, actors work themselves into deeper and deeper holes (or onto higher and higher peaks, if you're still imagining a fitness landscape).

Systems on biological or social landscapes aren't bouncing around on a fixed surface with fixed holes, however; rather these landscapes are constantly warping. They aren't just vibrating; the holes are shrinking or deepening, disappearing and appearing. A system may be resting comfortably in a deep hole one day and the next day find its niche has become quite shallow. It may bounce out of a shallow hole that later becomes deep. This happens because systems interact, they change, they compete; and as they do so, they deform each other's landscapes. Frogs develop sticky tongues and insects find their existence in jeopardy. The Americans developed the atomic bomb and the Japanese found themselves out of the war business. IBM® introduced 16-bit processors in 1981, and CP/M®, which was an operating system developed for 8-bit microcomputers, found itself out of buyers. Landscapes do not stand still, they change, and the changes bounce the systems that ride them from hole to hole—or they bounce them out of existence.

The less fit a network of systems is, the more the landscapes within the network perturb one another. Chaotic networks are unfit and must become less Chaotic to avoid wild fluctuations in their landscapes. Such landscapes deform one another so violently that fitness rises and falls at a rate that makes the peaks virtually impossible to climb (or descend, in the case of potential energy surfaces)—they change long before a given species can get to the top. Likewise, exceedingly stable networks are unfit and must become more vibrant. Their high levels of internal complexity (K) create conflicting constraints that leave numerous low peaks representing poor compromises, and their low levels of inter-competition do little to rectify the situation. Fitness is optimal in an intermediate range between Chaos and stability where peaks are as high as possible, where there are not so many shallow peaks that high ones become difficult to find, where peaks don't change so rapidly that they can't be climbed, and where there is sufficient vibrancy to bounce systems off shallow peaks and onto high ones.

Thus the dynamics of interacting landscapes, how readily each is deformed as populations interact, is crucial to fitness. Not only do the internal components of species (K) interact and evolve, but the landscapes on which species exist interact and evolve. It's a two-dimensional process: Species evolve, their landscapes evolve, and fitness is a function of both.

Network maturity is achieved when actors find good peaks from which they are difficult to dislodge. These peaks are not necessarily optimal, however, because the overall network of landscapes is likewise seeking a good peak, and what is optimal for the individual may not contribute to the fitness of the whole. Once the network of networks reaches a fit state, it will remain there.

Each actor in the broader network has found a viable niche, one that doesn't threaten the fitness of others. They have learned how to be fit, how to survive effectively in the community or cartel or niche. Moreover, the network has likewise found a high peak that is viable and stable and unflappable. Both system and network have evolved to the Edge of Chaos.

Fitness and Sandpiles

The mature network achieves an environmentally stable state (ESS), albeit a rather vibrant one. These systems can be perturbed, but not easily. Intruders had an easy time of it in the immature system, but not so in the fit network. Intruders haven't learned the ropes; their internal complexity is wrong, their competitive strategies are off. They find it difficult to compete and to invade the system.

Yet sometimes they do manage to invade, or sometimes the system loses an actor (extinction). When this happens the network is perturbed, and now we return to Bak's sandpile. The actors of a Complex community are linked together in a mutually supportive network, one with many redundant links and dead end paths among its inhabitants. When one of the membership is lost or when outsiders enter the system, the membership adjusts and absorbs, and does so quite effectively because of their fitness and because of the robustness of their networks. Perturbation will typically trigger a landslide, but it is controlled and likely small.

Nonetheless, the system is poised. The state at which it is most fit is poised on a precipice, just at the Edge of Chaos. Bak calls this a state of criticality. The network gains everything by existing here—fitness, stability, vibrancy—but it risks everything too. Perturbation triggers mostly small slides that are quickly absorbed by the moderately loose network of constituent entities. Occasionally, however, perturbations will find paths through the network and trigger somewhat larger slides and on occasion will trigger even major slides. If the system were Chaotic, perturbations would likely cause only major landslides because every intrusion or change in a tightly coupled system reverberates throughout that system. If it were deeply stable there would be no slides, no "life-empowering" change. With either Chaos or stability, there would be no power law distribution, just a flat line high or low (respectively) on the Y axis of a graph. Because the mature system is at the Edge of Chaos where it is sufficiently fit and sufficiently vibrant to deal with intrusion or loss, most landslides are small and only a very few are of any size. Even so, mature networks are exposed to the potential of devastation; it's one of the costs of fitness.

Power law distribution is a footprint, a clue, left behind by the Edge of Chaos. It indicates the presence of a system that is fit but active, one that resists change but that daily subjects itself to the possibility of major change. It exists because something systematic rather than random is going on—random, meaningless words generated by a monkey at a word processor, for example, leave no frequency pattern, but words in a novel do (Zipf's law: Words in a novel that are plotted by frequency describe a power curve). Similarly, random activity in nature leaves no pattern, but adaptive behavior does; that pattern is the power law distribution, and the force that generates the distribution also takes the system to the Edge of Chaos.

We have implied repeatedly that moderate coupling is the operant link between organizational theory and Complexity. We now hypothesize that social structures coevolve with other social structures, and the results include cartels, technologies, financial systems, organizations, and communities. We further hypothesize that these structures emerge and mature by adjusting their levels of complexity and competition, and by winnowing the number of competitors. All this is the product of adaptation to the Edge of Chaos.

▨ Organizations at the Edge: The Microcomputer Industry

Organizational theorist Phillip Anderson has written an interesting PEO perspective of the emergence of the microcomputer industry. We will summarize that story in the next few paragraphs, then reinterpret it using Complex Systems Theory.

The micro industry was born in the mid-1970s with the appearance of the Altair® microcomputer, a simple computer by today's standards that was produced by Micro Instrumentation and Telemetry Systems® (MITS) and debuted in the January 1975 issue of *Popular Electronics* magazine. The Altair was also among the first micros to fail.

There were a number of related technologies already available at the time that micros first appeared. Commercially available mainframe computers had been around since 1952, cathode tube technology emerged in the late 1920s, microprocessors were developed in the late 1960s followed immediately by hand-held calculators—these and many other pieces were developed prior to, and independent of, the development of the micro. The technologies were emerging as small packets in separate parts of a moderately coupled network of industries, and in 1975 the pieces precipitously came together as the microcomputer. This is Stu Kauffman's autocatalysis and John Holland's aggregation. The microcomputer was distinctly different from these constituent technologies and qualifies as a "species" in its own right, separate even from mainframe computers. Micros were clearly cheaper than computers, thus accessible by a broader audience. A more important defining characteristic, however, is that the architectures of micros compete more directly with one another than with the architectures of mainframe computers or calculators.

Architecture is related to the design of the computer's processor and determines the way the machine handles instruction. Architecture accounts for different operating systems and explains why programs written for Macintosh® won't run on IBM machines. The competition in the micro industry during its developmental stage had less to do with different manufacturers than with different architectures. There were, and are, two major micro architectures: that based on the Intel® chip and that based on Motorola's® processor. There were, however, a number of operating systems built around these basic architectures, including the Z80® chip, MOS Technology 6502®, CP/M®, the Apple® system, IBM DOS®, and systems for the Commodore®, Tandy®, Texas Instrument® (TI), NCR®, NEC®, Olivetti®, Wang®, and Xerox®. The early niche was crowded with architectures and operating systems.

IBM didn't enter the fray until 1981—a very long 6 years after the games began. It initially competed in the business market. IBM's operating system immediately shut down CP/M operating systems, which had been the fastest growing segment of the niche, and quickly became the largest and strongest player in the field. Apple had established a strong foothold in the educational market, although its VisiCalc® spreadsheet was quite popular in the business market. Commodore was active in the low-end, inexpensive home computer market, and dominated in Europe. Radio Shack® sold the Tandy, a machine based on the Z80 chip, through its retail outlet. It was successful because Radio Shack's support was everywhere, and the Tandy was a reliable machine. TI attempted to make inroads into Apple's educational market with limited success. Its major strength, however, lay in its chip production.

By the mid-1980s, IBM's architecture was dominant. To survive, other manufacturers adopted IBM's non-proprietary architecture and most of the then-existing architectures faded away. Today most computer manufacturers use the DOS architecture (or the Windows® variation of it).

Apple's architecture was the only other proprietary system to maintain a strong hold in the market. In the mid-1980s it introduced the Macintosh, with its simple and intuitive mouse-based point-and-click system. The Mac® immediately found a place in the niche with desktop publishing. IBM DOS, by contrast, was cumbersome and difficult to learn; and IBM was unable to master simplicity until Microsoft introduced a derivative operating system called Windows. This solution lay on top of IBM DOS, however, and was somewhat clunky before the introduction of Windows 95® and faster machines. Even with that, IBM-based operating systems have not been able to match the simplicity and elegance of Mac OS®, but Windows has been sufficiently satisfactory to ward off the Mac.

Micro-processors, the heart of a computer, have evolved through several technological generations. The earliest chips were able to handle 4 bits of information at a time. This was quickly replaced by 8-bit technology. Macintosh and IBM's initial entry was based upon 16-bit technology, and by the mid-1990s, 32-bit technology was dominant. The transition from 4-bit to 8-bit technology was fairly simple. Sixteen-bit technology was somewhat more difficult to achieve and 32-bit processors were even more difficult to develop. By the 1990s, chips were based on either the Intel Pentium processor or the Motorola Power PC processor. The next level of processor technology is expected to be quite difficult to achieve, and micros are instead differentiating themselves based on less dramatic features such as clock speed and CD technology.

There are a lot of lessons in this story, some of which we'll deal with later in the chapter. The emergence of microcomputers teaches a lesson about dramatic change, the type of change presented by Einstein's Island—our mind experiment from Chapter 1. The appearance of microcomputers seemed to be precipitous, explosive. There were few people dreaming of them in 1974; by 1976 all us dreamers wanted one. It was as if they appeared out of nowhere. But they didn't. The pieces were coming together long before micros were ever envisioned: Cathode tubes were being used in televisions and dumb terminals; microcircuits, microprocessors, and ROM and RAM memory storage chips were being used in hand-held calculators; computer language logic was well documented in the mainframe industry. All the pieces were down at the local Radio Shack waiting for someone to come up with the idea of putting them together. The micro, like most innovative changes, did not appear full-blown out of a void. It was built from the pieces of other innovations, and when a critical mass of development was achieved, someone imploded the pieces and micros were upon us—as if by magic. The same story can be told about copy machines, fax machines, the automobile, the discovery of oxygen by Joseph Priestly, the emergence of the Copernican universe, the downfall of the USSR, and the eruption of riot. The pieces are inevitably there, they simply need to achieve a critical level and come together.

The early micro niche was occupied by a large number of architectural species (S). The internal complexity (K) of most producers was probably rather low—however, the stories about one or two young engineers working out of a garage is an urban folkway, although MITS, the maker of Altair, did originate in a garage as a seller of mail order equipment for airplane and rocket enthusiasts. Nonetheless, many early producers were quite small and were driven by a few engineering personalities. A number of the early micros were kits produced by hobbyist companies (MITS) and companies producing scientific supplies (Heath®, Ohio Scientific®). Few companies emerged exclusively because of the micro revolution; Apple was the more important exception. Larger, more complex, companies emerged later, with IBM being perhaps the kingpin of high K complexity.

Early entries into the burgeoning niche competed directly with one another for markets, but the competition was diluted significantly by the fact that the field was wide open; there was plenty of market for everybody. By the late 1970s, contenders were dividing up the niche: Apple dominated the educational field and was an important player in business; Wang, NEC, and others struggled for dominance in the business arena; Commodore went after the low-end home market; and Tandy sought a broad market that included all the above. C (competition) had increased, but was being controlled at least somewhat by specialization. IBM put an end to all this, however; this manufacturer wanted it all, and eventually its architecture pretty much dominated in all sub-niches. C increased significantly when IBM showed up.

The number of manufacturers grew significantly during the 1980s but the architecture field was gradually winnowed out until it was dominated by only two major players, IBM DOS-based systems and Mac OS. Just as there are different types of canines in the dog world, there are many manufacturers of micros in the micro world. Even so, dogs represent a single species and modern micros have essentially two species (S): Mac and IBM.

There are other classes of species—the peripherals, for example—in the micro network, however, and the number of these species also had to be controlled in order for the micro network to stabilize and become fit. Each micro species dealt with the control problem by establishing standards for peripherals, add-ons, and the such. Mac in particular was noted early on for its standard look and feel; the way one cut and pasted text, for example, was the same from one word processor to another and from word processor to spreadsheet. By establishing such standards, Mac controlled variability in the software produced for its machines. Removable input/output media came in several forms during the early years; the first systems used cassette tape players; the $5\frac{1}{4}$-inch floppy was popular for a while; and TI experimented with ROM cartridges. The market eventually settled on the $3\frac{1}{2}$-inch diskette, but even that may eventually be replaced by CD drives. Mac went with serial output to peripherals and IBM went with parallel output. Technological solutions to different problems were reduced to a manageable few. As if by an invisible hand, S was brought under control by the last half of the 1980s.

Let's pull all this together. Early manufacturers were small and specialized, thus their internal complexity, K, was generally low. As the market developed, the complexity of players within the niche increased. IBM was clearly a megalithic, high K organization. In the early 1980s, the personalities around which Apple had been built and the family atmosphere that bonded it together were replaced by sophisticated business leaders and management strategies better suited to complex organizations—Apple lost its innocence. K was on the increase.

The nature of competition, C, likewise evolved. The market was initially broken into subniches: Apple dominated in education, Commodore went after the home market, IBM was interested in business clients, and Mac made a name in desktop publishing. By the late 1980s, however, these distinctions were blurring—IBM made significant inroads into public education and Mac had quite a few Fortune 500 clients. C was on the increase.

The number of species, S, in the network was initially quite high but was significantly reduced by the late 1980s. There were only two important contenders in the architecture arena, and each micro had controlled the number of related species in its niche by establishing standards for use of their machine.

In the beginning, then, K was low, S was high, and C was inconsequential. This is the profile of a network somewhat in the Chaotic regime. Between 1975 and 1981, K increased slightly, S remained about the same or increased slightly, and C increased—the system was still quite Chaotic but showed signs of moving toward the stable regime. The entry of IBM signaled dramatic increases in K and C, and significant drop in S. By the early 1990s, C was fairly high, there were only two major contenders (S was low), and K was rather high (although internal couplings within the two giants was almost certainly more moderate than tight). This is the profile of a network that is more stable than Chaotic, but there are elements of both regimes—it would seem to be at or near the Edge of Chaos?

The successful invasion of the emerging niche by IBM in 1981 is interesting. At that time the network had been developing for 6 years and was some distance up its fitness landscape. It should have been difficult to invade, but IBM did so with impunity. Three things can account for this. First, IBM was itself quite fit, undoubtedly more fit than the emerging network. True, its operating system was new and the champ in 1981, CP/M, had been around for a while, but IBM was trusted and respected in the business community. IBM already had an excellent reputation with computers, for it was a major supplier of mainframes. It had built-in networks of related technologies whose fitness rivaled and probably exceeded the network being constructed by the other micro producers. On balance, although IBM came late, it alone was probably stronger than the entire network of players that had emerged in the prior 6 years of development.

Second, IBM was a high K player and the other players in the network were generally low K. High K players typically have an advantage over low K players in an emerging network because they are better able to cope with an uncertain environment. On the other side of this coin is the fact that low K actors are aided by play against high K competitors, so IBM may have stimulated rather than depressed the subsequent success of Apple.

Third, and perhaps most important, the micro industry was hit by rather frequent, strong shock waves, or perturbations, during its first decade and a half, and IBM introduced one of those waves. The largest perturbations were created by advances in microprocessor technology (the smaller ones included Apple's introduction of floppy drives, the emergence of CD drives, and the appearance of hard drives, color monitors, and laser and bubble jet printers). As we discussed a few paragraphs earlier, the micro industry has seen several rather dramatic advances in the speed and handling capacity of its microprocessors. At each advance, the landscapes of existing players were severely deformed. Each time, network fitness dropped so precipitously that a number of contenders were forced out, but the lowered fitness also made it easier for new actors to appear (Anderson documents this nicely). IBM entered with the third such advance. The 16-bit processor it brought with it depressed the fitness of the existing landscape, which immediately forced the demise of the CP/M operating system, which had been based upon 8-bit technology. All this greased the way for IBM's invasion. The micro industry was experiencing the evolution of coevolution.

The phenomenon discussed in the last few paragraphs is similar to what Bak saw in his sandpiles. Periods of relative quiescence would be interrupted by what Austrian economist Joseph Schumpeter has called "gales of creative destruction." The gales that battered the early micro industry were rather violent because its network was not very fit, but each gale forced the system up increasingly higher fitness peaks (more on this a little later when we talk about patches).

Fitness in the micro industry was not just a function of improved technology, although that was certainly important. Fitness was also a function of the state of the entire micro network. Network fitness is the product of two interrelated activities: interdependence among actors of the network, and industry commitment to standardized strategies for addressing solutions. The first of these refers to moderately coupled relationships in which the success of each actor is dependent upon the activities of others. The second refers to agreement among, and inertial commitment to, certain strategies for solving common problems. The micro community, for example, "agreed" that $3\frac{1}{2}$-inch floppies were an appropriate storage strategy, and they have committed to the strategy at a level that discourages movement to another strategy. Such commitment allows the technology to advance its effectiveness as opposed to constantly experimenting with infant technologies.

There is one final lesson, this one brief, to be developed from the micro experience. The distance—in time, expenditure of resources, and difficulty—between major technological advances has expanded with each new change. Similarly, the magnitude or significance of changes has become increasingly smaller, focusing more on details such as clock speed or CD speed. This is consistent with what we have learned about fitness landscapes. Early steps up an emerging fitness peak can be large because everything is up and there's a long way to go to get to the top. As the trip progresses, the species looks around for better, more fit peaks, but the more fit the species becomes, the harder it becomes to find better peaks. Further, the better peaks that are found provide less and less advantage over current fitness. Eventually the species is reduced to taking small steps, and even those become increasingly infrequent. The future of a species, or in this case, micro technology, may see a breakthrough into dramatically new landscapes—we may, for example, see a future in which micros utilize many processors instead of just one—but as long as micros remain on their current path, Complexity Theory predicts that progress will continue to slow and to proceed in ever smaller increments.

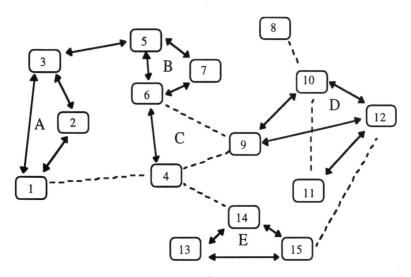

Figure 14.2. A moderately coupled network of networks. Bold, double-headed arrows indicate relatively tight links; dotted lines indicate weak links.

▥ Change and Networks

Let's envision all this talk of emergence and change from a different perspective. Think back to the chapters on loose coupling. Figure 10.1 illustrated loosely coupled networks, and that basic idea is elaborated upon in Figure 14.2, but this time the system is identified as moderately coupled.

In Figure 14.2 there are five small networks labeled A through E: A is composed of units 1, 2, and 3; B is 5, 6, and 7; C is 4, 6, and 9; D is 9, 10, 11, and 12; and E is 13, 14, and 15. Unit 8 is an isolate that is loosely coupled to D. Network C is more loosely coupled internally than are the other small networks, as indicated by the dotted lines. The small networks are coupled together into a larger network of networks by links that are generally weaker than are the links within individual networks.

Controlled Change

If disturbance occurs in network A, that change could migrate to B or C, but it would seem logical that it would go to B because of the stronger link between A and B. From either of these locations it could migrate to D, E, and to isolated unit 8. It not likely to migrate directly from A to D or E, however.

A is walled off from these networks by distance, by formal structure, by regulations, or by differences in roles, just as Kauffman's complex attractors were walled off from one another by forcing structures (see Chapter 7).

Because the networks are moderately coupled with one another, then, most disturbances will be controlled, absorbed. They will not propagate far from their origin. Some, however, will propagate farther into the network, not necessarily because they are more serious than other perturbations have been but rather because they hit the system just so. We discussed the Garbage Can Model of decision making in Chapter 10; we can apply that discussion here. Perhaps a perturbation (problem) in network A caught a decision maker just when a solution he or she had been itching to try out swirled to the top of his or her can. Moments later a person from network C just happened to walk into the office suite and was conscripted into the problem/solution issue by the decision maker. Meanwhile, actors 3 from A and 5 from B had lunch together and before they finished 5 was concerned about the problem. Then the actors in group D approached group B about the issue, and unit 5 said she had heard about the problem already, and discussion ensued. Through a series of happenstances, the perturbation is beginning to penetrate the network, and, like Brian Arthur's increasing return, the problem gains momentum.

The same general principles apply when the perturbation is an innovation. The model predicts that most innovation, like damage, will not radiate far from its source. Now, however, we focus on understanding how innovation spreads in a controlled, productive fashion rather than on how damage is prevented.

In a fit network of networks, one in which both the strength and number of couplings generate a limited number of relatively small, moderately coupled and stably interacting constituent networks (ESS at the Edge), innovation spreads along paths between systems that have logical relationships with one another. An innovation in packaging technology would be less likely to generate collateral change in a hospital's routine than it would in the routine of the provider of a packaged product. If the hospital used that packaged product or used some derivative of the product, it might eventually be affected by the innovation, but that would depend on a somewhat idiosyncratic mix of events and somewhat on tension that may exist in the network.

Network dynamics such as those just described protect the integrity of the broader network. Innovation goes no farther than is needed, for example, and affects only systems that logically should be affected. Imagine the pandemonium if hospitals were directly affected by every innovation in the packaging industry. Controlled dissemination helps assure that won't happen.

Further, the logical evolution of innovation minimizes damage to the fitness of the Complex network. The adjustments made to innovation by one part of a network are related to its own needs and to the needs of other entities that are affected by its behavior. Actors cooperate with one another to accommodate innovation because each is dependent upon functionally related actors for support, and because non-cooperation would disrupt the balance of conflicting constraints, thus lowering network fitness. Ordered cooperation—small pockets of self-indulgent but cooperative adaptation linked into a larger, self-indulgent but cooperative network—evolve.

In Chaotic systems, by contrast, networks are so tightly intertwined that controlled dissemination of innovation is improbable at best. Innovation spreads unpredictably and rampantly, in no logical sequence. Cooperation and deliberation are replaced by mimicry and spontaneity. Such innovation is destructive of the old order. During times of social upheaval, rioters pillage and burn indiscriminately, for something uncontrollable, Chaotic, is in charge. The innovations of Einstein, Copernicus, and Pasteur were so dramatic and the systems they usurped so tensely poised that major, science-changing adjustments were launched. Chaotic change can produce important social transitions, but the process is explosive and change is catastrophic (in the more technical sense of that word as defined earlier in this chapter).

The Complexity process, however, looks and feels rational, and in many ways it is. One can rarely predict when an innovation will catch on and spread and when it won't, but when an innovation does spread, it does so in a fashion that minimizes fitness damage and maximizes control.

Creating Change

There's another side to this innovation and network perspective: The nature of networks at the Edge actually enables, and in a sense, promotes, innovation. Karl Weick argued that the loosely coupled organization permits isolated units to experiment with novel structures or procedures without committing the resources of the entire system. The notion that innovation can emerge in relatively isolated sub-networks implies that innovation would have rough going if the larger network of structures had to be coordinated before it could emerge. That is, small, isolated structures encourage innovation but large, megalithic ones don't. Weick left the story here, but there is more.

Systems in a fit network are not isolated from one another, rather they are only semi-isolated and are interconnected in a web of controlled couplings. Individual systems are identifiable and are somewhat autonomous, and it is because of this, as Weick suggested, that innovation tends to emerge. Simple perceptions about the diffusion of ideas might assume that good ideas appear fully developed from these isolated units, catch on, and spread, while bad innovations languish, but that grossly oversimplifies matters. Rather, different events emerge in different parts of the network. Moderate interconnections among subsystems allow these different innovations and events to interact, they begin to find common niches, and ideas grow into ever bigger ideas. Innovation isn't born fully developed to diffuse throughout a network, rather pieces of innovation emerge within moderately coupled systems; they link a few at a time, then many at a time; and major innovation implodes out of the mass of activity.

In Chapter 3 we discussed autocatalysis, and illustrated by imagining ourselves tying together randomly selected buttons two at a time with pieces of string. Single buttons slowly became networks of two, then networks of three emerged, and so forth. At some point, however, a critical mass is achieved and suddenly relatively small networks became very big networks. This is the essence of what is being argued in this section. Small networks of innovations grow larger and larger, then at some critical mass they explode into very large networks. It happened with microcomputers, as we observed earlier. Numerous technologies emerged over the course of the 20th century—cathode tubes, microcircuits, memory chips, processors, electronic storage and playback, higher-order languages for binary instruction. These pieces began to link with one another in hand-held calculators, transistor radios, tape players, computer terminals, mainframe computers, and the such. In 1975 the networks achieved sufficient critical mass to implode, and the microcomputer resulted.

Replacing Old Networks

Much of the discussion to this point has implicitly presumed that there is little or no resistance to the emergence of a given *CAS,* that a void exists that the emerging system will occupy. This is largely true of technological innovation such as the micro revolution—although one might argue that the microcomputer had to push aside the typewriter and the manual ledger book. Often, however, a well-established system already exists within the niche, and that system may need to be thrown in the trash bin to make room for the new. I suspect that we commonly assume that this is not a problem; a better idea comes along and the old is simply discarded. Matters are hardly as simple as all that. There are plenty of examples lying around of great ideas that cannot make much inroad against older, less effective, but established ideas. High definition TV, for example, or laser disk (or DVD or even 8-mm tape) video technology, or cupped and slotted bicycle seats (we talked about this earlier in Chapter 11). One can, nonetheless, point to other cases where new or better ideas did supplant old ones—CDs have edged out tape cassettes, which earlier displaced vinyl records in the audio industry; rock displaced country swing and big band in the 1950s; free market economy replaced Communism in Eastern Europe in 1989; and digital car radio dials replaced manual band dials in the 1980s. It happens, but how? Some technologies hang on for years in the face of better technologies (VHS video, standard definition TV, manual car radio band dials), while others fall readily (tape stream storage for microcomputers, big band in the 1950s, eight-track audio tapes); why? Finally, why do the conversions from an old idea to a new so often occur suddenly rather than gradually?

Let's first tackle the question of why some ideas fall readily while others have tremendous, almost illogical staying power. The answer has to do with the nature of the network, or *CAS,* that has been built about the idea. Some networks represent tremendous, far-flung investment. The VHS industry illustrates: Millions of people have invested $150 to $400 in a VHS player; millions more have purchased VHS cameras; video stores have invested billions in the purchase of VHS movies; the movie industry itself reaps billions of dollars from the marketing of VHS; to do this, they have invested significant monies into expensive equipment needed to produce VHS tapes; the mining industry would lose significantly if there was significant decline in demand for the iron oxide used to coat video tape. Dismantling such a network is hardly an inconsequential affair, yet dismantling, at least in large degree, would occur if new technology were to replace it. Such industries are difficult to dislodge, even with significantly better ideas.

Other networks are less entrenched, or transition to new ideas can occur without major disruption. The eight-track audio phenomenon of the 1970s, for example, was not firmly entrenched, but more important, the conversion to cassette tape involved the same industries that had produced the eight-track. The change was minimally disruptive to existing networks. Other networks are easy to replace because—while they may be extensive and well estab-lished—they do not represent significant investment. Big band, for instance, was widely popular in the 1930s and 1940s, but was ravaged with impunity by rock and roll in the 1950s. Big band had extensive networks that included fans, radio, the vinyl record industry, record players, and performers. Of these, only the record industry represented significant investment, but it cost that industry no more to produce an Elvis record than a big band record. Record players played both styles with equal clarity, fans change their tastes for free, everyone was buying new records every few weeks anyhow, and performers can be replaced with minimal cost. That industry fell rather easily.

Just what is the process by which change occurs? The answer applies equally to ideas that fall readily and those that hang on tenaciously. One important requirement of change, as we've said frequently in this chapter, is the ability of a new idea to build its networks. Ideas, like the microcomputer, often emerge when different pieces emerge independently, reach a critical point, then collapse together—the autocatalytic dynamic. Yet an idea alone is insufficient, for it needs broader support and nourishment in order to survive. Micros needed retail outlets, software, peripherals, buyers, repair technicians, and practical uses—none of which existed in significant degree when this technology emerged in 1976. A second autocatalytic process had to happen to bring these pieces together. In some cases, the original event is sufficient to trigger the second; this was certainly the case with micros. In others, the original idea is just the start; the broader network must then be constructed, and the idea doesn't become fit, or see broad acceptance, until that network achieves critical mass. A new retailing idea, for example, may languish for years as an at-risk Mom-and-Pop outfit until sufficient networks of loyal patrons, stable suppliers, and related industries reach appropriate levels.

The creation of critical mass networks is technically sufficient to replace an old idea, but in reality there is more. First it is entirely practical for two or more ideas to coexist, to share an environment. That is the case with VHS, 8-mm, and VHS-C formats in the video tape industry; indeed, sharing is not at all uncommon. Holland notes that a defining characteristic of *CAS* is the degree of rich diversity that exists; there is room for more than one approach to a problem or need (*S* must be reasonable, however). There is also an element of the mystical about whether the better idea will catch on and spread. This is the essence of Per Bak's sandpiles: Change has a hit-and-miss quality about it. Success or failure often depends upon how and when a new idea hits; it's often the luck of the draw rather than the quality of the idea. Humans can, of course, help matters along. Aggressive marketing, for example, may tip the scale in favor of success. Even so, human intervention is typically potent only when operating from a strong foundation; that is, an existing network must be in place (as when an existing industry markets its new products) or the proponents of the idea must have built a sufficient network to allow themselves to be heard. Life® cereal was not on the road to flaming success in the 1960s; Mickey, the cute advertising wonder, salvaged it (one should ask how it was that Mickey was such a success, but we can only handle one example at a time). The makers of Life were sufficiently networked that they were able to pull this off. Mom and Pop would have needed extraordinary luck to do it.

Sometimes things are going on with an existing idea that contribute to its replacement. By the Renaissance, the Ptolemaic perspective of the solar system was struggling under the weight of rationalizations; there were too many heavenly things being observed that just didn't fit neatly into a terra-centric system. Copernicus resolved things nicely by placing the sun in the middle and moving Earth to third place out. Newtonian physics was under assault when Einstein came along. Closed theories of organizations were insufficient for explaining Organizational Dynamics, and Open Systems theories opened broad new explanatory vistas. Communism was heavily burdened with conflicting constraints that simply could not be resolved by central coordination; free market was the way out. When a fresh idea builds its network against an ambiance of deterioration in the old, entrenched idea, change is virtually assured.

The final question asked above is: Why does change often seem so precipitous? In 1994, the Republican party in the United States captured both houses of Congress and many state legislatures; the event was sudden and almost without warning. One day the Democrats were strong and in charge, the next day they weren't. Microcomputers appeared seemingly out of no-where in 1976. The USSR died suddenly and unannounced in 1989; in 1988 the Communist regime appeared a vibrant threat to the West, the next year it was gone. Why?

The answer for some precipitous events can be derived from Per Bak's sandpiles. Social systems are poised at the Edge of Chaos, and unpredictable, chance events can throw them over the precipice. Things that have limited impact on the system one day can cause major dislocation the next. Nowhere is this more dramatically evident than in the stock market.

It is probably more usual, however, that things are going on behind the scene that set the stage for sudden change. This something is tension in one form or another. The Black population of Los Angeles in the early 1990s was highly incensed by the Rodney King police brutality case that had been caught on videotape. The tension that existed over the affair was coordinated by media coverage—the video was shown nightly for weeks. The community, consequently, was in a high K state of interaction with the issues. The acquittal of the officers who were involved proved to be the trigger that released that tension. Tension built in pre-World War I Europe over colonies in undeveloped countries and over a rash of mutual defense treaties; that tension was released violently with the assassination of Archduke Ferdinand. Sudden change, then, is often a release of pressures that build up over time. The change is not without history, but often the history and the tension are unsuspected, thus when the tension breaks, people are surprised.

The same general principles apply to the sudden appearance of new scientific and organizational theories. Tension builds in the unanswered questions and challenges that arise about the old theory; concurrently, the different elements of a new theory begin to appear in diverse places and contexts. When these elements achieve a critical mass they implode into new theory, and the old finds itself precipitously out in the cold.

▓ Organizational Structure and Patches

In *At Home in the Universe,* Kauffman makes interesting arguments about the structure of social organizations. He asserts that flatter is better, that decentralized decision making increases organizational fitness, and that hierarchical authority is unable to maximize organizational effectiveness. Actually it isn't these conclusions that are interesting, for they have been debated often in the literature of organizational theory. Rather it is his reasons for drawing these conclusions that now attracts our attention.

Kauffman premises his arguments on his observation that, "[W]hen problems are very hard, thinking may not help that much. We may be relatively blind watchmakers" (p. 202). In complex organizations, there may be too many conflicting constraints among constituent parts for a central authority to resolve. From the perspective of fitness landscapes, there are far too many low peaks ever to find the few high peaks.

Kauffman approached the problem by asking us to imagine social structure as patchwork quilts. Some quilts are simply one large patch, some have many small patches, and others have a moderate number of patches. Each patch acts to achieve its own self-interest, even at the expense of other patches. The quilt as a whole, however, is seeking a compromised state of fitness among its patches that maximizes the fitness of all patches.

Quilts that are composed of many small patches attempt to coordinate too many conflicting constraints. There are simply too many possible combinations of wants and needs to find effective compromise, and fitness is trapped by too many small peaks. The system is Chaotic. Kauffman calls this the "Leftist Italian" phenomenon, after the many competing political parties in Italy.

Quilts with only one large patch can change only if the change is good for all the components of the quilt. This network becomes frozen on low local optima, unable to change and improve itself. This he calls the Stalinist limit after the strong centralized decision-making apparatus in Stalinist USSR.

The optimal structure is a patchwork somewhere between the Leftist Italian and Stalinist limits. Like the Leftist Italian quilt, this social web is still conflict-laden, but it is not so dynamic that order is prohibitive. To elaborate, we return briefly to our earlier discussion of potential energy landscapes—the fitness landscape turned upside down. Potential energy landscapes represent the search by physical systems for low energy states. Physical systems can get trapped in energy states that are separated from other energy states by high energy barriers. That is, they in are too deep to bounce out and seek even deeper holes. The system can only jump the barrier by temporarily increasing its level of energy, which, of course, is bucking the tide of entropy. This is accomplished by a process called annealing; molecules are vibrated or perturbed by some outside force (such as heat from a furnace), causing them to jump out of their holes. Annealing forces the system to jump from hole to hole in a search for ever deeper holes. If the landscape isn't so complex that deep holes are nearly impossible to find, the system will eventually settle into low, stable, energy states. This is what happens when a blacksmith tempers iron. The alternate heating and cooling of metal forces molecules to jump about on their potential energy landscape in search of low energy states; low energy states are stable and the process makes the iron stronger.

Kauffman argues that the same thing, in reverse, occurs on social fitness landscapes. If there are enough patches to present a reasonable number of good peaks but not so many that the search for them is impossible, then decentralized decision makers will eventually find a good fitness peak. Each actor, or patch, makes decisions and, in general, behaves in ways that are self-serving. Self-serving behavior on the part of one patch deforms the landscape of another patch, thus forcing it out of a local optimum. The patches bounce around the landscape, raining on each other's parades and climbing ever higher peaks. The mature system eventually achieves a fit landscape, one that resists perturbation.

At the end of Chapter 10, it was argued that imperfect decision makers bounce from mistake to mistake and peak to peak. Their mistakes are useful for they distort the peaks of others who are searching, forcing colleagues to find new peaks. The stupid in our midst are more than a little aggravating, but thank God for them. They are, after all, part of the larger irrational structure that makes us, ultimately, fit. Perfect decision making draws a system directly onto local optima where it is trapped by the smugness of the leaders who carried it there; imperfect decision makers anneal the organization, forcing it to bounce from solution to solution until tall peaks are found.

More Patches

The picture is a bit more complex than this—something that is certainly not surprising of a theory of Complexity. Kauffman found that if systems have low internal complexity (low K), the best results are found in the Stalinist limit. For simple problems with few conflicting constraints, there are not many small peaks on which to get trapped. This supports what Structural Contingency theorists have concluded: Routine systems, those with predictable raw materials and predictable manufacturing processes, are best served by centralized authority structures. Their environment, internal and external, is not terribly complex and their decisions are easy. The Stalinist approach works in this situation.

For more complex, rugged landscapes, however, organizations are better served if they are broken into smaller patches so that the system is near the phase transition between order and Chaos. Here the system is sufficiently rugged that good peaks are available but not so rugged that they are hard to find. Organizations at the Edge should be sufficiently vibrant and fluid to find the good peaks even though they are moving and deforming because of interaction.

Will knowledge of all this help social leaders? Kauffman argues that there are too many unknowns to allow us deliberately to choose maximally structured patches; the process must be allowed to find its own way to fitness. Knowledge should help us avoid the obvious mistakes, like trying to impose authoritarian leadership on organized anarchies, or failing to try to bring some sense of order to those same anarchies. Knowledge, he says, gives us a rough starting point, but beyond that our best strategy is to get out of the way and let the system seek its level. Sometime the best leader is one who enables rather than gets in the way.

Traditional Theorists on Patches

The phenomenon of patches has gone unspecified but not unknown in traditional organizational theory. Corwin, for example, was getting at the issue in his book, *The Organization-Society Nexus,* when he stated that the "invention of an entirely new approach is more likely to be facilitated by organic forms of organization based on decentralization, flexible rules, and the like" (p. 209). This is related to Kauffman's assertion that problems are sometimes too complex for humans to pre-specify. If you want the system to solve new problems with unique solutions, then turn it loose.

Roger Corwin, writing in 1987, sounds hauntingly like Kauffman and his conclusions from Complexity Theory:

> Every unit within an organization has unique problems. Therefore, all units are inclined to propose changes as a way of coping with their particular problems. However, a change that helps one unit can be detrimental to another. Therefore, when a unit makes a proposal, it will in turn stimulate counter proposals from others, in self-defense. (p. 209)

To this point Corwin has argued precisely what the patches hypothesis argues: Units make self-serving decisions that perturb the landscapes of other patches, who make counterproposals in self-defense.

He continues:

> In support of this proposition, positive relationships were found in one study between the rate of change in programs and (a) the organization's complexity and (b) the number of occupational specialties within it. . . . Given the resistance factor, it follows that the more highly differentiated an organization, the smaller the proportion of proposed innovations that will be adopted in their original form. (p. 209)

Here he argues that the more complex an organization, the more perturbations it experiences. This, as we now know, is a function of the number of conflicting constraints an organization is attempting to juggle. Highly complex organizations are likely never to stabilize on fit solutions, as Corwin hinted when he said that the more highly differentiated an organization, the fewer the number of innovations it adopts.

Patches or Power

Kauffman is a bit naive on this subject of social systems, but of course he is not an organizational theorist and can be forgiven his lapses. As we shall see, even his seemingly glaring oversights are amenable to the patches hypothesis.

His innocence is in assuming that social systems function only on a "fitness" landscape; that is, they are motivated only by effectiveness. Actually there are any number of human motivators, or preferences: There is the powerful power preference, the desire to control; there is the closely related growth preference, or the desire to increase the scope of one's control; there is status quo preference, or the desire to avoid change; and there is prestige preference, or the desire to be admired. Thus we can speak of power landscapes, growth landscapes, security landscapes, and prestige landscapes—to name only a few.

These more discretionary preferences are potent actors in the patches dynamic. People will resist change (the status quo preference) because it threatens their security or their power or simply because they are jealous of others who may have a better idea. Decisions are based upon selfish power agendas or even personal biases. The barriers between peaks on a landscape are composed of more than mere depressed fitness. Further, the peaks themselves are constructed of more than just effectiveness strategies. Rather they are composed of a complex mix of preferences, and the particular mix that defines a given landscape is intimately dependent upon a variety of conditions that can be only somewhat generalized and understood (perhaps we can say, for example, that governmental bureaucracies are primarily driven by power preferences, but that is not uniformly so, even within the same bureaucracy).

However, it really doesn't matter what the peaks are composed of, for the dynamics described by Kauffman still apply. Different preference landscapes, like different species, interact with and distort one another. The behaviors described by each landscape bounce from peak to peak and slowly work their way onto higher and higher peaks. Simultaneously, the landscapes themselves become fitter and fitter. Both individual behaviors and the "network of networks" converge onto a state where high peaks are found. Here different preferences are balanced relative to one another; they achieve the dynamic state of ESS that exists at the Edge of Chaos. Here there is a unique blend of power and efficiency and prestige and effectiveness and security. This blend maximizes the system's "fitness" in a broader sense of the word, a sense that includes all the preferences that drive humans and their behaviors.

▦ Change and *Star Trek*

We began Chapter 13 with a story from the TV series *Star Trek* (the original *Star Trek*) in which Captain Kirk had the opportunity to save a woman he had fallen in love with, but doing so would dramatically change the future—of which he was a product. We asked whether the future were all that brittle that it would change dramatically at the slightest perturbation. By implication we asked whether individuals were really all that important in the affairs of history, even humans to whom we ascribe historical importance, such as Winston Churchill or Genghis Khan. Do individuals shape history or are they merely along for a historical ride presented by complexly interactive events?

Churchill and Genghis Khan evoke the Great Man debate, and as such it is difficult to answer because we cannot manipulate the variables. We cannot put Churchill into World War II to observe what happens, then take him out and observe what happens. Would the RAF pilots beat Goering's Luftwaffe without Churchill's inspiring speeches? Would the British stiff upper lip have been so stiff without Churchill's resolve? Would another prime minister have been able to provide the level of international leadership required to guarantee appropriate levels of support? If Churchill had not been available, would we be eulogizing some other heroic leader today?

Evidence from Complexity Theory, however, suggests that society is far more robust than we credit it being. One could suspect that British resolve pre-dated Churchill, that there were many heroic leaders in Great Britain, that international support would have been behind them. I suspect that great leaders are elements of complex adaptive systems whose strength derives in part from the strength of their leaders (tags) but that derive primary strength from interactive forces.

Yet our central question drifts away from the classical Great Man debate and asks instead about the nature of change and stability in general. How does change emerge in a *CAS,* how does it spread, what dynamics permit change, what are the characteristics of change? In this chapter we found that *CAS* are poised on the edge of change and that the slightest breath of wind can topple them. Most breezes—even gales—have no effect, however, because *CAS* are, by definition, vast networks of interdependent structures, and such interdependency gives strength to a system. *CAS* are robust, not brittle. Nonetheless, a *CAS* is composed of moderately coupled units, thus the potential exists for change to spread throughout the network. If a perturbation hits the system just so, at just the right time, in just the right place, and if the system is in just the right state, the disturbance can work its way through much of the system. Alternatively, if a change has gained momentum and reached a critical level, it can reverberate throughout the system. Dramatic change is entirely within the realm of possibility. By taking the risk of being at the Edge, however, a system, oddly, protects itself from most dramatic changes, and, coincidentally, it receives added benefits of vibrancy, creativity, adaptability, and overall fitness.

So I suspect that a time traveler would have no more effect on the future than would a person living in an era legally. Dramatic change can be sparked by the resources at hand; it does not require a visitor from the future. According to Per Bak's theory, it doesn't even require a significant event, such as might be associated with a great person. Bak argued that massive change can emerge from small events, and that there is no predicting what size "landslide" a small event will precipitate—except that it will most likely precipitate a small slide. Neither Marty McFly (*Back to the Future*) nor Captain Kirk was any more or less potent a grain of sand than most people in the 1950s or 1930s; nor did they have the advantage of critical mass. The societies they visited were fit, stable, and characterized by many overlapping redundancies, thus the probability they would make a difference was remote. But it was possible.

CHAPTER 15

Researching Social Chaos
and Complexity

▓ Growth in Organizational Populations:
A Chaotic Model

Population Ecologists, theorists who use Darwinian Theory to describe social structure, have modeled organizational growth using the logistic equation (see, for example, Guastello, 1992, or Nielsen & Hannan, 1977). Swiss mathematician Cesaré Marchetti found numerous examples of logistic growth in social phenomena, including the productivity of Mozart and the work flow at airports. Biologists use the equation to model the growth of populations within ecological niches. The logistic equation can also model Chaos.

We discussed the logistic equation and its solution in Chapter 12, but will repeat a bit of that discussion here for review. The general logistic equation assumes that population size is determined by two factors: the carrying capacity of the organization's environment, and the growth rate of the organization. The equation is quite simple:

$$X_{new} = rX_{old}(1 - X_{old}) \qquad [15.1]$$

This type of equation is solved by iterating it. Let's set the initial value of X at 0.1 and set growth rate (r) at 1.8 (these starting values are arbitrarily chosen, although the initial X must be between 0 and 1 and r must lie between 0 and 4). The logistic equation can then be solved for the first iteration.

$$X_{new} = rX_{old}(1 - X_{old})$$
$$X_{new} = 1.8 \cdot 0.1 \cdot (1 - 0.1)$$
$$X_{new} = 0.162$$

The population that began at 10% of niche now fills 16.2% of its niche. This new value can be inserted into the right side of the equation as X_{old} to obtain a second-generation value for X_{new}:

$$X_{new} = 1.8 \cdot 0.162 \cdot (1 - 0.162)$$
$$X_{new} = 0.24436$$

The population increases to 24.4% of niche in this round. On the next iteration it will increase to 33% of niche, then 39.9%, 43.1%, and 44.1%. From there it will slowly creep up to 44.4444 . . . %. This, incidentally, is where the population with $r = 1.8$ will wind up, whatever its initial value. For values of r greater than 1 and up to about 2.9, you can determine where the population will stabilize by simply subtracting $1/r$ from 1 (e.g., $1 - 1/1.8 = 0.44444 . . .$).

As we illustrated in Chapter 12, these figures can easily be calculated and plotted on a computer spreadsheet. Figure 15.1 illustrates such a plot using the above calculations—with a few generations added, of course.

The baseline (or X axis) of Figure 15.1 represents time (or generation), and the vertical, or Y, axis represents population size. You can see that the population size takes about seven generations to reach the approximate area of equilibrium (the plateau at the top of the curve).

Figure 15.2 is a far different, and far more interesting, look at all this. In this figure, the Y axis represents population size at final equilibrium and the X axis represents increasing values of r, the growth rate. To illustrate, when $r = 2.5$, the population size stabilizes at 0.60—the population fills 60% of its niche. You can roughly confirm this in Figure 15.2; just draw a perpendicular line from 2.5 on the X axis to the graph line, then straight across to the Y axis. The line will intersect the Y axis at 0.60.

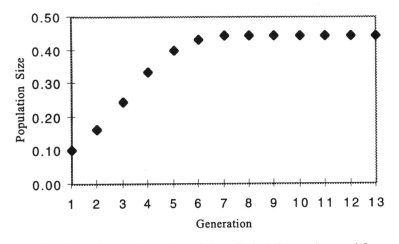

Figure 15.1. First 13 generations of growth from the logistic equation; $r = 1.8$, initial value of $X = 0.1$.

If a population's growth rate does not allow it to create at least one organism for every existing organism (in other words, if r in the logistic equation isn't at least 1), then the population dies out. This can be observed in Figure 15.2; equilibrium is a flat line at zero percent of niche for any r less than 1. Beyond $r = 1$, a population's equilibrium increases regularly with r.

As the growth rate approaches 3.0, the time required to reach equilibrium takes longer and longer (this cannot, however, be deduced from Figure 15.2). When $r = 2.8$, it takes 789 generations to achieve equilibrium (measured to 8 decimal places); if $r = 2.9$ it takes 1,699 generations; and at r equals 3.0, equilibrium does not stabilize beyond two decimal places after 10,000 generations! Then, at a birthrate that is slightly above 3, the equation does something interesting: It "bifurcates," or splits into two equilibrium points. At $r = 3.01$, the population occupies 63% of its niche in one time period, 70% the next, back to 63% on the third time period, and so forth. This is called period 2 equilibrium because the system requires two cycles to return to an original value.

You may want to switch your attention to Figure 15.3—which magnifies just the bifurcation range—for the remainder of this particular discussion.

At about $r = 3.46$ there is a second bifurcation; now the population is cycling among four different population sizes. If this particular phase 4 equilibrium represented the yearly infestation of mosquitoes, then once every 4 years the number of mosquitoes would be murderous (86% of niche), there

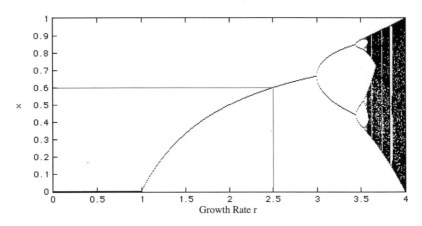

Figure 15.2. Bifurcation diagram of the logistic equation; r ranges from 0 to 4.

would be 1 year out of 4 in which the problem would be tolerable (41% of niche); 1 year would be quite high again (84%), and 1 year out of 4 would be almost tolerable (47%). Phase 8 bifurcation occurs at $r = 3.55$, phase 16 comes close on its heels at $r = 3.556$, and phase 32 begins at a birthrate of 3.569. This is followed quickly by phase 64, then phase 128, phase 256, and so forth.

Then something unusual happens: At $r = 3.57$, traditional equilibrium collapses and is replaced by seeming disorder. Logic would say this shouldn't happen: What looks like random behavior is generated by an equation that should provide perfectly predictable and simple results. It's like discovering that $2 + 2$ is far more complex than originally thought.

Appearances are deceiving, however, and this deception helps explain an important distinction between the disorder of Chaos and more common disorder. Imagine sitting in a grove of trees that have been deliberately planted in straight lines. This is order, the type one gets in the logistic equation when r is less than 3.5 or so. Such order is easy to identify because of its obvious regularity. Imagine now sitting in another grove, but this time you see nothing that looks orderly. You then rise above the trees and look down on them; sure enough, the pattern, as can be seen from this perspective, is random. This represents common disorder.

You can see where we're going with this. Now imagine yourself in still another grove, and again the pattern of growth appears random. Once more you rise above the grove, but this time you discover that the trees have been planted in some pattern, perhaps an "S" shape that folds back on itself, or a

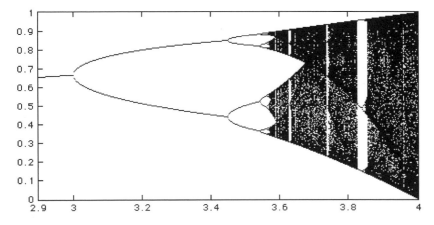

Figure 15.3. Bifurcation diagram for the logistic equation; *r* ranges from 2.9 to 4.0.

complex spiral. This is Chaos. The order is there, but it's difficult to observe without some special perspective. In a bit you will see this complex brand of order in the Chaotic range generated by the logistic equation when *r* is greater than 3.57.

Finding the Order: First We Need a Map

Before we can "find the order," we must talk about phase space portraits and Poincaré maps. We discussed phase space portraits in Chapter 2. These are plots of a system's motion without time being one of the variables. A pendulum's to-and-fro swing, for example, is usually plotted as an undulating line called a sine curve (such a plot assumes that the pendulum reverses direction instantaneously and that it is not slowed by friction). If, however, you were to ignore the time variable, and were to replace it on the *X* axis with the pendulum's position, then you would have a phase space portrait. A phase space portrait for the motion of a pendulum describes a circle.

This phase space portrait is more than a circle, it's an attractor. An attractor is an orbit to which motion gravitates. The process is represented in Figure 15.4; the arrows represent initial positions in the vicinity of the attractor that are moving toward that attractor. The practical side of this is easier to understand; if you flick a swinging pendulum, it will quickly return to its original trajectory. The trajectory is the attractor; when perturbed, a pendulum returns to that attractor.

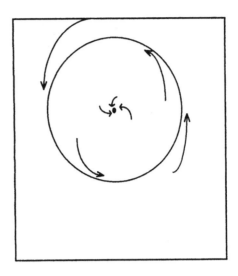

Figure 15.4. Phase space portrait of point and periodic attractors.

The circular attractor is called a periodic attractor because it repeats itself periodically. It's also called a limit cycle. There are a number of variations on the periodic attractor. For example, with three variables, it would look like a doughnut.

There are three other kinds of attractors. One is called the point attractor, and is also illustrated in Figure 15.4. This attractor, logically, is represented in phase space by a point. The point attractor is a system at rest; it is, for example, a pendulum that is not moving. The second type of attractor is the Complex attractor; we discussed it in Chapter 3. The third type of attractor is the Chaotic attractor, and this is what we're trying to work up to. There are, however, a few other things to discuss before we tackle Chaos.

Attractors in phase space are described mathematically by calculus. Calculus defines trajectories in terms of velocity and position at any given point in time. With it, one can trace the path of a cannonball or a planet and predict where either will be at some point in the future; one can succinctly describe the vibration of a guitar string; and NASA scientists use it to determine how to get a rocket to the moon. Calculus can reveal where an object will be and how fast it will be moving at any given point in time—that is, it monitors the moment-by-moment movement of that object.

Calculus is also difficult to master. Henri Poincaré, the famous mathematician who lived at the end of the 19th and first of the 20th centuries, had a simple idea for dealing with the difficulty. Calculus can track, say, the motion of the moon, but, Poincaré would assert, why go to the trouble? Why not insert the equivalent of a large sheet of paper into the moon's trajectory and observe where the object intersects the sheet? A significant amount of information could be derived from such a plot—which, for obvious reasons, is called a Poincaré plot. One could, for example, determine whether a system were stable, and that brings us to the reason Poincaré came up with the idea to start with. It's a story worth reciting, because it adds to what we are attempting to develop.

King Oscar's Reward

In the late 1800s, King Oscar II of Sweden was concerned about the state of the solar system—would the moon ever fall into the Earth, for example, or is it forever in a stable orbit? He was sufficiently interested in the issue that, in 1887, he offered a substantial reward to any scientist who could answer his questions about the solar system. In order for, say, the moon's orbit to be stable, it must, at some point in time, repeat itself. That is, it must intersect a given point at the same velocity and angular position at which it has inter- sected that point in the past. If this occurs, then the moon is in a repetitive orbit; if it intersects this point after five orbits, then it will do so again in five more orbits, then again five orbits after that, and so on forever. Such repetitive patterns are periodic, they are stable. If, on the other hand, the moon's orbit is not stable, there is every possibility that the future may see the Earth and the moon intersect at a common point. A collision is not a guaranteed thing in the absence of stability, but knowing the trajectory is periodic would sure be comforting.

So Poincaré came up with the intersecting plane idea. If the orbit were stable, then the fact would show up on the sheet. If, for example, the moon repeats itself every five orbits, there will be five points on the plane regardless of how long one left the plane in place. If the orbit were three dimensional—it spirals in its orbit, thus creating a doughnut shape if tracked for a period of time—it would create a neat little circle on Poincaré's plot.

There's another convenient sidebar to Poincaré's plot: The math needed to describe it is much simpler than calculus. An indecent background in high school algebra should do the trick. Such equations are called "finite difference equations"; in general, they look like this:

$$X_{t+1} = f(X_t) \qquad\qquad [15.2]$$

Now, like most equations, this one looks formidable, but it's not. It says, simply, that the next value of X is somehow related to the current value of X. In the equation, t refers to time, so $X_{(t+1)}$ is the next value of X; f refers to function, thus the next value of X is a "function" of the current value of X. If $f(Xt)$ is $1.5X$, then the next value of X is 1.5 times greater than the current value.

Our finite difference equations should have one other characteristic: They should be nonlinear. By this we mean simply that they shouldn't graph as a straight line. Chaos is about nonlinear equations, so it is sometimes referred to as *nonlinear dynamics*. The above example, with the function of X set to $1.5X$, is linear, so it doesn't qualify. It's a perfectly good difference equation, but it just won't do the things in which we are interested. One example of a nonlinear finite difference equation is $\phi(t + 1) = \phi + \tau + b \sin(2\pi\phi_t)$. Don't worry, you don't need to know much about this one. ϕ replaces X, which is no big deal—it's still a difference equation; this equation plots as a cross-section of a torus.

One difference equation that you do need to learn more about is:

$$X_{t+1} = rX_t(1 - X_t) \qquad [15.3]$$

Light bulbs should be coming on now; this is the logistic equation that we saw so much of in the previous section, except that X_{old} and X_{new} have been short-handed to X_t and X_{t+1}. Our logistic equation is a finite difference equation, and it plots a Poincaré map. This, then, is the tool we have been looking for to find Chaos.

As already discussed, difference equations are solved by iteration. You probably remember from high school that equations are solved by placing different values of X in the right side of the equation and solving for Y, which is in the left side of the equation. Each X,Y pair thus created is then plotted and connected by a smooth line. Difference equations, by contrast, are solved by selecting an initial value of X for the right side of the equation, solving for X_{t+1}, then substituting the solution back into the equation and repeating the process. The resulting X and X_{t+1} pairs can then plotted against each other (without connecting them with a line) to create a Poincaré map (maps that plot one generation against another like this are also called embedded maps). Figure 15.5 was plotted from the logistic equation with $r = 3.2$ and an initial value of $X = 0.1$. Notice that the spreadsheet portion of the figure shows more data points than are plotted in the graph; that's because the first 17 rows of data represent movement toward equilibrium and consequently are not plotted.

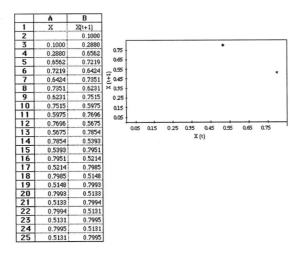

	A	B
1	X	X(t+1)
2		0.1000
3	0.1000	0.2880
4	0.2880	0.6562
5	0.6562	0.7219
6	0.7219	0.6424
7	0.6424	0.7351
8	0.7351	0.6231
9	0.6231	0.7515
10	0.7515	0.5975
11	0.5975	0.7696
12	0.7696	0.5675
13	0.5675	0.7854
14	0.7854	0.5393
15	0.5393	0.7951
16	0.7951	0.5214
17	0.5214	0.7985
18	0.7985	0.5148
19	0.5148	0.7993
20	0.7993	0.5133
21	0.5133	0.7994
22	0.7994	0.5131
23	0.5131	0.7995
24	0.7995	0.5131
25	0.5131	0.7995

Figure 15.5. Poincaré map of logistic difference equation with growth rate = 3.2. Spreadsheet shows values of solutions to the logistic equation.

These early values of *X* are not on the attractor, but are moving toward the attractor. This Poincaré plot shows two points, thus the attractor it represents is a period 2 attractor.

Sheets, Strobes, and Population Growth

We've said that Poincaré maps are like sheets of paper intersecting a trajectory. One can also create a map by taking "stroboscopic" shots of the trajectory. Say it takes 10 seconds for a pendulum to complete a back-and-forth swing; we can create a Poincaré map of this motion in either of the following ways:

- Hold the map in the orbit of the pendulum, in which case the pendulum will intersect it every 10 seconds.
- Observe the location of the pendulum every 12 seconds (or 15, or 5—whatever); do this long enough and the strobe will either begin to recycle through locations it had previously revealed or—if the momentum of the pendulum is out of sync with the speed of the strobe—the points will never repeat themselves and our snapshots will eventually reveal the entire trajectory.

Mathematically, then, you either hold the map within the trajectory of a phase space plot to see if the trajectory intersects it periodically, or you strobe

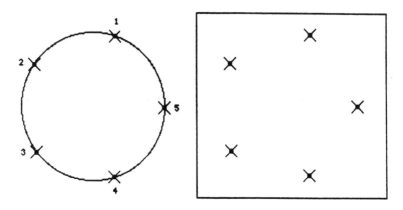

Figure 15.6. Phase space portrait of pendulum motion (10-second cycle) on left. "Stroboscopic" snapshots at 12-second intervals were taken to create Poincaré map on right.

the trajectory to see if the same points appear repeatedly. If a strobed trajectory is not periodic, the points that appear on the Poincaré map will eventually fill out the full trajectory drawn by a phase space portrait. An intersecting trajectory will leave a cross-section of the phase space portrait. The stroboscopic approach is illustrated in Figure 15.6.

The Poincaré plot created by our logistic equation represents stroboscopic pictures. If we converted the logistic equation to a differential calculus equation so that its motion could be plotted, it would draw a parabola in phase space. The motion of a population on the logistic parabola is a bit different than is the motion of a pendulum in its phase space. The pendulum moves completely around the circle, occupying every point once in its swing. A logistic population may move over the entire parabola, it may range over a limited range of the parabola, or it may be motionless. If it is motionless, then a strobe will pick up the population at the same place each time it flashes. If the population cycles consistently within a limited range, two points should be picked up by the strobe. If the motion is a bit more erratic, the strobe might reveal 4, or 8, or 16, points. The motion of the population can be so erratic, however, that the strobe never reveals the same point twice.

The nature of motion in a logistic population is determined by growth rate r. Values of r between 1 and about 3.2 yield motionless, period 1 trajectories (they map as a single point), but as r increases, the population

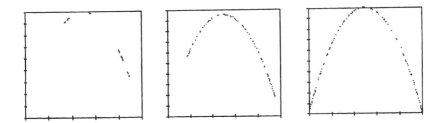

Figure 15.7. Poincaré maps of the logistic equation at different growth rates. From left to right, $r = 3.57$, $r = 3.8$, $r = 4.0$.

moves ever higher on the parabola (i.e., it stabilizes at ever-increasing sizes). When r is 3.2, population size bifurcates and two points are picked up on the parabola. As r increases above this point, the range over which the trajectory swings increases until it bifurcates again. At a growth rate of 3.46, the strobe reveals 4 points; at $r = 3.55$ it reveals 8 points; at 3.556, 16 points emerge, and so on.

When r reaches 3.57, motion becomes so erratic that it is nonperiodic; the same point is never strobed twice. Further, the stroboscopic points appear fitfully, first here, then there; we never know where to expect the next one. One might conclude by observing the emergence of data that the logistic with high r is a random number generator—yet when plotted, the data describe a regular parabola. It is randomly ordered, and random number generators based upon the logistic equation must be used with caution.

At $r = 4.0$ the maximum possible trajectory for the system is drawn on a Poincaré map. Any growth rate larger than 4 would attempt to create a trajectory that just isn't possible—the population is driven either to jump to 100% of its niche, which totally depletes resources and the system ceases to exist, or it eventually jumps to zero and the system ceases to exist.

Figure 15.7 illustrates the Poincaré maps for several Chaos-level growth rates. Note that the full trajectory is a parabola. This is the same plot that would be drawn by the differential calculus equivalent of the logistic difference equation; our strobe has simply filled in enough points on that trajectory to reveal its pattern. This should come to no surprise to those of you who paid attention in beginning algebra. The logistic equation can be algebraically converted to $X_{(t+1)} = rX - rX^2$; this is kissing cousin to the old high school standby, $f(X) = rX - rX^2$; and this is the formula for a parabola.

■ **Organizational Growth (Revisited):
Competition Model**

In Chapter 12, the chapter on organizational growth, we added an additional term to the logistic equation to represent the impact of a second, competing population. That second term is $aX_{old}Y$, and the new, modified equation is:

$$X_{new} = rX_{old}(1 - X_{old}) - aX_{old}Y \qquad [15.4]$$

We could equivalently write this equation in the slightly more condensed form:

$$X_{t+1} = rX_t(1 - X_t) - aX_tY$$

In the extra term, Y represents the size of the second population expressed as a percentage of carrying capacity (unlike X, Y is a fixed value), and a represents the success of the second population in frustrating the efforts of the first (a high value of a, for example, might suggest that Y is outbidding X for market sales). This new term multiplies X_t by Y to represent the degree of overlap between the two populations. If X and Y are both large, X times Y is likewise large; if X and Y are small, the product of their terms is small. The competition variable, a, is then multiplied times this coefficient of overlap in order to estimate the cumulative drain that is exerted by the presence of competition.

This logistic difference equation behaves very much like the regular logistic equation (see Figure 15.8). The major difference is that population sizes are shifted downward a bit—the greater the drain due to competition, the greater the shift, and drain increases with either a or Y. Thus the equilibrium point of the regular logistic with $r = 2.8$ is 0.64, but when competition is added with $a = 0.3$ and $Y = 0.5$, the equilibrium drops to 0.59.

The logistic with fixed competition, like the regular logistic, plots a parabola, but that parabola is compressed a bit to the left (compare Figure 15.8 with Figure 15.7). Furthermore, the growth rate of r is allowed to intensify a little beyond 4.0: At $Y = 0.5$ and $a = 0.3$, extinction doesn't occur until r exceeds 4.15. This trajectory never quite allows X to fill its niche—the best it does is about 95% of niche; this makes sense because some allowance must be made for the presence of a second population Y.

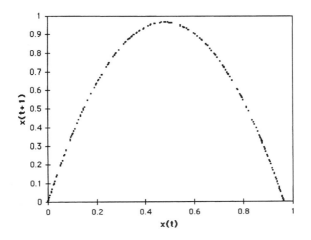

Figure 15.8. Logistic equation with competition term. The initial value of X is 0.01; the competitor, Y, is fixed at 0.5, $a = 0.3$, and growth rate is 4.15 (the maximum growth rate possible in this case).

Predator Organizations

By varying the competition equation, the impact that a predatory organization has on a given prey can be represented. In this scenario, the population size of the predator is not an issue—if the prey is depleted, the predator simply moves on to some other prey and its own population size doesn't suffer. While the predator is occupied with other interests, the prey can of course recoup its losses, but as it gains strength it draws the attention of the predator again, so there is a never-ending cycle of predatory depletion and recoupment. This sort of predator-prey relationship exists between some industries and their source of raw material. The fishing industry, for example, "preys" upon the fish in an area until the fish population drops to the point that further fishing is no longer profitable and the industry moves on to other grounds. Indeed, the equation we are about to describe is a variation of one derived by SUNY mathematics professor Edward Beltrami to explain just this relationship. The equation might also describe the impact of large user organizations on small feeder organizations, particularly if the feeder organizations deal with a limited but renewable resource—farms, for example, or the lumber industry. This equation is:

$$X_{(t+1)} = rX_{(t)}[1 - X_{(t)}] - bX^2_{(t)}/[1 + X^2_{(t)}] \qquad [15.5]$$

In this equation, r, as usual, refers to the growth rate of X; b, which is in the second term, refers to the feeding intensity of the predator. This variable b is the only direct reference in the equation to the prey. The remainder of the second term (following b) is an index of the potential yield to the predator. The actual yield is dependent upon both X and b. If X is high, the potential yield index is, of course, high. However, the predator must take advantage of the potential yield and that's where b comes in. If b is 0 (the predator isn't exploiting the prey), the ultimate size of the prey is determined entirely by the first half of the equation.

This model follows the usual route to Chaos with increasing growth rate, from fixed equilibrium to period doubling, then period 4, period 8, and so forth. When Chaos is achieved, the overall pattern, as was the case with previous models, describes a parabola.

Like the earlier competition model, X's range of behavior is restrained by the second system. In this case, however, the impact is more dramatic: When $r = 3.578$ and $b = 2$, X ranges from a low of near 0 to a maximum of 0.55 (see Figure 15.9; the plot is Chaotic, and any higher value of r will destroy the population). With the simple logistic model, X ranges almost twice as broadly, from 0% of niche up to 100% of niche. The range of X in the predator/prey equation does fluctuate somewhat with b, but except for the highest values of b, there is no particular pattern to the fluctuations. X expands and contracts about 10% at both the high and low ends as b changes, but it does so erratically. At large values of b, however, the system's orbit shrinks to the point that it ranges from only 10% to 30% of niche.

The value of b does not determine whether the system is Chaotic or periodic; only r can do that. When $r = 3.2$, the trajectory is periodic with period 2; by varying b, we can shift the equilibrium points to higher or lower levels, but for all values of b the system remains at period 2.

If b, the intensity of exploitation, increases too high, the target population is killed off, as you would expect. Interestingly, low values of b can, under certain circumstances, also lead to the extinction of a population. When growth rate is particularly high, say 3.63, the predator's feeding intensity (b) cannot drop below 3, for if it does, the prey will overfill its niche and die. The prey actually depends upon its predator to help it avoid over-crowding its niche! Social systems can control this problem by controlling growth rate, however; an industry, for example, can avoid creating excessively large inventories that could overextend its resources and lead to extinction.

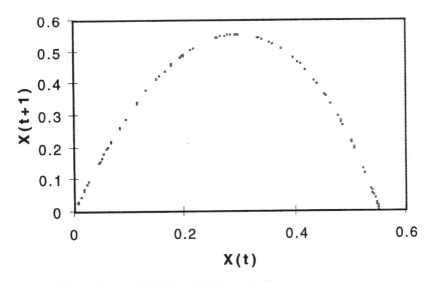

Figure 15.9. Predator model with $r = 3.578$ and $b = 2$.

Interacting Organizations Model

The growth equation can be further expanded to permit fluctuation of a second population, Y. To do this, two growth equations are needed: one to model the growth of population X and one to model the growth of Y. These equations are presented below (Equation 15.6). Each looks very much like the competition equation presented earlier: Both have a term at the end that represents competition from the other ($aX_{old}Y$ represents competition from Y and bXY_{old} represents competition from X). The difference is in how X and Y are calculated. It's a two-step process: First X_{new} is calculated for some initial value of X_{old} and some initial value of Y (you pick that value). This result is then plugged into the second equation, the one that calculates Y. The solution for Y is plugged into the next iteration of X, and so forth. In the equation for calculating Y, variable s is the growth rate of population Y (like r is the growth rate for X), and variable b represents the competitive advantage of X over Y.

$$X_{new} = rX_{old} (1 - X_{old}) - aX_{old}Y$$
$$Y_{new} = sY_{old} (1 - Y_{old}) - bXY_{old}$$

[15.6]

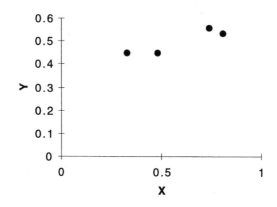

Figure 15.10. Poincaré map of period 4 stability with competing populations. From Equation 15.6; $r = 3.75$, $s = 2.5$, $X = Y = 0.1$, $a = 0.6$, and $b = 0.4$.

When we experimented with these equations earlier, in Chapter 12, we found that growth rate is an important determinant of market share; predictably, as a population's rate of growth increases, its percentage of captured carrying capacity increases. Further, we found that the population with the higher rate will experience the higher equilibrium point. This will be true even if we give the population with the smaller growth rate a bit of a competitive advantage. We also discovered in Chapter 12 that if we set $r = s$ and progressively increase the levels of competition, the overall equilibrium points for both populations decrease. Our experiments further showed that when Y's competitive advantage over X was increased (while maintaining growth rates at equivalent levels), X eventually ceases to exist (the opposite is also true, of course). Finally, we found that when growth rate is pumped high enough, the period-doubling phenomenon that we have come to be familiar with is exhibited.

The discussion in Chapter 12 was limited to growth rates that generate equilibrium or periodic results. If, for example, the growth rate for X is set to 3.75 and that for Y is 2.5 (initial value for both populations is 0.1, the competitive advantage for Y is 0.6 and that for X is 0.4), the X-Y system cycles through four states on a periodic schedule (see Figure 15.10; note that X is plotted against Y instead of against X_{t+1}). Population X is in the driver's seat in this example—its growth rate causes the period doubling because Y's growth rate ($s = 2.5$) isn't high enough to do so.

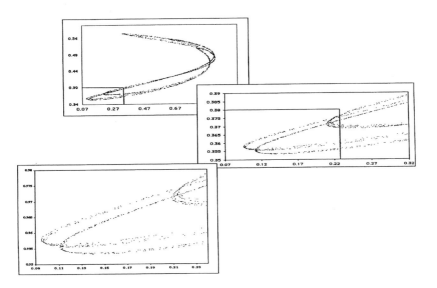

Figure 15.11. Poincaré map of Chaos within competing populations. From Equation 15.6; $r = 4$, $s = 2.5$, $X = Y = 0.1$, $a = 0.6$, and $b = 0.4$. Boxed areas are magnified in contiguous plots.

You should realize by now that period 4 isn't very far from Chaos. By r = 4.0, the two-population model is well within Chaos, as Figure 15.11 illustrates. Notice that Y's share of the niche doesn't fluctuate as much as does X's: Y, which has the more conservative growth rate, fluctuates from a little above 40% to about 65%, while X fluctuates from about 15% of market share to about 90%. X is paying for its prolific growth, but when times are good, they are really good. The wild, unpredictable fluctuations from period to period, however, have to be disconcerting for both populations.

Notice how the pattern in Figure 15.11 seems to be layered, like a pastry. As can be seen from the magnifications of the lower left edge of the image, there appear to be four layers. Later we will see an attractor called the Hénon attractor, which exhibits infinite folding.

Earlier in the chapter we identified two attractors, the point attractor and the periodic attractor. These attractors have several characteristics: They attract motion to themselves, they are finite, and they return eventually to a previously visited site in phase space. Attractors can be represented on Poincaré maps—point attractors map as a single point and periodic attractors map as a finite number of points. The Poincaré maps in Figures 15.7 through 15.9, and now Figure 15.11, represent strange attractors. Like point and periodic attractors, these attractors draw motion and they are stable; but unlike their cousins, their trajectories never visit the same site twice. How can that be, and if true, how can they be finite? Simple: For trajectories drawn by differential equations, it's the layers; for maps drawn by difference equations, it's the points and, at times, it's layers. Make the layers drawn by differential equations fine enough and you can cram an infinite number of them within a finite space. Make the points generated by difference equations accurate to an infinite number of decimal places, and you can place an infinite number of them on a Poincaré map. A highly magnified portrait of a strange attractor in phase space or on a Poincaré map will reveal even more layers or even more points. That's how a trajectory can be finite yet never visit the same site twice.

Three-Variable Competition Model

It's a simple matter to add a third competitor into our system of equations. The individual equations are a bit longer because each has to represent competition from two other systems. Other than that, they're quite familiar, and you should already know how to solve them.

The three-system equations are:

$$X = rX(1 - X) - aXY - bXZ - cXYZ \qquad [15.7]$$
$$Y = rY(1 - Y) - £XY - £YZ - çXYZ$$
$$Z = rZ(1 - Z) - åXZ - βYZ - ¢XYZ$$

Not surprisingly, we again obtain a Chaotic attractor when the growth rate for one or more populations is sufficiently high. In Figure 15.12, the growth rate for X is high enough to generate Chaos, but that for the other two populations is rather small. Even so, the three populations interact in a Chaotic pattern. X, with the largest growth rate, also fluctuates over the broadest range of behaviors ($0.001 < X < 0.93$). Populations Y and Z have the same growth rates (2.5), but because of the interactions of the various competitive factors, Y ranges a bit more broadly than Z and stabilizes at a lower level ($0.26 < Y < 0.51$, and $0.41 < Z < 0.61$, respectively).

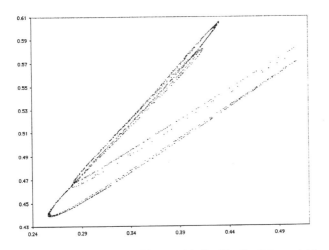

Figure 15.12. Three-variable competition model. $X = Y = Z = 0.1$, $r = 4.15$, $s = t = 2.5$, $a = 0.3$, $b = 0.5$, $c = 0.2$, â $= 0.2$, £ $= 0.4$, ç $= 0.1$, å $= 0.4$, $\beta = 0.4$, and ¢ $= 0.3$.

Cooperation Model

Cooperative interaction between formal organizations or other social structures can be modeled with the following pair of simultaneous equations. The first of the equations is the simple logistic equation with a competition term (X_tY) subtracted from it. The second equation calculates the cost to a second population of doing business with the first. Parameters p and c are constants that index, respectively, Y's profit and costs; pXY_t reflects the profit to Y of cooperating with X, and cY_t represents the cost that Y incurs in that relationship.

$$X_{t+1} = rX_{(t)}(1 - X_t) - X_tY \qquad [15.8]$$
$$Y_{t+1} = pXY_t - cY_t$$

I call this a cooperation model because Y's size is dependent upon the profitability of its doing business with X—despite the fact that it depletes X's resources. Y doesn't exist without X, so cooperation is parasitic. From another perspective, were one to define p and c as X's profit and cost, the equations would model exploitation. In this interpretation, Y is exploited by X in direct proportion to the size of Y; the larger the population of Y, the more intensively it is gathered by X. Edward Beltrami used these equations to model the gathering of fish, thus he saw it as an exploitation model.

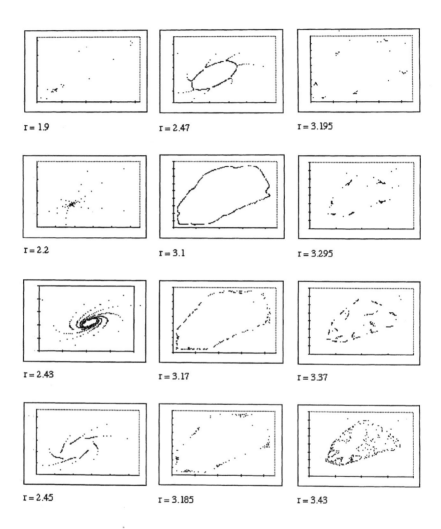

Figure 15.13. Increasing values of r, growth rate, for the profit-cost equation
(Equation 15.8). These particular renditions plot $X_{(t)}$ against $X_{(t+1)}$; similar plots
would be obtained if X were plotted against Y. Read from top to bottom, left to right.
$x = y = 0.1, p = 3.575, c = 0.1.$

The plots for this equation reflect some interesting diversity. The series
of Poincaré maps in Figure 15.13 shows what happens at different values of
r (the growth rate of population X). It is particularly interesting to watch these
maps being drawn on a slower computer—a dynamic I will try to describe.

The map is obtained when $r = 1.9$ first emerges in the upper right quadrant, then moves down a tail toward the lower left and spirals in to a point (in all illustrations, the initial values of x and $y = 0.1$, $p = 3.575$, and $c = 0.1$). A biological or social system with such a growth pattern quickly moves to a stable period 1 equilibrium where behavior is unchanging.

At $r = 2.43$ the maps looks like a spinning galaxy; the initial points draw the seven arms of the galaxy then merge into the oval and spin in a counterclockwise direction. Here the system appears to settle into a regular period 2 pattern, or limit cycle—but that is not the case, as will be seen in a moment.

At $r = 2.45$ the spiraling oval breaks up, then at $r = 2.46$ it reforms again; this time it is a bit larger than before. As before, the arms spiral counterclockwise into the oval, but this time they seem to switch directions abruptly upon reaching the oval and move in a clockwise direction. Also as before, the system almost settles into a limit cycle, but it doesn't quite close up. Rather, the oval is made up of seven different trajectories. When this image first begins to emerge, a point is generated for one of the seven arms, then a point is generated for the next arm (in clockwise direction), and so on. The arms form from the outside to the inside, then the process creates the pieces of the oval itself. The oval itself appears to move in a counterclockwise direction but that is illusory. Points are added in a clockwise sequence, with each segment receiving one point per pass, and the seven segments simply fill out counterclockwise. The system settles eventually into period 7 stability and not into a period 2 cycle. The oval discussed in the previous paragraph, that which emerges when $r = 2.43$, is drawn in a similar fashion, but it does not give the illusion of reversing directions. In both cases, the population sizes of systems described by these trajectories eventually settle and cycle among seven values.

At $r = 2.6$, an oval is formed. It begins as seven sections, then as points are added, the oval slowly takes shape. Motion of the emerging oval is clockwise.

When r reaches 3.37, the oval breaks into six loose clumps. A crude residue of the original oval can be discerned, but its original geometric shape is clearly broken and, interestingly, the system tends toward period 6 rather than period 7 stability.

By $r = 3.43$, the system is apparently Chaotic. This map looks roughly like a tortilla, with the edges of the shell folded over a hollow core. Three-dimensional rendering shows this to be the case. Figure 15.14 shows the form from several perspectives. It is generally deltoid in shape, with multiple folds in the pattern. The behavior represented by this trajectory would appear

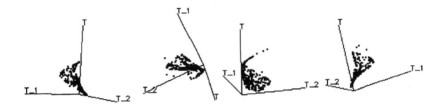

Figure 15.14. Three-dimensional rotation of cooperation models, Equation 15.8.

random from the perspective of those experiencing it. The behavior is, nonetheless, confined and patterned, both of which are indicative of Chaos.

More Chaos

A more complex strange attractor, called the Hénon attractor after its creator, Michel Hénon, is illustrated in Figure 15.15. The logistic system used to produce this map is:

$$X_{t+1} = 1 - 1.4(X_t)^2 + Y_t \qquad [15.9]$$
$$Y_{t+1} = 0.3X_t$$

The multiple folding typical of strange attractors is readily evident upon magnification of this Figure 15.15. The last frame magnifies a minute section of the attractor and reveals that what seemed to be a single line is actually composed of several smaller lines. Were one of these lines to be magnified, it would be found to be similarly constructed. Indeed, the pattern would continue to the limit of the computer's computing power.

■ Testing Social Systems for Chaos

Poincaré maps of real-world data can be generated by the same procedures used with the simulated data in the previous sections. If the data are univariate (if there is only a single variable, or a single stream of data, such as that obtained from the simple logistic equation), then one need merely plot X_t against X_{t+1}. If it is multivariate, like the data from simultaneous equations, then plot one variable against another.

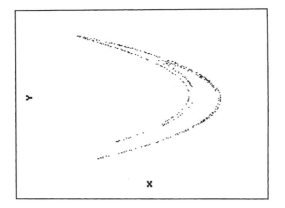

Figure 15.15. Hénon map.

The issue of identifying appropriate data is a bit of a problem in the social sciences. Such data must measure a dynamic over time; there must be some logical reason to assume that any given data point is deterministically related to the data that precede it; measurements must be reasonably accurate; and there must be a large number of measurements (at least 75 data points are needed, and several hundred plus are better). Repeated measures of a person's stress level (heart rate, for example) is good, but the IQ scores of a large group of students is not. The number of parking tickets issued by university campus police on each day during a school year might be appropriate if the number given on any one day is somehow deterministically related to the number given on previous days. Daily test scores of students using teacher-made tests is probably too imprecise, and daily test scores from a standardized test given to the same individuals each day will suffer a familiarity effect. A standardized test given daily to different members from the same population might work, however. Periodic measures of a population's growth rate is good, as are economic indices.

The physical sciences are adrift in such data; there are weather dynamics, concentrations of chemicals in a reaction, populations of animals, thermal convection data—the list is inexhaustible. Such data are readily available for at least two reasons: First, physical phenomena can be crisply measured, and second, physical scientists are schooled to think in terms of fluctuating dynamics. For similar reasons, such data are readily available to economists. Other social scientists are not schooled to think in terms of dynamical data, and at any rate such data are difficult to obtain. These obstacles can be overcome, however, as the few examples in the previous paragraph suggest.

Tools for Finding Chaos

Poincaré maps provide evidence of Chaos, but it is sometimes difficult to determine whether patterns on a map represent random behavior or Chaos. Traditionally, evidence of Chaos is provided by a system's correlation dimension, by its Lyapunov exponent, or by spectral analysis. The correlation dimension is a measure of fractal dimension. The Lyapunov coefficient is a measure of the average convergence or divergence of data points in a system. Spectral analysis folds a time series plot of a dynamical system back on itself every *n* cycles and measures the relative concurrence of those overlays. If a Chaotic system folds back on itself every 10 cycles, then 10-unit sections of the plot of this system should roughly overlap. Note that the correlation dimension, the Lyapunov exponent, and spectral analysis each measure, in varying ways, the degree to which a system stretches or folds back on itself.

These tools are premised upon a unique characteristic of Chaotic dynamics called near stability. Consider two dots on a piece of pastry. Were one to stretch the pastry, the dots would move apart; were the pastry then folded back on itself, the dots would return arbitrarily close to one another. Continue to stretch and fold the pastry, and the dots will return to the same general point in space for a number of cycles. Eventually, the points will lose track of one another and cease visiting the same region in space. This is near stability; the system almost cycles to a stable state, but not quite. Chaotic attractors can carry information about their initial conditions for only so long before it is lost. All three of the tools mentioned in the previous paragraph measure this phenomenon in one way or another.

A number of social scientists have identified problems with these traditional measures of Chaos (see, for example, Brock, 1986; Gilmore, 1995; Scheier & Tschacher, 1996). Among these are the facts that they tend to be somewhat insensitive to Chaos in small systems, they have difficulty with random noise, and the estimation of what are called scaling regions for these calculations is a subjective process. The limited data problem and the problem with random noise make them somewhat unsuitable for social data.

Two recently developed procedures offer promise for dealing with these shortcomings, particularly when these methods are considered together. The first is my own development; I call it the modified Poincaré map. This map helps one visualize near stability by mapping how points emerge. The second, called close return maps, is a more definitive topological procedure for identifying near stability. Not only are these procedures useful with small, noisy data sets, but both are well within the grasp of social scientists who typically are not prepared for the math required of other procedures.

Modified Poincaré Maps

The Poincaré maps created by some of the equations examined earlier (particularly the Chaotic maps from the cooperation equations) show a jumble of dots that are difficult to interpret. Chaos appears to be present—the maps are patterned, finite, and nonrepetitive—but the patterns are complex and difficult to evaluate. This is even more the case with live data, which are typically plagued by random noise. Patterns are easier to observe if the dots are connected as they are created. With modified Poincaré maps, then, data are treated as some sort of massive string art except that string is strung in the order that the anchors are placed.

The outcome must be carefully interpreted. It is tempting to assert that maps generated in this fashion represent actual dynamical trajectories, the same trajectories that would result from differential equations. This is not the case. Rather, these maps reflect patterns in the order that points emerge; they do not necessarily reflect the paths taken by a dynamic to get from one point to another. The parabolic attractor of the standard logistic equation illustrates. Figure 15.16 represents three different logistic attractors with $r = 4$ but with different initial values; as just described, the points that make up this attractor are connected as they are generated. This, and subsequent, figures show the lines smoothed for visual impact. There are differences among the attractors attributable to initial conditions—they wouldn't be Chaotic attractors if there weren't. Nonetheless, the general pattern of point emergence is the same in all three representations; the lines form something of a delta shape that tends to point toward the lower left corner.

The patterns observed in Figure 15.16 reflect near stability. If the points on the parabola had been generated in random locations, the lines would criss-cross in a haphazard manner. Instead, points that begin on the apex of the parabola tend to remain on the apex for a while, and those that begin low on the legs jump back and forth across the legs while inching their way upward. This behavior is not periodic because the trajectories never return to a previously visited location; rather, the dynamics exhibit slowly dissolving periods of near periodicity. They return to the same general area of the image for a while, and then move on to some other pattern or to an interlude of random behavior.

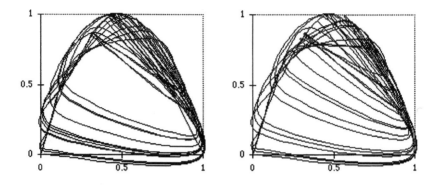

Figure 15.16. Modified Poincaré maps of the simple logistic equation with $r = 4.0$ but with different starting points for X.

Figure 15.17 illustrates the modified Poincaré map with live data, in this case Apple® Computer stock information. The daily increase or decrease in sales volume, labeled delta volume, is plotted; delta volume$_t$ is plotted against delta volume$_{t + 1}$. The repetitive, deltoid-shaped patterns in these figures suggest Chaos, but it is unclear whether points on the trajectories return to

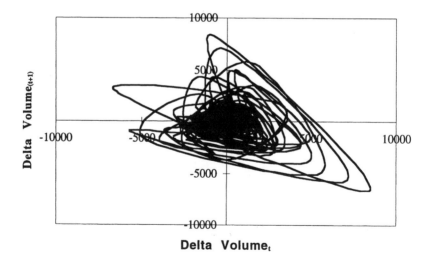

Figure 15.17. Modified Poincaré plot of daily changes in volume sales for Apple Computer stock between 1/4/94 and 12/30/94. Delta volume refers to daily increase or decrease in sales.

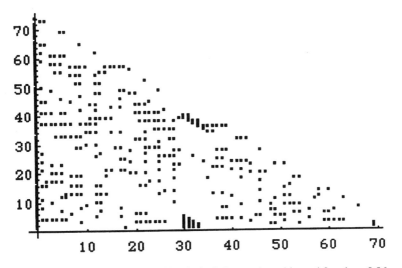

Figure 15.18. Return map generated by the logistic equation with $r = 4.0$ and $e = 0.06$.

roughly the same locations in space as is expected of Chaotic systems. It appears that trajectories tend to loop in one location for several cycles then jump to a different location and repeat the pattern—notice, for example, how the large loops shrink at their "nose" while continuing to overlap on their flanks—but more substantive evidence is needed. These maps will prove valuable, and we will return to them shortly.

Return Maps

Recent work with a topological approach provides more definitive data regarding the presence or absence of Chaos (Gilmore, 1995; Mindlin, Hou, Solari, Gilmore, & Tufillaro, 1990; Mindlin, Solari, Natiello, Gilmore, & Hou, 1991). This procedure, which is called the return map, reveals unambiguous images of patterns of folding that may exist in a data set. From it, one can determine not only the presence or absence of Chaos, but can get some rough idea of the degree of periodicity in the system.

Figure 15.18 is a return map of 75 data points generated by the logistic equation. Despite the very small size of the data set, Chaos is clearly evident in the horizontal lines of this map. Each of the horizontal lines represents near periodic behavior, or trajectories that return close to previously visited points.

Random systems will also generate points on a map, but the points will be spread haphazardly across the map; they will not cycle repeatedly to the same locations and generate the horizontal structures observed in the logistic map.

The y axis of these maps, labeled T, denotes the length in cycles of a given return; thus the horizontal lines at approximately T = 4 represent close return every four generations. If we are modeling the population growth dynamics of mosquitoes, then we are seeing near return every 4 years. The X axis, labeled i, represents the observation index and, consequently, the number of generations over which a close return extends. The point at i = 1 and T = 4 in Figure 15.18, for example, represents the first 4-year cycle in a Chaotic near return; the point at (2,4) represents the second 4-year cycle, and so forth. This particular Chaotic return lasts for six cycles before the stretching process obliterates any predictive information implicit in close return.

The procedure for generating such maps is fairly simple. In effect, it applies one, and if needed, two screens over the data in a dynamical system. The first screen blocks data that are not within a certain critical distance of other data points. The second screen blocks out random noise. All this is accomplished with the following algorithm:

• Calculate the absolute difference between every other data point (point 2 minus point 1, point 3 minus point 2, etc.), then every second data point (3 – 1, 4 – 2, etc.), every third data point, and so on; continue to the final data point (the last datum minus the first). This will produce an $n \times n$ (less $0.5 \times n$) triangular array of data. Each row of the data represents a given cycle length; the first row represents a cycle of 1, or the difference between every other data point, the second represents a cycle of 2, or the difference between every second point, and so forth.

• Find the maximum value in the difference array and multiply it by some small fraction. The fractional value is derived by experimenting; if too large, the resulting map will be dense and uninterpretable; if too small, there will be an insufficient number of points plotted. The fraction will typically lie between 0.01 and 0.1. The value obtained by multiplying the maximum value by this fraction is a critical value labeled ε. This is the first of the two screens; points will be plotted on the return map only if the difference values from step 1 are smaller than ε.

• Compare each of the first-cycle datum from step one with ε; if a given datum is less than ε, graph a point at the coordinates for the difference data. If a given datum is greater than ε, plot a blank at those coordinates. Thus, for example, if the fifth difference in the cycle 1 data is less than ε, a point is plotted at (5, 1); if the sixth difference is greater than ε, a blank is plotted at

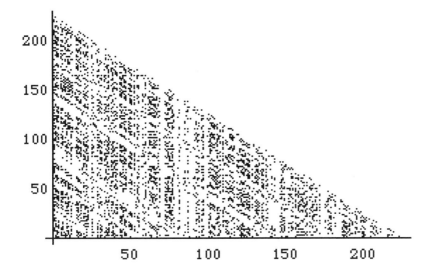

Figure 15.19. Return map of delta volume data from Duke Power stocks during the first 225 days of 1994; *e* calculated with a multiplier of 0.01.

(6, 1). Cycle 2 data are then compared with ε and plotted at (i, 2). In general, cycle T data create a row of blanks or points at (i, T); each line of data is length $n - T$. The result is an $n \times n - (0.5 \times n)$ triangular map similar to Figure 15.18.

Close return maps are generally robust against noise. If, however, it is suspected that the original data are so noisy that Chaos is masked, then recalculate the original data (before differences are calculated) as the mean of each datum plus the next *x* data points. Gilmore (1995) illustrated by introducing noise into a known Chaotic system. Without averaging, the system plotted as randomly distributed points; with averaging, the original structure was largely restored.[5]

Close Return in Live Data

Figure 15.19 is a close return map of delta volume for Duke Power® stock data. The Apple data used earlier (in Figure 15.17) made a good modified Poincaré map, but their return map was only so-so; in contrast, the Duke data made a better return map but a so-so Poincaré map. Both the Duke Power data and the Apple data produced deltoid shaped Poincaré maps (as did other stock data sets examined) and produced similar return maps.

Original volume data, rather than delta volume, were used for the return map. The multiplier used to generate ε is 0.01; data are not averaged for noise. The Chaotic returns are rather clear despite a somewhat heavy background of noise (random dots); the near return at about T = 160 is particularly pronounced. Most returns are rather short, however. Chaos is present, but in many cases it flashes only briefly, then its information is gone.

Because of the heavy background of noise in this plot, the second of the screens discussed above was applied: Each data point in the original delta volume set was averaged with the three points that followed it. The averaging screen helped somewhat, for horizontal lines were a bit easier to observe. Some detail in the close return map was lost, however, and averages over a larger range of data points made matters even worse. On balance, the best plots seem to be the original ones without averaging.

Revisiting the Modified Poincaré Maps

Much of what has just been discussed can be illuminated by the modified Poincaré map generated earlier in this chapter. In the maps generated for the simple logistic equation, for example Figure 15.16, one can fairly clearly see trajectories that begin on the lower right legs, move to the lower left legs, then upward to the top of the parabola, then back again to the lower right leg where the trajectory is roughly repeated. Little wonder, then, that the logistic return map exhibits such strong evidence of Chaos; the trajectories return repeatedly to the same general areas of the Poincaré plot.

The delta volume map of Apple Computer stocks (Figure 15.17) is not so clear. The largest trajectories, those that extend farthest into the lower right quadrant of the modified Poincaré map, approach each other on their flanks, but few trajectories are involved and the close return is of short duration. The patterns in the smaller core of this map suggest that this may be happening at many different scales. Trajectories loop in the same general direction and pass close to one another for short periods of time, then jump to a different trajectory. For the period of time that they closely approach one another, they generate close returns that show up as horizontal lines in the return maps.

However, as these trajectories shift from one pattern to another, a jumble of haphazard intersections and near passes inevitably appears. Instead of a neat, orderly pattern of trajectories such as that seen in the modified Poincaré map for the logistic equation, different patterns criss-cross with no consistent motif. The individual patterns themselves—the sets of deltoids that loop in sync for a while then dissolve—likely show on the return map as Chaos.

Different sets of deltoids may even, at times, be related in a complex, Chaotic dance. Quite likely, though, these relationships are chance and create the random noise seen in the return map. Such intimate but non-Chaotic relationships among different trajectory sets may explain why we were unsuccessful at removing noise—perhaps the noise generated by the overlap can only be degraded by degrading the Chaotic patterns themselves.

■ Complexity Analysis: Counting the Groups in a System

In Chapter 7 we looked at several social data sets to determine whether evidence of Complex stability could be identified. Studies of informal relationships among families in several Central American villages and in group homes for delinquent girls in the United States revealed structures consistent with Stu Kauffman's predictions from Boolean networks: The number of cliques was close to the square root of the total number of participants in the studies. We also examined the number of sections in tax-supported, public personnel agencies and found reasonably good evidence of the square root principle.

Charles Proctor, who did the studies of villages in Central America, used principal components analysis to identify village substructure. Principal components analysis (PCA) is a procedure for reducing a large set of items to a few clusters of items based on the underlying structure of data. Such clusters are often difficult, if not impossible, to identify without such manipulation. One might, for example, administer a set of questions that are thought to measure IQ to a group of children. Data reduction might reveal a cluster of questions that deal with spatial reasoning, another that deals with math reasoning, and so forth. This type of data reduction is a particular type of principal components analysis called factor analysis; it reduces data to clusters that can be identified and named. PCA itself is used to identify the complete structure underlying a data set and not just to identify constructs, so it will typically reveal a larger number of clusters than will factor analysis.

The basic idea behind principal components analysis can be illustrate with a simple two-variable system. If one variable is plotted against another on an *X-Y* coordinate graph, a cloud of points representing coordinate pairs is obtained (see Figure 15.20). The initial axes in this graph are in the normal position at 0° and 90°. There appear to be two clusters in this plot, and indeed that is the case. If the axes are rotated (maintaining their relationship at right

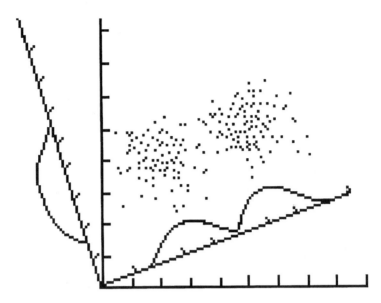

Figure 15.20. Representation of rotation in principal components analysis; based upon work by Simon Haykin.

angles to one another), the clusters can be clarified. Imagine a strong light source above the graph, and another to its right. The light casts a shadow of the coordinate pairs on the respective axes. The shadow on the Y axis shows nothing but a single clump of points, but that on the X axis (particularly after rotation) clearly shows two clumps. That is, a projection of the coordinate pairs onto the rotated axis reveals two clusters of items. Principal components analysis works in just this manner. Correlation matrixes are plotted, then their axes are rotated to create maximum separation among the clusters.

In statistics, principal components analysis is usually applied to a set of variables collected from a large set of subjects. An attitudinal scale might be administered to several hundred individuals, for example; PCA would reveal the structure underlying the questions on that scale. Complexity Theory reverses this notion, however. Here, a group of subjects is given a large set of questions, and PCA is used to identify the response patterns among subjects. In the usual statistical application, variables, such as attitudes, are the focus of interest; in Complexity Theory, the individuals are the focus of interest. Subjects (such as people) instead of questions, are the variables, and the researcher seeks to understand how subjects cluster in response to their reactions to the questions.

I tested this procedure using a database of attitudes among engineering students at a large university. The original data set was organized in the usual manner, with one column per variable and one row per student response. Then the data were transposed so that there was one column per student and one row per question. By doing so, each student, rather than each question, became a variable. There were 41 attitudinal items, which is small for this procedure. Up to 550 variables (students) were available, but with only 41 items (cases), results for so many variables can be tenuous. To be blunt, 41 cases are too few to produce dependable results even with fewer variables, so findings should be treated with caution.

Experiments were conducted with 25, 36, 49, 64, and 100 variables (students). Several samples of each N were drawn from the population of students in the database. The number of clusters obtained in each run was consistent with Kauffman's square root principle: 25 variables consistently yielded 3 to 4 clusters; each sample of 36 variables yielded 5 clusters; 49 variables gave either 7 or 8 clusters; 64 gave 9 clusters, and 100 variables yielded 13 to 14 clusters. Students cluster naturally, as if by an invisible hand, into attitudinal sets, and, although the results should be considered tentative, the number of clusters is an exponential function of the number of students evaluated.

With PCA, one would normally assume that the number of factors that emerge in a population is largely fixed, but in our experiments, the number of factors was clearly a function of N. I hypothesize that the attitudinal "attractors" present among larger samples of students are also present in smaller samples, but that, with the smaller samples, unidentified clusters explain too little variation to be revealed. From a Complexity Theory perspective, using $N = 49$ (7-8 clusters) and $N = 64$ (9 clusters) to illustrate, at least one subaggregate lurks, in primitive form, among the aggregates for $N = 49$, but it has not accumulated sufficient resources to establish its identity. In PCA, accumulated resources would refer to explained variation. From a more conceptual perspective, the subcluster of students is not large enough to be recognized or to exert its presence when $N = 49$. Perhaps some students are dissatisfied with the textbooks used in classes. There may not be enough concerned students in a sample of 49 for that dissatisfaction to be evident; 64 students, however, do provide sufficient mass for PCA to recognize the concern.

A scree plot of eigenvalues helps explain what is happening. Each cluster or factor in a principal components analysis has an associated eigenvalue, and eigenvalues are directly related to the amount of variance accounted for by a

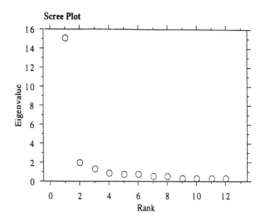

Figure 15.21. Scree plot of student data; $N = 25$.

factor. Scree plots graph eigenvalues by their magnitudes, with the largest eigenvalue plotted first, and so forth (see Figure 15.21). The resulting plot is a power curve—a fact that should ring some bells (see Chapter 14), but more on that in a moment. PCA typically uses the largest of two criteria to decide how many factors to identify as significant: Eigenvalues greater than 1 or 75% variance rule (the first X factors to account for 75% of the variance are identified). Any factors with an eigenvalue less than 1 or that account for the last 25% of variance are of negligible importance. They haven't garnered enough variance to be recognized. The dynamic we are describing here is precisely that dynamic we ascribe to autocatalysis and Complex Natural Teleology. When the data set is sufficiently large that a critical number of variables—students, in the above example—exists for a given factor, they will be recognized as a factor.

As we observed in the last paragraph, a scree plot of eigenvalues describes a power curve. The early factors account for much of the variance and later factors account for little. In the student data, the early factors were the dominant attitudinal clusters; later clusters garnered fewer resources (energy, concern, attention, people). The first factor, for example, might represent students who are concerned about instructional issues, and the ninth cluster might revolve about concerns over textbooks. A large amount of importance would be attached to the unifying issue of this first group and relatively little to that of the ninth. The same general dynamic underlies other power law distributions. The Zipf distribution, for example, observes that some words in a language see a great deal of usage and others see very little. If words are plotted by level of usage, a power law distribution results. Similarly, if factors are plotted against amount of variance explained (eigenvalue), we get a power law distribution. This is a footprint of Complexity.

■ Research on Chaos and Complexity

In this chapter we've developed equations for describing social Chaos, we've looked at procedures that can be used to identify Chaos in social system data, and we have discussed procedures for identifying Complex social structures. It is now time to revisit Einstein's Island.

16

Epilogue on Einstein's Island

We began this book by posing a thought experiment: Would Einstein have derived his famous theorems if isolated from birth on a deserted island with his mother and a library of books (current as of his birth). We assume that his brilliance was innate, thus the only thing he lacked was interaction with other academics and with the discoveries that transpired after his birth.

Our first response should properly be, "I don't know." This is not meant to be a denouement, nor is it meant to be flippant. Like the blind scientists in Chapter 2, we cannot know reality, we can only postulate about it. Niels Bohr said,

> We should doubtless kill an animal if we tried to carry on the investigation of its organs so far that we could describe the role played by single atoms in vital functions. . . . The minimum freedom which we must allow organisms in this respect is just large enough to permit it, so to say, to hide its ultimate secrets from us. (quoted in Pais, 1991)

Science is like trying to explain how a pocket watch works without being able to take the watch apart. One derives hypotheses based on observations, then tests those hypotheses to determine whether they consistently explain or predict the watch's behavior. Science, then, is our best shot at explaining reality, it is not reality itself. What Bohr said about the biological sciences is many times more descriptive of the social sciences.

However, we can now say how Chaos Theory and Complexity Theory perceive reality in this thought experiment. Both see structure and behavior as the product of interactive dynamics. Newtonian physics, which ruled prior to Einstein, was supported by a vast network of scientists who taught their science to their students, whose journals dominated the scientific landscape, who rejected science that didn't march to their drumbeat, whose hypotheses couldn't see beyond the confines of Newtonian physics. The tapestry of this physics derived strength from its interdependent structure. Newtonian physics was a complex adaptive system that emerged from the dynamics of Complex Natural Teleology in the 1600s.

Think about how difficult it would be to switch from gas driven to electric powered automobiles. The extensive infrastructure that supports the gasoline engine would have to be dismantled and a new infrastructure constructed for electric cars. For all that, the switch from a horse driven society to a gas driven one likewise waited some time after the invention of internal combustion engines for the development of an infrastructure of service stations, gasoline producers, auto sales networks, and auto producers. The television was invented in the 1920s, but didn't catch on until the 1950s; it awaited the construction of a supporting infrastructure and faced formidable competition from radio. Cable TV exploded onto the market only after enough cable was laid to develop sufficient revenue for widespread dissemination. In each of these illustrations, the technology is not sufficient in and of itself: Success requires more than a better idea, it requires a network of support. Old networks, with all their commitments and interdependencies, have to be dismantled before new technologies or ideas or movements or cultures can take hold, and that is no trivial task.

The same general idea was true of Newtonian physics and Einstein's relativity: The existing infrastructure had to be dismantled and a new one constructed. The dynamics are a bit different than with new technologies. Newtonian physics was ultimately crushed by its own limitations, for it simply could not be forced to explain the physics of very fast or very small objects (extremely small things are the province of a still later science called quantum physics). Its hypothesis that an "ether" existed that carried light beams would not hold up under Michelson and Morley's experimentation. Newtonian physics stumbled over Lorenz's observations regarding shrinkage of rigid bodies and Maxwell's work with electromagnetism. At the end of the 19th century and the beginning of the 20th, Newton was under attack; scientists were dismantling an old infrastructure and laying the framework for a new one. When that process achieved some critical mass, Einstein came along, pulled the pieces together, and, with brilliant insight, discovered relativity.

The new infrastructure, however, emerged during the years that *our* Einstein was marooned on his island. He was not part of that network and was not privy to its findings. Thus we can conclude that he would not have produced his momentous theorems, and today someone else would wear his mantle of genius (for it was inevitable that Newtonian physics would give way to the new physics—indeed, David Hilbert was working on a theory of relativity at the same time as Einstein).

The dynamic that our Einstein would have missed out on is called phase transition by Complexity Theory. Systems derive strength from networks of support and from existing commitments. Organizational theory calls this inertia; it has also been called culture. Cultures define the worldview of their participants; Newtonian physics defined the proper set of hypotheses for its scientists and blinded them to alternative hypotheses; a social clique defines the correct way to dress, the right things to say, and the proper people to be seen with; a highway rat pack holds its participants captive to the will of the whole. Culture and inertia, then, are networks of events, ideas, and people that derive lasting strength from the interdependency of their participants. Such networks resist change and will typically remain viable and appear strong almost to the day of their demise. That is, apparent change is not necessarily gradual; one does not see the old order slowly fade away and the new order gradually strengthen. Rather, matters are precipitous; the old dies suddenly and the new emerges overnight. This is phase transition.

There are behind-the-scene dynamics that presage a phase transition explosion, however. Back there, the old order is being chipped away. It can tolerate the chipping for it possesses considerable redundancy and robustness. At the same time, a new order is taking root, building its network piece by piece. The building process is autocatalytic; that is, each new piece combines with other pieces to catalyze ever-newer structure. The process is slow, laborious, with little observable result at first. Yet eventually it reaches a critical point where one new piece, one new idea, one brilliant insight, one new pair of Kauffman's linked buttons, creates explosive growth.

A graph of this whole process looks almost like a big Greek letter Chi; it's actually a pair of logistic plots moving in opposite directions, with time represented on the X axis and strength (of behavior, structure, organization, idea) on the Y axis (see Figure 16.1). One line, then, represents a system that begins strong, declines slowly for a while, then takes a fitness plunge. The

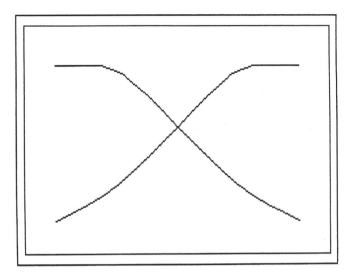

Figure 16.1. The decline of an existing network and the emergence of a new one.

other line represents a system that is doing just the opposite: It begins weak, gains strength slowly, then grows explosively to a fit equilibrium point.

The real Einstein was part of the explosion, indeed he was the spark and the flame thrower. He was also privy to, and part of, an emerging network of new knowledge, knowledge that simultaneously destroyed the old order and built the new. He existed in a rich intellectual environment, one that undoubtedly debated the disturbing findings about Newtonian physics. He read the journals and the books on the emerging issues. He was part of the academic community and that community was changing.

Our marooned Einstein was not part of the movement. Like Gene Rosellini, the eccentric wilderness hermit introduced in Chapter 14, it is unlikely that he could have changed the scientific landscape in isolation. Rosellini attempted to "prove" that the primitive side of mankind has been lost to centuries of civilization, that we can no longer survive off the wild. What he proved instead (if he indeed proved anything) was that humans cannot survive under any conditions without a support network of other humans. Similarly, Einstein could not have created new theory without a community of academics building the support structure for his discoveries. Without the likes of Michelson and Morley and Maxwell and Lorenz, Einstein was just another brilliant Newtonian physicist.

▨ Complex Systems Theory

The point of all this has to do with the nature of complex adaptive systems, or *CAS*. Such a system is strong and robust; its many interdependencies and complex networks of behavior and support imbue it with a degree of fitness and strength that resists perturbation, invasion, and usurpation. This was the state of Newtonian physics in the 19th century, the USSR for most of the 20th century, the vinyl record industry prior to the 1970s, radio entertainment in the 1920s, 1930s, and 1940s, the Democratic party in the United States prior to 1994, equestrian transportation prior to the 20th century, U.S. automotives prior to the Japanese invasion of the 1970s, the stock market prior to 1987. It continues to be the state of democracy, the automotive industry, standard definition television, the VCR industry, the microcomputer industry, and the public education model. Each (and of course the list is far from inclusive) emerged initially just as Einsteinian physics emerged: Bits and pieces began to form, or aggregate; the aggregations found each other to form meta-aggregates; and so on. Eventually the mass of linkages reached a critical mass, and all the meta-aggregates imploded into the super-aggregate with which we are familiar. Such implosions are typically precipitous; they appear almost overnight and seemingly out of nowhere.

They tend to die the same way, seemingly healthy one day and gone the next. Michael Crichton's best selling novel *The Lost World* (his sequel to *Jurassic Park*) was about this issue of Complexity Theory and extinction, but Crichton "sold out" to Newtonian causality in the end—his dinosaurs were dying from an infection of prions, or Mad Cow disease. According to Complexity Theory, real extinctions—whether biological or social—more typically result from one of two phenomena. Either the system experiences an unlucky mishap that catches the network just so and reverberates throughout the system, or a better system emerges at the same time as, or because, the old system is crumbling (in a variation of this, a new system can emerge and be so compelling that it undermines the old). Radio entertainment, vinyl records, and equestrian transportation were undermined by more compelling ideas; the new ideas built their networks of interdependency, and when they achieved critical mass, they precipitously drove out the old. Newtonian physics, the USSR, and the Democratic party in the United States lost touch or crumbled under inconsistencies and failures, and new *CAS* emerged and took their places. The stock market took a nose dive in 1987 because it was caught just so—Per Bak's sandpile phenomenon.

All this is attributable to complex social systems. Complex adaptive systems emerge from the dynamics of Complex Natural Teleology—a process that summarizes interaction among autocatalysis, teleology, physics (other than that associated with autocatalysis), and natural selection. The *CAS* is a differentiated network of sub-networks, each of which maps a given part of the *CAS*'s environment. The sub-networks are moderately coupled into a holistic system that transcends the summed capabilities of the parts. The *CAS* is fit because of the strength attributable to network, because each subaggregate evolves to a state of fitness that serves the needs of that subaggregate while simultaneously accommodating the needs of other subaggregates, and because the system evolves its internal and external couplings in such a way that good fitness peaks are available to the system as a whole. It is because the *CAS* is what it is, experiencing the dynamics that it does, that emergence and extinction occur as they do.

▓ Other Puzzles

In the conclusion to Chapter 1, a number of puzzles were posed. Some of them seemed perhaps trivial while others seemed truly perplexing. All of them, however, asked questions that could be answered by Complexity Theory, and the reader should now find them neither trivial nor perplexing. Why indeed did the USSR collapse so suddenly in 1989? How did the stock market manage to surprise us with a nose-dive in 1987? If evolution (or free-market capitalism) is really just a matter of the survival of the fittest, then why should it ever produce anything other than ruthless competition among individuals? Was Churchill right, that history is "just one damn thing after another"? Why is it so difficult to implement our 5-year strategic plans as they were designed to be implemented? Why do organizations sometime make bad decisions when issues are far from ambiguous? How is it that social systems, like mobs and rumors, are coordinated as if controlled by an invisible hand? How does social order emerge, anyhow? Answers can be found in our discussions of phase transition, in Brian Arthur's increasing returns, in Stu Kauffman's coevolutionary simulations and fitness landscapes, in Per Bak's sandpiles, in Edward Lorenz's butterfly effect, in our discussions of the nature of dynamic stable states, in "survival of the cooperative," in Craig Reynolds's flock of boids.

   Churchill was wrong: History is not one damn thing after another. Social life on this planet is a beautifully serene, stable network of interdependencies. Like the writer of Ecclesiastes in the Old Testament said, there is a time and a place for everything within that serene network. Just as the seasons come and go with regularity, history ebbs and flows with haunting strains of déjà vu.

But Churchill was also right: History is one damn thing after another. Each season brings its surprises, stock markets collapse without warning, and dictators appear out of nowhere to embroil us in destructive conflict. Social life is stable but dynamic, regularly undulating yet forever surprising us. Churchill is both right and wrong because society balances itself on the brink of Chaos. It is poised such that the slightest event can, potentially, create havoc. Yet it walks this tightrope because it is here that society is most robust, and only here could it survive calamities. The Edge of Chaos is indeed a strange place.

Notes

1. Boolean algebra, developed by mathematician George Boole about 1850, allows one algebraically to manipulate logical statements. The answer to such a statement is either true or false. "If A AND B, then C" is a Boolean expression that states that C is true only if both A and B are true. "If A OR B, then C" states that C is true if either A or B is true. Boolean logic is most commonly used in computer programming.

2. We define a specialist as one who performs a specific task; such a person requires only enough training to perform that task. The term *specialist* might be used differently by other theorists. Max Weber, for example, defines it much as we do. Richard Hall (1991), however, defines specialist as a highly trained individual with a broad range of skills—which is our definition of a generalist.

3. This works for Chaotic systems—Complex systems are somewhat more stable and predictable than are Chaotic ones, however. The Lyapunov exponent has been applied with some success to Complex social systems such as stock markets; more research is needed to determine its applicability to more overtly Complex systems such as those observed in formal organizations.

4. Existing literature on Chaos theory and social organization has made much of "sensitive dependence on initial conditions," or the "butterfly effect." Essentially, these arguments have invoked the butterfly effect to suggest that organizational behavior is highly unpredictable. Sensitive dependence is certainly a cornerstone of Chaos theory and is undoubtedly its best known tenant (moviegoers may remember the reference to it by the mathematician in *Jurassic Park* when he defined Chaos theory for the other characters), but Chaos theory involves much more than this. More important, to the extent that social systems are Complex rather than Chaotic, the butterfly effect is muted, more stable. Moreover, it is compromised by the fact that Complex attractors are loosely coupled—small and relatively isolated. To wit, social theorist should be cautious about indiscriminate reference to this phenomenon.

5. A word of caution: Plots generated by this algorithm should not be re-sized unless they can be re-rendered in postscript; otherwise, the relationships among points will be distorted. Further, the graphs generated from the stock volume data for this chapter could be reproduced accurately only with a 600 dpi (or finer) printer; detail may be lost with anything less than a 600 dpi printer.

Annotated Bibliography of
Books and Articles

Arthur, W. B. (1989). The economy and complexity. In D. L. Stein (Ed.), *Lectures in the sciences of complexity* (pp. 713-740). Redwood City, CA: Addison-Wesley.

Reading level: moderate
Brian Arthur argues that economy is better modeled by increasing return (them that has, gets more) than by decreasing returns, which is more traditionally accepted in economic circles. Increasing returns means that it is not necessarily the best product or service or technology that will rise to dominance, rather it is the product or technology that has an initial advantage in the market that is more likely to succeed. He provides numerous examples, and presents arguments about why this is true.

Bak, P. (1996). *How nature works*. New York: Copernicus.

Reading level: easy to moderate
This book represents a discussion of his criticality hypothesis that is geared to the general reader. Bak describes his sandpile experiments and the principles underlying them. He then applies the results to diverse phenomena, including highway traffic patterns, earthquakes, Conway's Game of Life, cognition, and economics. Presents an excellent discussion of the power law distribution.

Bak, P., & Chen, K. (1991). Self-organized criticality. *Scientific American*, pp. 46-53.

Reading level: easy to moderate
Per Bak argues that change is nonlinearly related to cause, and that it comes in many different scales. Demonstrates by dropping sand a grain at a time onto a scale and measuring the size of "sand slides." Observes a fractal dimension to the distribution of slides.

Baker, G. L., & Gollub, J. P. (1990). *Chaotic dynamics: An Introduction.* Cambridge, UK: Cambridge University Press.

Reading level: moderately difficult
Baker and Gollub introduce chaos to a fairly sophisticated but uninitiated audience. Their coverage of strange attractors, correlation dimension, spectral analysis, Poincaré maps, sensitive dependence, basins of attractions, bifurcation, phase space, logistic equations, and Lyapunov exponents is mathematical, but not oppressively so. Includes the code for a number of computer programs in the appendix.

Beltrami, E. (1993). *Mathematical models in the social and biological sciences.* Boston: Jones and Bartlett.

Reading level: moderate
Presents a number of mathematical models of social and biological dynamics. Of particular interest is his discussion of variations on the logistic equation.

Briggs, J., & Peat, F. D. (1989). *Turbulent mirror.* New York: Harper & Row.

Reading level: easy
An interesting book about Chaos that devotes roughly half its pages to Complexity Theory without actually calling it Complexity. The chapters in the first half of the book are numbered from largest to least (Briggs understandably invokes Lewis Carroll's imagery often); here he discusses Chaos Theory. The chapters in the last half of the book are numbered normally; here is discusses how order emerges out of interaction (Complexity Theory).

Cronbach, L. J. (1988). Playing with chaos. *Educational Researcher, 17*(6), 46-49.

Reading level: easy
Lee Cronbach was probably the first major social scientist (outside the field of economics) to write of the potential of Chaos for understanding

social phenomena. This article is primarily a review of Gleick's popular book, *Chaos,* but Cronbach also muses about how Chaos might be applied in social science research. He argued, however, that much of the initial work will be metaphorical because social scientists (his specific audience was educators) aren't prepared to do the type of math demanded by Chaotic analysis.

Feigenbaum, M. (1978). Quantitative universality for a class of nonlinear transformations. *Journal of Statistical Physics, 19, 25-52.*

Reading level: difficult
The important article in which Michael Feigenbaum develops the Feigenbaum constant, or the rate at which period doubling decomposes into Chaos.

Gilmore, C. G. (1995). A new test for chaos. In R. R. Trippi (Ed.), *Chaos and nonlinear dynamics in the financial markets* (pp. 383-415). Chicago: Irwin Professional.

Reading level: moderate
Gilmore develops a topological technique for analyzing Chaotic structure, one that is particularly useful for the relatively small data sets available in the social sciences. The algorithm is discussed, as are techniques for neutralizing random noise. Gilmore reanalyzes several previous studies and clarifies their results with the return map.

Gleick, J. (1987). *Chaos: Making a new science.* New York: Viking.

Reading level: easy to moderate
The classic that popularized Chaos. This book introduces the reader to the Lorenz attractor, Chaos in the logistic equation and Feigenbaum's universality, Mandelbrot sets and fractal geometry, and Poincaré maps.

Goodwin, B. (1994). *How the leopard changed its spots: The evolution of complexity.* New York: Scribner.

Reading level: easy to hard
For the most part, this is a biology text, hence the "hard" rating of reading level above. However, the introductions to several of Goodwin's chapters, and his last two chapters, are useful for social scientists. Here he discusses the reductionist versus holistic debate, cooperation versus competition, emergence, his version of the autocatalytic process, and human culture.

Hénon, M. (1976). A two-dimensional mapping with a strange attractor. *Communications in Mathematical Physics 50,* 69-77.

Reading level: difficult
The article in which Michael Hénon introduces the famous Hénon attractor, which is generated by two simultaneous difference equations on a Poincaré Map.

Holland, J. H. (1995). *Hidden order.* Reading, MA: Addison-Wesley.

Reading level: easy
John Holland, called by some the father of the field of genetic algorithms, describes how complex adaptive systems (*CAS*) interact to generate order. He describes an artificial life simulation called Echo, and describes strategies for expanding our understanding of CAS. His discussion in Chapter 1 of aggregation, tags, and building blocks is particularly useful.

Kauffman, S. A. (1993). *The origins of order.* New York: Oxford University Press.

Reading level: moderately difficult
Stu Kauffman's seminal work on Complexity theory. He argues that natural selection is incapable of creating the amount of order observable on earth, that instead order is free, the natural outcome of interaction. He proposes a role for selection that is largely secondary: Order emerges from interaction, then selection molds it. His discussions cover such things as rugged landscapes, morphology, and phase and parameter space.

Kauffman, S. (1995). *At home in the universe: The search for the laws of self-organization and complexity.* New York: Oxford University Press.

Reading level: moderate
A simpler and more readably version of his 1993 work, *The Origins of Order.* Appropriate for those wanting a less technical discussion of his argument that order is free. His discussion of patches and change in the final chapters is particularly interesting for social scientists.

Langston, C. G. (1986). Studying artificial life with cellular automata. *Physica, 22D,* 120-149.

Reading level: moderate
Chris Langston, who is perhaps the driving force behind the popularity of Complexity Theory, shows us how different forms of order emerge using cellular automata (anyone familiar with John Conway's "Game of

Life" is familiar with CA). Cellular automata is a simulation that occurs on an extended chess board. Cells on the grid are alive or dead depending upon the state of their neighbors. Langston controlled the probability that cells would live or die; he found that when the probability of death was high, pockets of repetitive or unchanging stability emerged. When the probability of death was low, Chaotic instability swirled across the board. At a middle point, however, loosely connected pockets of dynamic activity—Complexity—appeared.

Lauwerier, H. (1991). *Fractals: Endlessly repeated geometric figures.* Princeton, NJ: Princeton University Press.

Reading level: moderately easy
An excellent, easy to understand introduction to the mathematics of fractal geometry. Perfect for the novice. Includes computer program codes in the appendix.

Levy, S. (1992). *Artificial life: The quest for new creation.* New York: Random House.

Reading level: easy
Describes the quest to simulate life with a bottoms-up logic, as opposed to the top-down logic of artificial intelligence. Bottoms-up logic specifies adaptive rules for individual units of a system, then turns those units loose to interact with one another. Computerized simulations demonstrate that such strategy leads to spontaneous order and enables the system to deal with environmental problems with surprising effectiveness.

Lewin, R. (1992). *Complexity: Life at the edge of chaos.* New York: Macmillan.

Reading level: easy
One of a handful of books that popularized Complexity Theory in the early 1990s, this is probably still the best introduction to the subject. Levy introduces his topics through the eyes of the key researchers of the subject, including Chris Langston, Stu Kauffman, Heinz Pagals, James Farmer, John Holland, and Craig Reynolds.

Lloyd, A. L. (1995, June). Computing bouts of the Prisoner's Dilemma. *Scientific American,* pp. 110-115.

Reading level: not rated
Lloyd provides computer code for competing bouts of the simulation, Prisoner's Dilemma.

Lovelock, J. (1988). *The ages of Gaia: A biography of our living earth.* New York: Norton.

Reading level: easy
Lovelock, who is considered heretical by many biologists, argues that life, rather than existing because environmental conditions are favorable, actually manipulates that environment to make it favorable. In a computer simulation, he demonstrates that a world devoid of life becomes increasingly hot. When colored flowers are introduced, however, the temperature stabilizes at a livable level.

Mandelbrot, B. B. (1983). *The fractal geometry of nature.* New York: Freeman.

Reading level: moderately difficult
Benoit Mandelbrot's classic book provides what may be the first major advance in geometry since Euclid. He argues that nature is not composed of stylized lines and circles; rather nature is convoluted, broken, fractal. Discusses fractal dimension, measures of the length of borders between countries, fractal landscapes and artwork, and percolation. Beautifully illustrated; the pictures alone are worth the cost of the book. Mandelbrot alerts the reader to sections that are particularly difficult, and has written in such a way that these sections can be skipped over without loss.

Marion, R. (1992). Chaos, topology, and social organization. *Journal of School Leadership, 2*(2), 144-177.

Reading level: easy to moderate
Discusses the logistic equation within the context of information theory. Demonstrates Ruelle's procedure for generating Poincaré maps from univariate data, demonstrates the stability of chaotic systems exposed to random noise, and discusses possible applications of Chaos in the social sciences.

Martien, P., Pope, S. C., et al. (1985). The chaotic behavior of the leaky faucet. *Physics Letters, 110A*(7, 8), 399-404.

Reading level: easy
A classic experiment reproduced in numerous science labs for high school and college students. Martien and colleagues measured the time

lapse between drips of water from a leaky faucet and plotted the intervals. A strange attractor emerged.

May, R. M. (1976). Simple mathematical models with very complicated dynamics. *Nature, 261,* 459-467.

Reading level: moderately difficult
Robert May's classic article on Chaos in the logistic equation. Analyzes what happens to the output of this difference equation as lambda (or growth rate) approaches 3.57.

Nielsen, F., & Hannan, M. T. (1977, June). The expansion of national educational systems: Tests of a population ecology model. *American Sociological Review, 42,* 479-490.

Reading level: moderately difficult
Nielsen and Hannan demonstrate that the logistic equation models the growth of public education during the first half of the 20th century.

Nowak, M. A., May, R. M., et al. (1995, June). The arithmetics of mutual help. *Scientific American,* pp. 76-81.

Reading level: easy
Reports on simulation experiments with Prisoner's Dilemma in which many different "actors" play against each other simultaneously and repetitively, and each "remembers" the behavior of its opponents in the previous round. His results show a pervasive tendency toward cooperation.

Peterson, I. (1988). *The mathematical tourist.* New York: Freeman.

Reading level: easy
This book discusses a number of mathematical topics, but two chapters, one on Chaos and one on fractal geometry, are of interest. Both discuss core issues in a language that is easily grasped by beginners.

Poundstone, W. (1992). *Prisoner's dilemma.* Garden City, NY: Doubleday.

Reading level: easy
Poundstone's book is as much a biography of noted mathematician John von Neumann as a treatise on the simulation, Prisoner's Dilemma. He

traces the invention of Prisoner's Dilemma, discusses its many forms, presents the basic tenets of game theory, and discusses how game theory was used by nuclear weapons cold war strategists during the 1950s.

Prigogine, I. (1997). *The end of certainty.* New York: Free Press.

Reading level: moderate to difficult
Prigogine presents compelling evidence that traditional scientific notions of time-reversibility are destroyed by Chaos Theory. He attributes this to two observations: unmeasurable initial conditions and sensitive dependence upon initial condition, and unpredictable resonances among interacting units.

Prusinkiewicz, P., & Lindenmayer, A. (1990). *The algorithmic beauty of plants.* New York: Springer.

Reading level: moderate
Because of the beautiful illustrations, this is a coffee table book—despite the serious nature of its topic. The book presents genetic algorithms (actual computer code) for the generation of fractal images.

Reynolds, C. (1987). Flocks, herds, and schools: A distributed behavioral model. *Computer Graphics, 21,* 25, 32.

Reading level: moderate
In this article we learn about "Boids," a bottoms-up, computerized simulation of bird flocking. "Bottoms-up" refers to localized rules rather than global coordination; each entity responds according to simple rule sets guiding its behavior. The discussion illustrates basic principles of Complexity Theory.

Schroeder, M. (1991). *Fractals, chaos, power laws.* New York: Freeman.

Reading level: difficult
Good introduction to some of the basic mathematics of Chaos, including correlation dimension, Hausdorff dimension, fractals and time series data, universality, and Markov process. Applications to such events as stock markets, percolation, and population distribution are available. Includes a chapter on cellular automata.

Sterman, J. D. (1988). Deterministic chaos in models of human behavior: Methodological issues and experimental results. *System Dynamics Review, 4*(1-2), 148-178.

Reading level: moderately easy
Sterman modified two business simulations, one a stock management game and the other a beer distribution game, to collect data on decision points. When the data was plotted, images similar to known strange attractors emerged.

Stewart, I. (1989). *Does God play dice: The mathematics of chaos.* Cambridge, MA: Basil Blackwell.

Reading level: easy to moderate
This book makes Chaos accessible to the mathematically impaired. Conceptually develops key concepts, such as phase space, topology, fractals, Poincaré maps, differential calculus, and difference equations.

Trippi, R. H. (Ed.). (1995). *Chaos and nonlinear dynamics in the financial markets.* Burr Ridge, IL: Irwin.

Reading level: moderately difficult, but varies
A collection of articles on Chaos in financial systems. Focuses particularly on efforts to measure such Chaos.

Tufillaro, N. B., Abbott, T., et al. (1992). *An experimental approach to nonlinear dynamics and chaos.* Redwood City, CA: Addison-Wesley.

Reading level: difficult
Discusses Chaos relative to a program in a software package that accompanies the book. Code for several other programs is available in the appendix.

Waldrop, M. M. (1992). *Complexity: The emerging science at the edge of order and chaos.* New York: Simon & Schuster.

Reading level: easy
Waldrop's book is as much a discussion of the Santa Fe Institute for the Study of Complexity as it is a treatise on Complexity. In addition to the usual topics in Complexity Theory, this book introduces the reader to

efforts in economics, particularly the interesting work on increasing returns by Brian Arthur.

Zaslavsky, G. M., Sagdeev, R. Z., Usikov, D. A., & Chernikov, A. A. (1991). *Weak chaos and quasi-regular patterns* (A. R. Sagdeeva, Trans.). Cambridge, UK: Cambridge University Press.

Reading level: difficult
Discusses the phase transition between stability and Chaos as a band of dynamics in which islands of stability float within seas of Chaos—and vice versa. Illustrates with a interesting application of a difference equation for forced pendulum motion.

References

▓ PREFACE

Arthur, W. B. (1989). The economy and complexity. In D. L. Stein (Ed.), *Lectures in the sciences of complexity* (pp. 713-740). Redwood City, CA: Addison-Wesley.

Gilmore, C. G. (1995). A new test for chaos. In R. R. Trippi (Ed.), *Chaos and nonlinear dynamics in the financial markets* (pp. 383-415). Chicago: Irwin Professional.

Goldstein, J. A. (1995). The Tower of Babel in nonlinear dynamics: Toward a clarification of terms. In R. Robertson & A. Combs (Eds.), *Chaos in psychology and the life sciences: Proceedings of the Society for Chaos Theory in Psychology and the Life Sciences* (pp. 39-47). Mahwah, NJ: Lawrence Erlbaum.

Goodwin, B. (1994). *How the leopard changed its spots: The evolution of complexity.* New York: Scribner.

Kauffman, S. (1995). *At home in the universe: The search for the laws of self-organization and complexity.* New York: Oxford University Press.

Prigogine, I. (1996). *The end of certainty.* New York: Free Press.

▧ CHAPTER 1

The Edge of Organization

Arthur, W. B. (1989). The economy and complexity. In D. L. Stein (Ed.), *Lectures in the sciences of complexity* (pp. 713-740). Redwood City, CA: Addison-Wesley.

Bak, P. (1996). *How nature works.* New York: Copernicus.

Briggs, J., & Peat, F. D. (1989). *Turbulent mirror.* New York: Harper & Row.

Cartwright, T. J. (1991, Winter). Planning and chaos theory. *Journal of the American Planning Association, 57*(1), 44-56.

Cronbach, L. J. (1988, August-September). Playing with chaos. *Educational Researcher, 17*(6), 46-49.

Einstein, A. (1988). *The meaning of relativity* (5th ed.). Princeton, NJ: Princeton University Press.

Geller, H. A., & Johnston, A. P. (1990, January-March). Policy as linear and nonlinear science. *Journal of Educational Policy, 5*(1), 49-65.

Gell-Mann, M. (1994). *The quark and the jaguar.* New York: Freeman.

Gilmore, C. G. (1995). A new test for chaos. In R. R. Trippi (Ed.), *Chaos and nonlinear dynamics in the financial markets* (pp. 383-415). Chicago: Irwin Professional.

Gleick, J. (1987). *Chaos: Making a new science.* New York: Viking.

Goldstein, J. A. (1995). The Tower of Babel in nonlinear dynamics: Toward a clarification of terms. In R. Robertson & A. Combs (Eds.), *Chaos in psychology and the life sciences: Proceedings of the Society for Chaos Theory in Psychology and the Life Sciences* (pp. 39-47). Mahwah, NJ: Lawrence Erlbaum.

Goodwin, B. (1994). *How the leopard changed its spots: The evolution of complexity.* New York: Scribner.

Guastello, S. J., Dooley, K. J., & Goldstein, J. A. (1995). Chaos, organizational theory, and organizational development. In F. D. Abraham & A. R. Gilgen (Eds.), *Chaos theory in psychology* (pp. 267-278). Westport, CT: Praeger.

Holland, J. H. (1995). *Hidden order.* Reading, MA: Addison-Wesley.

Kauffman, S. (1995). *At home in the universe: The search for the laws of self-organization and complexity.* New York: Oxford University Press.

Langston, C. G. (1986). Studying artificial life with cellular automata. *Physica, 22D,* 120-149.

Lewin, R. (1992). *Complexity: Life at the edge of chaos.* New York: Macmillan.

Lorenz, E. (1993). *The essence of chaos.* Seattle: University of Washington Press.

Marion, R., & Weaver, K. (1997, March). *Modified Poincaré maps and return maps: Tools for analyzing social chaos.* Paper presented at the American Educational Research Association Annual Conference, Chicago.

Reynolds, C. (1987, July). Flocks, herds, and schools: A distributed behavioral model. *Computer Graphics, 21,* 25, 32.

Sterman, J. D. (1988). Deterministic chaos in models of human behavior: Methodological issues and experimental results. *System Dynamics Review, 4*(1-2), 148-178.

Waldrop, M. M. (1992). *Complexity: The emerging science at the edge of order and chaos.* New York: Simon & Schuster.

Willey, T. (1995). Testing for nonlinear dependence in daily stock indices. In R. R. Trippi (Ed.), *Chaos and nonlinear dynamics in the financial markets.* Chicago: Irwin Professional.

Wolfram, S. (1984, September). Computer software in science and mathematics. *Scientific American,* pp. 188-203.

■ CHAPTER 2

Chaos and Organization

Brager, G. (1969, August). Commitment and conflict in a normative organization. *American Sociological Review, 34,* 482-491.

Lorenz, E. (1964). The problem of deducing the climate from the governing equations. *Tellus, 16,* 1-11.

Prigogine, I. (1996). *The end of certainty.* New York: Free Press.

Ruelle, D. (1989). *Chaotic evolution and strange attractors.* Cambridge, UK: Cambridge University Press.

Ruelle, D., & Takens, F. (1971). On the nature of turbulence. *Communications in Mathematical Physics, 20,* 167-192.

■ CHAPTER 3

Organization at the Edge

Briggs, J., & Peat, F. D. (1989). *Turbulent mirror.* New York: Harper & Row.

Codd, E. F. (1968). *Cellular automata.* New York: Academic Press.

Jacob, F., & Monad, J. (1961). Genetic regulatory mechanisms in the synthesis of proteins. *Journal of Molecular Biology, 3,* 318-356.

Kauffman, S. A. (1995). *At home in the universe: The search for the laws of self-organization and complexity.* New York: Oxford University Press.
Langston, C. G. (1986). Studying artificial life with cellular automata. *Physica, 22D,* 120-149.
Levy, S. (1992). *Artificial life: The quest for new creation.* New York: Random House.
Lewin, R. (1992). *Complexity: Life at the edge of chaos.* New York: Macmillan.
Lorenz, E. (1964). The problem of deducing the climate from the governing equations. *Tellus, 16,* 1-11.
Reynolds, C. (1987, July). Flocks, herds, and schools: A distributed behavioral model. *Computer Graphics, 21,* 25, 32.
Waldrop, M. M. (1992). *Complexity: The emerging science at the edge of order and chaos.* New York: Simon & Schuster.
Wolfram, S. (1984, September). Computer software in science and mathematics. *Scientific American,* pp. 188-203.
Zaslavsky, G. M., Sagdeev, R. Z., Usikov, D. A., & Chernikov, A. A. (1991). *Weak chaos and quasi-regular patterns* (A. R. Sagdeeva, Trans.). Cambridge, UK: Cambridge University Press.

▓ CHAPTER 4

Shifting Historical Premises to the Edge of Chaos

Ashby, W. R. (1960). *Design for a brain* (2nd ed.). New York: John Wiley.
Axelrod, R. (1984). *The evolution of cooperation.* New York: Basic Books.
Bauer, M., & Cohen, E. (1983). The invisibility of power in economics: Beyond markets and hierarchies. In A. Francis, J. Turk, & P. Willman (Eds.), *Power, efficiency and institutions.* London: Heinemann.
Buckley, W. (1967). *Sociology and modern systems theory.* Englewood Cliffs, NJ: Prentice Hall.
Cannon, W. B. (1938). *The wisdom of the body* (Rev. ed.). New York: Norton.
Dahrendorf, R. (1959). *Class and class conflict in industrial society.* Stanford, CA: Stanford University Press.
Francis, A. (1983). Markets and hierarchies: Efficiency or domination? In A. Francis, J. Turk, & P. Willman (Eds.), *Power, efficiency and institutions* (pp. 105-116). London: Heinemann.
Gibbs, J. W. (1902). *Elementary principles in statistical mechanics.* New York: Scribner.

Gimeno, J., Folta, T. B., Cooper, A. C., & Woo, C. Y. (1997). Survival of the fittest? Entrepreneurial human capital and the persistence of underperforming firms. *Administrative Science Quarterly, 42*(4), 750-783.

Goodwin, B. (1994). *How the leopard changed its spots: The evolution of complexity.* New York: Scribner.

Grandori, A. (1987). *Perspectives on organizational theory.* Cambridge, MA: Ballinger.

Hannan, M. H., & Freeman, J. (1977). The population ecology of organizations. *American Journal of Sociology, 82,* 926-964.

Hoy, W. K., & Miskel, C. G. (1991). *Educational administration: Theory, research, and practice* (4th ed.). New York: McGraw-Hill.

Kauffman, S. A. (1993). *The origins of order.* New York: Oxford University Press.

Langston, C. G. (1986). Studying artificial life with cellular automata. *Physica, 22D,* 120-149.

March, J. G., & Simon, H. A. (1958). *Organizations.* New York: John Wiley.

Margulis, L., & Sagan, D. (1986). *Microcosmos.* Oxford, UK: Oxford University Press.

McKelvey, B. (1982). *Organizational systematics.* Berkeley: University of California Press.

Nowak, M. A., May, R. M., & Sigmund, K. (1995, June). The arithmetics of mutual help. *Scientific American,* pp. 76-81.

Packard, N. H., & Bedau, M. A. (1992). Measurement of evolutionary activity, teleology, and life. In C. G. Langston, C. Taylor, J. D. Farmer, & S. Rasmussen (Eds.), *A-Life II: Vol. 10.* Santa Fe Institute Studies in the Sciences of Complexity. Reading, MA: Addison-Wesley.

Parsons, T., & Shils, E. A. (Eds.). (1951). *Toward a general theory of action.* Cambridge, MA: Harvard University Press.

Perrow, C. (1981). Markets, hierarchies and hegemony. In A. H. Van de Ven & W. F. Joyce (Eds.), *Perspectives on organizational design and behavior* (pp. 371-386). New York: John Wiley.

Pfeffer, J., & Salancik, G. R. (1978). *The external control of organizations: A resource dependence perspective.* New York: Harper & Row.

Thompson, D. (1961). *On growth and form.* Cambridge, UK: Cambridge University Press.

Webster, G., & Goodwin, B. C. (1982). The origin of species: A structuralist approach. *Journal of Social Biological Structure, 5.*

Weick, K. E. (1979). *The social psychology of organizing.* Reading, MA: Addison-Wesley.

■ **CHAPTER 5**

A Nonlinear Redaction of Open Systems

Arthur, W. B. (1989). The economy and complexity. In D. L. Stein (Ed.), *Lectures in the sciences of complexity* (pp. 713-740). Redwood City, CA: Addison-Wesley.

Bloomfield, B. P. (1986). *Modelling the world: The social constructions of systems analysts.* Oxford, UK and New York: Basil Blackwell.

Buckley, W. (1967). *Sociology and modern systems theory.* Englewood Cliffs, NJ: Prentice Hall.

Forrester, J. W. (1969). *Urban dynamics.* Cambridge: MIT Press.

Forrester, J. W. (1971). *World dynamics.* Cambridge: MIT Press.

Gell-Mann, M. (1994). *The quark and the jaguar.* New York: Freeman.

Holland, J. H. (1995). *Hidden order.* Reading, MA: Addison-Wesley.

Katz, D., & Kahn, R. L. (1966). *The social psychology of organizations.* New York: John Wiley.

Kauffman, S. A. (1993). *The origins of order.* New York: Oxford University Press.

Kauffman, S. A. (1995). *At home in the universe: The search for the laws of self-organization and complexity.* New York: Oxford University Press.

Langston, C. G. (1986). Studying artificial life with cellular automata. *Physica, 22D,* 120-149.

Leavitt, H. J. (1964). *Managerial psychology.* Chicago: University of Chicago Press.

Lorenz, E. (1964). The problem of deducing the climate from the governing equations. *Tellus, 16,* 1-11.

Maruyama, M. (1963). The second cybernetics: Deviation amplifying mutual causal processes. *American Scientist, 51,* 164-179.

Prigogine, I. (1996). *The end of certainty.* New York: Free Press.

Seiler, J. A. (1967). *Systems analysis in organizational behavior.* Homewood, IL: Irwin/Dorsey.

Smith, J. M. (1986). *The problems of biology.* Oxford, UK: Oxford University Press.

■ **CHAPTER 6**

Structural Contingency Theory: Differentiation and Awareness

Blau, P. M. (1970). Decentralization in bureaucracies. In M. N. Zald (Ed.), *Power in organizations.* Nashville, TN: Vanderbilt University Press.

Blau, P. M., & Schoenherr, R. A. (1971). *The structure of organizations.* New York: Basic Books.

Crozier, M., & Friedberg, E. (1977). *L'acteur et le système.* Paris: Editions du Seuil.

Grandori, A. (1987). *Perspectives on organizational theory.* Cambridge, MA: Ballinger.

Hage, J., & Aiken, M. (1972). Routine technology, social structure, and organization goals. In R. H. Hall (Ed.), *The formal organization* (pp. 55-72). New York: Basic Books.

Holland, J. H. (1995). *Hidden order.* Reading, MA: Addison-Wesley.

Kauffman, S. A. (1995). *At home in the universe: The search for the laws of self-organization and complexity.* New York: Oxford University Press.

Lawrence, P. R., & Lorsch, J. W. (1967). *Organization and environment.* Cambridge, MA: Harvard University Press.

Parsons, T. (1960). *Structure and process in modern society.* Glencoe, IL: Free Press.

Van De Ven, A., Delbecq, A., & Koenig, R. (1976). Determinants of coordination modes within organizations. *Administrative Science Quarterly, 41*(2), 322-338.

▒ CHAPTER 7

Footprints of Complexity: The Nature of Order

Blau, P. M., & Schoenherr, R. A. (1971). *The structure of organizations.* New York: Basic Books.

Forsyth, E., & Katz, L. (1960). A matrix approach to the analysis of sociometric data: Preliminary report. In J. L. Moreno (Ed.), *The sociometry reader* (pp. 229-235). Glencoe, IL: Free Press.

Goodwin, B. (1994). *How the leopard changed its spots: The evolution of complexity.* New York: Scribner.

Gullahorn, J. T. (1960). Distance and friendship as factors in the gross interaction matrix. In J. L. Moreno (Ed.), *The sociometry reader* (pp. 506-517). Glencoe, IL: Free Press.

Haykin, S. (1994). *Neural networks: A comprehensive foundation.* New York: Macmillan College.

Kauffman, S. A. (1993). *The origins of order.* New York: Oxford University Press.

Kauffman, S. A. (1995). *At home in the universe: The search for the laws of self-organization and complexity.* New York: Oxford University Press.

Loomis, C. P. (1960). Informal groupings in a Spanish-American village. In J. L. Moreno (Ed.), *The sociometry reader* (pp. 490-493). Glencoe, IL: Free Press.

Moreno, J. L. (Ed.). (1960). *The sociometry reader*. Glencoe, IL: Free Press.

Proctor, C. H. (1960). Informal social systems. In J. L. Moreno (Ed.), *The sociometry reader* (pp. 484-489). Glencoe, IL: Free Press.

Weiss, R. S., & Jacobson, E. (1960). The structure of complex organizations. In J. L. Moreno (Ed.), *The sociometry reader* (pp. 522-534). Glencoe, IL: Free Press.

▨ CHAPTER 8

Resource Dependency: The Emergence of Order

Arthur, W. B. (1989). The economy and complexity. In D. L. Stein (Ed.), *Lectures in the sciences of complexity* (pp. 713-740). Redwood City, CA: Addison-Wesley.

Coser, L. (1956). *The functions of social conflict*. New York: Free Press.

Dawkins, R. (1976). *The selfish gene*. New York: Oxford University Press.

Gerlach, M. (1987). Business alliance and the strategy of the Japanese firm. In G. R. Carroll & D. Vogel (Eds.), *Organizational approaches to strategy*. Cambridge, MA: Ballinger.

Grandori, A. (1987). *Perspectives on organizational theory*. Cambridge, MA: Ballinger.

Holland, J. H. (1995). *Hidden order*. Reading, MA: Addison-Wesley.

Katz, D., & Kahn, R. L. (1966). *The social psychology of organizations*. New York: John Wiley.

Kauffman, S. A. (1995). *At home in the universe: The search for the laws of self-organization and complexity*. New York: Oxford University Press.

Lewin, R. (1992). *Complexity: Life at the edge of chaos*. New York: Macmillan.

Lovelock, J. (1988). *The ages of Gaia: A biography of our living earth*. New York: Norton.

McKelvey, B. (1982). *Organizational systematics*. Berkeley: University of California Press.

Packard, N. H., & Bedau, M. A. (1992). Measurement of evolutionary activity, teleology, and life. In C. G. Langston, C. Taylor, J. D. Farmer, & S. Rasmussen (Eds.), *A-Life II: Vol. 10*. Santa Fe Institute Studies in the Sciences of Complexity. Reading, MA: Addison-Wesley.

Pfeffer, J., & Salancik, G. R. (1978). *The external control of organizations: A resource dependence perspective.* New York: Harper & Row.

Stinchcombe, A. L. (1965). Social structure and organizations. In J. G. March (Ed.), *Handbook of organizations* (pp. 142-193). Chicago: Rand McNally.

Wesson, R. (1994). *Beyond natural selection.* Cambridge: MIT Press.

▓ CHAPTER 9

Organizations in Wonderland: Enacted Environment

Casti, J. (1994). *Complexification.* New York: HarperCollins.

Holland, J. H. (1995). *Hidden order.* Reading, MA: Addison-Wesley.

Kauffman, S. A. (1993). *The origins of order.* New York: Oxford University Press.

Prigogine, I. (1996). *The end of certainty.* New York: Free Press.

Weick, K. E. (1979). *The social psychology of organizing.* Reading, MA: Addison-Wesley.

Whitehead, A. N. (Ed.). (1978). *Process and reality.* New York: Macmillan.

▓ CHAPTER 10

Coupling at the Edge

Cohen, M. D., March, J. G., & Olsen, J. P. (1972, March). A garbage can model of organizational choice. *Administrative Science Quarterly, 17,* 1-25.

Grandori, A. (1987). *Perspectives on organizational theory.* Cambridge, MA: Ballinger.

Holland, J. H. (1995). *Hidden order.* Reading, MA: Addison-Wesley.

Kauffman, S. A. (1993). *The origins of order.* New York: Oxford University Press.

Kauffman, S. A. (1995). *At home in the universe: The search for the laws of self-organization and complexity.* New York: Oxford University Press.

Kuhn, T. S. (1970). *The structure of scientific revolutions* (2nd ed.). Chicago: University of Chicago Press.

McPherson, R. B., Crowson, R. L., & Pitner, N. J. (1986). *Managing uncertainty: Administrative theory and practice in education.* Columbus, OH: Merrill.

Pfeffer, J., & Salancik, G. R. (1978). *The external control of organizations: A resource dependence perspective.* New York: Harper & Row.

Weick, K. (1976). Educational organizations as loosely coupled systems. *Administrative Science Quarterly, 21*(March), 1-19.

▨ CHAPTER 11

Darwin and Organizations, Goats and Monkeys

Alchian, A. (1950, June). Uncertainty, evolution, and economic theory. *Journal of Political Economy, 58,* 211-221.

Aldrich, H. E. (1971). Organizational boundaries and inter-organizational conflict. *Human Relations, 24,* 279-293.

Aldrich, H. E. (1979). *Organizations and environment.* Englewood Cliffs, NJ: Prentice Hall.

Arthur, W. B. (1989). The economy and complexity. In D. L. Stein (Ed.), *Lectures in the sciences of complexity* (pp. 713-740). Redwood City, CA: Addison-Wesley.

Brittain, J. W., & Hannan, M. H. (1980). Organizational proliferation and density dependent selection. In J. R. Kimberly & R. H. Miles (Eds.), *Organizational life cycles* (pp. 291-338). San Francisco: Jossey-Bass.

Brown, A. E., & Jeffcott, H. A. (1960). *Absolutely mad inventions.* New York: Dover.

Emery, F. E., & Trist, E. L. (1965, February). The causal texture of organizational environments. *Human Relations, 18,* 21-32.

Grandori, A. (1987). *Perspectives on organizational theory.* Cambridge, MA: Ballinger.

Hannan, M. H., & Freeman, J. (1977). The population ecology of organizations. *American Journal of Sociology, 82,* 926-964.

Hooton, E. (1946). *Up from the apes.* New York: Macmillan.

Kauffman, S. A. (1993). *The origins of order.* New York: Oxford University Press.

Lewin, R. (1992). *Complexity: Life at the edge of chaos.* New York: Macmillan.

McKelvey, B. (1982). *Organizational systematics.* Berkeley: University of California Press.

Wright, S. (1931). Evolution in Mendelian populations. *Genetics, 16,* 97-159.

Wright, S. (1932). The role of mutation, inbreeding, crossbreeding and selection in evolution. In *Evolution: Selected papers* (W. B. Provine, Ed.; pp. 161-171). Chicago: University of Chicago Press.

◾ CHAPTER 12

Pushing the Envelope: Limiting Organizational Expansion

Grandori, A. (1987). *Perspectives on organizational theory.* Cambridge, MA: Ballinger.

Guastello, S. (1992). Population dynamics and workforce productivity. In M. Michaels (Ed.), *Proceedings of the Annual Chaos Network Conference: The second iteration* (pp. 120-127). Urbana, IL: People Technologies.

Marchetti, C. (1986). Stable rules in social behavior. In *IBM Conference.* Brazilia: Brazilian Academy of Science.

McKelvey, B. (1982). *Organizational systematics.* Berkeley: University of California Press.

Nielsen, F., & Hannan, M. T. (1977, June). The expansion of national educational systems: Tests of a population ecology model. *American Sociological Review, 42,* 479-490.

◾ CHAPTER 13

Changing Complex Organizations

Anderson, P. (1995). Microcomputer manufacturers. In G. R. Carroll & M. T. Hannan (Eds.), *Organizations in industry* (pp. 37-58). New York: Oxford University Press.

Barnard, C. I. (1938). *The function of the executive.* Cambridge, MA: Harvard University Press.

Carlson, R. O. (1965). *Adoption of educational innovations.* Eugene: University of Oregon, Center for the Advanced Study of Educational Administration.

Carroll, G. R., & Hannan, M. T. (1995). *Organizations in industry.* New York: Oxford University Press.

Chin, R. (1967). Basic strategies and procedures in effecting change. In E. L. Morphet, R. L. Johns, & T. L. Reller (Eds.), *Educational organization and administration concepts, practice and issues.* Englewood Cliffs, NJ: Prentice Hall.

Corwin, R. G. (1987). *The organizational-society nexus: A critical review of models and metaphors.* New York: Greenwood.

Deal, T. E. (1985). Cultural change: Opportunity, silent killer, or metamorphosis? In R. H. Kilmann, M. J. Sexton, & R. Serpa (Eds.), *Gaining control of the corporate culture*. San Francisco: Jossey-Bass.

Edelman, M. (1967). *The symbolic uses of politics*. Urbana: University of Illinois Press.

Halpin, A. W., & Croft, D. B. (1962). *The organizational climate of schools*. Chicago: University of Chicago, Midwest Administration Center.

Holland, J. H. (1995). *Hidden order*. Reading, MA: Addison-Wesley.

Katz, D., & Kahn, R. L. (1966). *The social psychology of organizations*. New York: John Wiley.

Kauffman, S. A. (1995). *At home in the universe: The search for the laws of self-organization and complexity*. New York: Oxford University Press.

Kindergarten education, 1957-68. (1969, March). *NEA Research Bulletin, 47*(1), 10.

Lawrence, P., & Dyer, D. (1980). *Toward a theory of organizational and institutional adaptation*. A working paper, Harvard Business School.

McKelvey, B. (1982). *Organizational systematics*. Berkeley: University of California Press.

Moch, M. K., & Morse, E. V. (1977). Size, centralization, and organizational adaptation of innovation. *American Sociological Review, 42*, 716-725.

Mort, P. (1958). Educational adaptability. In D. H. Ross (Ed.), *Administration for adaptability* (pp. 32-33). New York: Metropolitan School Study Council.

Ouchi, W. (1981). *Theory Z: How American business can meet the Japanese challenge*. Reading, MA: Addison-Wesley.

Owens, R. G. (1991). *Organizational behavior in education* (4th ed.). Boston: Allyn and Bacon.

Peters, T. J., & Waterman, R. H. (1982). *In search of excellence: Lessons from America's best run companies*. New York: Harper & Row.

Rogers, E. M., & Rogers, R. A. (1976). *Communications in organizations*. New York: Free Press.

Schein, E. H. (1985). *Organizational culture and leadership*. San Francisco: Jossey-Bass.

Selznick, P. (1949). *TVA and the grass roots*. Berkeley: University of California Press.

Selznick, P. (1957). *Leadership in administration*. New York: Harper & Row.

Snyder, R. C. (1988). New frames for old: Changing the managerial culture of an aircraft factory. In M. O. Jones, M. D. Moore, & R. C. Snyder (Eds.), *Inside organizations: Understanding the human dimension* (pp. 191-208). Newbury Park, CA: Sage.

Weick, K. (1976, March). Educational organizations as loosely coupled systems. *Administrative Science Quarterly, 21*, 1-19.

CHAPTER 14

Change and Stability at the Edge

Aiken, M., & Hage, J. (1970). *Social change in complex organizations*. New York: Random House.

Anderson, P. (1995). Microcomputer manufacturers. In G. R. Carroll & M. T. Hannan (Eds.), *Organizations in industry* (pp. 37-58). New York: Oxford University Press.

Arthur, W. B. (1989). The economy and complexity. In D. L. Stein (Ed.), *Lectures in the sciences of complexity* (pp. 713-740). Redwood City, CA: Addison-Wesley.

Bak, P. (1996). *How nature works*. New York: Copernicus.

Bak, P., Tang, C., & Wiesenfeld, K. (1989). Self organized criticality: An explanation of $1/f$ noise. *Physical Review Letters, 59,* 381-384.

Blau, J. R. (1995). Art museums. In G. R. Carroll & M. T. Hannan (Eds.), *Organization in industry* (pp. 87-114). New York: Oxford University Press.

Corwin, R. G. (1987). *The organizational-society nexus: A critical review of models and metaphors*. New York: Greenwood.

Gell-Mann, M. (1994). *The quark and the jaguar*. New York: Freeman.

Holland, J. H. (1995). *Hidden order*. Reading, MA: Addison-Wesley.

Kauffman, S. A. (1993). *The origins of order*. New York: Oxford University Press.

Kauffman, S. A. (1995). *At home in the universe: The search for the laws of self-organization and complexity*. New York: Oxford University Press.

Krakauer, J. (1996). *Into the wild*. New York: Villard.

McKelvey, B. (1982). *Organizational systematics*. Berkeley: University of California Press.

Raup, D. M. (1991). *Extinctions: Bad genes or bad luck?* New York: Norton.

Schroeder, M. (1991). *Fractals, chaos, power laws*. New York: Freeman.

Weick, K. (1976, March). Educational organizations as loosely coupled systems. *Administrative Science Quarterly, 21,* 1-19.

West, B. J. (1996). Fractal statistics: Toward a theory of medicine. In C. A. Pickover (Ed.), *Fractal horizons* (pp. 263-295). New York: St. Martin's.

CHAPTER 15

Researching Social Chaos and Complexity

Beltrami, E. (1993). *Mathematical models in the social and biological sciences*. Boston: Jones and Bartlett.

Brock, W. A. (1986). Distinguishing random and deterministic systems: Abridged version. *Journal of Economic Theory, 40,* 169-195.

Gilmore, C. G. (1995). A new test for chaos. In R. R. Trippi (Ed.), *Chaos and nonlinear dynamics in the financial markets* (pp. 383-415). Chicago: Irwin Professional.

Guastello, S. (1992). Population dynamics and workforce productivity. In M. Michaels (Ed.), *Proceedings of the Annual Chaos Network Conference: The second iteration* (pp. 120-127). Urbana, IL: People Technologies.

Haykin, S. (1994). *Neural networks: A comprehensive foundation.* New York: Macmillan College.

Hénon, M. (1976). A two-dimensional mapping with a strange attractor. *Communications in Mathematical Physics, 50,* 69-77.

Marchetti, C. (1986). Stable rules in social behavior. In *IBM Conference.* Brazilia: Brazilian Academy of Science.

Mindlin, G. B., Hou, X., Solari, H. G., Gilmore, R., & Tufillaro, N. B. (1990). Classification of strange attractors by integers. *Physical Review Letters, 64,* 2350-2353.

Mindlin, G. B., Solari, H. G., Natiello, M. A., Gilmore, R., & Hou, U. (1991). Topological analysis of chaotic time series data from the Belousov-Zhabotinskii reaction. *Journal of Nonlinear Science, 1,* 147-173.

Nielsen, F., & Hannan, M. T. (1977, June). The expansion of national educational systems: Tests of a population ecology model. *American Sociological Review, 42,* 479-490.

Proctor, C. H. (1960). Informal social systems. In J. L. Moreno (Ed.), *The sociometry reader* (pp. 484-489). Glencoe, IL: Free Press.

Scheier, C., & Tschacher, W. (1996). Appropriate algorithms for nonlinear time series analysis in psychology. In W. Sulis & A. Combs (Eds.), *Nonlinear dynamics in human behavior* (pp. 27-43). Singapore: World Scientific.

▨ CHAPTER 16

Epilogue on Einstein's Island

Pais, A. (1991). *Niels Bohr's times, in physics, philosophy, and polity.* Oxford, UK: Clarendon.

Name Index

Subject Index

About the Author

RUSS MARION grew up in North Carolina where he received four degrees in education and educational administration from the University of North Carolina at Chapel Hill. He has been a public school teacher and a school principal; he helped develop an administrative software package for public schools in North Carolina; and he currently is an associate professor of Educational Leadership at Clemson University in South Carolina. Marion's current research interests include nonlinear social dynamics (as witnessed by this book), school finances and student achievement, and mathematical modeling of social dynamics. He has published articles on social chaos in the British journal *Management in Education* and in the *Journal of School Leadership,* and has spoken on the subject at a number of scholarly conventions. He maintains a Web site dedicated to studying social chaos and complexity (www.hehd.clemson.edu/complex/Cmplxdex.htm) and teaches a graduate-level course at Clemson University on applications of Chaos and Complexity Theory to formal social organizations.